# Content with My Wages

## A Sergeant's Story:

### Book I - Vietnam

Also by the author:

Content With My Wages-A Sergeant's Story: Book II-The War On Drugs
Content With My Wages-A Sergeant's Story: Book III-Afghanistan

(To be published in 2015)

# Content with My Wages

## A Sergeant's Story:

## Book I - Vietnam

Gregory H. Murry
Master Sergeant, U.S. Army (Retired)

No End To Publishing Company
Austin, Texas, USA

Library of Congress Cataloging-in-Publication Data

Murry, Gregory H.
Content With My Wages-A Sergeant's Story: Book I-Vietnam/Gregory H. Murry
Includes index.

ISBN: 978-0-9903976-0-1

First Printing

No End To Publishing Company LLC
P.O. Box 151136
Austin, Texas, USA 78715
noendtopublishing.com

Manufactured in the United States of America

***And some serving in the military also questioned him,***
***Saying, and we, what shall we do? And he said to them,***
***"Extort nothing from anyone by force,***
***nor take anything by false accusation,***
***and be content with your wages."***
***Luke 3:14***

**To**

Those who went, and among them are: Jose Garcia, Donnie Gunby, Peter Clark, Jack Hyland, Rodney Floutz, Don Gilliland, Ed Christiansen, Dennis Howley, Bill Williamson and the men of the 1st Battalion, 16th Infantry who were always ready to accomplish the mission, no matter how difficult, no matter how great the sacrifice, their duty came first.

and especially to those who didn't come back.

**Semper Paratus**

# Contents

## June 17th, 1967

I was numb when the pilot pulled pitch and the Huey's skids broke contact with LZ X-Ray. The helicopter skimmed across the ground picking up speed, banked to the right and we flew over the trees that ringed the landing zone. I scanned the ground through the trees, looking for the VC anti-aircraft gun that I was sure was there waiting to shoot us down. I was anticipating the bullets, the crash, and the fire that would do to my body what had already happened to my soul five hours before.

I was the weapons squad leader of 2d Platoon, Alpha Company, 1st Battalion, 16th Infantry, 1st Infantry Division. The day before, we had received a number of replacements bringing us up to full strength, forty-two men. Now the remnants of the platoon were on the helicopter with me, all eight of us.

The high pitched whine of the turbine engine made it impossible to hear anyone talking unless they were shouting in your ear—but no one was talking. The only other member of my squad, Donnie, was leaning back against the rear wall of the compartment, staring straight ahead.

The air grew cooler as we gained altitude and when we reached 1500 feet it was cold. We weren't going far though, about five miles, to the artillery firebase at Chi Linh; and after a few minutes of flying the helicopter began to drop as we approached the road next to the base that also served as an airstrip.

As for the rest of our comrades, the wounded and the dead, they were on other helicopters taking them to the hospital or to the morgue. Many men's lives ended on that piece of ground in Vietnam, June 17th, 1967, where I asked God to make the news of my death easy on my parents. But I was still alive, for how long I couldn't know, but nevertheless, under a sentence of death.

APPROACHES TO SAIGON
1966-1967
Battles
0
30 MILES
0
30 KILOMETERS
CAMBODIA
Loc Ninh
Phuoc Long
III CORPS
Hwy. 13
Bunard
Quan Loi
An Loc
QL-14
Ap Gu
Prek Klok II
War Zone C
QL-13
QL-22
Suoi Tre
OP Junction City
Dong Xoai
Xom Bo I-II
Prek Klok I
Nui Ba Den
OP Billings
Tay Ninh
War Zone D
Dau Tieng
Ap Bau Bang
Saigon R
Lai Khe
Bong Trang
Ben Suc
Ben Cat
QL-1
OP Cedar Falls
Iron Triangle
Cu Chi
QL-1
QL-13
Xuan Loc
Bien Hoa
Long Binh
Saigon
IV CORPS
(U.S. Army)

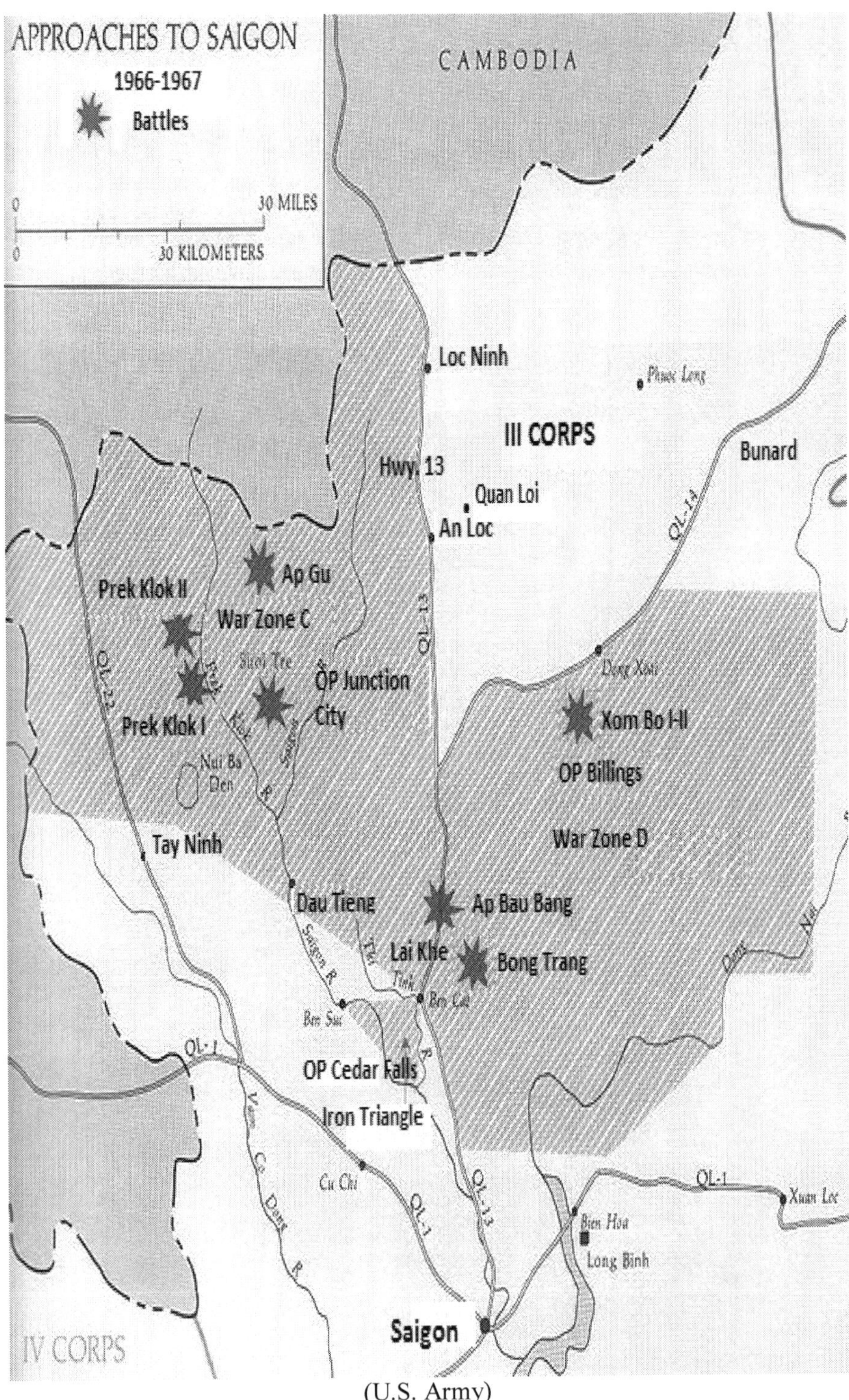

# Author's Note

This is the first of a war memoir trilogy I have written for a particular audience, the infantry sergeant. If you're neither a sergeant nor infantry, read on at your peril. The officer/sergeant relationship can be boiled down to this: the officers use what is working and the sergeants fix what is broken. If my outlook appears to you to be a bit negative, I will respond that I am a product of my environment.

I began writing this narrative in 2006 after I returned from my third war, Afghanistan, and had retired from the Texas Army National Guard. Most of what I saw and heard in 1966 and 1967, lay dormant in the back of my mind, except for the flashbacks, which are part of what is now called PTSD. After Vietnam I passed through one event after another through the rest of the Sixties: the 'lost years' in Mexico, Central and South America and Texas in the seventies, police work and the War on Drugs in the eighties and nineties, and finally the War in Afghanistan in 2003 and 2004. Now I'm sharing what I saw along the way.

A pilot once told me that our eyes are the least reliable of our sensor organs. As a former police officer who took statements from several 'eye witnesses' of the same event, I can attest to that pilot's observation. I wrote these accounts based on what I think I saw so long ago. The dialog is approximate in most cases but some of it is exactly what was said, but I have removed most of the expletives.

The language used by the infantry soldier is heavily laced with a peculiar word beginning with the letter 'f.' It is a 'magical vocabulary expander' and can be used as a noun, a verb, an adverb or an adjective. It is compounded with other words and the multitudinous ways it can be used to express the thoughts and emotions found in the infantry are still being explored.

There was a species of lizard that lived in the jungle where we sought our enemy. It used this word followed by 'you' as it's mating call. I wonder if like a parrot, the lizard learned this expression from hearing us reply to suggestions that we re-enlist or extend our tour. It's interesting to note however, that the frequency of our usage usually decreased as the amount of incoming fire increased and the tone became a more reverent expression.

I am an avid reader of military history. One of my favorite books is "Galahad," a memoir by Colonel Charles Hunter of the WWII Marauders in Burma. He quotes author John Steinbeck, who said at his Nobel Prize acceptance speech, that the writer "is charged with exposing our many grievous faults and failures, with dredging up to the light our dark and dangerous dreams for the purpose of improvement."

In the pursuit of my own dark and dangerous dreams, I made a lot of mistakes and at times I was derelict in my duty. Why I came home from Vietnam and why much better men than I didn't, is for God to explain. For the sake of their memory and my duty as a veteran, all I can say is that I tried to be a better sergeant.

***What has been is what will be,***
***And what has been done is what will be done,***
***And there is nothing new under the sun.***
***Ecclesiastes 1:9***

# Preface

When I retired from the Texas Army National Guard, after twenty-seven years of service between 1963 and 2005, I felt compelled to write an end of career after action report. I wrote this to be a memoir, a history and an after action report or critique of the operations described. As a memoir, it is a record of my own actions and failures, what I saw and did in Vietnam—my confession.

As military history, I hope to add to the body of information available for those who will study the effort made by the U.S. and its allies to defeat a state-sponsored insurgency and build a nation. It wasn't the first time we did something like this nor will it be the last.

As an after action report or critique, I'm using hindsight developed during the years I spent in the Army after Vietnam to point to some areas where a small unit leader might learn a lesson from history. By listening to Santayana, one might escape the self-condemnation that comes from doing something and then finding out later that you should have known better.

Writing the memoir was fairly easy. I typed a stream of consciousness into my computer and did what I could to organize it into what passes as literature. Then I did some searches on the internet and found some of the men I served with in Vietnam forty years before. I emailed the manuscript to them for fact checking. That part was easy.

Then, for the purpose of context, I decided to add some history. In order to do this I did some research to update my knowledge of the war. More than 55 years had passed since I first heard about Indochina and there have since been thousands of books written about the Vietnam War in English, French and Vietnamese.

The internet has been an explosion of knowledge about everything under the sun and research is as easy as clicking a mouse and rolling the wheel. In doing so, I found myself following a trail of footnotes through the cyber-jungle to a huge can of worms. As a result, the after action report or critique aspect of my writing becomes somewhat of an indictment. I invite you to follow in the trail of footnotes to see what I discovered about the war, while I share what I experienced.

### Report Writing

I wrote many reports when I was a police officer in the 1980's. The bottom line in police reports is truthfulness of facts. You can be prosecuted for perjury if you write a false report.

When I left the police department to help the Texas National Guard start their Counterdrug Task Force, one of my duties was to write the after action reports of our special operations on the border. At the end of every operation we would have to send a report to the National Guard Bureau stating what we had done, how we had done it, and what were the results. The National Guard Bureau would compile these reports and use the data to prepare reports to the Congress, mainly for the purpose of policy and budget. These reports were used by the Congress to interact with the Executive branch to further determine and define policy.

I would write the report; my superiors would red-line certain things, make some additions and give it back to me to make the corrections. In the beginning there were a lot of red-lines through the information I entered, showing the mistakes we had made and the difficulties that arise when conducting joint inter-agency operations. I argued that it was our responsibility to give them the facts so that they could have a true picture. They would end the argument by ordering me to make the corrections. I needed the job so I did.

Eventually I got the point; we don't air our dirty laundry. My superiors felt that there was no need in troubling the people on the Potomac with the problems we had encountered in Texas due to our own ineptitude, because after every operation we would conduct a real after action review and make sure that we got it right the next time. After a few years, I was convinced that this was what we do in the Army, for the good of the service. At the same time, I would hear the young operators remind each other that "if you're not cheating, you're not trying."

As a sergeant, I wasn't charged with being the ethical standard bearer for the organization; and while I did fight some battles over ethical issues while leaning on the point of my sword, the 'it's all good' after action reports were a minor irritation to my conscience and eventually faded out completely. None of this troubled me until I started writing my own history.

What is history? What are its sources? Why do academics insist on documentation of sources? Is it so that those studying history will feel comfortable in accepting what has been written as truth? "What is truth?" asked Pontius Pilate of the Author of Truth before he caved in to political pressure and delivered Him up to be crucified.[1]

## The Study of War Is the Study of Human Nature

**Brigadier General S.L.A. Marshall**

Samuel Lyman Atwood Marshall holds a unique place in U.S. Army military history. During his service in the Pacific during WWII, Marshall discovered that by interviewing a group of soldiers after a battle he could discover the 'truth' about what had taken place. While he has been the subject of some controversies, including his claims that some soldiers don't fire their weapons in combat, his 'Post Combat Interview' technique became the foundation of the modern After Action Review or AAR.[2]

The U.S. Army doesn't define truth in its leadership doctrine; but FM 22-100, the leadership manual, defined integrity as "the uprightness of character and the soundness of moral principles, the quality of absolute truthfulness and honesty …an indispensable trait in a leader."

FM 21-13, The Soldier's Guide, a small handbook issued to every recruit states: "You must be honest because there is absolutely no room in the military world for dishonesty or half-truth…a dishonest person can damage the esprit de corps of a unit and the morale of the members of that unit."[3]

The U.S. Army, like every army before it, has learned through experience that its members have weaknesses of character which create problems during the execution of its mission. The Army attempts to address these problems by extolling the desired virtues of a soldier in its leadership and soldiers manuals. By reading them one can see that the emphasis is on courage; one paragraph is on physical courage and the rest of the manual on moral courage and ethics. These manuals raise high the moral and ethical standards of the military service.

At the other end of the spectrum are the Manual for Courts-Martial and the Uniform Code of Military Justice. It is the standard by which all unsanctioned conduct in the military is measured. This compendium of laws and procedures exists because while everyone agrees that the high moral and ethical standards of military service are good, no one has ever been able to meet them all the time or completely. In order to see human nature for what it is, it is necessary to look beyond the military exhortations to see the condition of every recruit the day he takes the oath that puts him under those standards. As Marshall put it, the study of war is the study of human nature.

***...But let God be true and every man a liar...***
***Romans 3:4***

There are many explanations dealing with failures in human conduct. Since we are discussing human nature as understood by the U.S. Army, then we must consider the source of its laws. The U.S. military justice system is a mirror of the civilian legal system with additions to deal with military situations. The U.S. legal system follows the traditions of English Common Law which derived much of its concepts from the Holy Bible.

The Bible tells us that the Law was given by God to Moses on Mount Sinai and the children of Israel were the first to misunderstand God's intention. In Exodus 24:3 they declared, "All that God has said we will do." Paul clears this up in Romans 3:20 when he says, "...for through the law is the clear knowledge of sin." In case some would misunderstand this, in verse 23 he says, "For all have sinned and fall short of the glory of God." For the purpose of this discussion then, we could say that the result of the failure to meet the moral, ethical and legal standards defined in the leadership manuals and prosecuted in the UCMJ are offenses that the Bible calls sin.

What are the psychological effects of the knowledge of sin? Titus 1:15 says, "All things are pure to the pure; yet to those who are defiled and unbelieving nothing is pure, but both their mind and their conscience are defiled." The conscience is the moral sense—the faculty of judging the moral qualities of actions, or of discriminating between right and wrong, particularly applied to one's perception and judgment of the moral qualities of his own conduct.[4]

Accordingly, it would seem that anyone telling a lie would be troubled in mind and conscience; but Paul explains in 1st Timothy 4:2 that "By means of the hypocrisy of men who speak lies, of men who are branded in their own conscience as with a hot iron." The point here being that if you tell enough lies, the effect on your conscience is like the burning of the skin with a hot iron; the nerve endings are destroyed and you have no feeling there. Nonetheless, there seems to be a need in most men to confess things that have troubled their conscience.

A confession is a voluntary statement made by a person charged with the commission of a high crime or misdemeanor, communicated to another person, wherein he acknowledges himself to be guilty of the offense charged, and discloses the circumstances of the act or the share and participation which he had in it. Many times this is at the end of a person's life, a 'deathbed' confession. As I began writing my own confession, my research led me to others' confessions.[5]

Is any of this necessary for the preface of a memoir? It depends. If the purpose of the after action review is to identify unit strengths and weaknesses and to determine what could be done to improve performance, then it requires that the truth be told. In telling my story I hope to provide some useful information to those who will follow in the military service. My memoir is a personal confession, but the history I found requires me to include critiques. My conclusions would have been better served back then by confession. As my comrade Jose (Joe) Garcia, who you will meet in these pages, says, "Confession is good for the soul."

# Acknowledgments

When I finished writing a first draft, I looked for some of the men I served with and found two members of my squad, Jose (Joe) Garcia and Donnie Gunby. I asked them to read it for the purpose of confirming the historical accuracy. When I asked them if they could add anything from their own recollections, Jose provided several written narratives and a number of photographs which he graciously allowed me to use. When I visited Donnie in 2013, he also gave me some of his memories of those days.

Because leadership is the number one factor in combat, I wanted my company officers to have a look. They shared the same hardships with us in the field while bearing the heavy burden of command in combat.

The first, Dennis Howley, the Alpha Company Commander from August to November 1966, has reviewed the manuscript and provided me with some written observations which I have added to the narrative. He also designated the 'F' word a "magical vocabulary expander."

The second, Bill Williamson, Alpha Company Commander from November 1966 to June 1967, corresponded with me numerous times and also provided me with some written observations which I have added to the narrative.

Peter Clark, a member of our platoon and later one of Bill Williamson's radio-telephone operators, provided several written narratives and a sketch which have also been added. He is an excellent writer and he has been encouraged by me and others to write his own memoirs.

Neil Skiles, a machine gunner and later a squad leader in third platoon gave me the 'rest of the story' regarding an ambush patrol during the Tet Truce of 1967. Jack Hyland, who spent two years with the 1-16 Infantry, including a year with the battalion's Recon Platoon, gave me some of his recollections. Don (Doc) Gilliland, our platoon medic, reminded me of certain unpleasant events.

I corresponded with BG (Ret) Bill Mullen III and LTC (Ret) Jim Holland with regard to my presentation of the Battle of Bong Trang on August 25th, 1966. We were not able to see eye-to-eye but I think they'll agree that the battle was one for the books. Chuck Mundahl, a member of the patrol that started the battle of Bong Trang, gave me some details that were left out of the histories.

Dr. Lewis Sorley, one of the best historians of the Vietnam War, took the time to read an uncorrected proof of my manuscript and encouraged me by writing that he was favorably impressed and thought it was publishable. Thank you, sir.

I want to thank my comrades from later wars who read this manuscript and provided me with valued feedback. Among them are: Colonel James Sansone U.S. Army (Retired); Major Max Krupp, U.S. Army Special Forces; CSM 'Action' Jackson, U.S. Army Special Forces (Retired); SFC Thomas Payne, U.S. Army Special Forces (Retired).

There was another person who helped me through the entire ordeal of writing this story and desires to remain anonymous. For her I thank my God and her God.

Of course, all opinions and mistakes are mine.

# Abbreviations
## (And other useful information)

| | |
|---|---|
| AAR | After Action Report or Review |
| Abn | Airborne |
| AIT | Advanced Individual Training |
| AO | Area of Operation |
| APC | Armored Personnel Carrier |
| Arty | Artillery |
| ARVN | Army, Republic of Vietnam |
| AT | Annual Training |
| Avn | Aviation |
| AWOL | Absent Without Leave |
| Bde | Brigade |
| BMNT | Begin Morning Nautical Twilight (Dawn) |
| Bn | Battalion |
| CAAR | Combat After Action Report |
| Cav | Cavalry |
| CHICOM | Chinese Communist |
| CIA | Central Intelligence Agency |
| CIB | Combat Infantryman Badge |
| CMB | Combat Medic Badge |
| CMH | Center of Military History |
| CO | Commanding Officer |
| CQ | Charge of Quarters |
| Div | Division |
| DZ | Drop Zone-Parachute |
| EENT | End Evening Nautical Twilight (Dark) |
| Engr | Engineer |
| FAC | Forward Air Controller |
| FDC | Fire Direction Center |
| FNG | 'Blanking' New Guy |
| FO | Forward Observer for mortars or artillery |
| FPL | Final Protective Line (Machine gun in the defense) |
| H+I | Harassment and Interdiction |
| HQ | Headquarters |
| ID | Infantry Division |
| Inf | Infantry |
| Intel | Intelligence |
| KIA | Killed in Action |
| Klick | Kilometer |
| KP | Kitchen Police (Dish Washer) |
| LRRP | Long Range Reconnaissance Patrol |
| LZ | Landing Zone-Helicopter |
| Mech | Mechanized |
| MIA | Missing in Action |
| Mil | Military |
| NDP | Night Defensive Position |

| | |
|---|---|
| NLF | National Liberation Front |
| NVA | North Vietnamese Army |
| Opn | Operation |
| Optempo | Operations Tempo (the rate of missions) |
| ORLL | Operational Report-Lessons Learned |
| P-38 | C-ration can opener |
| PIR | Parachute Infantry Regiment |
| Plt | Platoon |
| POC | Point of Contact-Location of fighting |
| POW | Prisoner of War |
| R+R | Rest and Recuperation |
| RCT | Regimental Combat Team |
| Ret. | Retired |
| RON | Rest Over Night |
| RTO | Radio-Telephone Operator |
| RVN | Republic of Vietnam |
| S+D | Search and Destroy |
| SF | Special Forces |
| SITREP | Situation Report |
| Sortie | One aircraft's flight |
| Sqdn | Squadron |
| T+E | Traversing and Elevation |
| TOE | Table of Organization and Equipment |
| TOT | Time on Target-Planned simultaneous impact |
| TRP | Target Reference Point |
| VC | Viet Cong-Vietnamese Communists |
| WHA | Wounded, Hostile Action |
| WIA | Wounded in Action |
| XO | Executive Officer |

Time: Times are designated using the 24 hour clock or military system of time. After 1200 (Noon) comes 1300 and so on.

Unit abbreviations are as noted:

| | |
|---|---|
| 1st Battalion, 16th Infantry | 1-16 Infantry |
| A Company, 1-16 Infantry | A-1-16 Infantry |
| 1st Squadron, 4th Cavalry | 1-4 Cavalry |
| 1st Battalion, 5th Artillery | 1-5 Artillery |

Battery, Company and Troop letter designations are addressed as:
A-Alpha, B-Bravo, C-Charlie, D-Delta

Ranks, when abbreviated, use the modern abbreviations except for Spec-4/5:

| Rank | Pay Grade | Abbreviation |
|---|---|---|
| Enlisted (EM) | | |
| Private | E-1, 2 | PVT |
| Private First Class | E-3 | PFC |
| Specialist Forth Class | E-4 | Spec-4 |
| Specialist Fifth Class | E-5 | Spec-5 |

Non-Commissioned Officers (NCO)

| | | |
|---|---|---|
| Corporal | E-4 | CPL |
| Sergeant | E-5 | SGT |
| Staff Sergeant | E-6 | SSG |
| Platoon Sergeant | E-7 | PSG |
| Sergeant First Class | E-7 | SFC |
| Master Sergeant | E-8 | MSG |
| First Sergeant | E-8 | 1SG |
| Sergeant Major | E-9 | SGM |
| Command Sergeant Major | E-9 | CSM |
| Sergeant Major of the Army | E-9 | SMA |

All Sergeants are addressed as 'Sergeant' except for First Sergeants and Sergeants Major.

Warrant Officers

| | | |
|---|---|---|
| Warrant Officer | W-1 | WO |
| Chief Warrant Officer 2 | W-2 | CWO 2 |
| Chief Warrant Officer 3 | W-3 | CWO 3 |
| Chief Warrant Officer 4 | W-4 | CWO 4 |

Chief Warrant Officers 2 thru 4 are addressed as 'Chief.'

Officers

| | | |
|---|---|---|
| 2nd Lieutenant | O-1 | 2LT |
| 1st Lieutenant | O-2 | 1LT |
| Captain | O-3 | CPT |
| Major | O-4 | MAJ |
| Lieutenant Colonel | O-5 | LTC |
| Colonel | O-6 | COL |
| Brigadier General | O-7 | BG |
| Major General | O-8 | MG |
| Lieutenant General | O-9 | LTG |
| General | O-10 | GEN |

2d and 1st Lieutenants are addressed as 'Lieutenant,' or LT,
Lieutenant Colonels and Colonels are addressed as 'Colonel.'
All General officers are addressed as 'General.'

# Introduction

## The End of the Road

On April 30, 1975, a North Vietnamese Army tank crashed through the gate of the Independence Palace in Saigon. The President of the Republic of Vietnam announced the unconditional surrender of his country. Colonel Bui Tin, a senior NVA officer told him, "Although the war is ended today, all Vietnamese are victors. Only the American imperialists are the vanquished. If you still have any feeling for the nation and the people, then you can consider this day your own happy day, your day of victory."[6]

## The Road to War

America's military involvement in Vietnam began during WWII when Office of Strategic Services (OSS) operatives parachuted into northern Vietnam to arm and train a small band of Vietnamese communist anti-Japanese resistance fighters led by Ho Chi Minh and Vo Nguyen Giap. When the Japanese surrendered, Ho declared Vietnamese independence. Then the French returned to reclaim their former colony and were soon engaged in an eight year war with Ho Chi Minh's forces, the Viet Minh. The Cold War's geo-political concerns, the fear of a communist takeover in France, forced the U.S. to tacitly support the French effort to reclaim their colonies.[7]

In 1950, President Truman approved logistical support to the French. In 1954 President Eisenhower approved covert bombing and aerial resupply, using repainted U.S. Air Force planes, in support of French troops at Dien Bien Phu. In the aftermath of the French defeat, Eisenhower began a massive aid program to the newly established Republic of Vietnam.

In 1961, President Kennedy inherited Eisenhower's program in Southeast Asia, increasing the number of advisors and aid. A year after Kennedy's assassination in 1963, President Johnson, while campaigning for the presidency, said, "We are not about to send American boys nine or ten thousand miles away from home to do what Asian boys ought to be doing for themselves." Johnson was elected by the largest margin in U.S. history with sixty-one percent of the popular vote, running as the 'peace candidate' against Senator Barry Goldwater.[8]

*And this is the writing that was inscribed: mene, mene, tekel, and parsin.*
*This is the interpretation of the matter: mene,*
*God has numbered the days of your kingdom and brought it to an end*
*Daniel 5:25-27*

# Chapter 1-My Road to War

### The Writing on the Wall

Due to a series of most unfortunate events, my road to war began the moment I was born. It was a time of unprecedented turmoil on the earth. As soon as I could read I took an interest in the news of the day and the events mentioned shaped me and the generation that would go to war in Vietnam.

I was conceived in the spring of 1945 during a brief wartime reunion of my parents in San Francisco, California. My father was the first mate on a cargo ship that was supplying the troops fighting in the Pacific and my mother was working as a secretary for a Navy pre-flight training program at a college in the San Francisco Bay Area. They were part of the national mobilization which had unified the country, enabling the impending defeat of Germany, and Japan.

In the spring of that year, Allied troops were advancing in every theater. Italy had already surrendered; Germany would do so in June; and after two of its cities were vaporized by atomic bombs, Japan would do the same in September.

As World War II came to a blazing end, the writing was on the wall for the European empires. The British, Dutch, and French were on the brink of ruin and their colonies in Asia, Africa and the Middle East were demanding independence. The Russian Empire, though devastated by the German invasion, was now expanding into Eastern Europe after defeating Germany and its allies.

I was born in January of 1946. One of the first of the baby-boomer invasion, I was brought into a world that appeared to be at peace; but that was an illusion. While my parents and the rest of the nation were worried about housing, jobs, their kids, the Russians, and Negroes; millions of people around the world were struggling for survival as the old order crumbled.

### A New World Order

The new world order now consisted of three 'worlds;' the U.S. and its allies, the U.S.S.R. (Russia) and its subjects, and the non-aligned countries of the 'Third World.' As the colonies became independent, these countries with their natural resources and people would be wooed by the great powers; and if the suitor was unsuccessful, they became targets for agitation, subversion and even invasion.

The Russian Empire had grabbed most of Eastern Europe and now cast her eyes on the rest of the world. The result of this was a wave of fear in the U.S., the fear of an idea.

People's loyalties were publicly questioned on television, but this fear was not without cause. According to the communist ideology, radical changes in the social order and a redistribution of the wealth would have to take place. These changes were implemented by force. Millions of people were murdered, starved or worked to death in the new 'Workers Paradise.'[9]

## The Cold War

Two months after I was born, in an attempt to awaken the world to the threat posed by Russia, Britain's wartime Prime Minister, Winston Churchill, now voted out of office, gave his 'Iron Curtain' speech at a small college in Missouri. It was a declaration of war, the 'Cold War.'[10]

At the end of WWII there were twelve million Americans in the armed forces. Two years later, after a massive demobilization, there were one and a half million in uniform. In June of 1948, as the Cold War warmed up, the Selective Service Act required all men from eighteen to twenty-six years of age to register for the draft. The 'military obligation' was defined as an eight year combination of active, active reserve, and inactive duty. After high school, young men had the choice of being drafted into the army or joining another service. Going into the service for two years of active duty became part of the culture. In July of 1948, President Truman integrated the armed forces by executive order.[11]

## Civil Rights

There were other writings on the wall, this time closer to home. Since the end of the Civil War, black people faced a life of absolute segregation in the South and various forms of de-facto segregation in the rest of the country. Hispanics faced prejudices in the Southwest: children were punished if they spoke Spanish at school and signs saying, "No Mexicans" were seen on restaurant windows.[12]

From the day I entered kindergarten, our teachers taught us to say the Pledge of Allegiance. Every morning, standing together with our right hand over our heart, we faced the flag and recited the words that bound all Americans in a common belief that our flag represented liberty and justice for all. Of course, in kindergarten these words didn't mean much; but we all knew them by heart.

My father grew up in central California. His grandfather was a cowboy and a cattleman. Once when I was traveling with him we had a flat tire. He didn't have a jack and while he was considering the next move, a car pulled up next to us. A black man got out and asked my father if he could help. I could sense that my father was uncomfortable but I didn't know why.

He told the man that everything was OK, but I blurted out that we didn't have a jack. The man smiled at me, opened his trunk and pulled out a jack. My father then allowed him to jack up our car and the man helped him change the tire. When they were finished the man offered my father a swig of some liquid in a gallon jar which my father refused. He offered the man a five dollar bill for his help but the man refused to take it. He put his jack away and drove off. My father was angry, but he wouldn't say why; and he never spoke of the incident again.

## Duck and Cover

After the Soviet Union successfully detonated an atomic bomb and China fell to the communists, the U.S. government began an all-out civil defense campaign to prepare for nuclear attacks. In kindergarten I was trained to deal with the unthinkable by practicing to duck under my school desk and cover my head when I saw a bright flash.

Plans were published for family fall-out shelters and the ethics of sharing with less-prepared neighbors was debated. The fear of total annihilation became part of the culture.[13]

## The Korean War

North Korea, backed by the Soviet Union, invaded South Korea in June of 1950. Divided by the victors of WWII, Korea became a battle of the wills between Russia, China, and the West, led by the U.S. With the advent of atomic weapons it was thought that the days of extended infantry combat operations were over. Then the U.S. became engaged in another infantry shooting war in Korea.

After initial successes, the North Koreans were cut-off and routed by General MacArthur's brilliant landing at Inchon. They were pursued north toward the Chinese border. Thinking that the U.S. intended to restore the Government of Chiang Kai-shek, Communist China sent 500,000 'volunteers' to Korea.[14]

I was up early one morning and joined my father at the kitchen table. He had finished breakfast and was preparing for the long ride to San Francisco in a car pool with other men who had left the most exciting times of their lives and were now working boring jobs; my father's was in the insurance business.

He was smoking a cigarette and drinking a cup of coffee while listening to the news on the radio. I sat down quietly, having learned not to bother him during his morning ritual. The announcer was talking about a place called Korea. He said that all was quiet with only routine patrol activity. I waited until the commercial before asking him what a patrol was. He looked at his watch, stubbed out his cigarette, looked back at me as he stood up and said, "It's war."

## What is War?

From that time on I tried to find out everything I could about wars, armies, and battles. I had resisted learning how to read, to the despair of my mother, until I found out that there was a wealth of information about these things in the books at the library. My parents were astonished at my sudden interest in reading and took me to the local library on a regular basis. My father subscribed to Time Magazine and often had to search for it in my room when he wanted to read it.

My second source of information was the continual stream of propaganda films made during the war that were being shown on a new device called the television. For several years, my father resisted our entreaties to buy one. All our neighbors had one when he finally gave in, after my sisters and I promised that we would only watch it for an hour a day. During the summer when there was no school and my father was at work, my mother was unable to hold the line against my demand for more TV time, and I must have seen every war movie ever made.

When I wasn't reading about war or watching "Victory at Sea," and "The Big Picture," I was patrolling the nearby hills for enemy soldiers preparing to attack. The boys in the neighborhood would choose sides for war games and we built forts and had pear fights during the harvest time. My mother had a large bell that she rang as hard as she could when it was time for dinner. Frequently, I got lashes on my bare butt from my father's razor strop after arriving several hours late for dinner, claiming that I hadn't heard the bell.[15]

## Indochina

When my mother took me with her to shop at the grocery store, I would run to the magazine rack and look at the large picture magazines. They would be filled with photographs of the war in Korea and another place called Indochina. My mother was mildly interested in the latter because of her French heritage and would look at the pictures for a moment before pulling me away so she could go home and cook dinner.

The U.S. and its allies had managed to hold the line in Korea but refused to send troops to help the French regain control of their colonies in Indochina. Instead we quietly provided overt and covert logistical support for her war against the Viet Minh. After the cease-fire in Korea, the French withdrew their contribution to that war, an infantry battalion, and sent it to participate in their last ditch fight to hold on to their colonies in Southeast Asia.

The climactic battle at Dien Bien Phu, an attempt by the French to draw the Viet Minh under General Vo Nguyen Giap into attacking their fortified positions that were supported by artillery and airstrikes, was a disaster. The Viet Minh moved men and material to the battlefield in a logistical effort that astonished the world. Using artillery pieces, given to them by the Chinese who captured them in Korea, they hammered the French positions and then overwhelmed them with waves of infantry.[16]

A few days after the fall of Dien Bien Phu in May 1954, the 'Korea' battalion was swallowed up in a series of ambushes on Route 19 between An Khe and Pleiku, places that would become well known to the U.S. in the next decade.[17]

On 21 July, 1954, the Viet Minh and the French signed the 'Agreement on the Cessation of Hostilities in Viet Nam.' There was a second document, which provided for, among other things, the division of the country pending a nationwide vote that would decide whether there would be reunification or permanent division. Although most parties agreed with this in principal, it was never signed. Indochina became North and South Vietnam, divided at the 17th Parallel. The CIA began covert operations in the north with the goal of disrupting the communist consolidation of power there.

In October 1954, Ho Chi Minh and his troops took over Hanoi and northern Vietnam. The country was devastated by the wars. The refugees who fled to the south had looted and destroyed essential services. The main source of rice was in the south and no longer available. China and the Soviet Union began providing aid while Ho attempted to carry out land reform. They held tribunals and between ten and fifteen thousand people were killed, 'erroneously' by their government.[18]

## South Vietnam

In the south, the last emperor of Vietnam, Bao Dai, appointed Ngo Dinh Diem, a Catholic, as the Prime Minister of South Vietnam, a country populated by Buddhists, Taoists, and Confucianists. The CIA operations in the north convinced the Catholics there to flee to the south and a million of them did, giving Diem a strong anti-communist constituency. The plight of the refugees fleeing to the south on U.S. Navy ships received a great deal of media coverage and the Catholic Church added their voice to the call to save these people from the communists.[19]

The U.S. began to support South Vietnam. By August of 1954, the U.S. Military Assistance Advisory Group had 342 men in the south. Infiltration and subversion by agents of the North had begun and any dissent was ruthlessly suppressed by the government forces of South Vietnam. During the rest of the fifties, Diem consolidated his rule and the U.S. supported him with aid programs and military assistance.[20]

### Southern California

In 1954, as the French survivors of Dien Bien Phu were being marched into captivity, my family moved from the hills of east San Francisco Bay to the beaches of Southern California. It was here that my research on all things related to war was suddenly interrupted by something I saw at the main beach of Corona del Mar. Men were standing on long planks and riding waves that towered over them. They were surfing! Just like Mr. Toad, when he saw his first motor car in "The Wind in the Willows," this was my epiphany and I had to have a surfboard.[21]

### Civil Rights (2)

In 1954 the U.S. Supreme Court ruled that segregation in public schools was unconstitutional. This would lead to some brutal confrontations at Little Rock High School and the University of Mississippi.

In December of 1955, Rosa Parks refused to give up her seat to a white passenger on a bus in Montgomery, Alabama. This incident led to a bus boycott and publicized the hypocrisy of the U.S. attitude toward racial equality. This was the beginning of the end of institutional racial segregation in the United States.[22]

In 1957, U.S. troops from the 101st Airborne Division were sent by President Eisenhower to enforce the law in Little Rock and the civil rights movement continued to gain momentum in the 'land of the free and the home of the brave.' In 1962, the Mississippi National Guard joined the U.S. Marshals in a pitched battle with segregationists at 'Old Miss when an Air Force veteran named James Meredith tried to enroll.'[23]

Much of this was shown on the nightly television news and I was at a loss to understand any of it. My mother thought that racial discrimination was terrible and my father didn't say anything. I became interested because up to this point I thought everybody was happy in the U.S.A.

### My Career Decision

At school, I gave the impression to my teachers that I wasn't interested in the subjects they were teaching. How right they were. In a kind of pre-PTSD experience, my mind was preoccupied with war history and surfing fantasies. My parents sought help and I was diagnosed with what they now call ADD or attention deficit disorder.

My father told me repeatedly that if I didn't study I would end up digging ditches. When I saw the movie, "To Hell and Back," starring Audie Murphy, and saw that soldiers had to dig foxholes, my father's predictions about my future helped me to decide on a career, I would join the army and serve in the infantry.[24]

## The Army

I continued following the news of the day by watching television and reading the magazines at the store. There were full color pictures of the atom bomb testing in Nevada. Troops were sent there as guinea pigs to prove that the Army could function on the nuclear battlefield. In order to stay relevant with the competition for budget, the infantry went nuclear and fielded the Davy Crockett that could launch a small atomic projectile one and half miles. Our weekly news magazine announced that the first 'atomic division,' the Pentomic Division, would be the reorganized 101st Airborne, commanded by Major General Westmoreland.[25]

By now I had begun to follow U.S. politics. President Eisenhower's term was coming to an end and there was a kind of expectation that a change was coming. In 1959 General Maxwell Taylor, the Chief of Staff of the Army, resigned in frustration with the New Look policies of the Eisenhower administration which emphasized a 'massive (nuclear) response' to Soviet aggression. With the Air Force claiming the lion's share of the defense budget and the thought of all-out nuclear war in response to lesser threats, he published a book in 1960, "The Uncertain Trumpet" which influenced the presidential campaign of John F. Kennedy to adopt a strategy called the 'flexible response' to the 'brushfire wars' that were continuing to spring up around the world.

Taylor became Kennedy's principal military advisor after the election. He convinced Kennedy that the army could deal the guerrilla wars springing up around the world. With Gavin and Ridgway retired, Taylor was now the 'Godfather' of the airborne 'mafia.'[26]

## Vietnam

In the north, Ho Chi Minh continued to consolidate his revolution. Land reform was proving unpopular and when his home province revolted, he sent a division of his army to put it down. In 1956, the deadline for the plebiscite on the question of reunification passed. In the south, when Diem, backed by the U.S. and knowing that Ho Chi Minh would win the vote for reunification, refused to abide by the Geneva Agreements and insurgency began in earnest in the south. In May, 1959 North Vietnam took control of the insurgency with reunification of the two Vietnams now the goal.[27]

## The Promise

Along with my parents and millions of other Americans I watched the televised debate between Richard Nixon and Senator Kennedy. Kennedy won the young people with his quick wit and brilliant smile. He was elected president in November of 1960.

In his inaugural address he answered Nikita Khrushchev's pledge that the Soviet Union would support wars of national liberation, by declaring that the U.S. would, "pay any price, bear any burden, meet any hard ship, support any friend, and oppose any foe, to insure the survival and success of liberty." Nine days later, Radio Hanoi announced the forming of a 'National Liberation Front' for South Vietnam. Viet Minh were now called Viet Cong.[28]

The Kennedy administration became known as Camelot and it seemed like there was nothing the Americans couldn't do. From JFK came a call to the youth of the country to "ask not what your country can do for you, but what you can do for your country." Fifty mile hikes were declared the standard for physical fitness and he even set a ten year goal for landing men on the moon.

## Another Type of War

In 1961 Kennedy decided that U.S. credibility required a stand in South Vietnam. He directed the armed forces to develop a counter-insurgency capability and insisted that military officers receive training in counter-insurgency tactics. When the Army chief of staff told the president that, "any good soldier can handle guerrillas," he was replaced. He authorized the U.S. Army Special Forces to wear the Green Beret and following his directive, the Navy created the SEAL teams and the Air Force 'Air Commandos' were resurrected.[29]

The Viet Cong (VC) guerrilla attacks increased in South Vietnam and Kennedy responded by sending more advisors and Special Forces. By the end of 1961, there were 3200 U.S. military personnel in South Vietnam and 27,000 VC insurgents. The U.S. Air Force was flying combat missions in support of South Vietnamese ground forces and their U.S. advisors. In January 1962 the Air Force began defoliation missions using Agent Orange. By the end of 1962 there were 11,000 U.S. military personnel in South Vietnam and an estimated 25,000 trained VC guerrillas and 150,000 VC 'sympathizers.'[30]

## Ap Bac, South Vietnam

In January of 1963, near the village of Ap Bac, 2,500 ARVN soldiers fought with 300 VC who stood their ground for a day. The VC shot down a number of U.S. helicopters, killed several U.S. advisors and more than fifty ARVN's. They left three of their own dead when they retreated during the night. When General Harkins the MACV commander proclaimed the battle a victory, young American war correspondents wrote opposing stories in the U.S. newspapers.[31]

I followed all these events with interest. When I tried to discuss them with my surfing friends they had no idea what I was talking about and decided I was crazy. I was doing so poorly in school that I dared not ask for information from my teachers and I was in constant trouble at home. As a result, I read whatever I could get my hands on at night and tried to get to the beach whenever I wasn't at school.

## High School

After repeating the eighth grade, I was enrolled in a Catholic high school which asked me not to return after my freshman year. As a sophomore, surfing, girls, and military history were my main interests. Since they didn't tie-in with the education process, I was suspended and finally expelled after the school compared the various hand writings on all the 'he was sick' notes from my 'parents' that had covered my surfing trips to the beach. For my junior year, my parents sent me to a boarding school in Arizona because the California schools were tired of me.

## The Arizona Army National Guard

In March of 1963, during my junior year in high school, I joined Company B, 3d Battalion, 158th Infantry of the Arizona Army National Guard. After I was sworn in, the Guard issued me uniforms and field gear. We had drill every Tuesday night and a weekend drill once a month.

That summer I attended annual training (summer camp) with my unit at Fort Huachuca, Arizona. It was the most exciting two weeks of my life. I was issued an M-1 Garand rifle and carried it everywhere we went. During the first week we had classes in garrison. I learned how to make a bunk the 'army way' and how to lay out my equipment for an inspection. A regular army advisor with little patches that said 'airborne' and 'ranger' taught me bayonet drills.

On the weekend, most of the company went on a spree in the desert oasis of Naco, Arizona. It was a typical border town and since most of their activities took place in Mexico, I was privileged to experience an 'old army' tradition the 'Short-Arm Inspection,' that has since gone the way of the horse cavalry.

We stayed in the field for the second week and fired our rifles, the M-1919A2 BAR, and the M-1919A6 Machine Gun. Even though I hadn't been to basic training, I participated in all the training events. We did day and night live-fire attacks on a hill, first by squad, then platoon and finally the whole company with the mortars and recoilless rifles.

On payday I stepped in front of the CO and rendered my very best RAF salute. I then received some personal saluting instruction from my squad leader before I got paid. Later, as we rode back to Phoenix in the back of a truck, I was reviewing all that I had learned at summer camp. My squad leader had told me that I did a good job and I had enjoyed the rough humor of the troops. It was then that I decided to skip my senior year of high school and attend basic training where I was sure to learn what I needed to know for a career in the Regular Army. When we returned from Fort Huachuca, I asked to be sent to basic training.

## Basic Training

I took basic training at Fort Ord, California in September 1963. President Kennedy had granted draft exemptions to married men that same month but many of the married men in my basic training company missed the date on the Executive Order by several days. I didn't understand why they were so unhappy. Later, when student deferments were introduced, the 'fairness' of the system was completely compromised and many of those who were drafted felt like they had been screwed.[32]

Since I had already done everything an infantryman would ever do in training I thought I was a veteran. While the rest of my platoon complained about how hard it was I would tell them that this stuff was easy. My attitude didn't enhance my popularity with the platoon.

I would have done better in 1st Platoon which was made up entirely of Eskimos, members of the Eskimo Scout Battalions of the Alaska National Guard, stationed on the little islands in the Bering Sea close to Russia. Most of them didn't speak English and wouldn't have been bothered by my incessant babbling, about all things army.

## Drill Sergeants

My drill sergeant, SFC Bernard Chase, took a special interest in my personal hygiene. One morning during inspection he noticed that I hadn't shaved. The rest of the platoon was delighted when he grabbed me by the throat and shaved me with his pocket knife.

One of Sergeant Chase's many concerns was supply conservation. He had the entire platoon watch as he demonstrated how we were to use one sheet of toilet paper when we wiped. After folding the paper a number of times until it looked like a spearhead, he pulled off a small piece of the tip and put it behind his ear. He then unfolded the paper and put his index finger in the hole.

He demonstrated the wipe with gestures and then squeezing the paper around his finger, he slid it forward showing us how to clean our finger. He disposed of the larger piece of paper and took the small piece from behind his ear and showed us how to use it to clean the fingernail.

Sergeant Chase wasn't amused but the whole company got a laugh when I fell out for a Class A inspection forgetting that I was wearing the white socks that I used when running a buffer on the center aisle of our barracks. The first sergeant noticed them and directed me to stand on an elevated platform in front of the formation with my Class A trousers rolled up to my knees.

For the regular army at Fort Ord, the atmosphere was like the news of an awesome party in Laguna Beach to a bunch of surfers. Young officers with the blue and white Combat Infantryman Badge (CIB) sewn on their fatigues were strutting around Fort Ord. Every day I heard my drill sergeant asking the company clerk if his orders for Vietnam had come.

Regardless what the novelists say, most soldiers are excited by the prospects of going to war. Besides being the place where young manhood is tested, the opportunities for career enhancement are an irresistible motivation to many professional military men. General Westmoreland was quoted later as saying that "The Russian Army was envious of the U.S. Army officer corps for gaining all that combat experience."[33]

## Change of Command

The day before I graduated from basic, President Kennedy was shot in Dallas, Texas. We were being tested on a hill overlooking the main post when we heard the news. No one seemed alarmed but there was a lot of whispered speculation about the extent of his injuries and who did it. Then we saw the flag at the main post go to half-staff, announcing a change in seasons for our country and the rest of the world.

The next day, for graduation, we joined every other soldier on Fort Ord and stood in formation on the runway of the old Army Airfield. There we heard an officer announce that Lyndon Johnson was the President. For our parade, we marched back to the barracks and were dismissed.

My basic training company's first sergeant wore a unit patch on his right shoulder with a big red one. "What's that patch stand for?" I asked him, figuring that if the question made him angry he couldn't do much to me because I had my orders. "Sonny," he said, "that's the best damn division in this sorry-ass'd army."

### Advanced Individual Training

My orders for advanced individual training, or AIT, had to be wrong. I was assigned to a clerk-typist course instead of infantry training. Believing the orders to be in error, I went through the entire chain of command until I was standing at attention in front of a full bird colonel, who while sympathetic to my desire to be an infantryman, assured me that there was no mistake and that my unit in Arizona had wanted me to be a clerk. I had no choice but to go to clerk typist school where I quickly gained notoriety as the worst clerk in the army, and was eventually awarded the MOS of file clerk, lower than a clerk-typist.

### Covert Operations

In February of 1964, while I was pretending to learn how to type, the U.S. military began its covert operations against North Vietnam under the codename OPLAN 34A. These operations included dropping unconventional warfare teams by parachute into North Vietnam and commando raids on coastal installations. At the same time the U.S. Navy ran intelligence gathering patrols off-shore.[34]

### Surfing

When I finished my six months of active duty, I still had some unfinished business on the coast of California. And as I was still mad about the clerk school business, I sent my regrets to my unit in Arizona and joined a unit of the California Army National Guard. I spent the next year flipping burgers, salting French fries and surfing at my favorite spot, Trestles, which was 'Off Limits' on Camp Pendleton Marine Base.

I was now over six feet tall and a little clumsy; in my estimation I hadn't gotten very good at surfing but I refused to give up. One of my high school friends who had a car took me to the beach a number of times that year. There we practiced infiltration techniques to counter the defensive tactics of the MPs.

Because of complaints about surfers 'mooning' the train that passed close to the beach two times a day, the Marines at Camp Pendleton had escalated their campaign to keep the surfers from enjoying one of the best point-breaks in California. This cut down on crowds and there were several times when we had the waves all to ourselves.

The year before, I had been caught by some clever MPs who had suddenly appeared while we were sitting on the beach. We ran into the water with our boards, paddled out past the breakers, and flipped them off. They left, but then they low-crawled through the sand and were waiting when I tried to retrieve my glasses which were hidden with my t-shirt under a clump of seaweed. I paddled in and grabbed them; that's when they grabbed me and confiscated my surfboard.

To get my board back, I had to go with my mother to the Provost Marshal's office where a Marine Master Gunnery Sergeant ranted and raved at my mother about the despicable things that the surfers were doing on his beach. "Let me show you what they're doing," he shouted, as he pulled a large photograph from the top drawer of his desk and thrust it in my mother's face. In the photo was a line of surfers, backs to the train with their trunks down to their ankles, spreading their cheeks and smiling between their legs. On the way home, I promised my mother that I would never be caught there again.

My friend was a prudent man and made sure that when we snuck onto the base we hid his car in the deepest part of the jungle behind the beach. We would stop before a wall of thick vegetation and take our boards out of the trunk. Then he would drive his car as far as he could into the wall of vegetation. I showed him what I had learned from the Army about camouflage. We made sure that no one could see his car and we even brushed out our tracks on the dirt road near our hiding places. We always walked to the beach on the smaller trails that were not so well known and we never got caught by the MPs.

It was one of those beautiful southern California days—hot, sunny, almost no wind and the waves were six to eight foot blue faces and glassy when we paddled out to the break at Lower Trestles. We were the only ones out. The sets were coming about every three or four minutes. When the next set came, my friend caught the first wave and dropped down the face.

I turned my board toward the beach and waited for the next wave to go by. When it did I got on my knees and began to paddle toward the shore for the wave that was approaching behind me. I felt myself being lifted up as it caught up to me and suddenly I was being pushed forward.

I had caught a wave with maybe an eight foot face. I stood up and rode my board straight down to the bottom, turned hard to the right and went right back up to the top. I ran to the nose to keep from going out of the wave, backpedaled, cutback and went straight down to the bottom again. There I made another right turn, trimmed and suddenly I realized I was really surfing.

The wave walled up for the section that is to the right of the peak. I set the trim of my board and rode across the section with the wave breaking right behind me. It was so good! When I pulled out a long way down the line where the wave petered out; I was electrified. All those years I had been trying to do what I had just done! I shouted, splashed the water; I had a little celebration all by myself.

When I paddled back out I saw my friend taking off on a set wave. He was really surfing well. Instead of wishing I could do the same, I raised my fist and shouted "whaa hoo!" as he rode by. The next wave I caught, I did pretty much the same thing but when the wave started walling up for the section, I walked forward and got my first real nose ride. I didn't hang five or ten but I was within six inches of the nose and I stood there while my board carried me across that wall of water. I must have ridden twenty waves that day and by the time we left I was on a high that would last for several days. All the way home I told my friend about each ride until he finally told me to shut up. I know he was sharing my stoke but there was only so much he could take.

We went to Trestles every day during that swell. One day we saw James Arness, the actor from the TV show, "Gunsmoke," surfing at Upper Trestles, and on another day, we saw a fellow I knew from Newport who was making surfing films. While we were talking to him, a jeep full of Marines drove up the beach. Since they weren't MPs we watched warily to see what they wanted. When they waved I walked over and talked to a lieutenant who just wanted to watch the surfing. He was on a training exercise nearby, "Guerrilla warfare training," he said, looking out to sea toward Southeast Asia.

## Vietnam

Meanwhile, the news reports coming out of South Vietnam were bad. The advisory effort was not sufficient to defeat a growing insurgency supported by North Vietnam. The South Vietnamese Army suffered defeat after defeat at the hands of guerrilla forces that melted away after inflicting heavy casualties.

Step by step, President Johnson attempted to persuade the North Vietnamese to stop backing the insurgency in the south by increasing the level of violence. In August of 1964, while covert operations against North Vietnam continued, the U.S. claimed that the North Vietnamese had attacked U.S. Navy ships in international waters, and launched airstrikes against North Vietnam. The airstrikes destroyed half the North Vietnamese Navy. Congress passed the Gulf of Tonkin resolution which granted Johnson authorization to use conventional forces in Southeast Asia without a declaration of war.[35]

In September, Montagnard tribes revolted and killed fifty ARVN troops at a U.S. Special Forces camp. That story was featured on the front page of National Geographic Magazine. The Green Berets, President Kennedy's great hope for countering these guerrilla bands were unable to overcome the larger problems of increased North Vietnamese Army infiltration into the south, and an inefficient and corrupt South Vietnamese government and military.

## Politics

After the Cuban Missile Crisis in October of '62, the fear of nuclear war weighed heavily on the country. The presidential election of 1964 had Lyndon Johnson running as the 'peace' candidate against Senator Barry Goldwater. In a campaign speech in Akron, Ohio, he told the country, "We are not about to send American boys nine or ten thousand miles away from home to do what Asian boys ought to be doing for themselves." LBJ was elected by a landslide.[36]

## Vietnam

North Vietnam responded to our covert operations with a few of their own. In November the VC attacked Bien Hoa Air Base, twelve miles north of Saigon and killed five Americans and two Vietnamese, while wounding many others. The VC also destroyed six B-57 bombers and damaged twenty more aircraft. At the end of the year, 416 American servicemen had been killed in Vietnam since 1957.

The VC hit Camp Holloway in the Central Highlands at Pleiku in February 1965. Eight Americans were killed, 126 wounded, and twenty-five aircraft were destroyed or damaged. [37]

## Johnson Sends the American Boys

President Johnson authorized the introduction of U.S. combat troops to guard the air bases and in March, 3,500 Marines made an amphibious landing at Da Nang, South Vietnam. They were welcomed by Vietnamese girls who gave them lei's, as if they were landing in Hawaii, and by some Army advisors with a large sign saying, "Welcome, Gallant Marines."

Shortly after this, the 173d Airborne Brigade left their home on the island of Okinawa to perform similar duties at the air base at Bien Hoa, just north of Saigon. The mission of these units was defensive but little by little, their patrols ranged further and further until they were conducting what would come to be called 'search and destroy' operations.[38]

### The Regular Army

On June 1st, 1965, at the beginning of the summer surfing season, I demonstrated my commitment to an Army career by enlisting in the regular army. Not because I couldn't wait any longer to get to the war but because I had just been released from the county jail where I had spent thirty days for an accumulation of unpaid speeding tickets; tickets which I threw out the window as I sped away from several encounters with the police.

I knew that if I stayed around I'd soon be back in jail so I raised my hand the same day I was released from incarceration. The recruiter, citing some regulation, made me take four years instead of three because of my recent crime spree. My father was at sea and my mother made me promise to enlist for Europe so I could get some 'old world' culture.

I went in through the Los Angeles Induction Center which was quite a zoo in 1965. The next day, because I was a Private E-2, I was put in charge of a group of men and told to take them to Fort Polk, Louisiana. Once again, thinking that I was a veteran, having been to basic training and having done live fires with the Guard, I expected to be given some important task while waiting for my Infantry AIT course to start.

The army agreed and put me on KP at the South Fort Polk Officers Mess for thirty days. Every morning at 0400, the CQ would wake us up for KP. We would work until 1900. After a quick shower we would go to the beer club next to our transit barracks and drink 3.2 swill until they closed. Often we would pass out on the lawn between the club and the barracks. No problem: the CQ would check the lawn. After burning my fingers on a hot pan I was given a new job: escorting one of my fellow KPs to the stockade after he got tired of KP and went AWOL.

### 11b-Infantry

Finally I took a bus to North Fort Polk and Infantry AIT. North Fort was buzzing as the cadre attempted to cope with the flood of recruits that summer. I was pretty sure I was going to Germany because of my enlistment contract but the word going around was that Vietnam was the destination for the draftees and anyone else who hadn't requested airborne school. Because of my exalted rank, I was made an 'acting jack' platoon sergeant in an 11b infantry company. For the next two months we trained for fighting the Russians in Europe. I guess I did OK with my duties because I was promoted to PFC the day we graduated.

While we were training, rumors were flying. The Marines and the 173d Airborne Brigade had already deployed to Vietnam. On 28 July, President Johnson announced in a televised news conference that he was sending 50,000 more troops to Vietnam, including the Airmobile Division. Later we found out that this included the Big Red One (1st Infantry Division), and a brigade from the

101st Airborne Division was also heading that way. Most of the men I trained with at Fort Polk that summer were assigned to either the 1st Cavalry Division or the 1st Infantry Division which were both trying to build up their remaining brigades prior to sending them to Vietnam that fall.

### The Cold War-West Germany

After passing through Infantry AIT at Fort Polk, Louisiana, I received orders assigning me to the 7th Army in West Germany. I flew to Frankfurt, missing the troopship experience, where I was assigned to the 4th Armored Division. Once again due to my PFC rank I was put in charge of five other men and we took a train to Goppingen in Southern Germany. When we arrived at the station I stood up, stretched, and before I could alert my troops, the train took off. At the next station we went through a nightmare of currency exchange, sign language, and a lot of "Ja, ja, ja!" exchanges with the locals before we caught the next train back to Goppingen where we jumped off like paratroopers as soon as it stopped.

After more processing I was taken to Bamberg in Northern Bavaria in the back of a deuce and a half. When we finally arrived, the driver lowered the tailgate and said, "So you're going to Pork Chop's outfit, well, good luck." After processing through battalion, I was assigned to Company A, commanded by Captain James R. Davis, of the 2nd Battalion, 54th Infantry, commanded by LTC Joseph G. Clemons Jr. who was played by Gregory Peck in the movie "Pork Chop Hill." There I was schooled in the ways of the mechanized infantry.[39]

This was the frontline of the Cold War. Rumor had it that our mission was to fight our way to Berlin when the balloon went up. We had classes on nuclear, biological, and chemical warfare. The nuclear battlefield was an interesting concept especially when we discussed the use of the dosimeter which would tell us how much radiation we had received after a nuclear attack. If the radiation reached a certain level we would attack the nearest enemy troop concentration in a 'heroic' effort to kill as many of the enemy as possible because we wouldn't survive the radiation dose we had received.

We kept a basic load of ammunition in our M-113 APCs, called 'tracks' and once a month we would be awakened at 0400 by a klaxon blasting repeatedly as we grabbed our field-gear duffle bag and ran to the arms room to draw our weapons. From there we would run to the track park and prep our APCs for movement. Our platoon sergeant liked to beat the battalion recon platoon out of the track park so as soon as we had everyone we would roar out of the Kaserne and head for an assembly area in the woods. Sometimes this would be the start of a field problem but usually we returned to the Kaserne by the afternoon.

Several times a year the battalion would drive the vehicles to a rail head, load them on a train and go to a major training area like Grafenwoehr or Hohenfels where we would stay for a few weeks and train. According to the old-timers, our unit was always in the field during Oktoberfest, a yearly beer drinker's festival in Munich. This was due to past outrages by American infantrymen unused to the alcohol content of the German beer.

When we drove our APCs down the public roads, the German civilian vehicles would dart in and out of the spaces between our 'tracks' as they tried to pass. We had these paddles that were painted with a red symbol on one side and a green one on the other. When a civilian vehicle pulled into the space behind our track, the air guard, standing up in the open cargo hatch and facing to the rear, was supposed to look forward and see if it was safe to pass. When it was, he was supposed to wave the green paddle.

The Germans ignored the paddles and took their chances, which pissed off the GIs. In retaliation, we would signal a green sign when we saw on-coming traffic. The Germans were wise to this and would give us the finger before pulling out when they thought it was safe.

## Maneuvers

We had a lot of maneuvers in the German countryside. The length of them was determined by the amount of money allocated for maneuver damage. A tank hitting a patch of ice and sliding into a German house could cost a lot of money. The big one that year had us facing the 24th Infantry Division with a river between us. After a few days we were told to remain where we were because we had reached the limit of maneuver damage money.

One night my squad was chosen to patrol across the river on a small bridge and sneak into a town that was on the south side of a much larger bridge. There we found two M-114 APCs idling with no one on guard. Our squad leader climbed on one of them and stuck his head down the open hatch and made note of the radio frequency. Then he woke up the troops and made them our prisoners.

He directed one of our guys to get in the driver's seat and drive us across the bridge to our lines with our prisoners. While we were crossing the bridge, one of the prisoners jumped off the back and ran for his side. Several of us shot him in the back with our blanks and we returned in triumph with two other prisoners. Our squad leader took the prisoners to the river, and cranking a TA-312 telephone, encouraged them to talk. One of them kept hollering, "We're on your side!"

Whenever we stopped and set up near a German town, the kids would come out to see what the 'Ami's' were up to. We would give them money to buy brotchen, kase, and bier which we hid in the camo nets on top of the track. Once, after several days in the field with little sleep, the LT was sitting in the cargo compartment with the platoon sergeant and the squad leaders looking at a map when one of the beer bottles slid out of the net above and dropped onto the center of the map. Our quick thinking platoon sergeant grabbed it like a German hand grenade and tossed it out the top hatch before the LT could focus on the forbidden item. "What was that?" he asked and the platoon sergeant assured him it was nothing while pointing to the map and asking the LT a question about our location which of course totally distracted the LT. The platoon sergeant didn't forget however and we all tasted a little pain.

## Vietnam

When it became clear that the U.S. would not invade North Vietnam because it feared another Chinese intervention like what happened in Korea, both sides determined that the strategy of attrition, which is not a strategy per se, was the way to win the war. North Vietnam saw it as the means to bring about a political solution demanded by the people of the United States after they lost the will to fight. The U.S. reasoned that North Vietnam would lose the will to fight when we killed more of their soldiers than they could replace.[40]

In November two battles took place in the Ia Drang Valley of the Central Highlands between troops of the 1st Cavalry Division and the People's Army of Vietnam, later called the North Vietnamese Army (NVA). The first battle, involving the 1-7 Cavalry at LZ X-Ray, was highly publicized as a great victory for American arms. The U.S. claimed a kill-ratio of ten enemy dead for every U.S. soldier killed. The 10-1 kill-ratio became the gold-standard for U.S. commanders. The second battle, near LZ Albany, was less publicized because it was a disaster for the 2-7 Cavalry with 155 Americans killed and 124 wounded.

## The 'Old' Army

Garrison life in Germany was definitely old army and the bulletin board outside the orderly room kept us advised of our duties. We checked it several times a day to see if we had Guard Duty, KP or CQ runner. Guard duty was a company level production. The guard posts were at the battalion's ammo dump in the nearby woods. There were eight posts which required an armed man at each one for two hours. The next shift or 'relief' would exchange any information and the first relief would be driven back to the guardhouse. Four hours later they would return to their post for another two hours. Wintertime guard duty in the snow was rough; but God help you if you fell asleep.

Guard mount was an inspection done by the officer of the day and the sergeant of the guard. There was a serious competition to be chosen as the best turned-out soldier on guard mount. The winner was given the title of "Colonel's Orderly," and spent the night in the guard house, sleeping. Carrying our spit-shined boots, we would bring our freshly starched fatigues to the bottom floor of the barracks where we would carefully put them on, 'breaking starch.'

The inspection consisted of weapons inspection, uniform appearance and knowledge of both practical infantry and esoteric army information. The time I won, the deciding question was, "what are the sizes of the three flags flown on an army post?" During that evening I questioned the sergeant of the guard about what my duties would be the next day.

He, along with most of the NCO's was nervous when Colonel Clemons was around. The colonel had recently put out an order prohibiting anyone from sitting on the APC commander's cupola. The colonel saw a sergeant from another company sitting on one and busted him, one stripe, "and that guy was with him on 'Pork Chop Hill,' said the sergeant, shaking his head. He told me to stay awake and answer any questions with "yes sir" or "no sir."

The next morning I reported for duty at battalion headquarters and was given a chair outside Colonel Clemons' office. There I waited for him to give me an important mission but I was ignored until about 1500. He came out of the office and I sprang to attention. He looked me over for a moment before asking me, "Murry, did you ever play any basketball?" I was about to tell him all about surfing but he didn't look like he would be interested and remembering what the sergeant of the guard said, I said, "Yes, sir." He nodded and walked out the door. I was disappointed that I hadn't made a better impression on him and decided the next time he addressed me I would tell him what I really felt.

KP came around regularly. The CQ runner would wake you at 0400. If you moved quickly and were the first KP at the Mess Hall you were given the duties of DRO (dining room orderly). The next KP's did trays and the last man got pots and pans and the grease trap. I hated KP and pulled pots and pans more often than DRO. There I amused myself by making up verses to a popular song of the day "Baby the Rain Must Fall." 'Some men climb a mountain; some men swim the sea. Some men fly above the sky, while others pull KP.'[41]

Bed check was at midnight every night unless you had a pass. Friday night 'GI Parties' and Saturday morning inspections with junk on the bunk were routine. Pile caps, starched fatigues, infantry blue ascots with blue knight insignia, and spit-shined boots were the uniform of the day.

Payday activities ended with the smart soldier buying shoe polish and Brasso at the PX before heading to the club or downtown until the money was gone. The rest went straight to town and after they were broke, borrowed money from the ten for twenty on payday loan-sharks or pulled someone's weekend guard duty or KP for ten dollars.

The company clerk had a serious scam going. He would charge money if you wanted to take leave but not use any of your thirty days of leave that the army gave you each year. While the CO was getting a shave and a hair cut from the company barber, the clerk had him sign the papers without looking at them.

The overall leadership climate in the 7th Army rewarded those soldiers who looked good and showed a lot of enthusiasm for whatever training or maintenance event was scheduled. Our combat training was less than realistic. For the young soldier like me, it seemed like war was fun. The combat veterans among us attempted to influence our thinking but it was difficult for them to express their opinions about some of our training for fear of being considered subversive.

### Automatic Rifle Marksmanship Training

I was made an automatic rifleman and issued an M-14E2 with a selector switch that allowed me to fire it on full auto, quite prestigious in those days. We were out on the range and Colonel Clemons took a personal interest in my training. He jumped in the firing position with me and said, "You're holding your weapon the wrong way." I looked at him while he directed me to put my left hand on the comb of the rifle stock rather than using it to hold the front hand grip on the forend of the stock. Then he said, "Rest your cheek on your hand."

"Oh no sir, that's the way you fire the old BAR," I said brightly, proud of the fact that I had fired one with the Arizona Guard. I rushed ahead before he could speak, "This is the M-14E2, the army's new automatic rifle, and you're supposed to use the front hand grip when you fire it." His face turned slightly red and he looked me straight in the eye; "Just do what I said!" I did and resumed shooting while he stood next to me watching as my marksmanship improved. He jumped out of the hole, satisfied that he had done his part to improve his unit and went on his way. All was well until the next day when the first sergeant jacked me up.

"Who the hell do you think you are, arguing with the battalion commander," was how the one-way conversation started. "I'm sending you to the Mannheim Stockade for three months and I want you to take a good look at what goes on there, because the next time you argue with the colonel, you'll end up inside!"

I was thinking that stockade time was a little stiff for a discussion of marksmanship techniques but I needed to get away from the first sergeant before he added any more pain so I said, "Yes, First Sergeant," and scurried away. I found my squad leader who told me to talk to the platoon sergeant.

Sergeant Taladay told me that I was being assigned as a 'TDY' stockade guard and that it was actually pretty good duty. "You mean I'm going to be an MP," I said belligerently, because I hated MPs. "Couldn't you get him to send someone else, I like it here, and I don't like MPs." He laughed and said, "Pack your bags, you're leaving tomorrow."

## MP Duty

The next day I took the train from the Bamberg Bahnhof. I carried a duffle bag and my automatic rifle. No one, at least none of the frauleins, seemed to pay attention to an armed GI on the train and that was disappointing. That afternoon I arrived in Mannheim and caught a shuttle bus to the Coleman Barracks and the Mannheim Stockade.

The MP sergeant whose section I was assigned to was contemptuous of infantrymen and he probably sensed that the feeling was mutual. He assigned me to a PFC who was feeling the power as he told me how things were in the most important unit in the European Theater, the MP detachment that guarded the Mannheim Stockade.

The stockade was filled with troops who had run afoul of some rule and were now paying for it. Many of them were from the 509th Airborne Infantry, the only mechanized airborne brigade in the U.S. Army and stationed nearby. Alcohol and alarm clock failures were some of the contributing factors for many of the incarcerated paratroopers.

There were also murderers, rapists and other felons waiting to be shipped to the 'Big House' at Fort Leavenworth. While they were waiting they succeeded in making the Mannheim Stockade seem like the 'Big House' of Europe. Suspected snitches were beaten and more than once I saw blood pouring down the shower drain from cuts made by small pieces of razor blade that had been pushed into someone's bar of soap. The hot water anesthetized their skin as they soaped up, cutting themselves over and over.

One night, the night before a shipment to Leavenworth, the entire stockade population gave the 'bad boys' a send-off. All night long the prisoners rioted in their cell blocks and sang with one voice the chorus to the pop hit, The Land of a Thousand Dances. Na na-na-na na, na-na-na na, na-na-na na, na-na na, na-na-na! went on for hours. An infantry company was called to guard the outside perimeter until morning when everything went back to normal. Other than the usual bad vibes from my partner because I refused to harass the prisoners like the MPs did, all was quiet until Easter.[42]

## Easter Sunday

On Easter Sunday morning, my partner and I were assigned to the chapel. He was even less friendly than usual because I had been promoted to Spec-4 a week before and now outranked him. He tried to tell me that my rank meant nothing there because he was an MP but I ignored him.

When the chapel was filled, the MP sergeant told me to go across the hall from the chapel and get a prisoner from the solitary confinement block. I was told to sit with the prisoner in the rear pew while he attended the service. My partner was assigned a position along the wall on the right side of the room near the door.

I did what I was told and was sitting next to the prisoner when the chaplain came out to start the service. With the gentle words, "Peace be unto to you," the prisoners in front jumped to their feet as one and started toward me, climbing over the pews. This didn't seem like it was part of the service and I guessed that this was the reason the guy next to me was in solitary confinement; it was not for being bad in the stockade but for protective custody. All this passed through my mind in a nanosecond. Then I was on my feet and pushing him down the pew toward the door of the chapel.

As I began moving I saw my partner moving even faster as he hauled ass out the door, down the stairs and through a guarded gate, leaving me to fend for myself. The rest of the prisoners were right behind me as I pushed my charge toward the door. As we moved across the floor, the men behind me were throwing their fists as hard as they could over both of my shoulders and landing them on the back of my prisoner's head. Not one touched me except in a grazing way. I saw a butt-can rack hit my man on the head hard enough to break it but again, nothing touched me.

When we got to the door I pulled it open and pushed him through and across the hall to the solitary confinement block where another TDY infantryman was standing ready on the other side of the bars. He unlocked the door and I pushed my prisoner through. Then together, with me pulling the bars and him pushing, we managed to lock the cellblock door. I turned around to the mob of prisoners who seemed to be disappointed that their buddy was now out of their reach.

"Let's get back inside, the chaplain is waiting to finish the service," I said. That got a laugh and they turned around and went back to their seats. Of course the chaplain was long gone so we sat there quietly for a few minutes until we heard the sound of many boots running up the stairs outside.

The door flew open and twenty MPs led by my section sergeant and including my partner, stormed in with nightsticks raised. They stopped and stared at the quiet scene for a moment until the sergeant said to me, "Where's your prisoner?" "Well," I said, "he got tired of the service so I took him back to his cell."

This brought some snickering from the rest of the prisoners and the MPs started shouting "At ease!" before herding them back to their cells. My partner wouldn't even look at me and several days later I was transferred to the Heidelberg Army Hospital to guard a prisoner being treated there. That was some soft duty. I remained there until my time was up and I returned to my unit in Bamberg.

## DA-1049

Because of the unit's outstanding leadership and especially that of SSG Elmer Taladay, our platoon sergeant, my squad and our company won the U.S. Army Europe (USAREUR) high score for the Rifle Squad Proficiency Tests at

Grafenwoehr in the spring of 1966. As a reward, we were given a free week at the General Patton Hotel in Garmisch-Partenkirchen. The morale in our company was excellent, making me believe that it was like this everywhere in the army.

Meanwhile, war fever was running high. Barry Sadler's hit song, The Ballad of the Green Berets was blaring out of every Gasthaus jukebox near our base. The Army had issued a series of correspondence courses on counterinsurgency warfare, known as the 'be a Green Beret by mail course' of which it was said that after finishing the courses you had to jump off a footlocker blindfolded and eat a worm before you could wear the green beret. Of course I signed up and soon began learning the secrets of the Special Forces.[43]

Many of the older NCO's had already been ordered back to the states to fill out the units being sent to Vietnam. Since I was a Spec-4, I was made a squad leader, then the platoon sergeant. During that summer a number of young Vietnam veteran sergeants with CIB's began arriving in Germany.

With the introduction of the regular army to Vietnam, it looked like the war would soon be over and I didn't want to miss my chance for combat experience and glory. So I asked around how I too could go to Vietnam. It wasn't difficult and the company clerk typed out the single page form after trying to dissuade me, either because he genuinely cared for my welfare or because he was lazy. While I did learn some useful lessons in Germany, I was hardly the battle-ready jungle warrior that I thought I was when we filled out my DA Form 1049, volunteering me for a transfer to the U.S. 1st Infantry Division in South Vietnam.

**Where do wars and fightings among you come from?**
**Are they not from this, from your pleasures**
**that war in your members?**
**James 4:1**

# Chapter 2-The War in Vietnam

### On War

Carl von Clausewitz, the German military philosopher, gave a great deal of thought to the nature of war within the context of a nation: The more powerful and inspiring the motives for war... "the more closely will the military aims and the political objects of war coincide, and the more military and less political will war appear to be.

"On the other hand, the less intense the motives, the less will the military element's natural tendency to violence coincide with political directives. As a result, war will be driven further from its natural course, the political object will be more and more at variance with the aim of ideal war, and the conflict will seem increasingly political in character."[44]

### North Vietnam

Vietnam was a mystical land, its values embedded in a village culture. To the Vietnamese, the land was sacred and they worshiped their ancestors as the source of their lives, their fortunes, and their civilization. They had a long history of struggle against the Chinese empire. In 1954, after seventy years of French rule, the Vietnamese were attempting to create a nation and adapt their society to the modern world. For a better understanding of the vast cultural differences between Vietnam and the west, please refer to Chapters One and Two of "Fire in the Lake," by Frances Fitzgerald.[45]

**Ho Chi Minh**, the president of North Vietnam, left Indochina at the age of twenty and traveled the world. He became a revolutionary while visiting the U.S., France, Russia, and China. He returned in 1941 and created the Viet Minh as an army of liberation. He fought the Japanese and then the French after the Japanese surrendered in 1945.[46]

**Vo Nguyen Giap** was a history teacher and dedicated revolutionary. Ho Chi Minh assigned him the task of leading the Viet Minh. In an amazing validation of the 'on-the-job' training method, Giap was responsible for training and leading the army that defeated the cream of the French army at Dien Bien Phu.[47]

In 1954, Ho Chi Minh and the government of North Vietnam had two goals: the consolidation of their revolution after the defeat of the French and the reunification of the two Vietnams. Agrarian reform resulted in small scale revolts in the north. The first goal took some time to achieve, but by 1959 they were ready to begin work on the second. By mobilizing the entire country for total war, they eliminated any dissent and went at their second task with a national will.[48]

## Their Supporters

The two most powerful communist countries, Russia and China, were rivals for the leadership of the world-wide communist revolution. The Soviet Union was talking of 'peaceful coexistence' with the capitalist nations of the west. At the same time they were covertly supporting 'wars of national liberation.' They would become North Vietnam's main supplier of weapons and ammunition. China, in the midst of its 'cultural revolution,' was a long-time enemy of the Vietnamese; but it was fearful of a strong American presence on its southern border and would do what it could to support North Vietnam.[49]

## The United States of America

The United States was a land of amazing contradictions. A victor of WWII, and the leader of the free world, it was enjoying an unprecedented wave of prosperity. The mainstream politics of both the liberals and the conservatives embraced an anti-communist dogma. The American Communist Party promoted Marxist Leninist socialism and was active in the labor union and civil rights movements; but fought among themselves over the Maoist challenge to Russian dominance of the communist movement.

The civil rights movement had awakened the African-American and Hispanic citizens (about fifteen percent of the total population) who began to demand their voting rights and an end to segregation. The baby boomer generation was coming of age with a huge shift in moral values which caused great turmoil in American family life. There was an unpopular military conscription of eighteen year-old males not going to college and a burgeoning anti-war movement on the college campuses. The leadership of the country felt that in the midst of all this upheaval we should go to war.

**Lyndon B. Johnson**, President of the United States, a politically ambitious Southern Democrat, was confronted with unprecedented turmoil in the country. His 'Great Society' initiatives sought to correct some fundamental domestic issues. The momentum of the civil rights movement forced him to enact the Voter Rights legislation that changed America. Medicare and his War on Poverty sought to address some of the economic contradictions of the society.

A massive breakdown of traditional family values occurred among the youth, centered around the colleges and universities, fueled by drugs and music. In the middle of all this social change, Johnson also inherited the previous administration's attempts to counter the communist threats to Southeast Asia, most specifically to the Republic of South Vietnam.

**Robert S. McNamara**, the Secretary of Defense, was a Harvard professor of accounting who served in the Army Air Corps during WWII. After the war he went to work for the Ford Motor Company, and fourteen years later, he was the first man from outside of the Ford family to be named president of the company. After seven weeks as president of Ford, McNamara was appointed Secretary of Defense by President Kennedy, and later, retained by Johnson.

McNamara introduced his 'improved' business practices and systems analysis to military planning and strategy. In doing so, McNamara accelerated the cultural shift in the armed forces from leadership to management.

By making numbers: number of bodies, percentages of people, land and infrastructure under control, etc, the measure of success, he forced men, who should have been combat leaders, to be accountants. In February, 1966, he told the commander of U.S. forces in South Vietnam, General Westmoreland, that the measure of Westmoreland's success would be determined by when he reached the 'cross-over' point—when he was killing the VC faster than they could replace their losses.[50]

## U.S. Army Leadership

U.S. Army leadership doctrine was based on the experiences of the veterans of WWII. With the enormous and rapid expansion of the armed forces after Pearl Harbor, came the need for a top-down centralization of leadership. Soldiers were expected to respond immediately to any order, no questions asked. After WWII, the Army sought to change this, recognizing that soldiers were more educated and had some capacity to think for themselves.

The leadership manual of 1951 stated, "There are two kinds of leadership, authoritarian and persuasive. One who is predominantly of the authoritarian type normally is recognized by the dogmatic use of authority or power. The persuasive type of leadership takes into consideration the human element with all its complexity and with all its differentiation of the physical, mental, and moral capabilities and limitations of the individual. To a great extent, the persuasive leader bases his skill in leadership upon example and ability, with high standards of discipline and efficiency for himself as well as for his followers. This manual is concerned solely with the development of the persuasive type of leadership." Regardless of what the manual said, and most soldiers never saw the leadership manuals, the authoritarian method was alive and well in 1966.[51]

Military leadership is defined by the character of its leaders. Doing one's duty, a word defined in the manual as, "A moral or legal obligation; a responsibility, [which] is an indispensable characteristic of a leader." Human nature imposes continual assaults on a leader's sense of duty with tendencies toward arrogance, ambition, and pride.[52]

The example set by his superiors, his strength of character, and his moral compass, is all a man has to guide him as he advances from one level of responsibility to another. The leadership culture of a nation is developed over a long period of time, but the climate changes more quickly when the leadership changes. President Johnson, an ambitious man, set the tone for the military climate of leadership during the escalation of the war. The military leaders had no choice but to acquiesce to his political schemes in order to remain in his favor.

## The U.S. Army Senior Leadership

**General Earl Wheeler**. Wheeler succeeded General Maxwell Taylor as Chairman of the Joint Chiefs of Staff. He was a consummate staff officer with no infantry combat experience. He thought he knew the political ways of Washington and Lyndon Johnson played him like a fiddle.[53]

**General Harold K. Johnson.** The Army Chief of Staff, and a two war combat infantry leader, he along with the other service chiefs resented the way McNamara and his deputies changed the leadership dynamic of the Defense Department from civilian control to civilian command. He was a strong advocate of a counterinsurgency strategy rather than a war of attrition.[54]

**General William Westmoreland.** The commander of U.S. forces in Vietnam, he graduated from West Point in 1936, the First Captain of his class. Six years later he was a lieutenant colonel in the 9th Infantry Division, commanding a field artillery battalion which received a Presidential Unit Citation in North Africa. During the invasion of Sicily his battalion was attached to the 82nd Airborne Division where his leadership and initiative were appreciated by Generals Matthew Ridgway and Maxwell Taylor. When the 9th Division landed in Normandy, he was the executive officer of division artillery and promoted to full colonel. At the end of the war, still an artillery officer, he commanded the 60th Infantry Regiment.[55]

As soon as he returned to the States he went to jump school and joined 82nd Airborne Division where General James Gavin gave him command of the 504th Parachute Infantry Regiment. He was now a full-fledged member of the airborne 'mafia' that would lead the army for the next 15 years. In 1952, Westmoreland was promoted to brigadier general while commanding the 187th Airborne Regimental Combat Team during the last year of the Korean War.[56]

His next assignment was in the Pentagon where he was educated on the business of running the Army. Working in the G-1 Personnel section, he helped Chief of Staff Matthew Ridgway deceive the Secretary of Defense with a shell game showing the Army with nineteen divisions when it only had seventeen. He attended a management course at Harvard University, and Ridgway received a glowing report on Westmoreland's performance among up and coming business leaders attending the same course. General Maxwell Taylor, the next Army Chief of Staff, made Westmoreland his Secretary of the General Staff.[57]

After four years at the Pentagon, Westmoreland commanded the 101st Airborne Division before returning to West Point in 1960 as the superintendent. He was promoted to Lieutenant General at Fort Bragg and commanded the 18th Airborne Corps. In 1964 he replaced General Paul Harkins as Commanding General, Military Assistance Command, Vietnam (MACV).[58]

## South Vietnam

The Republic of Vietnam was hastily conceived and heavily subsidized by the United States after the French left Indochina. The Buddhist majority revolted against the Catholic rulers periodically, while the Montagnard tribes in the hills plotted to create their own autonomous region. In 1963, a military coup, orchestrated by the U.S., overthrew the civilian leadership and this began a series of coups by the Generals. There was military conscription for all those who hadn't been taken by the Viet Cong and were unable to bribe their way out of it. Much of the land was owned by absentee landlords and entire village populations were being relocated from their ancestral homes to refugee camps.[59]

The South Vietnamese Army or ARVN was led by men appointed to their positions based on their perceived loyalty to the current president of the country. The soldiers were mainly conscripts. The army was trained by U.S. advisors, using conventional tactics from WWII and Korea, to defend against an invasion by North Vietnam. The ARVN were armed with U.S. weapons from those wars. They carried the M-1 Garand rifle with an eight round clip, the M-1 Carbine with a thirty round magazine, the BAR with a twenty round magazine and the M-1919 .30 caliber machine gun. Their leaders were afraid of taking casualties because of career considerations and the soldiers deserted when they could.

## The Allies

The U.S., seeking allies, invoked the Southeast Asia Treaty Organization (SEATO) agreement and was rebuffed. Some of the SEATO allies reluctantly made small contributions to the U.S. effort. The Australian Task Force, bolstered by an artillery battery from New Zealand, was the second largest contributor. The Philippines sent a civic action unit and Thailand sent troops, both at U.S. expense. The largest contributor and not a member of SEATO, South Korea, sent two army divisions and a marine brigade, all expenses paid for by the United States.[60]

## The 1st Infantry Division: 1965-1966
### The Big Red One

When I joined the regular army in June of '65 the 1st Infantry Division, commanded by Major General Jonathan Seaman, was preparing to send its 2d Brigade to Vietnam. Seaman said he "tore that division apart" to make the 2d Brigade the best possible brigade out of his own resources.

On July 14th, 1965 the 2d Battalion, 16th Infantry conducted an amphibious landing at Vung Tau and then moved by air to Bien Hoa, just north of Saigon, where they established their first base at Long Binh which would later become the largest American base in Vietnam. During that summer, amid massive personnel turmoil caused by soldiers being discharged when their time was up and new soldiers coming to the division from their initial training, the rest of the division was cobbled together and sent by ship to Vietnam.

The Army Chief of Staff favored a counterinsurgency approach to the war. He recommended this concept to General Westmoreland who argued that he planned to use the division and the 173d Airborne Brigade to defend Saigon by taking the fight to the enemy main force units in War Zones C and D which were north of Saigon. A compromise was reached; the 1st and 3d Brigades would face north to deal with the main-force VC units in War Zones C and D. The 2d Brigade would take up Operation LAMSON (Revolutionary Development), the winning of the hearts and minds of the people.[61]

Counterinsurgency included social programs such as education and medical treatment. During the day they appeared to be successful but after dark everything changed when the VC leaders in the village took over. The division attempted to counter the VC activities by conducting ambush patrols around these villages, hoping to kill the VC, who moved from village to village maintaining their control over the people.

The 1st Battalion, 16th Infantry landed at Vung Tau on 9 October, 1965 and moved to a base camp at Ben Cat, a few miles south of Lai Khe, which later became their permanent base camp. The entire 1st Infantry Division was in Vietnam by November.[62]

The division established base camps at Phouc Vinh, thirty-four miles north of Saigon, and Lai Khe, thirty miles north of Saigon, with the division headquarters nine miles north of the capital at Di An. Running north through the middle of this area was Highway 13 and securing it was General Seaman's top priority.[63]

## The Viet Cong and the NVA

The enemy forces of the B2 Front that was facing the advancing Americans were estimated to be 16,000 main force Viet Cong and North Vietnamese soldiers in two divisions, the 5th and the 9th. The 9th Viet Cong Division consisted of the 271, 272, and 273 Regiments and would be the 1st Infantry Division's primary target, and vice-versa.

The senior leaders of the Viet Cong and the North Vietnamese Army had years of combat time fighting the Japanese and defeating the French in the first Indochina War. Many of them had fought in the same areas for twenty years. All of them were hardened by war and jungle living. They lived on little food, moved quickly for long distances, taught the younger soldiers discipline and all they knew about this kind of warfare.[64]

Most of the young VC and NVA were country boys from an agricultural society. They grew up working in the family rice paddies and knew little of the world beyond the boundaries of their village. Armed with the excellent family of Russian small arms such as the SKS semi-automatic rifle, the AK-47 assault rifle, the RPD light machine gun, and the RPG rocket propelled grenade launcher, they were formidable fighters when directed to fight. Organized in three-man cells, they were required to practice a form of self-criticism after every battle and they would remain in combat until they were killed or victory was achieved.[65]

## NVA/VC Intelligence

The North Vietnamese were orchestrating a revolutionary war strategy in South Vietnam. This required the total mobilization of the people in the north and in the areas under their control in the south. They used a combination of persuasion, coercion, intimidation, and terrorism to rally the rest of the population. Revelations since the war have reported enemy agents in every level of the Saigon government and the military. All U.S. operations were cleared with them, which means that there was little operations security. Every Vietnamese was a potential spy. The KPs in our mess-halls, the barber who ran his straight-edge razor across our throats, the girls in the bars and boom-boom parlors, the people who sold us bread and soda pop on the roads, everyone could be recruited and/or coerced into the VC intelligence attack on our campaign.[66]

They were practiced at the art of deception. All of the revolutionary leaders in Asia were students of "The Art of War," a collection of ancient Chinese military philosophy which had been passed down through the centuries. The writers were masters of intelligence operations and our enemies read their ideas carefully. The "Art of War" told them that all warfare is based on deception and they went at it with a will.[67]

In order to counter our aerial and ground recon efforts, camouflage schemes were employed. From the individual fighter covered with vegetation to the tying together of bushes and tree tops to conceal fire lanes, trails and camps, the VC were masters of concealment. In both the 1st Infantry Division area and the area occupied by the 25th Infantry Division, enemy tunnel warfare operations were used successfully to defeat our recon efforts.[68]

If that wasn't enough, in 1969, a unit of the 1st Infantry Division, working with a communications intelligence unit, overran a small enemy radio intercept operation and captured its personnel and records. The enemy unit had been operating in that area for a number of years. They used captured U.S. radios and they were English speakers.

Voice encryption or 'scramblers' were not available in those days for the backpack radios of the infantry and our attempts to encode or 'shackle' our grid coordinates didn't seem to give them much trouble. Their records showed that they had been able to listen to our radio traffic, plot our locations on their maps, and generally keep up with our plans and intentions in real time. Not only were they listening, they were also intruding, calling for artillery fire from American guns onto American troops.[69]

## The American Soldiers

Major General Seaman was a West Point graduate who served as an artillery battalion commander in Europe and the Pacific during WWII. He remained in the artillery branch and it appears he had an unremarkable career until he was given command of the 1st Infantry Division and sent to Vietnam.

The field grade officers who led the 1st Infantry Division in Vietnam, the brigade and battalion commanders, were usually veterans of WWII and/or Korea. What motivated them to serve in Vietnam, other than the obvious, that they were career soldiers, is subject to debate. Both LTC Anthony Herbert and COL David Hackworth wrote about 'ticket punching,' the quest for assignments that would enhance an officer's potential for promotion.[70]

To be fair, that was the way the system worked in those days and these men were products of the Army culture of those times. If you wanted to advance in your chosen profession, you had to have command time in combat. The 1970 Army War College Study on Military Professionalism called this 'optimum career patterns.' The participants in the study called it 'ticket punching.'

Their biggest complaint revolved around the "ambitious transitory officers, marginally skilled, engulfed in producing statistical results, fearful of personal failure, too busy to talk to or listen to subordinates, etc." Leading units in combat was a big 'punch' and there were officers standing in line to get a combat command, so many that a command tour was usually six months in order for more officers to get this vital punch.[71]

The company commanders and platoon leaders were generally new to combat. The most difficult job, platoon leader, was given to the man with the least military experience. They were usually full of youthful exuberance and idealism which in many cases was short-lived. These officers usually had six months in a command position before moving to a staff job. They were supposed to be balanced by their senior NCOs who presumably were experienced with combat in WWII and Korea.

The senior sergeants serving in Vietnam in the early days of the war were usually veterans of WWII and/or Korea. Some of them had done tours in Vietnam as advisors. The Army had been transferring them to Vietnam from places like Germany and Korea since 1965. By 1968 there were severe shortages of squad leaders, platoon sergeants and first sergeants in the Army. Many of them had seen heavy combat in earlier wars and were hoping to find a nice job in Saigon, but found themselves in front of a platoon of kids commanded by an eager beaver second lieutenant. Out of shape and close to retirement, theirs would be an ordeal of epic proportions.

The squad and fire team leaders bore the brunt of the leadership challenge for the ambush patrols and other small unit actions. Eventually, after the older sergeants were used up, the small unit leaders were all home-grown. Placed in positions of responsibility without the stripes and the pay, PFCs led fire teams and Spec-4s led squads. Familiarity with their men made it difficult to enforce discipline and lack of training left many of them unprepared for dealing with situations that were beyond their experience.

The U.S. Army of 1966 was made up of two-thirds volunteers and one-third draftees. They came from a largely industrial society. The recruits had eight weeks of basic training and eight weeks of infantry training before they were sent to Vietnam. The training was to prepare men to fight the Russians in Europe.

While in training they usually slept in barracks, they never dug a fighting position; and if the temperature was too high or too low, training was curtailed. The rifle used for marksmanship training was the M-14. The rifle issued to them in Vietnam was the M-16 which quickly gained a reputation for unreliability. They also carried the M-60 machine gun, considered quite reliable and the 40mm M-79 grenade launcher, not suited for operations in thick vegetation.

There was little done to prepare them, and nothing was done to acclimate them for jungle warfare. Their leaders practiced a gravity-driven method of discipline and correction: everything rolled downhill. Their 'tour' of duty would be one year, unless it was shortened by illness, debilitating wounds or death.

### South Vietnamese/U.S./Allied Intelligence

Counterinsurgency warfare is much like police work. Without specific information from a trusted source, you are very limited in your ability to establish an advantageous contact with your enemies. The U.S. search and destroy operations which were conceived without specific intelligence were not productive. In most of the battles of those early days, the enemy usually initiated the contact and then broke it off at the time and place of his choosing.

The U.S. and its allies attempted to find the enemy using every technological tool at its disposal. Everything from satellites, U-2 spy planes and a multitude of lower altitude aircraft took pictures, listened for enemy radio transmissions, and utilized radar and infrared technology to 'see' enemy troops below. At night, photo recon planes dropped flash-flares over suspected enemy locations. R+D came up with something called the 'people-sniffer' that was supposed to be able to detect people in the jungle from a helicopter flying overhead.[72]

On the ground, the intelligence organizations were looking. From field interrogation to large interrogation centers, VC suspects were put through the ringer in an attempt to get 'actionable intelligence' on the whereabouts of the enemy. The signal intelligence people were listening to every radio frequency used by the enemy and trying to get a 'fix' on enemy transmitter locations. Special Forces teams and long range reconnaissance patrols were out there looking. Each battalion had its own recon platoon out there looking. Large search and destroy operations had battalions of infantry out there looking.[73]

All of these efforts were supported by thousands of photo-interpreters and intelligence analysts, the people whose mission it was to find the enemy and determine his intentions. The information gathered was used to generate thousands of vague reports that were filled with the 'P' words: possible, possibly, probable, and probably. These reports were used to show that efforts were being made to find the enemy. Since that couldn't be done they read and generated thousands of more reports.[74]

Due to self-imposed security restrictions, timely information flow to the troops in the field was limited. Often, when they actually had something, security classifications prevented the dissemination of useful information. When it was passed down, the information was usually overtaken by events.

There is a very small window of opportunity in counterinsurgency operations. The hot tip on an enemy troop concentration, received by a unit that can act on it 30 minutes after the information is received, is most likely useless information. The result of these intelligence failures meant the American troops would spend many days trudging through the jungle between contacts with the enemy; those contacts they did have would almost always be initiated by the enemy.[75]

## The Fighting Begins

From the time they landed, the men of the division had been engaged building their base camps and conducting local security patrols. Clearing the highway for large military convoys moving men and material north would become a routine mission for the division. The first major battle of the 1st Infantry Division was fought at Bau Bang, a few miles north of Lai Khe, on Hwy. 13.

In November 1965, during a road clearing mission, the VC 272d Regiment attacked an overnight defensive position consisting of a 2-2 Infantry company, a 1-4 Cavalry troop, and a 2-33 Artillery battery. The attack began just as these units were beginning their morning activities. The infantry held their ground, the cavalry charged into an attacking VC battalion, and the artillery battery lowered their tubes and fired directly into the attacking enemy formation. The enemy retreated with their wounded, leaving their dead and weapons on the battlefield.[76]

A week later the 272d Regiment attacked 2-28 Infantry a few miles north of Bau Bang while they were moving toward an overnight defensive position. The VC left more men and equipment as they retreated into the nearby jungle. These two battles resulted in American casualties of twenty-six KIA and 141 WIA. Enemy casualties were estimated at 286 KIA and undetermined WIA.[77]

In December, the 271st and 273d VC Regiments overwhelmed an ARVN regiment in the Michelin Rubber Plantation. Two infantry battalions with artillery were sent to help the ARVNs. The 2-2 Infantry was attacked by the 272d VC Regiment. After a four hour battle, the battalion counted 301 bodies after the VC retreated. Their own losses were 39 KIA and 119 WIA.[78]

The tempo of operations was increased and 1966 saw the Division in the field constantly, searching for the 9th Viet Cong Division. The enemy forces eluded them through January, but on the morning of 24 February, the 271st and 273d Regiments, supported by a local VC battalion attacked the 1st Brigade's base camp at Tan Binh.

The 1-26 Infantry, B Company, 1-28 Infantry, B Troop, 1-4 Cavalry, and two batteries of the 1-5 Artillery defended the camp, with the artillery firing directly into the attacking enemy units. The enemy left 142 dead and many weapons when they retreated and the Americans reported eleven KIA and 74 WIA.[79]

In March, again near Bau Bang, the 272d Regiment attacked a defensive position of the 2-28 Infantry. A VC company walked into an American ambush on their way to the battlefield which alerted the perimeter to an impending attack. Three assaults followed and then the VC retreated into the jungle. Their losses were estimated to be 199 dead while the U.S. reported fifteen KIA.[80]

## General William DePuy

In March, General Westmoreland stood up a new organization, the II Field Force, a Corps type command, to be over the 1st Infantry Division, the 173d Airborne Brigade, and the newly arrived 25th Infantry Division. He gave this command to Major General Seaman and placed his MACV operations officer (J3), Brigadier General William DePuy, in command of the 1st Infantry Division.

A highly decorated battalion commander of the 90th Infantry Division in WWII, DePuy considered himself an expert on infantry tactics. Much of these tactics he learned from the German Army while fighting them during WWII. He was also a practitioner of covert operations, having served with the CIA during the Korean War. One of his assignments at the Pentagon just prior to his transfer to MACV was Director, Counterinsurgency and Special Warfare for the Deputy Chief of Staff for Operations (DCSOPS).[81]

DePuy had already played a major, though hidden, role in the events leading up to the Gulf of Tonkin incident that was used by President Johnson to justify a major escalation of the war, the introduction of American combat troops in Vietnam. He was also an architect of Westmoreland's strategy of attrition and the 'search and destroy' tactics to attain it.[82]

The counterinsurgency strategy of 'clear and hold,' or the 'oil spot' concept of securing the civilian population, did not interest him because he said, "We didn't know how to do counterinsurgency very well and we had white faces." He wanted the ARVN forces to do that job, but, since we had trained them, and 'winning the hearts and minds of the people' was only practiced at that time by the communists in Vietnam, this would be a losing proposition.[83]

Both Westmoreland and DePuy came of age in the European Theater during WWII. Westmoreland was an artilleryman and DePuy an infantryman. Neither of these men ever served in combat at the battery or company level nor had they ever fought in the jungle, nor had they fought guerrillas. The culmination of their war experience was the dash across France with Patton's Third Army—the gold standard for army leaders in years to come. They would take the expertise they had developed and refined in fire twenty years earlier in Europe and use it to try and destroy Ho Chi Minh's jungle fighters.

## General Nguyen Chi Thanh

General Thanh left Hanoi and arrived in South Vietnam in 1964. He was a 'political' General and it doesn't appear that he ever saw any infantry combat. He discarded General Vo Nguyen Giap's recommendation that a mix of guerrilla warfare and big unit fighting should continue until the south was deemed ready for a general uprising that would put an end to the Saigon regime.

Instead, Thanh pushed for a big unit war against the ARVN and its American advisors. Thanh was the perfect match for Westmoreland and DePuy. He wanted big battles with the South Vietnamese Army, hoping to destroy it before the Americans introduced combat troops to the war.

He continued his 'Big Unit' war tactics when the 1st Infantry Division arrived and continued to throw his troops against U.S. firepower until his death in July of 1967. After his death the hard-liners in Hanoi approved launching the General Offensive/General Insurrection resulting in the TET Offensive of 1968.

General Thanh's tactics were simple: "One slow, four quicks" described: slow planning, quick advance, quick attack, quick battlefield clearance, and quick withdrawal. Thanh said, "A battle should last only 15 to 20 minutes." He directed the use of the slogan, "Grab the enemy's belts to fight them," for all VC and NVA forces on the battlefield. Thanh's tactics were a perfect match for General DePuy's 'rules for combat.'[84]

## DePuy's Rules for Combat

DePuy took command of the 1st Infantry Division on 15 March, 1966. On the 27th of March he published this tactical directive for his subordinate commanders: "The term 'pinned down' is no longer part of the vocabulary of the 1st Division. During the first five to ten minutes of a meeting engagement, the chances are the VC will have the advantage. He will initiate combat at the place and time of his choosing--usually from prepared positions.

"After the first five to ten minutes, the combat advantage will begin to shift rapidly in favor of 1st Division forces as additional fire power is brought to bear. Under NO circumstances, repeat, NO circumstances will the forward element in contact withdraw in order to bring artillery fire on the VC. The base of fire will stand fast and reinforce if necessary. Contact will be maintained if necessary throughout the night."[85]

## General DePuy Takes Charge

General DePuy knew Westmoreland wanted to use the U.S. troops to fight the enemy forces that had been overwhelming the best ARVN units. While serving as the MACV Operations Officer, DePuy believed that General Seaman wasn't aggressive enough in his efforts to make contact with the enemy. He said, "I knew the difference between what the division was doing and what was expected of it. It was clear to me that he (Westmoreland) wanted me to get cracking.[86]

"It was my idea to go after the Main Forces wherever they could be found and to go after them with as many battalions as I could get into the fight—what was later called 'pile-on.' To do that required a very agile and fast moving division, a division which was, in fact, airmobile. My initial efforts were to create just such a division."[87]

General DePuy's command style was different from General Seaman's. Seaman's command post was at the division headquarters; DePuy's was in a helicopter circling the battlefield. Since many of Seaman's officers remained with the division, he heard about the negative things being said about his tenure as division commander before DePuy took over. BG James Hollingsworth, DePuy's assistant division commander, was quoted as saying that he and DePuy had been sent there "To clean out the damn 1st Division and organize it."[88]

That they did. Hollingsworth got the ball rolling when he relieved Seaman's former aide. By December of 1966, they had relieved nine lieutenant colonels and two majors; seven of the LTCs were battalion commanders. Terms such as being "DePuyed" and "the midnight Chinook" were used to describe the consequences of running afoul of them. Lower ranking officers and NCOs also felt their wrath and a climate of 'career-fear' fell upon the division.[89]

## DePuy Gets 'Cracking'

### Operation Abilene

DePuy's first opportunity to 'get cracking' came when he launched Operation Abilene, a two brigade search and destroy mission. On 11 April, C-2-16 Infantry made contact with a small element of the D800 VC Battalion. After medevacing their wounded, Charlie Company began to set up a night defense perimeter, about 100 meters from the D800 base camp. Around sunset, the VC attacked with mortars and heavy machine guns before launching several ground assaults. The fighting continued through the night.

The next morning Charlie Company counted forty-one dead VC in front of their positions. Their own losses were 34 KIA and 72 WIA. Charlie Company went into the fight with 134 men and came out with 28. General Harold K. Johnson, the Army Chief of Staff came to Vietnam shortly afterwards and told DePuy that, "The American people won't support this war if we keep having the kind of casualties suffered by Charlie Company."[90]

Operation Birmingham followed Abilene in the last part of April and continued until 16 May. Two brigades were moved into Tay Ninh Province near the Cambodian border. There were several contacts resulting in the estimated deaths of 425 VC and the capture of 130 weapons. U.S. casualties were 62 KIA and 324 WIA. He sent the 3d Brigade to Loc Ninh on 19 May where three battalions conducted search and destroy operations until 26 May with no contact.[91]

## Operation El Paso II/III

On 2 June, DePuy launched Operations El Paso II/III. The first contact was at Ap Tau O on 8 June, when the 272d VC Regiment ambushed Alpha Troop, 1-4

Cavalry on Highway 13, 85 miles north of Saigon near Quan Loi. The VC lost 93 men and the U.S. forces lost 14 KIA and 37 WIA. On 11 June the 2-28 Infantry fought with a battalion of the 273d VC Regiment north of Loc Ninh. The VC lost 98 dead and the U.S. losses were 33 KIA and 33 WIA.

On 30 June, once again north of Loc Ninh on Highway 13, the 271st VC Regiment ambushed B Troop, 1-4 Cavalry. C Troop fought their way into the battle and the two Cav troops held their ground while airstrikes and artillery hammered the VC on both sides of the highway. The 2-18 Infantry conducted an air-assault nearby and the VC retreated, then returned two days later and attacked the 2-18 Infantry perimeter.

The infantry held their positions while airstrikes and artillery pounded the VC. When they retreated they left seventy-eight dead and the total for the three day fight was 270 VC dead. The U.S. casualties were nineteen KIA and ninety-four wounded. The U.S. troops captured forty small arms and twenty-three crew-served weapons. The VC knocked out a helicopter and eleven armored vehicles including four tanks.[92]

### Minh Thanh Road

Believing that he could lure the VC into attacking the Cav again, DePuy sent B and C Troops, 1-4 Cavalry and Bravo Company, 1-2 Infantry down Route 245 from An Loc toward Minh Thanh. This was a clever trap laid by DePuy based on information given to him by his G2 (Intelligence) officer LTC LeGro.

LeGro was aggressively collecting information from many sources. From a prisoner captured by the Special Forces, he learned that the 272d VC Regiment was moving along Route 245. The prisoner said he was on his way to dig holes along the road when he was captured. LeGro was also getting daily reports from a signals intelligence unit that was following the same VC unit by direction finding their radio signals.

LeGro and DePuy decided to tell the ARVN District Chief that they were sending a troop of the Cav to escort some engineers and their equipment from Minh Thanh to An Loc. They reasoned that whatever they told the ARVNs would quickly reach the ears of the VC. DePuy staged five infantry battalions and most of the division's artillery within striking distance of the suspected ambush site. Airstrike and artillery concentrations were planned.

At 1100 hours on 9 July, as the column continued southwest on Route 245, the VC sprung their ambush with three battalions of the 272d VC Regiment firing from the north side of the road. The Cav and infantry pulled into a defensive perimeter and fought for their lives. The airstrikes and artillery were bringing effective fire on the VC almost immediately and DePuy maneuvered his infantry units in an attempt to surround the VC regiment and annihilate it.

When the enemy retreated into the jungle, they left 239 dead, eight prisoners and fifty-four weapons. U.S. Casualties were reported as 25 KIA and 113 WIA. Operation El Paso II/III continued through September and resulted in 825 VC dead, the destruction of hundreds of base camps and supply depots, and the capture of tons of rice and other supplies.[93]

DePuy was especially pleased with the results of the Minh Thanh Road battle and the way it had been brought about. He even wrote a lengthy article for the division newspaper. He hoped to lure the VC into traps like this again and he had his G2, LTC LeGro working day and night toward that goal.

### Effort verses Results

General DePuy had his maneuver elements in the field almost continually, trying to find and engage the VC with his superior firepower. Every night Arc-Light B-52 bombing runs shook the ground like an earthquake and left long straight lines of bomb craters, which, when filled with water looked like iridescent turquoise jewels from the air. During the nightly shooting sprees, harassment and interdiction (H+I) fire missions rained down thousands of artillery shells on suspected enemy locations in the jungle such as trail junctions in what were called 'free-fire zones.'[94]

Years later, General DePuy looked back on his efforts to engage the VC in battle. "I guess I was surprised a little bit, too, after I took over the division, about the difficulty we had in finding the VC. We hit more dry holes than I thought we were going to hit, they were more elusive than I had expected and they controlled the battle better. They were the ones who usually decided whether or not there would be a fight."[95]

### En Route to Vietnam

In August, my battalion was at Grafenwoehr when I was notified that my orders for Vietnam had arrived. Sergeant Taladay, my platoon sergeant, had also received orders for Vietnam and he drove us back to Bamberg. I was excited but he was not. He had fought with the 2d Infantry Division in Korea and knew the deal. I shook his hand, and thanked him for schooling me. Then, like it happens so often in the Army, we went our separate ways and I never saw him again.

I had to be in Frankfurt the next day. So I stacked my unit issue of field equipment at the supply room door, caught a cab to the Bahnhof with my duffle bag and took the last train to Frankfurt. They put me on the first thing smoking and everyone on that plane was going to Vietnam. After a day of processing at Fort Dix and a night of drinking in the club, I was issued a travel voucher for a flight from New York to Los Angeles.

I came home on 22 August and spent a two week leave with my family. My mother made me get a portrait photograph in my dress uniform so she would have something to remember me by if I got killed. Of course she didn't say as much and I never gave it a thought. While I was partying with my friends and proudly telling anyone who appeared to be interested that I was going to war, events were taking place near a small village named Bong Trang in South Vietnam that would have a long and telling effect on my unit of assignment.

*"Believe me, nothing except a battle lost can be half so melancholy as a battle won"*
*The Duke of Wellington after Waterloo*

# Chapter 3-August 25th, 1966

### August 25th

Early in the morning of August 25th, 1966, during a road clearing operation named Amarillo, an ambush patrol from Charlie Company, 1-2 Infantry of the 1st Infantry Division's 1st Brigade made contact with the Viet Cong's Phu Loi Battalion. Charlie Company and a platoon from C Troop of the 1-4 Cavalry moved toward the patrol to help and were soon in heavy contact with the VC.

After Charlie Company was reinforced by the rest of the 1-2 Infantry and the 1-26 Infantry, elements of the 3rd Brigade including the 1-16 Infantry and the 2-28 Infantry were sent to the fight. This was roughly one-half of the 1st Division's combat power.

This battle was one of the largest and least publicized of the Vietnam War. In its aftermath, there would be fundamental changes in the way the 1st Infantry Division, and eventually the entire U.S. Army, would fight in Vietnam.

Years later, the 1st Brigade commander Colonel Berry said that ultimately 3,000 U.S. troops were committed to the fight against the 500 Viet Cong of the Phu Loi Battalion. The battle that ensued is now known in the history books as the Battle of Bong Trang. But for those who were there it will forever be known as the battle of August 25th.[96]

### The Fog of War

The Duke of Wellington, the victor of the battle at Waterloo, once pointed out that a battle was rather like a military ball, full of interesting incidents that none of the participants could later put into chronological order, much less reconstruct them into a coherent story. Von Clausewitz called the cause of this puzzle, 'The Fog of War.' The battle of Bong Trang on August 25th left similar challenges to the military history detachment of the Division.

Ironically, S.L.A. Marshall, the man who had done much to dispel the effects of the fog of war, visited the 1st Infantry Division headquarters four months after the battle. He was there to train the members of the military history detachment in the art of the 'post combat interview,' using past actions chosen by the Division for study. Suffice to say, the Battle of Bong Trang was not among those chosen. The events of August 25th and 26th had profound effects on the morale of the survivors of this battle in the unit I was assigned to in September. To show why, I have attempted here to describe what happened during those days.

There is some information about this battle, some written while the smoke was still in the air, so to speak, and other accounts that were recorded in personal memoirs, official interviews and oral history projects over the years. Much of the later information conflicts with the reports made soon after the battle. In the next chapter I will show some details that were either unavailable or omitted from the official history.

## After Action Reports

The 1st Brigade's Combat After Action Report of 18 December, 1966 was the basis for the official history published in 2000. In the section titled, Commander's Analysis, the 1st Brigade Commander, Colonel Sidney B. Berry, Jr. said that his brigade was victorious. The Viet Cong (VC) also declared this a victory. In December, 1966, the 173rd Airborne Brigade captured an undated 'Circular' which contained lessons for future actions from the 'victory' on August 25th. They claimed 700 American casualties, four aircraft downed, fourteen APCs destroyed, twenty-three weapons and 'lots of plans of operations captured.' Both of these reports could be categorized as wishful thinking.

## History and Eyewitness Accounts

In an attempt to further illuminate what happened during those two days in August, 1966, I have inserted excerpts of the history of the battle as it was compiled by John M. Carland in "Stemming the Tide," the eighth volume in a series called "The United States Army in Vietnam," published by the U.S. Army's Center of Military History. The original footnotes are included with their original numbers annotated as (Fn 48, etc).

Interwoven through the Army's history are the narratives of two of my comrades. The first, Dennis Howley, is a former Alpha Company, 1-16 Infantry company commander. The second, Peter Clark, was an automatic rifleman with the 2d Platoon, Alpha Company, 1-16 Infantry. Peter Clark had been with Alpha Company for two months on August 25th.

## Fighting the Phu Loi Battalion
**By John M. Carland**

As the southwest monsoon season reached its peak, General DePuy's campaigns accounted for nearly half of the theater's large unit operations during August and September. One of his objectives was to harry the enemy along Highway 13, as well as on other roads in Binh Long and Binh Duong Provinces. For the most part this worked-the Viet Cong did not contest the raids, except during Operation AMARILLO.[97]

The operation began in late August as a routine road security mission. Colonel Berry's 1st Brigade joined South Vietnamese regulars and Regional and Popular Forces in clearing Routes 1A and 16 from Phuoc Vinh, the brigade base camp, south to Di An, the division headquarters, and in providing protection for elements of the 1st Engineer Battalion, which were working on the roads. Berry's force consisted of Colonel Prillaman's 1st of the 2d Infantry, with the latter's executive officer, Maj. Richard D. Clark, in command during his absence; Lt. Col. Paul F. Gorman's 1st of the 26th Infantry; and Captain Slattery's Troop C, 1st of the 4th Cavalry. The force established two artillery bases a little more than thirty kilometers north of Di An: Artillery Base 1, at the hamlet of 80 La; and Artillery Base 2, about two kilometers to the south. Both were near Route lA, allowing for easy resupply. Elements of the 1st Battalion, 5th Artillery, provided fire support.[98] The topography and vegetation offered less than ideal operating conditions. Heavy underbrush cloaked the gently rolling countryside, limiting visibility to little more than twenty meters, and trees impeded the movement of armor. On the other hand, the landscape offered good cover for enemy soldiers, who maintained myriad trails and fortifications in the area as well as platforms for observation and sniping.

Little happened during Amarillo's first two days. On 23 August Major Clark's 1st of the 2d Infantry patrolled southward from Artillery Base 1, covering about eight kilometers. Colonel Gorman's 1st of the 26th Infantry, south of Clark, moved even farther south along Routes 1A and 16, securing the roads for future convoys. During the evening of the twenty-fourth Captain William J. Mullen III, commander of Company C, 1st of the 2d Infantry, sent out a fifteen-man patrol from Artillery Base 2. The men were to remain in the field overnight, looking and listening for Viet Cong. As darkness closed in, they settled about five kilometers west of the firebase.[99]

At dawn on the twenty-fifth the patrol moved east toward the firebase. The day turned out to be one of the few in August when rain did not fall, but the ground remained wet and soggy. Although the troops were unaware of it, they had begun their day inside a large enemy base area. They were about to find more Viet Cong than they might have thought possible.[100]

The situation began to develop just after first light, when enemy soldiers-later identified as belonging to the crack Phu Loi Battalion and the separate local force C62 Company-attacked the patrol. After an initial exchange of fire, the Americans took cover in a nearby bunker and trench line and called for help. Immediately, Major Clark ordered the remainder of Captain Mullen's Company C and the 2d Platoon, Troop C, 1st of the 4th Cavalry, to the rescue. From Artillery Base 2 eighty-five men and seven armored personnel carriers headed out, led by a tank breaking trail. Captain Mullen directed the column's movement from a helicopter overhead.[101]

Meanwhile, the commander of the besieged patrol reported that insurgents had breached the trench line. With the Viet Cong threatening to overrun him, he called in artillery on his own position. The fire broke the momentum of the attack. No Americans were injured by the artillery, but the patrol had sustained 5 wounded and its machine guns were out of action. Still faced with what seemed by then to be a full enemy battalion, the surviving members separated. Nine of the men, led by Pfc. Dennis L. Peterson, hid together in an unoccupied bunker, while the others struck out on their own.[102]

While the patrol struggled, Colonel Berry and General DePuy enlarged the relief force. Around 0830 Berry instructed Major Clark to detach his two other companies from road-clearing duties and move them in the direction of the battle. Colonel Gorman's 1st of the 26th Infantry received the same instruction— "move to the sound of the guns."[103]

Berry also placed Gorman's Company C under Clark's control. Over the next two hours DePuy put two more battalions at Berry's disposal: Colonel Wallace's 1st of the 16th Infantry and Lt. Col. Elmer D. Pendleton's 2d of the 28th Infantry. Both deployed from the airstrip at Lai Khe.[104]

> **Peter Clark:** *"Hot and dry, like any other August day in Lai Khe. The mission was a company sized day patrol just outside the base camp. We trudged down the sandy paths through the rubber, past the sandbag bunkers*

*along the perimeter, and out through the wire. Cutting across the shallow rice paddies to the north-west, we entered the jungle in two parallel lines, following a compass heading that the point guys were given. I was a rifleman in Second Platoon, two months in country. Actually I was my squad's designated automatic rifleman, which meant that I carried a folding bipod for my M-16 in a canvass sheath and a steel box of 500 rounds of 5.56 ammo. This distinction was a result of my having fallen asleep on an ambush patrol, and being discovered by my squad leader, a tough, skinny black lifer E-5...*

*"After an uneventful (hot, sweaty, buggy) couple of hours, everybody in a single line following the guy in front through jungle with no more than a few yards of visibility in any direction, we abruptly changed direction and were told to hustle our asses. An hour or so later we emerged at the edge of a waist-deep rice paddy, a klick or so west of Lai Khe... The paddy berm ran into a red dirt road, and a bunch of deuce and a half's rolled in from the left. We loaded up and were driven back to Lai Khe. I was pleased as punch -- what a great deal, a free ride. Our lucky day! Nobody had told us anything different at that point.*

*"In a few minutes we pulled up on the company street. A big pile of c-ration boxes greeted us in front of the barracks. "Three meals each, move your asses, fall in by platoons." After I had gotten my chow I was just pulling delightful dry socks on when the deuce-and-a halfs pulled up in front of the tents. My sergeant stuck his head in and, in classic fashion, provided additional motivation for me to get my ass on the truck; it is not easy to get dressed and tie jungle boots and re-apply the sixty or so pounds of gear, to say nothing of the box of 500 5.56 rounds, and get on a truck which was already moving. The next stop was the Lai Khe chopper pad.*

*"Once off the trucks, we were chivvied into chopper loads and lined up along the tree-line parallel to the PSP airstrip. We sat down, smoked, ate some C's, and maybe some of us dozed. I still didn't have a clue as to what was going on. Most of us didn't have much interest in the destination, figuring it would be the same old shit -- and there wasn't anything we could do about it, anyway. Even after two months, I'd been down this road sufficiently often for my native curiosity to be atrophied. We'd find out when we got there.*

*"When a whole shitload of choppers are coming in, the first sign is a deep sub-sonic vibration in the air, felt rather than heard. This resolves into the rhythmic chukka-chukka-chukka of the blades, soon overlaid by the angry whine of the turbines. The first birds appeared over the tree-line at the left end of the strip, one after the other, nosing up to lose speed and moving down the line of the PSP.*

*"Dirt and debris stung our hands and faces as the sergeants got us on our feet and moving towards the right bird. Avoiding the deadly tail rotors, we climbed over the skids and scrambled into the body of the Hueys, either siting on the floor in the middle or on the edge with our boots on the skids. I got a place in middle and wedged the ammo can between my legs. After a minute or two the whole row of choppers raised up, put their noses down, and took off for the treeline, clearing the tops of the rubber by a couple of feet and swinging to our left.*

*"Looking out the open doors on both sides, I could see lots of Hueys before and behind us, and another flock coming in to pick up more troops. Wherever Second Platoon was going, it was going to have lots of company. The chopper ride was uneventful, and the reason I remember it at all was the damn ammo can. With one hand holding my M-16 and another bracing against the swerving of the chopper, the ammo needed to be gripped between my legs to keep it from sliding out the open doors."*[105]

While Colonel Berry and General DePuy shuffled units, Captain Mullen's relief column was already moving toward the beleaguered patrol. Around 0900 Mullen joined his command on the ground. A short while later, believing that his men were approaching the patrol but still unsure of its exact location, Mullen left a platoon at a small clearing to guard his rear and pushed the rest of his column deeper into the base camp. By then, his force had moved a little over four kilometers from Artillery Base Two.[106]

Then things began to go wrong. The tank leading Mullen's convoy and one of the M-113s broke down and fell out of line. At almost that moment the Viet Cong attacked the security platoon in the clearing, inflicting heavy casualties. Receiving a frantic call for help, Mullen wheeled his vehicles around and raced toward the fight. But no sooner had the troops entered the clearing when they were pinned down by heavy fire.[107]

The clearing, which became the center of the action for the remainder of the day, was the perfect place for an ambush. Barely large enough for a single helicopter to land, it was surrounded by tall trees and clogged with thick underbrush and vines, nice cover for the Viet Cong. As the bullets flew, three of Mullen's M-113 commanders were killed or wounded. As the leader of Troop C's 2d Platoon, Sgt. Wilbur J. Barrow, reported, "Every time we tried to get out, we were hit by mortars and hand grenades." As the commanders fell, Barrow continued, "Privates were taking command of the tracks and calling me to ask for help. My answer to them was to pick up their wounded and take salt pills and drink water, and pray, pray, pray! There was no help for anyone."[108]

Mullen, who had taken cover in a small trench line at the clearing's northern edge, was more hopeful than the sergeant. Believing that his force could withstand the onslaught, he felt that this was an opportunity to hit the Viet Cong while they were massed and recommended that Major Clark delay any reinforcement until American firepower could be brought to bear all around. Clark rejected the advice, and Colonel Berry endorsed his decision. "The commander of an infantry company under attack," Berry said later, "hardly had the perspective to decide for or against a relief attempt."[109]

By noon that day, 25 August, the units that Berry had selected as a relief force were en route to Mullen. Company A, 1st of the 2d Infantry, was about two kilometers away and maneuvering northwest toward the fight. Captain Johannesen's Company B, 1st of the 2d Infantry, and Captain Slattery's Troop C, 1st of the 4th Cavalry, had linked up two and a half kilometers northeast of the battle and were moving southwest. The force included part of the battalion command group, but not Major Clark, who was overhead in his helicopter. Company C, 1st of the 26th Infantry, was advancing north toward the action.[110]

As these reinforcements converged on Mullen, additional forces were preparing to pile on. Colonel Pendleton's 2d of the 28th Infantry moved eastward from Lai Khe, first on foot and then by helicopter, to occupy blocking positions directly north of the battle. Colonel Wallace's 1st of the 16th Infantry helicoptered about twenty-five hundred meters west of Mullen's clearing and pushed east. Meanwhile, Colonel Gorman, his command group, and Companies A and B, 1st of the 26th Infantry, had joined up with the armored personnel carriers of Troop A, 1st of the 4th Cavalry, and were preparing to enter the battle from the south. Thick jungle, soggy ground, and caution born of a certainty that the Viet Cong were nearby made progress slow.[111]

> **Peter Clark:** *"We landed on a cold LZ some minutes out of Lai Khe, in a typical open area surrounded by bamboo and low jungle. The ground was dry, sandy, and covered with clumps of grass and shrubs. After re-assembling, the platoon took up positions along the woodline for a bit.*
>
> *"Another flight of choppers came behind us, and we moved out in two parallel columns through the brush. Both columns were on a sandy, rutted trail, almost a road, and were moving pretty quickly.*
>
> *"A stream of close support aircraft were circling in the same direction: F-100 Super Sabers, Canberra's, and Phantoms, as well as Hueys, FACs, and LOACHes. As we moved along we could hear the tearing-fabric sound of the Huey gun-ships' machine guns and the occasional detonation of a large bomb, as well as the drumbeat of artillery battery missions. No question there was some heavy shit going down, and that was where we were going."*[112]

Around noon, after moving rapidly west across mostly open ground, Johannesen's Company B and Slattery's Troop C were slowed by dense jungle and formed up in a column. Since they had only the vaguest notion of where the embattled platoon was, they advanced toward the sound of circling helicopters. Close to 1300, after taking what Colonel Berry called "an interminable time," the two units neared the clearing. The infantrymen then separated from the mounted troops and began to sweep southwest toward Mullen against stiff opposition. Heavy automatic weapons fire from Viet Cong in the trees and incoming mortal' fire pinned them down. When a grenade injured Johannesen, his intelligence officer, Capt. George M. Downs, replaced him. Company B made three unsuccessful attempts to break through, but with each try more and more men were wounded or became separated. Only fourteen made the last charge. By then, Captain Downs himself was wounded and almost everyone was exhausted. Clark's communications officer took charge.[113]

Slattery's cavalry troop found the going easier. Encountering almost continuous sniping, the troopers were well secured in their tanks and armored personnel carriers and made their way steadily through the underbrush. As they neared the clearing, Slattery realized that Mullen's situation was precarious. Heavy enemy fire had downed an Air Force medevac helicopter in the clearing, making it impossible for other helicopters to land. But when Troop C broke through, the situation brightened. In order to keep the organization streamlined, Major Clark immediately put all units in or near the clearing under Mullen's command.[114]

*and pounded the guy in turret. "Cease fire! Fucking cease fire!" The guy in the turret stopped shooting and the officer yelled, "Don't shoot unless you have a fucking target! I don't want to take any more dead GIs out of there!" Just as he finished the track exploded in a fireball and the guy in the turret went flying through the air.*

*"I found myself near one end of the clearing, with the downed Huey to my left, and a small trench or depression to my front, and beyond that, a solid wall of dense jungle with some bamboo. The burning APC was to my right, and I think another APC a few meters beyond that. The ground was dry and sandy and littered with leaves and branches as well Army gear. A couple of dozen GIs were lying under the brush around the sides of the clearing, many of them without helmets or weapons. Most had the black bandannas of the 1/2."*[123]

Berry took further steps to ease the pressure on the 1st of the 2d Infantry by ordering Wallace's battalion to attack north. It would be a difficult maneuver. The 1st of the 16th Infantry had to turn ninety degrees in heavy jungle, with Company B on the left, Company A on the right, and Company C and the battalion command group in the rear.[124]

**Dennis Howley:** *"During my air time and after A/1/16 made contact, Col Berry (1st Bde) called on Cmd channel which I was connected asking for napalm "to break contact" – obviously Berry knew nothing about Charlie or he would have known they were and had been pulling out leaving a rear guard to kill Americans as they arrived in the killing zone. AF refused but opted for 500 pounders, which were dropped killing some in A/1/16..."*[125]

But an enemy assault preempted Wallace's attack. As the Americans moved into position, the right platoon of Capt. Peter S. Knight's Company A came under heavy fire from Viet Cong well entrenched in a deep bunker system immediately to the company's front. Hit with 57-mm, recoilless rifles, .50 caliber machine guns, grenade launchers, and small arms, Captain Knight ordered his troops to advance and committed his reserve platoon. As they closed with the enemy, Knight was killed leading an attack on a machine gun and all of his officers were wounded.

**Peter Clark:** *"Soon after the track exploded a heavy machine gun opened up from somewhere beyond the wall of jungle to my right front. We were in a slight defilade from that direction, and the rounds seemed to be cutting through the trees and brush overhead. Our platoon sergeant, whose name I forget, jumped up and yelled, "Let's get that fucking gun!" and ran into the jungle towards the sound of the firing.*

*Oh shit, I thought, but got to my feet and followed him, along with several other guys from Alpha. I left the can of ammo behind at this point, figuring that whatever trouble I'd get in would be less onerous than having to claw through jungle and fight one-handed.*

*The machine gun and other small arms fire increased, and several Alpha guys went down. The guy next to me, a SP4 named Martinez, was hit in the left arm above the elbow, breaking the bone and leaving a nasty mess. He collapsed, and I carried him back to the relative safety of the clearing. "Oh God it hurts, it hurts," he said. I put my field dressing over the wound, covering the protruding bone as best I could. I yelled for a medic but got no response. An abandoned aid bag was lying a few feet away. I crawled over and dragged it back to Martinez, and rummaged through it, finding some morphine ampules. I gave him one in the right shoulder and stuck the needle through his collar, and bent it like a safety pin. I was too squeamish to write the time on his forehead with blood, which I remembered from training as the proper next step.*

*I never saw Martinez again, and I've worried for the last 40 years that maybe he didn't get his next shot because some medic saw the ampule and didn't know whether he was due because I didn't write the time. But at that point Martinez was saying "Don't leave me, it's cold." I figured he might be going into shock, and covered him with a poncho. "Hey, man, this is a million dollar wound, you're going home, you're going to be all right." "Do you think so?" He asked. "Please stay with me." But the training kicked in: leave the wounded for the docs, get on with the mission. Attractive as the little pocket of apparent safety was, I grabbed my M-16 and took off after the rest of the platoon, all of whom by now were either wounded or had disappeared into the jungle.*

*The sarge and the other guys had charged somewhat to the right, I thought, so I ran towards the jungle where I thought I would be on their left flank. Within a few steps over the little depression, however, the jungle became too thick to penetrate. I got down and commenced the low crawl, straight out of basic training; within a couple of meters, however, the vines and brush were too thick to crawl through. I had a civilian sheath knife which I used to cut the vines and stems that were holding me up. Somebody from the platoon said later they saw me 'flat fucking doing the low crawl with a knife in my teeth' and while I don't recall biting the knife it could have happened.*

*I managed to work my way a few meters into the brush, but couldn't see any GIs -- visibility was maybe two meters at best. The heavy machine gun was still firing intermittent bursts and I tried to steer in that direction. After a fair amount of crawling I could see a thinning of the brush to my front. A few more meters and I could see the body of Matt Miedema, lying on his stomach and facing me. His right leg was gone below the knee and he had multiple wounds from a high caliber weapon. He was a handsome blond kid from another platoon, and his nickname was Dutchy. I crawled a little closer and saw that Dutchy was lying in a path partially cleared through the jungle by an APC, which I could see stopped at the end of its path about ten meters to my right. A couple more dead GIs were lying between me and the APC, but I couldn't see either of their faces. I found out later they were from another battalion. For the first time I experienced the quality of stillness which surrounds the dead. Even at a glance there was no question that these guys were gone.*

*The machine gun was continuing to fire sporadically from somewhere in the thick brush on the other side of the path made by the APC, which was just as wide as that vehicle, maybe three meters. I couldn't see a muzzle flash, but the rounds were definitely incoming and I could hear them going through the foliage. At that point I figured that crossing the APC path was not a smart thing to do. I switched to automatic and fired a magazine in short bursts towards the brush where I thought the machine gun was located. The firing stopped but a grenade landed a meter or so away from me. The explosion kind of lifted me up, blew a lot of dirt and shit on me, and my GI glasses disappeared, but otherwise I didn't seem to be hurt, although my ears were ringing.*

*I reloaded and fired another magazine into the brush at my front. Another grenade landed further away, and exploded again without doing me any harm. I still had not a clue as to the whereabouts of the guy chucking the grenades, except that he had to be somewhere in front of me and pretty close. I put in my third magazine and started to fire when a third grenade landed about two feet from my face. It was just out of reach. I could see the grain on the short little wooden handle, which looked like bamboo, and the scoring on the otherwise smooth metal business end. It was hissing and a thin stream of smoke was coming out of it. Oh shit, I thought, turned my head so my helmet was facing the grenade, and pushed my face into the dirt. There was a little pop, and when I peeked out the grenade was sitting quietly -- a dud. This was the point at which I decided discretion was the better part of valor, and tried to back up in the direction I had come, which turned out to be easier said than done.*

*My entrenching tool was fastened to the back of my butt pack, and a tough, woody vine had wrapped around it, underneath the cover, and was preventing me from backing up. I tried to ease forward but found I couldn't get enough slack to slip the tautly stretched vine over the handle of the entrenching tool. Nor could I reach the vine to cut it. Finally I was able to detach the entrenching tool cover from my pack, and slither backwards. No more grenades were thrown. Whether the Viet Cong were out of grenades or simply chose to disengage at that point I will never know. Rather than dragging my entrenching tool back with me I abandoned it at that point, the first piece (but sadly not the last) of government property which I failed to conserve during my tour."*[126]

Meanwhile, Company B began its push, moving forward almost two hundred meters against little resistance. Rather than disperse his forces too far, Colonel Wallace stopped the unit's forward movement. While it idled, awaiting developments, the enemy withdrew. The impetus for large-scale action on both sides seemed spent.[127]

As Wallace's fight petered out, the last of the American reinforcements began arriving at the clearing. Colonel Gorman rode in on an M48, and Colonel Berry climbed aboard to shake his hand. At that moment, Berry recalled, "a machine gun opened up on us, and we unceremoniously scrambled off the tank, dashed across the clearing, and jumped into the VC trench I was using as a CP." Shortly afterward, Berry placed Gorman in charge of all companies in contact with the insurgents and returned to his helicopter to resume control of the 1st Brigade. He had played an unusual role that day but was convinced that he had done the right thing: "I was at the critical place at the critical time, where the commander should be."[128]

**Peter Clark:** *"Although I tried to retrace my path back to the clearing, when I did emerge from the jungle, I was in a different location, similar in character to the clearing I had left, but without any Alpha soldiers in evidence. A handful of 1/2 troops and other elements, including some artillery and track crews, were occupying a series of VC bunkers and trenches. By now the day was winding down, and the firing had become sporadic. I asked the GIs if they know where the 1/16 was, and nobody knew anything. There was no obvious leader in evidence. "Goddam, you still have grenades!" was the dominant response.*

*"I shared my grenades and my ammunition, as most of the guys had pretty much used theirs up. While I wished I had my box of 5.56 ammo, I wasn't going to go looking for it, or anything else, in the rapidly falling darkness. I was invited to join four other GIs in a four foot deep and perhaps eight foot square bunker, which had a kind of roof made from bamboo and leaves. As the jungle became as dark as only nighttime jungle can, we traded stories. The others included an older E7 from the 1/2, and a couple of younger guys. We established that we pretty well represented the United States geographically and the sergeant gave us a pep talk about how Americans together could handle anything the VC could throw at us."*[129]

As the sun set, the Americans prepared three night laagers. The 1st of the 2d Infantry, the 1st of the 26th Infantry, and a portion of the 1st of the 16th Infantry remained in the clearing, where they established a unified position under Colonel Gorman's command. The rest of Colonel Wallace's 1st of the 16th created a perimeter about four hundred meters to the north. Colonel Pendleton's 2d of the 28th Infantry stayed in its blocking positions still farther north. Throughout the night, artillery and a flare ship kept the battlefield illuminated.[130]

**Peter Clark:** *"The sergeant had heard that Alpha's captain had been killed, and most of his officers were dead or wounded. The sense all of us had was that we had had our asses kicked and that we could expect an attack during the night or at dawn. There was a determination to defend ourselves in place, though there really was no alternative. We shared a couple of cans of Cs, set up a guard rotation, and spent an anxious night. Other than artillery firing H and I, which was often close enough to send shrapnel spinning over our heads, the night was uneventful.*

*As the jungle began to become visible once more, we prepared for a dawn attack. A chorus of what must have been insects or frogs made me think of the clickers the VC were reputed to use to pass signals at night, but in any event there was no incoming fire from the enemy. Almost as scary was the artillery which started to become a pretty constant and close barrage."*[131]

The next day, 26 August, started poorly. Colonel Berry called for an east-to-west napalm drop in the narrow slot between Gorman and Wallace, and the jets screamed overhead with their deadly payloads. The first thirteen canisters landed on target, but the fourteenth hit a tree and careened toward the waiting Americans.

**Peter Clark:** *"This was followed by the scream of jet aircraft coming in at treetop level. Five hundred pound bombs and napalm fell all around us. One napalm canister landed behind us and we were literally roofed over with fire. I deeply regretted the loss of my entrenching tool as I used my helmet to improve the depth of the corner of the bunker as we cowered under the friendly fire. (I later read accounts of this incident, which was about the only part of the battle which got press coverage. The napalm had landed on or near an area where a large bunch of dead GIs had been laid out, and those deaths were initially blamed on the napalm. As far as I know only a couple of GIs were actually killed or wounded by the Air Force)."*[132]

Burning jelly splattered across Colonel Gorman's command group, igniting a map in the colonel's hands. Despite the accident, Gorman requested that the bombing continue. The twenty-second canister fell short, killing 2 Americans and wounding 14. Deciding that his luck had run out, Berry called off further strikes.[133]

For the rest of the day Berry and his men concentrated on finding the Viet Cong. Gorman's battalion moved north against the fortified position that Wallace had been primed to attack the previous afternoon, but the area was empty. Meanwhile, Wallace's men moved east and then searched to the south. There they found the bodies of six members of Mullen's lost patrol. That was the bad news. The good news was that, on 26 August, the other nine who had taken refuge in the bunker made their way to Landing Zone BLUE, where they received a warm welcome. It was a last eventful moment in the operation. AMARILLO ended five days later, with no further action.[134]

**Peter Clark:** *"At some point the explosions dwindled and ceased, and we emerged from our holes. I collected most of the remaining water from my bunker mates and made a canteen cup of C-ration coffee, which I warmed with some heating tablets, and, in an episode of clumsiness which I will regret forever, spilled most of when I climbed out of the bunker. We did all get a couple mouthfuls. By this point some officers were checking on the survivors, and I discovered some Alpha troops who had spent the night nearby. While I was looking for somebody from Second Platoon I noticed that none of the dead GIs covered with ponchos were Dutchy -- they all had two feet.*

*"I asked a lieutenant if anybody had found him, and apparently no one had. I said I could try to find him, and with a couple of guys from his platoon (I think First Platoon) I went around the clearing until I found what looked like the track of an APC. Just a few meters up the track we found Dutch, and a bit further along the bodies of the other GIs I had seen, as well as the APC. The First Platoon guys went back for some ponchos and we carried our brothers back to the clearing. At about that point some guys from the Second Platoon appeared and I was reunited with the new command structure, which*

*chewed me out for losing my entrenching tool and gas mask, which had gotten buried in the bunker when I was trying to get very deep very quickly after the napalm strike. Fortunately for me no one remembered the can of 5.56 ammo, and as my squad sergeant had been wounded and never returned to the platoon, that issue never arose.*

*"As I was leaving the bunker area I saw two captured VC, who looked like nothing more than skinny old men. They were kneeling with their hands tied behind them, in dirty pajamas, and surrounded by officers and RTO's and gawking GIs. Somebody told me they had been in a tunnel which had collapsed when an M-48 ran over it. They were the only VC, dead or alive, that I saw during or after the fight. Probably the RVN's killed them later. You could tell they were scared but calm. I hope they didn't suffer.*

*"The new sergeant made us clean up and shave, and while I thought it was chickenshit it did make me feel better and more like a soldier. I learned then that Jim Emerson, our SP4 machine gunner, and Felix Pacheco, his assistant gunner, had been killed along with Captain Knight and SSgt. Amburgey. I'm still amazed Alpha only had five dead, as we had many seriously wounded guys. Emerson was a tall, skinny draftee with GI glasses from Washington State. He was a decent, helpful guy who never lost his temper that I knew of, and was endlessly patient with me and the other rookies in the platoon. Pacheco was quiet and cheerful, also a good comrade and friend. I didn't know Amburgey well, but he did his job and took care of the troops.*

*"Captain Knight was a soldier out of another era, soft-spoken, gentle, but endlessly competent. A former Army varsity footballer, he was built like a tank and seemed just as indestructible. He cared about his men and his mission, I think in that order. I had great trouble believing him dead while the rest of us somehow survived."*[135]

During the nine-day operation the battle casualties were high on both sides. The Americans suffered 41 killed, 34 on 25 August. Berry's men accounted for 54 enemy dead and possibly another 92, with the Air Force adding 45 more by body count and possibly another 30. Shortly after the operation a South Vietnamese intelligence source reported that the enemy actually had lost 171 men: 101 from the Phu Loi battalion, 60 from the C62 Company, and 10 laborers. Whichever figures were accurate, the Viet Cong had suffered severely. Out of a force estimated to be around five hundred men, either figure meant that the Phu Loi Battalion and the C62 Company were down to about half strength.[136]

In evaluating his brigade's performance during AMARILLO, Colonel Berry praised the aggressive patrolling of the 1st Battalion, 2d Infantry, which had generated the fight on 25 August. He claimed that as a result of the soldiers' efforts and performance, the brigade had been "victorious" in this "major battle" against the "elite Phu Loi Battalion." Berry's assessment was, perhaps, too generous.[137]

**Dennis Howley:** *"...I assumed Command of A-1-16 the night of August 25th, 1966, the day in which Capt Pete Knight...was killed as he moved against a dug in VC MG position with an empty rifle and a grenade in his* *hand. ...The fact that Pete Knight with an empty rifle and grenade was going after a VC MG position alone reflected that fact that he had no functional company any more...just scared, shocked troops. [I'm] not sure how many [were] killed as they walked into the kill zone or how many the USAF 500 pounders killed, but do know and saw at least 2 platoons had been seriously chopped up like 1/2 WIA/KIA!!*

*"According to the "history," the After Action Reports, 9 Americans were killed and 80 wounded---but I saw a mound of dead American bodies on August 26th that had 30-40 American dead and Westmoreland stood right next to it!! According to the "history" After Action Report 15 VC/body count and over 170 killed and WIA's out of the total Phu Loi Bn strength...total BS, we got waxed!!! There were no "spider holes" or men in trees...they were professionally dug in positions on ground level, you could not see them and they had good fields of fire et al...professionals waiting for the lambs to walk in for the slaughter...Several days later as C.O. I watch the A-1-16 formation addressed by Col Berry about the "victory"...don't know if he made general but he was sure working on it..."*[138]

The patrol's presence in the Phu Loi Battalion's base camp, not its patrolling ability, triggered the fight. Indeed, a report penned by Colonel Prillaman characterized the fight as "essentially a meeting engagement in which neither side was prepared for or really wanted heavy contact." The isolation of Company C's patrol, he added, "forced us to fight, and the invasion of their base camp forced the Viet Cong to hold their positions in the face of a strong US effort." Although still satisfied that his brigade won the day, Berry himself acknowledged many years later that "we ultimately committed about 3,000 American soldiers against about 500 Viet Cong. The VC had several advantages, principally well constructed, heavily fortified positions in jungle terrain they knew intimately. We thrashed our way almost blindly into the enemy's base camp and fought him on his home ground under conditions favorable to him."[139]

*But there is nothing covered up which will not be revealed, and hidden which will not be known*
*Luke 12:2*

# Chapter 4-August 25th, 1966-Redux

### The Problems with Military History

When I compiled the preceding chapter, I did some searches on the internet for the source documents mentioned in the footnotes of "Stemming the Tide" by John Carland. In following this trail of footnotes I found another story. Security classifications can explain the omission of certain information available to Mr. Carland but I'm forced to conclude that career concerns and professional reputations are the explanation for the omissions of the rest of the story. It's my belief that the battle was the result of a very clever counter-trap laid by the Phu Loi Battalion and General DePuy fell for it lock, stock, and barrel.

### Finding the Enemy

Ostensibly, Operation Amarillo began as a simple road clearing operation. Moving supplies is always a major concern but the logistician's work was not what the tacticians were focused on. General DePuy was a man in a hurry. Attrition, killing the enemy faster than he could replace his losses was the strategy and finding, fixing, and finishing the main force VC and NVA units was the mission. General DePuy was often frustrated in his quest for mission success. Finding the enemy was the one single problem that the technology and firepower available to him couldn't solve; but DePuy had a few tricks up his sleeve.

The Viet Cong were also pursuing a strategy of attrition, killing American soldiers until the American people forced their government to withdraw from Vietnam. The VC didn't have the technology and firepower available to the Americans but they were experienced jungle fighters; skilled in ambushing, sniping, mining roads and booby-trapping trails; and their intelligence operations were brilliant.

One of the VC units operating in Amarillo's area was known by the intelligence people as the Phu Loi Battalion. This was a popular name for VC units because it commemorated an incident at a prison in Phu Loi where it was alleged that the RVN government poisoned and killed hundreds of imprisoned VC. In naming them the Phu Loi Battalion, the VC leaders were reminding the troops of their duty to avenge these 'martyrs' to the cause. The unit was also called Quyet Thang II or 'Determined to Win.'[140]

### The Radio Game

LTC William LeGro was the G2 (Intelligence) officer for the 1st Infantry Division. He was conducting aggressive intelligence operations in an attempt to find the enemy. General DePuy based all his operations on LeGro's information, which was mainly gained through SIGINT; "We based all our operations on Bill LeGro's intelligence...Signal Intelligence was our primary source...long range patrols sometimes verified such intelligence..."[141]

In an oral history interview given in 2005, LeGro described one of these intelligence operations, a radio game gambit. Prior to August 25th, he arranged to have one of the new standard infantry radios, an AN/PRC-25, that had been 'jarked' by the CIA, to be 'lost' by an infantry battalion operating near the Phu Loi Battalion's suspected base area. The radio had a hidden transmitter that would allow it to be located by special direction finding equipment and it appears that the scheme worked.[142]

## LRRP

On August 24th, Charlie Company 1-2 Infantry was positioned at Artillery Base Two, close to the located position of LeGro's 'special' radio. Captain William J. Mullen III, the company commander of C-1-2 Infantry had recently formed his own long range reconnaissance patrol (LRRP), called them the 'Leopards' and issued them 'Tiger Suit' fatigues. Being authorized to form a long range reconnaissance patrol at the company level would require approval from battalion and it seems likely that no one would do this unless permission came from Division. General DePuy already had formed a provisional LRRP unit in April of 1966 and attached them to the Division's 1-4 Cavalry Squadron.[143]

Choosing a leader and some troops, issuing them distinctive uniforms and calling them a long range reconnaissance patrol does not make LRRPs. Long range recon patrolling is very difficult to do well and it is extremely dangerous. Most soldiers are not able to perform this duty; that is why the LRRP's are considered elite. Colonel Charlie Beckwith, a commander of the 5th Special Forces Group LRRP's, Project Delta, said that selection of personnel was the single most important factor in forming a LRRP Team.[144]

In the early days of the war, these types of recon units were mostly ad hoc creations based on the need to find the enemy. Typically the commanders would choose some 'Ranger' qualified officers and NCO's to perform this task. The ranger training at Fort Benning was a leadership course using a light infantry scenario under extreme physical conditions. It had nothing to do with the techniques of long range patrolling. The 5th Special Forces Group ran a three week 'Recondo' school which taught many of these skills, but the school wasn't available for U.S. troops until September 1966. Even with individual training, the time needed to train a team depends on the experience of the team leader and the support he receives to allow him to train his men.[145]

## The Ambush Patrol

On August 24th, between dusk and dark, the 15 man patrol from C-1-2 Infantry left their battalion perimeter and moving west, entered the jungle. Some of the explanations and cover stories for this patrol are as follows:

1. According to the Intelligence section of Col. Berry's CAAR, the patrol's mission was to ambush enemy soldiers. According to the Execution section it was to locate VC personnel, bases and materials.

2. According to James Holland, a C-1-2 Infantry platoon leader, in a short story posted on the 1-4 Cavalry web page, the squad sized ambush patrol was ordered to watch a designated area for 4 days.

3. In the October 2007 edition of "Vietnam", a war history magazine, is an article entitled, "The Battle of Bong Trang" by James Holland. In the article, Mullen is quoted as saying, "We briefed Colonel Prillaman (the 1-2 Infantry commander) and got support to the point where I was able to line up an overflight for Fortune Smith [the sergeant who was to head up the ambush]. This was simply a pre-planned ambush in the event the opportunity arose." He told Smith that the side-operation would be "configured…as a combat patrol." Mullen made sure that an artillery forward observer (FO) named Sergeant Glasscock would be along to give the detachment quick access to heavy support. He also beefed up the patrol with GI's from the company's reconnaissance squad. This too would have been an ad hoc unit as there was no 'reconnaissance squad' at the company level table of organization and equipment.[146]

## Ambush Patrols

Ambush Patrols a nightly were routine in the 1st Infantry Division and all of the ambush patrols conducted by the Division were pre-planned. When the 1-16 Infantry was in the field, a rifle squad with a machine gun crew and a medic would be sent from each platoon to ambush a road or trail in the vicinity of their perimeter. The ambush patrol in the movie, "Platoon" was a reasonable depiction of these patrols except for the contact, which was rarely made.[147]

Usually, ambush patrols were positioned by the company commander or the battalion operations officer in consultation with the S2 and battalion commander. The patrols navigated by dead reckoning, using a compass azimuth and pace count to take them through the dark to a spot in the jungle where a trail had been noted on a map, usually no more than a thousand meters distance from their unit. There they functioned more as a long range listening post and they were there to ambush any enemy troops that might be moving toward their unit's night defensive positions for an attack.

They responded to hourly requests for situation reports by keying their radio twice to indicate all was well. At dawn they would return to the perimeter. Ambush patrols were a nightly routine in the 1st Infantry Division, but this patrol was anything but routine.

This is the only case known by me that an ambush patrol leader got an overflight prior to going out or one where an artillery FO was assigned to accompany the patrol. Since Sgt. Glasscock was there we can assume that he had pre-plotted artillery concentrations based on specific target reference points—grid coordinates that were given to the artillery fire direction center of the artillery battery co-located with C-1-2 Infantry. This practice allows almost instant and accurate artillery fire support for a unit in contact; the only requirement is that the FO knows where he is.

## The Ambush Patrol (2)

The patrol left the perimeter at 1930 hours, about twenty minutes after sunset and moved into the jungle. On the 24th, the sunset was at 1908 hours and EENT (dark) came at 1955 hours. The moon was in its first quarter and it set at forty-nine minutes after midnight.

This was during the Monsoon or rainy season so it was probably cloudy although there is no mention of rain on the 24th. Suffice it to say, in that vegetation, it was dark. The remaining light only lasted a short time and soon it was pitch black. The grid coordinates for their destination were more than 4000 meters from their start point. Here are some of the descriptions of the patrol's movement:

1. According to James Holland in a story on the 1-4 Cav's web page; "On the way to their ambush location, they became lost and requested permission to 'coil up' (spent the night) where they were and move to their ambush site when the sun came up. The next morning, they realized that they were inside an enemy base camp."

2. According to the magazine article by James Holland, "After moving several thousand meters, Sergeant Smith called a halt and established a night perimeter, though the patrol had not reached the ambush location. Smith told the men that he wanted to avoid other ambush patrols...The night before, when Smith decided to coil up, he had unknowingly chosen the middle of a base camp for the VC Phu Loi Battalion."

3. According to Colonel Berry's CAAR, the patrol moved from the Artillery Base at XT 2887379 to XT 842387, about 4500 meters. The next morning the CAAR reports their location as XT 865382, a little more than 2000 meters from their starting point.[148]

4. Finally, according to Chuck Mundahl, a member of the patrol, Sergeant Smith called a halt when the point man found several sticks tied in the shape of an arrow on a path pointing in the direction they were going. Sergeant Smith decided to stop there and proceed the rest of the way in the morning.[149]

### The Ambush Patrol (3)

The next morning the patrol found the Phu Loi Battalion, hardly a target for an ambush patrol. What happened next is described by several different sources:

1. According to the Intelligence section of the CAAR, the fighting began at 1700 hours on the 25th when they found themselves in contact with the Phu Loi Battalion; I'm sure they meant 0700. The Execution section said that it began at 0630 when the Tiger Patrol reported contact with the VC and that they were receiving mortar fire. Ten minutes later the 1-26 Infantry was informed that the C-1-2 Infantry LRRP patrol had become engaged with an estimated VC battalion. At 0759 the patrol reported that they were receiving grenades, machine gun, and small arms fire, and that the VC were in the trench-line with them. Artillery was called in from Arty Base 2 and adjusted by the FO with the patrol. The patrol called artillery fire on its position when they were about to be overrun. Five men had been wounded and their machine guns disabled. Airstrikes were called in and artillery began firing concentrations to block avenues of escape.[150]

2. According to Holland's story on the 1-4 Cavalry web page, "When the sun came up that squad found that they had walked into a battalion sized base camp. They were surrounded by VC and fought their way into a VC bunker where they set up a defense. When they found themselves in that predicament they called back to the company for help. We initiated air and artillery strikes in support of them and at the same time asked for help from the 1/4 Cav."[151]

3. According to Holland's magazine article, "The next morning the patrol moved out. Mundahl, at the back of the column, recalls that they walked only a few minutes before he heard "children's voices." Then came the pop-pop of small arms fire. Mundahl had yet to see the enemy, but grenades were going off, bullets were flying by, and he heard high pitched screams. "What the hell did they do—shoot a bunch of kids?" Mundahl said to no one in particular. Then Sergeant Smith shouted, "They're everywhere!" He meant the Viet Cong, whose voices Mundahl had mistaken for those of children. The GI's scrambled into a nearby trench…The ditch was a vacant communications trench within a camp that held at least 500 VC. The patrol was surrounded. The enemy began mortaring the Americans' position, wounding several GI's. [Sergeant] Smith called for countermeasures, and soon American artillery was blasting the ground around the trench…Men shouted that the fire was too close. Smith shifted the big guns…With the grenades going off around the trench; Sergeant Smith passed the word to the patrol to hold on: "Captain Mullen's coming with the Cav."[152]

### The Battle of Bong Trang

C Company, 1-2 Infantry, reinforced by a platoon from the 1-4 Cavalry, began to move west, riding on the Cavalry's APCs, toward the patrol's location. Mullen controlled the movement from a helicopter overhead for a time, then landed and was with his unit on the ground. He left two platoons to guard the open area behind them. A tank and an APC were disabled by mechanical failure and abandoned. Around the same time Mullen got a call from a platoon he had left at the open area who reported that they were under attack. Mullen ordered his men to return to the clearing.[153]

### The Decision Point

At this point, Capt. Mullen realized that it would be futile to continue to assault into the thick vegetation. He had lost radio contact with the patrol but knew that they were in a trench where they might survive the bombardment if they weren't already dead. He recommended to the colonels and generals circling above him in their helicopters that reinforcing be delayed until the artillery and air had pounded the camp. Instead, after MG DePuy ordered the grand maneuver, the result was what we in the infantry call a massive cluster-blank, with units firing into each other and airstrikes which dropped bombs and napalm on U.S. troops.

### When Will They Ever Learn?

It's my belief that the man on the ground is better able to determine what's needed than a man flying above a heavily wooded area in a helicopter. From an armchair quarterback's perspective it looks to me like Captain Mullen had the better grasp of the situation when he recommended to the men in the air that they delay reinforcements until artillery and airstrikes had dealt with the enemy force.

His recommendation was rejected by Maj. Clark, Col. Berry, and though not mentioned, General DePuy. Berry was quoted as saying, "The commander of an infantry company under attack hardly had the perspective to decide for or against a relief attempt."[154]

This illustrates one of the major leadership failures of the U.S. Army in Vietnam. Two distinguished combat leaders, Lt. Col. Anthony Herbert and Col. David Hackworth both wrote about their disdain for this practice. Herbert said, "The rule of thumb in the infantry had always been to be at the critical place at the critical time...not up at 1,500 feet, giving directions...The bird-men may have been commanders in the technical sense of the word, but they weren't leaders, and the grunts knew it." Hackworth said, "Where was the...company and battalion commanders? Where was the brigade commander? ...most likely they would be on the scene as well, overhead in choppers, all of them issuing orders and playing what became known as the Great Squad Leader in the Sky, creating absolute chaos in an already confused situation."[155]

This practice was a trademark role of General DePuy. LTC Alexander Haig, DePuy's operations officer during the battle of Bong Trang, wrote that DePuy was, "the best squad leader, platoon commander, and company commander in the division...[He] liked to talk by radiotelephone directly to platoon leaders and company commanders in the heat of battle while circling overhead in his helicopter."[156]

This 'command and control' method continues to kill soldiers and create chaos for no good reason. Pete Blaber described a similar situation during the 2002 battle in the Shahi Khot Valley of Afghanistan during Operation Anaconda. There, he, a senior special operations commander on the ground, was overruled by an Air Force General at Bagram Airbase, hundreds of miles away but hovering vicariously over the battlefield watching a remote video feed from a drone. SEALs, Rangers, and Air Force personnel all died because the deputy JSOC commander knew better than the man on the ground. This is the premier special ops unit of the U.S. military; you'd think that they would, if anyone could, learn the lessons of history.[157]

### The Battle of Bong Trang (2)

Berry and Clark realized that the situation was out of control on the ground. They landed and while they were discussing the situation, Clark was killed. Berry then took over and described the hours that followed as a time when he, "ran around like a crazy man getting things going." It appears to me that the reason he was running around was because the radio nets on the ground were jammed by everyone trying to transmit at the same time.

The final offensive action of that day by the 1-16 Infantry was the right flank company's attempt to attack through the left flank company's position. Meanwhile the enemy cast their vote and after designating some brave rearguard elements, they did what guerrilla fighters always do under the circumstances and left while assuring that they would inflict many more casualties.[158]

At around 1600, Berry put LTC Paul Gorman in command of the forces on the ground and resumed command of his brigade. That night Gorman tried to prepare a sketch of what unit was where using radio messages, runners, and staff officers; "there was mass confusion, particularly as to the whereabouts of the various parts of the 1st Battalion, 16th Infantry. All night long Americans as individuals or small groups were milling around trying to find their parent units. I was worried about firing on friendlies and every time there was a burst of fire we'd try to figure out who was shooting at whom."[159]

Throughout the night, flares provided some illumination and the artillery continued to pound the enemy positions. The commanders planned a dawn attack preceded by airstrikes. The next morning, the Air Force dropped 30 napalm bombs on the suspected VC positions. An infantryman from C-1-2 Infantry, PFC John Johnston, said that "Our Air Force dropped napalm on us because some dumbass threw a red smoke grenade when we marked our position with smoke. When they dropped the napalm, the gooks left."[160]

After the airstrikes and their effects were dealt with, Gorman ordered his battalion to assault. As soon as they began to move they received a "terrific blast of fire from the north, it was the 2-28 Infantry, much closer to us that I had imagined. I had to get them to cease fire so that we could resume our attack." When they resumed the attack the enemy was gone and they secured the area.[161]

One of the members of the ambush patrol, PFC Dennis Peterson, came out of the jungle and led others to the wounded survivors. Another member, a machine gunner named Sexton, crawled into an open area and was picked up by a helicopter. They were brought out and the bodies of the dead members of the LRRP team were found later in the VC camp. SSG Fortune Smith and SGT Glasscock are listed as KIA on August 25th and the 'recon' squad leader wasn't identified. Neither Smith nor Glasscock received a posthumous decoration other than the Purple Heart.[162]

Peterson and the other survivors have never publicly made known what exactly transpired during their ordeal. Peterson received a Silver Star and another man received a Bronze Star with V device, posthumously. It seems evident that the LRRP team leader and the squad leader had a disagreement on what to do after the fighting went on for a while and the LRRP team tried to escape and evade, unsuccessfully. Probably for the sake of the families and perhaps for the reputations of the leaders, this episode is being kept close-hold by the leadership and survivors.

### The Combat After Action Report

The Combat After Action Report is a cover story on many levels. The first page of the twenty-three page document, dated 18 December 1966, is addressed thru the 1st Infantry Division Commander, Major General William DePuy to the MACV Commander, General Westmoreland. It gives the dates and a brief summary of Operation Amarillo and the reporting officer's name, Colonel Sidney B. Berry, Jr, 1st Brigade Commander. It lists a task organization which includes the added units that took part in the battle and then the first major sub-section, Intelligence. Please pay close attention to section (e).

**Intelligence:** The Intelligence section starts with the enemy situation and section (a) goes right to the battle. It mentions the patrol that initiated the fight and that the enemy was well dug-in and fled after "stubborn and determined resistance." It then goes on to speculate that "the badly defeated battalion and its attachments" disappeared in various directions and was now believed to be back in the same general area. Section (b) says that the Phu Loi Battalion had 384 men.

It lists the subordinate units and the heavy weapons that were believed to be carried by them: four 81mm mortars, one 75mm recoilless rifle, five 60mm mortars, two 57mm recoilless rifles, and one .50 caliber machine gun. Also listed are ten AN/PRC-10 radios, the U.S. military's backpack radio that was replaced by the AN/PRC-25.

Section (c) states that there had been increased VC activity along Route 16 in the two weeks prior to convoy operations and Section (d) describes the terrain as flat with dense vegetation which could limit visibility to two meters and conceal the trails, fortifications and other structures.

## CAAR (2) The Phu Loi Battalion Base Camp

Section (e) gives some detail regarding the fortifications of the Phu Loi Battalion base camp. It says that they were well constructed and consisted of open and covered trenches and fighting positions. The overhead cover was considered especially well-constructed. The firing apertures were two to three inches above ground level, and it was noted that this made "it extremely difficult to obtain hits into the position." The fighting positions were mutually supportive and arranged in depth. The entire camp including the above ground structures and the furniture got high marks from whoever wrote this section.

## Another View

Captain Rudolf H. Egersdorfer, the S2 for the 1-26 Infantry investigated the Phu Loi Battalion's camp after the fight. Observing in an interview that the defenses were "awesome" he said: "They were designed around large bunkers capable of holding twenty or more men, with deep trenches radiating out to smaller fighting bunkers, all connected by trenches in a ring. The firing apertures were narrow and low, so small that no American could use a weapon through them. The fields of fire were really fire tunnels, cut by clearing lanes in the underbrush nearest the ground, and tying the bushes above together. No GI walking through such a lane could know that from the belt down he was perfectly visible to the VC in the bunkers…

"The bunkers themselves were masterpieces. They were built not of large logs, like we Americans usually used, but of laminated layers of saplings, arm thick, with three or more feet of dirt packed on top.

"They were neat, durable, and equipped with creature comforts like picnic tables. I really believe that the only way we could have driven them out is with flame, and preferably very precise flame throwers." The location of the camp, so close to the road, and the quality of its fortifications, make it appear that the VC built it as their version of General DePuy's defensive positions, specifically for a fight.[163]

## CAAR (3)

The last Intelligence sub-section (f) covers civil affairs and psychological warfare. The BS bombers dropped 480,000 leaflets during the operation and tapes were played along Route 16 with themes "varied to meet the situation." The themes were "Stay in your hamlets, Surrender, and Chieu Hoi (defect)." With toilet paper in short supply I'm sure the leaflets were a welcome relief to the locals and the VC. There is no mention of any Chieu Hoi's or surrenders.

**The Mission:** The next section 'covers' the mission: The 1st Brigade, in coordination with various RVN forces, clears and secures Route Red and conducts search and destroy operations and resupply convoys during the period of 20-25 August 1966. In parentheses it states, ("This operation was initiated by the 1st Brigade after coordination with the 1st Infantry Division.") This is a most unusual phrase and I have not seen it in any other report like this. It also contradicts the G2's statement that [the 1st] Brigade was directed to send a reconnaissance—what he called a reconnaissance in force. This statement in the CAAR appears to me, based on the evidence shown later in this chapter, to be Berry's covering for people above him in the chain of command.[164]

**Concept of The Operation:** The concept of the operation follows and it describes each phase of the road clearing operation with no mention of the battle. Section (b) tells us that the 1st Battalion, 5th Artillery provided and coordinated fire support, that armed helicopters would escort the convoys, and that Air Force FAC's would be on station.

**Execution:** This is probably the most appropriate term for what is described in the next six pages of single spaced, small font type. Probably compiled from the staff duty journals of the various units involved, it gives a day by day, hour by hour, and moment by moment record of whatever the radio operators in the CP's were able to record. People talking on the radio while under fire can be difficult to understand. So, whoever constructed this section had a job of work. Remember, there were no personal computers in those days.

Much of this section has been covered elsewhere but I'll highlight a few things that were of interest to me. At 1330 hours on the 25th, two APC were hit and 'disabled,' one by mortar and/or grenades, and one by 75mm recoilless rifle fire. The 75mm recoilless rifle weighed at least 114 pounds and there was no trace of it when the camp was searched afterward. Some short time after 1635 hours A-1-16th Infantry came under fire by VC forces using besides small arms, 57mm recoilless rifle[s] and .50 caliber machine gun fire. One 57mm recoilless rifle was later captured but no .50 cal.

Three 60mm mortars and 84 high explosive shells were also captured, indicating that either the trees overhead prevented the mortars from being fired or the VC mortar and recoilless rifle crews, who were not under overhead cover, felt some heat that day. The 1330 report is the first mention of VC mortar fire besides the report from the patrol at the beginning of the battle; this may indicate when the VC began their rearguard actions.

I was impressed with the documentation of what are called 'friendly fire' incidents. Of course, the patrol's calling for artillery fire on their own position was a gutsy move that speaks of the desperate situation they were in and would not be considered friendly fire.

Several of the incidents mentioned took place the night of the 25th. At 1845 hours, elements of B-1-16 Infantry received "a heavy volume of small arms, automatic weapons, and mortar fire, from east to south, probably from friendly elements with 2 WIA's. At 2105 hours the 1-16 Infantry received an artillery shell in their perimeter adjusted by the 1-26 Infantry.

The napalm strike on the 1-2 Infantry CP at 0730 hours, the morning of the 26th, resulted in 2 killed and 14 wounded, mostly men of the 1-16 Infantry. On the 27th at 0825 hours, a patrol from B 1-16 Infantry was taken under heavy fire by a patrol of the 1-26 Infantry resulting in two WIA's. The 'blast' of friendly fire from the 2-28 Infantry on the 1-26 Infantry as they began their attack after the napalm strike on the morning of the 26th is not mentioned, nor are some others that must have occurred but were impossible to sort out.

**Fire Support:** Section 8 covers supporting forces. During the operation, the artillery fired 8869 rounds of 105mm, 1538 of 8-Inch (possibly a typo) and 680 of 175mm high explosive shells, most of them on August 25 and 26. The Air Force flew eighty-five strike missions with 256 sorties.

## The VC Counter-Gambit

**Results of Operation:** Section 9 tallies the results. Along with the captured weapons and ammunition is a list of enemy equipment and material. Toward the end of a long list of inconsequential items are two AN/PRC-10 radios and a PRC-25 radio. The AN/PRC-25 radio would have been a valuable piece of equipment for VC signal intelligence operations. Why was it left in the camp?

Was it a coincidence that Colonel LeGro called his 'special' radio a PRC-25 in his interview and it was listed this way in the CAAR rather than correctly as an AN/PRC-25? Did the VC figure out the radio game and use it as a lure? It seems clear to me that the VC knew the radio was jarked, used it to draw the U.S. forces to attack the camp, and left it behind for obvious reasons.[165]

LeGro seems to dissemble when asked about who would follow up on the information [gained] from triangulating and locating that [Phu Loi Battalion base.] He says "well, we would report it to—gave the information to the G3 and if he wanted to do something about it he could send somebody in there. Actually, I don't believe that we did exploit that directly." This contradicts DePuy's word that, "we based all our operations on Bill LeGro's intelligence...Signal intelligence was our primary source...long range patrols sometimes verified such intelligence..."[166]

There was something else: LeGro was asked if he or the Division troops were able to exploit the fact that they were standing right on top of the Phu Loi Battalion's home headquarters. He replies that he didn't pick up any documents, (numerous documents were found), but he did mention an 'intelligence operation' that was encouraging the executive officer and a number of soldiers of the Phu Loi Battalion to Chieu Hoi, but the operation went 'sour.'

When asked what happened he said he believed it was compromised by an American officer, Major Robert Schweitzer, of the Division, who worked closely with the Vietnamese. That officer had ordered the sergeant in charge of the intelligence operation to read him into what was going on. LeGro suspected that if Schweitzer hadn't gotten involved it might have worked.[167]

This must have been a source of contention between LeGro and DePuy because when DePuy referred to Schweitzer in his interview he said, "in the case of Colonel Schweitzer, we had the perfect man. He spoke Vietnamese, was the bravest man I ever met, was a man of enormous initiative and energy, was wounded a number of times, and had the confidence of the Vietnamese at every level to the extent that they would assign forces to him at his request without his even telling them what he was going to use them for; and, there would be no intelligence leaks of any kind.'' Most of DePuy's senior officers, including Schweitzer, retired as general officers, LeGro retired as a colonel.[168]

As to the actual technique used for the radio gambit, great care would be necessary to convince the VC commander that a newly fielded AN/PRC-25 radio could fall into their hands without being part of some ploy. In 1957, the French used a similar trick to kill a rebel leader in the Algerian War for Independence. Knowledge of these kinds of ploys gets around in the 'secret world.' I don't know to what lengths LeGro went to in order to deceive the VC but I believe that the scheme backfired and while the surprise appearance of the patrol that morning threw off the planned VC ambush, General DePuy played into their hands with his brilliant 'pile on' maneuver.[169]

## CAAR (4)

**The Body-count:** The U.S. casualties are undisputed and were reported as forty-one KIA and 196 WIA. Heavy casualties were sustained by some of the units taking part in this battle. A-1-16 Infantry lost its Company Commander that day and several others KIA and a large number of wounded. The VC casualties were added, imagined, extrapolated and finally totaled with a claim that ARVN intelligence officers stated that a total of 171 VC were killed in the battle. The body-count remains suspect due to another indicator, the six captured enemy small arms: two BAR's, one U.S. .30 caliber carbine, one .45 caliber submachine gun, one Chinese bolt action rifle, and one M-16 rifle.[170]

David Hackworth said in his autobiography, "About Face," that a 4:1 body-count to weapons captured ratio was a reasonable [assumption]. My math tells me this was a 28.5:1 ratio. If you think I'm being nit-picky about the body-count, please educate yourself by taking a look at the 1970 Study on Military Professionalism done by the U.S. Army War College. On page B-1-10 under the sub-heading 'Integrity' the reports states, "One of the most violent reactions we got was from the body-count, particularly from young combat arms officers recently back from Vietnam, '...the President of the United States was making decisions on totally invalid information...Nobody out there believes the body-count,'" etc, etc, etc.[171]

**Administrative Matters:** By the time the reporting officer's typists got to Section 10, Administrative Matters, they must have been wore out. After two pages of insignificant captured materials and significant losses, they covered logistics, that is, supply, maintenance, and treatment of casualties, with two small paragraphs and not much detail. Transportation was also covered with little verbiage but detailed statistics. The convoys, what the whole operation was for, moved 294 cubic yards of gravel, eighty-eight cubic yards of sand, 2240 bags of cement, roofing material and forty-five round wall Quonset Hut sections.
The big ticket items were 5492 8-Inch, 3552 175mm, and 15,490 105mm artillery shells along with 1250 4.2 inch mortar rounds. Oh, and eighty-three truckloads of PX supplies and forty-nine truckloads of construction materials for an ice plant.

**Communications:** The next sub-section is communications. It is marked N/A (not applicable). That's laughable. Perhaps because of the extent of the communication problems this section was probably written by the commo officer and classified. The problem of jammed networks by more than one person transmitting at the same time caused many problems over the years in Vietnam. The enemy had some electronic capabilities, but in firefights, the enemy was us. I don't know if anyone developed an SOP for these situations but it would have been helpful. I like the technique of the RTO monitoring the radio, while the leaders direct the fight and the CO makes radio contact for inquiries and orders.

**Commanders Analysis:** Here Colonel Berry concluded that the brigade was victorious because of three 'salient' factors: Artillery and air support, the skill of the CO, 1-26 Infantry, in the maneuvering of the reinforcements, and the skill, training, initiative and physical stamina of the individual soldiers needed in order for US forces to be successful.

In section 'e' he reiterates his interpretation of Herbert's rule of thumb mentioned previously, that the commander must be at the critical place at the critical time which is where CPT Mullen was. For DePuy, Berry, and Clark, after overruling Mullen's decision on how to fight the battle, this place was in the air until everything was FUBAR and then Clark and Berry went to the ground.[172]

**Lessons Learned:** In the first section Berry admires the way that the 1-26 Infantry managed to find transportation for their move to the battle. The next section lauds the use of armor by the same battalion and posits their future use, dependent, of course, on their level of maintenance. Then he goes into how armor should be used on future attacks on fortified base camps in the jungle.

The section on fire support is cautiously revealing when he says, "closing one infantry unit on another already engaged in the jungle is an inherently very difficult undertaking since one or both elements are likely to take fire from the other and the confusion redounds to the benefit of the enemy." This was interesting because DePuy's Big Red One Battle Principals, Number 3 states: 'Complicated schemes of maneuver have no place in jungle warfare.'[173]

He concludes this section by mentioning that the tactic of surrounding an enemy force in the jungle presents the most difficult case for friendly fire control. He says that command and control must be maintained from the air unless the commander is needed on the ground, and then he needs someone in the air to control him on the ground. If the commander is on the ground he recommends having a photographer with a Polaroid camera in the air, dropping him pictures of the battleground! Seriously…?

**The Lesson Learned:** Though not described in the CAAR, there was a lesson learned. From then on, when 1st Infantry Division forces found an entrenched enemy unit in the jungle, rather than conducting frontal assaults, from then on they would maintain contact in a defensive posture and call for sustained, massive airstrikes and artillery before attempting to move into the enemy positions.[174]

## Generals

Where was General DePuy during this battle and afterwards? For some of it, he was circling the battlefield in his own aerial command post. Later, he landed in the clearing and met with BG Hollingsworth and General Westmoreland. No narrative mentions him talking to the troops afterwards. Why he is not mentioned in any of the CAAR's is open to interpretation but it appears to me that he had no desire to be associated with the maneuver decisions made on August 25th.[175]

On the third day of the battle at Gettysburg during the U.S. Civil War, after Robert E. Lee ordered the disastrous assault on the Union center led by Pickett's Virginians, he personally addressed General Pickett and the survivors as they retreated from the high-water mark of the Confederacy, saying to Pickett and heard by men standing nearby, "General, your men have done all that men could do; the fault is entirely my own."[176]

LTC Arthur Fremantle, a British officer observing Confederate operations saw Lee speaking to the soldiers passing him saying, "never mind, all this will come right in the end; we'll talk it over afterwards; but, in the meantime, all good men must rally..." Fremantle wrote, "Very few men failed to answer his appeal and I saw many badly wound men take off their hats and cheer him."

To a brigade commander, General Wilcox, Lee said "General, all this has been MY fault—it is I that have lost the fight and you must help me out of it the best way that you can." Then Fremantle wrote, "In this manner I saw General Lee encourage and reanimate his somewhat dispirited troops, and magnanimously take upon his own shoulders the whole weight of the repulse. It was impossible to look at him or to listen to him without feeling the strongest admiration, and I never saw any man fail him..."[177]

## The General's Confession

Years later General DePuy, in an interview with LTC William J. Mullen III, who was then a student at the Army War College, referred to the battle without being asked, saying; "Well, we might as well talk about that battle on August 25th." Without waiting for Mullen to reply, he summarized the details of the maneuvers and ended with, "I presided over this very gory and unsuccessful operation. The VC made monkeys out of us."[178]

Please try and imagine what it must have been like for Mullen, who apparently held a great deal of respect for DePuy, to be sitting there talking to the man who was now, thirteen years later, admitting that he was behind the decision to ignore Mullen's recommendation to hold off on the reinforcing move until the artillery and air had finished the VC resistance. The result of that decision being forty-one dead GI's and 196 wounded, many of those from Mullen's company.

What is even more striking to me is that Mullen never mentioned trying to get permission from Berry, or DePuy, who was circling overhead, to pull back and pound the VC camp with airstrikes and artillery before trying to go in. Instead he says that he tried to tell DePuy by radio that they were in contact with something big and to go ahead and try the doughnut thing [surround the VC camp]. Mullen says to DePuy, "well I'm happy to discover that you tried to do just that. I have thought all along that these companies which kept coming in—which was nice to see— screwed up all the fire support, and made a bit of a mess of it."

This is a good example of the difficulties of drawing any useful conclusions from military history. Mullen's loyalty to DePuy, the man who approved Mullen's DSC for his actions during the battle, and who appears to have tied him in knots back then; now those knots keep him from asking the question that I would have been most interested in which was; Why, why, why? Remember, this interview was published by the U.S. Army's Center for Military History.

## Once An Eagle

In 1968, Anton Myrer, a Marine Corps veteran of WWII in the Pacific, wrote an epic war novel, "Once an Eagle," which became an instant best seller in the military. The two main characters represent two extremes of the types of people you meet in the military, with most of us somewhere in-between. The hero, Sam Damon, is always being told to swallow his ethical code for the good of the service between bouts of physical and moral courage that we all wish we could emulate when the time comes. The villain, Courtney Massengale exemplifies the ticket punching careerist, climbing to the top of the army hierarchy over the dead bodies of his troops.

What no one seems to get is that 'Sad Sam Damon' failed his own code when he didn't prefer charges against his corps commander, Massengale, who was responsible for the destruction of his division. Massengale broke his word when he took Damon's reserve force and used it for a grandstand play while leaving Damon without the backup he was counting on. When Damon has a meeting with Massengale in the hospital after the battle, after some sparring, he asks him why, "Why did you do it?"

When Massengale claims it was all a misunderstanding, Damon fights back by saying that he has copies of the messages and witnesses. Massengale and he go back and forth, with Massengale threatening to ruin Damon's career; then Massengale brings up the old bottom line, that Damon should drop it for the good of the service. Damon resists compliance until Massengale offers a unit citation for his division and reminds Damon that the war isn't over.

Damon considers that his reconstituted division will have to fight again and if he is gone, who will lead them? Damon caves in and Myrer implies that in Damon's doing so, we had Vietnam. I loved that book along with many other vets but it took three readings to see that Sam was just like the rest of us, willing to live with the lie and even tell it for the good of the service and his own career.[179]

## The General's Quandary

Prior to the battle of Bong Trang on August 25th, 1966, in April of that year, 134 men from C-2-16 Infantry went into a fight with the VC during Operation Abilene and twenty-eight walked out. General Harold K. Johnson, the Army Chief of Staff, visited with DePuy shortly after that battle and warned him, "The American people won't support this war if we keep having the kind of casualties suffered by Charlie Company."[180]

DePuy's next higher was the II Field Force commander, Major General Jonathan Seaman. Seaman had no love for General DePuy, who had replaced him as commander of the Big Red One. Both Harold K. Johnson and Seaman felt that DePuy had relieved too many senior officers and Johnson had told him so in a meeting on Christmas Day, 1966. Johnson told him that he was supposed to train his subordinates, not relieve them. DePuy's assistant Division Commander, BG Hollingsworth was also at this meeting and argued with Johnson saying, "I had the idea that you were going to train them and we were going to fight them over here and save soldier's lives."[181]

DePuy was famous in Vietnam for relieving subordinates who screwed up and got people killed. He relieved at least nine Lieutenant Colonels, a career ender for them, during his time with the 1st Infantry Division. Just before bringing up August 25th in the interview, DePuy discussed them: "Well, I guess I have to say that I'm fairly well convinced that once a man has made a bad mistake, not of judgment, but of incompetence, and revealed himself by his actions, actions that are the consequence of a general weakness in command, then there is very little you can do to change him at that stage in his life." When discussing one of them he said, "In the case of another one, I really should have relieved him the first time he failed but I gave him another chance, and he killed a lot more people —our people."[182]

While DePuy rejected Johnson and Seaman's views, no doubt because he disagreed and because he enjoyed the total confidence of General Westmoreland, the MACV commander, they seemed to worry him. According to Colonel Berry, during the meeting on Christmas Day, Johnson told DePuy, "I can't afford another Big Red One...I need division commanders who make the best of the human material they are assigned." Berry said he never saw DePuy so dejected. Hackworth wrote that when he was visiting DePuy's headquarters at Di An with S.L.A. Marshall in December 1966, DePuy took him aside and said, "Hack...I'd like you to do me a favor if you get a chance when you talk to the Chief [Johnson]. Just tell him I'm a good man..."[183]

## S.L.A. Marshall

In the fall of 1966, S.L.A. Marshall, a renowned military historian and LTC David Hackworth, a distinguished combat leader in Korea and Vietnam, came to the war zone for the purpose of training the combat historians in the techniques of the post combat interview. The idea was that these interviews would be used to analyze the techniques, tactics, and procedures for future improvement. The units they visited would recommend the actions to be examined.

After two weeks with the 1st Cavalry Division, they came to the 1st Infantry Division headquarters at Di An. One of the actions Marshall covered was the inspiration for the title of his book, "Ambush." On December 11, 1966 a platoon from C-1-16 Infantry was ambushed near Soui Da, close to Tay Ninh. Only three men were left to tell the story so the post combat interview didn't take long.[184]

I suppose that the logistics of assembling the participants of August 25th were perhaps too daunting to consider that action for the Marshall treatment and so they spent most of the time covering more recent actions including Operation Attleboro. Hackworth wrote extensively about the visit and had some disparaging things to say about life in the Division headquarters and the Division's senior leaders. One result of Marshall's and Hackworth's work was the Vietnam Primer, a summary of lessons learned. In the first chapter Marshall extols the post-combat interview and its benefits:

*"Soon after [an] engagement, any combat unit commander can do this same thing: group interview his men until he knows all that happened to them during the fire fight. In their interest, in his own interest, and for the good of the Army he cannot afford to do less. There is no particular art to the work;*

*so long as exact chronology is maintained in developing the story of the action, and so long as his men feel confident that he seeks nothing from them but the truth, the whole truth, then the needed results will come...*

*Special rewards come to the unit commander who will make the try. Nothing else will give him a closer bond with his men. Not until he does it will he truly know what they did under fire. Just as the combat critique is a powerful stimulant of unit morale, having all the warming effect of a good cocktail on an empty stomach, and even as it strengthens each soldier's appreciation of his fellows, it enables troops to understand for the first time the multitudinous problems and pressures on the commander. They will go all the better for him the next time out and he will have a much clearer view of his human resources."*[185]

## A Critical Lesson

As can be seen from the testimony of the men who were there, the leadership decisions resulted in disaster, hardly a smoothly orchestrated tactical triumph. At the heart of the matter is the responsibility of leaders to determine what happened and provide accurate feedback to their troops for the purpose of improvement. Anything less creates cognitive dissonance in the ranks and leads to feelings of mistrust and hopelessness.

FM 21-13, The Soldier's Guide, a small handbook issued to every recruit states: "You must be honest because there is absolutely no room in the military world for dishonesty or half-truth...a dishonest person can damage the esprit de corps of a unit and the morale of the members of that unit." Whoever wrote the Soldier's Guide knew what they were talking about, it's too bad that everyone didn't read it.

One veteran of this battle, when asked by an officer, who should have known better, what it was that the soldier didn't like about the Army, replied, "They're always handing you a bucket of shit and telling you it's a basket of roses!"

*"Shall your countrymen go to war while you sit here?"*
*Numbers 32:6*

# Chapter 5-September 1966: Part I

### Shipping Out

I took a bus to the Bay Area and reported to the Oakland Army Terminal to wait for shipment. The army was using troopships in those days and I was looking forward to a long sea cruise across the Pacific. Since there was no information about when we would leave, my main activity was dodging the work details while showing up for manifest calls.

After three days my name was called; I boarded a bus for Travis Air Force Base and a plane ride to Vietnam. The plane took us to Hawaii but they didn't let us go anywhere while they refueled. The next stop was Clark Field in the Philippines. We got off the plane while they refueled and waited in the passenger lounge. I saw a Philippine Army soldier sitting on a bench waiting to go somewhere. He was wearing a small camouflage cowboy type hat, camouflage fatigues and he was holding an M-1 Garand rifle. He had live ammunition and I realized that we were entering a region were people were trying to kill each other.

When we returned to the plane, they announced that the next stop would be Saigon, the capitol of South Vietnam. We flew over the ocean for a long time but eventually I saw land in the distance. I could see smoke rising from the green vegetation here and there. Soon, everyone on the plane was looking out the windows. The plane landed at Ton Son Nuit Airport in Saigon. The heat and humidity were intense. As we walked toward the passenger terminal another group of soldiers passed us on their way to the same plane we came in on. Some of them called over to us as we passed with encouraging remarks such as, "Short!" and "You'll be sorry!"

### Saigon

We loaded into a bus with metal mesh screens on the windows. The driver took delight in telling us that the screens were there to prevent hand grenades from coming into the bus. Our destination was the 90th Replacement Battalion in Long Binh where we would be processed into the war. It was too late in the day for the trip so we spent the night in a tent city called Camp Alpha.

The driver closed the door and drove a short ways to the camp. The streets were crowded with every kind of transportation known to man. Pedestrians ran through traffic and vendors stood in the street selling food. "Cutta, cutta," a sergeant next to me kept yelling out the window. "What does 'cutta' mean," I asked him. "It's Korean, you know, cutta chogie." I guessed he thought because I was a Spec-4, I was coming from Korea. I kept myself from informing him that we were in Vietnam and tried to take in the spectacle that was the streets of Saigon in 1966. I was watching everywhere for VC but didn't see any as we lurched through the streets on our way to Camp Alpha.

Camp Alpha was the reception area for all personnel assigned to Military Assistance Command, Vietnam (MACV). General Westmoreland must have been busy that afternoon and wasn't able to welcome us personally to his command, so he sent a sergeant. The sergeant was pretty busy too, so he directed us to some tents nearby and told us to stay there until someone gave us further instructions. I joined the others, found a cot to lie on, and using my AWOL bag for a pillow, took a nap. I woke up sometime later to a commotion in the tent and followed some others to a chow line for supper. After chow I found a bulletin board and read through the various memorandums including some signed by General Westmoreland himself.

Of course, me being a Spec-4, I wasn't invited into Westmoreland's inner or even his outer circle of confidants. The bulletin board was a way for the commanders to keep the troops informed and on notice. There were a multitude of policies on the wear of the uniform, malaria pills, off-limits establishments, etc., etc., etc. Later when I got to my unit, the bulletin board was less cluttered with the petty concerns of the rear echelon military forces (REMFs).

The climate of the Army generally and specifically in Vietnam was one of career considerations taking precedence over everything else in most situations. As long as you read the bulletin board and didn't get caught doing something stupid you were maintaining your career and if you managed to look good or did something brilliant or heroic you might be able to advance your career. General Westmoreland set the tone and the rest of us had to figure it out.

## General Westmoreland

In June of 1964, General William Westmoreland took command of MACV. He was the fair haired hope of the conventional armed forces. Tall, sharp, and handsome, he was right out of Hollywood casting. A three war veteran, his dress uniform displayed a Combat Infantryman Badge over six rows of ribbons held up by master parachutist wings.

When I got there he had been in Vietnam for more than two years. He had determined that he needed U.S. troops to do the heavy lifting because the South Vietnamese Army was getting its ass handed to it during most of their contacts with their cousins on the other side. The President and the Pentagon agreed, so the build-up of U.S. forces continued. When I arrived there were more than 200,000 U.S. troops in South Vietnam.

The country was administratively divided by the Vietnamese government into four 'Corps' areas. The Marines had the northern most area, designated 'I' and pronounced 'eye' Corps, the 1st Cavalry Division was in II Corps and the 1st Infantry Division and 173d Airborne Brigade were in III Corps as part of the capitol defense plan. The 9th and 25th Infantry Divisions would soon arrive; the 25th would go to III Corps and the 9th to the IV Corps area of the Mekong Delta.

Up until now, most of the troops were in support of the combat units and most of the combat units were being used to protect the support troops and installations. In those days the 'tooth to tail' ratio was about 15 to 1, meaning that there were 15 support troops to every combat arms soldier. These support troops were commonly known as REMFs; Rear Echelon Military Forces, or words to that effect. Westmoreland had made the case that he needed many more troops before he could take the offensive and he was getting them.

## The 'Repple Depple'

They kept us in the tents at Camp Alpha for the night and the next day we were taken by bus to Long Binh and the 90th Replacement Battalion. As we passed through the city, the air was thick with diesel fumes from the many military trucks on the road. Horns sounded almost continuously as taxis and private vehicles jockeyed for position in the great Saigon Gran Prix. The cyclos, a backward tricycle with two seats in the front had replaced the rickshaw. They were everywhere.

The major roadside attraction was the Vietnamese women in their Ao Dai's, a form-fitting traditional costume. Every time we passed a group of them, the men on the bus began whistling and shouting like they were back in high school, which is where most of them were a year ago. Like good girls everywhere they ignored us while breaking into giggles.

After about an hour we drove through the gate of the 90th Replacement Battalion; everyone had to pass through here on their way to the war. While we waited for an assignment to a unit, the infantry personnel were assigned to guard duty at night. We were issued an M-14 rifle, a couple of twenty round magazines and we sat in shacks on the perimeter watching for the enemy. Long Binh was well protected and nothing happened while I was there. During the day we had to attend a few classes on Vietnamese culture and watch a movie, in which President Johnson's explanation of "Why Viet-Nam?" did nothing to relieve the boredom.

One of the main topics of conversation was the length of time we would be in Vietnam. The tour of duty was one year for army personnel. The Marine Corps, ever vigilant for an opportunity to show that they were more motivated, more dedicated, etc., than the Army, made their tour thirteen months. Command tours for most officers were set at six months in order to give more officers command experience; essential credentials for future advancement. The six month and one year tours would strip the Army in Vietnam of its most experienced men over and over; prompting one man to say that the U.S. hadn't been in Vietnam for twelve years, it had been there one year, twelve times.[186]

I met a sergeant who was returning for a second tour. He told me about his experiences with an advisory team. "Look at that guy's boots," he said, pointing at a soldier in faded jungle fatigues who was walking by. I looked at his jungle boots. "See how they're all reddish?" he said. I looked again and saw that they did have a red tint to them. "He's been up north where the action is."

"Up north," I thought, "where the action is, that's where I want to go." That's what I was thinking as he continued with his monologue about his experiences. "Up north, that's where my boots will turn red, where the action is."

## Orders

After a few days my name was called at the morning formation. I went to an office where I stood in line until my name was called again. A clerk gave me a copy of my orders and I saw that I was being reassigned to a replacement battalion in Cam Ranh Bay. I was sure that this was a mistake because the 1st Infantry Division was operating in III Corps and Cam Ranh Bay was in II Corps. I told the clerk that I was supposed to go to the 1st Infantry Division; he looked at me with annoyance and told me to move out and go where I was sent. I was mad but I left the office and went outside.

I remembered that I had seen a group of small tents nearby that served as offices and sleeping areas for liaison personnel from the major commands in the area. I walked over and found a tent with a sign that said: 1st Infantry Division, The Big Red One. I stuck my head inside and saw a black staff sergeant with a big Fu Manchu mustache sitting at a field table with a monkey on his shoulder.

He looked pretty mean and asked me what I wanted. I showed him my 1049 and my orders for Cam Ranh Bay. He smiled and told me that he would take care of it. We talked for a while and I found out that he was a short-timer with a month to go. He had been a LRRP and was working here for a month until he went home. When I tried to find out more about his combat experiences, he stood up and told me to come back in the morning.

The next morning I reported to the liaison sergeant and he gave me new orders assigning me to the 1st Infantry Division. That afternoon, I got on a bus with some other soldiers and we were driven to Di-An, the HQ for the Division. On the way, we drove through an area controlled by the Korean Army; their gate guards were very impressive, snapping to attention and shouting out something in their language. The U.S. sentries were not as impressive when we drove through the gate of the 1st Division base camp.

## The 1st Infantry Division

The 1st Infantry Division had its headquarters in Di An. It consisted of three brigades, each with three battalions of infantry. There was a squadron of armored cavalry, five artillery battalions, and battalions of engineers, medics, signalers, maintenance people and aviators. The Division was spread out in base camps all over northwestern III Corps.

The bus driver dropped us off at the Division's replacement company and we went through more paperwork with the clerks. I put most of my pay into a savings program and kept fifty dollars a month for my expenses. If I made it home alive, I was going to buy a car.

They issued us two pair of jungle fatigues but no jungle boots; the supply people said they were out. We were told that we would get our boots when we got to our unit. I happened to look into one of the Southeast Asia or SEA Huts that served as barracks for the clerks and saw that each bunk had at least two pairs of jungle boots under it. When I finally got to my unit and saw guys walking on patrol wearing black leather boots with the soles separated from the uppers and held together with commo wire wrapped around the toe of the boot, I remembered the two pairs of jungle boots under each clerk's bunk at Division.

## 1st Battalion, 16 Infantry

After two days at Division, I was assigned to the 1-16 Infantry, commanded by LTC George M. Wallace, and part of the 3d Brigade. It was based at Lai Khe in a rubber plantation on Hwy 13. There were two other infantry battalions in Lai Khe, the 2-2 Infantry and the 2-28 Infantry along with some artillery and aviation units at its airfield.

Because road travel was much more dangerous as you went north, I was flown to Lai Khe in a U.S. Army Caribou. It was a great transport, like a mini C-130. The Air Force was mad about the Army having a twin engine transport. Later that year, they took them away and if you wanted to fly in a Caribou, you had to fly Air Force.

We landed at the Lai Khe airstrip and waited; sitting in the hot sun on our duffle bags outside the airfield's flight operations. Eventually a soldier pulled up in a weapons carrier and announced that he was here for anyone assigned to the 1st of the 16th. Three of us climbed in the back with our gear and he drove us to the battalion headquarters.

The 16th Infantry was an old regular army regiment. It was part of the 1st Expeditionary Division, which became the 1st Infantry Division in World War I. It had stormed ashore in the first wave onto Omaha Beach in Normandy on D-Day and penetrated the German defenses, opening the way off the beach. The regiment's nickname was 'Rangers.' The 1st Battalion had a headquarters company and three rifle companies.

I was assigned to Alpha Company, located in the Southwest section of the base camp. While we did more paperwork, a clerk told us that the battalion was out on an operation named Danbury. The duty driver took me to Alpha Company later that afternoon. We crossed the airstrip and a poorly paved road, Highway 13, which ran north and south through the base. The Caribou that had brought us here was gone. The driver followed a dirt road and drove through row after row of rubber trees. The trees had long diagonal scars on their trunks and a small white porcelain bowl held by a wire stand driven into the tree.

## Alpha Company Headquarters

We passed an artillery battery on our left. Then the road curved around to the right and we entered Alpha Company's area. There was a row of partially completed SEA huts on the left and several completed ones on the right. "Here you are," said the driver as he pulled to a stop. I jumped out and grabbed my duffle bag. "Good luck," he said and drove off.

I looked around the company area. It seemed deserted. There was a guidon on a pole, hanging listlessly in the heat of the day in front of one of the buildings on the right. That had to be the company headquarters, so I left my duffle bag on the ground outside and knocked on the door.

No one answered, so I walked in. The headquarters building looked like a scene from a scary movie where everyone on earth had disappeared. There was a wooden desk with some papers scattered around on the top and several large brown paper bags leaning against the wall filled with what looked like personnel records. I found out later that the bags were the file cabinets. There was an open door leading to the next room where I found more desks with papers scattered on them and on the floor.

I continued walking through the building to the back door; I was starting to get a little tense. Then I heard some talking coming from the building behind the one I was in so I walked over to it and knocked on the door.

"What the blank do you want?" a voice said. I waited for the voice to tell me to come in but there was silence. "I've been assigned to this unit and I'm reporting in," I said to the voice behind the door. "Go to the supply room," the voice said, "It's to your right."

## The Supply Sergeant (1)

I went to the building to my right and there was a wide, open window with a counter. I could see rifle racks and boxes of supplies. I knocked on the counter and after a minute a figure appeared in the dim light. He was bare from the waist up and he looked like he had been sleeping. "You the new guy?" he asked. I told him I was. He said he was the supply sergeant and didn't offer to shake my hand.

He told me that the company was up near the Cambodian Border and wouldn't be back for a few days. The first sergeant would be back later that afternoon and then I could find out what platoon I would be going to. He had started to turn around and go back to his cot when I asked him if I could get a rifle because the people at battalion had taken the one that was given to me for the flight. He considered this for a moment and then said, "Sure."

He walked back to the rifle racks, grabbed an M-16 and laid it on the counter. Then he grabbed a sandbag full of empty magazines. "Here," he said, dropping them on the counter. "You can get your ammunition from the ammo tent over there," he said, pointing to his left. He turned again to go back to his cot. "Don't I have to sign for the rifle," I asked. Without turning around he said, "Don't worry about it" and continued into the gloom. I wanted to ask a lot more questions but I could tell that it would only serve to annoy him and you never want to annoy the supply sergeant if you can help it.

## The M-16 Rifle

I took the rifle and sandbag full of magazines and walked in the direction of the ammo bunker. I stopped after a little ways so I could look at my new rifle. It was the first time I had ever held one. It was much lighter than the M-14E2 I carried in Germany. It had a black stock, pistol grip and hand guards that were made out of plastic. There was a carrying handle on the top of the receiver. I looked it over and found the charging handle. When I pulled it back a small door sprung open and I could look into the chamber. I found a switch on the left side with three positions, Safe, Semi, and Auto. Unlike in Germany, where I had the prestigious position of automatic rifleman, here everyone had a fully automatic rifle.

Of course I had heard and read about the M-16. The Special Forces had them and they were being issued to the infantry in Vietnam before I got there. Usually the army takes great pains to train the soldier on the rifle he will carry. He is taught to shoot and maintain it, but this was war on the fly.

**Dennis Howley:** *"I left the Ranger LT and a squad minus behind when we went into a night logger...they hid as we pulled out, expecting VC to come out at night. They had set a claymore in a tree but had not connected it when out walked a Charlie, who stared at the claymore in the tree trying to figure out what it was. Our stay-behind cut loose FULL AUTOMATIC!! Scared hell out of Charlie but no one hit him. I asked later, believing in "one shot one* *kill" why they went to full auto; the rifles had never been zeroed!! The next day in our logger A-1-16 zeroed all the rifles on a 25 meter range we created."*[187]

## Pass the Ammunition

I continued on a path that led into the rubber trees. There was a tent that was about fifty meters from the nearest hut, the ammo tent. It was a little eerie there, surrounded by rubber trees with no one around; well, I couldn't see anyone around. The tent door was open so I cautiously peeked inside. The window flaps were rolled up and there was enough light to see what looked like the infantryman's Aladdin's Cave.

Inside were stacks of light colored wooden crates containing thousands of rounds of 5.56mm M-16 ammunition. Other crates contained cans of 7.62mm link M-60 machine gun ammunition. There were crates of 66mm Light Anti-Armor (LAAW) rockets, 40mm M-79 grenades, hand grenades, Claymore mines, trip flares, and smoke grenades. In a corner near the door were blasting caps and C4 plastic explosive.

I couldn't believe it, all this ammo lying around with no one guarding it. In Germany they counted every round and here there were open cans of ammo and loose rounds lying on the ground. I was indignant for a moment, but I was soon overcome by all the things that were available. I wanted to take some of everything, but I didn't have any place to store it. I grabbed several bandoleers of 5.56, stuffed them in my sandbag along with two Mark II pineapple hand grenades and decided to come back for more later.

I sat down on the low wall of sandbags that surrounded the tent and started to load my magazines. There were at least twenty and I thought that was a little excessive. We only used five, twenty round magazines in Germany. Like most soldiers, I judged everything that was new to me with old information. Later I was told to carry at least three hundred rounds of ammo, four hundred was better.

I loaded five magazines and put one of them in the magazine well of the rifle. I pulled back the charging handle and let it go. The bolt flew forward pushing a bullet from the magazine and seating it in the chamber. I made sure the selector switch was on safe, picked up my sand bag and walked back through the rubber trees toward the orderly room.

I was locked and loaded in a combat zone. I began scanning the tops of the trees, looking for snipers. The rubber trees were not that tall and the vegetation was thin so I was pretty sure that I would see one if a sniper was there. I looked for enemy ambushes on my left and right as I approached the orderly room.

My duffle bag was still lying on the ground in front of the orderly room. I had forgotten all about it. I inspected it carefully to make sure that the Viet Cong hadn't booby-trapped it. Then I sat on it and waited for the first sergeant to show up. I was starting to feel hungry, so I pulled out the C-ration that they gave me at the replacement battalion and ate it.

It was really hot outside in the sun, so I moved my bag and rifle into the deserted orderly room. I put my bag against the wall, sat down and leaned against it. I looked my rifle over some more; I held it to my shoulder and practiced aiming at a knothole across the room. I did this a few times until I started getting sleepy. Eventually I laid the rifle on my lap and rested my eyes for a moment.

## The First Sergeant

The next thing I knew, someone was kicking my boots and I heard a voice saying, "What the blank are you doing in my orderly room?" This had to be the first sergeant. I jumped to my feet and the rifle that was still on my lap flew forward and hit the first sergeant's boots. This set him off on a cuss fest while I bent down and secured my weapon. I looked up at the first sergeant and told him I had been assigned to A Company.

"Give me your orders and close that dust cover," he said. I looked around the room for a dust cover; the only dust cover I knew about was the blanket that covered the pillow on a military bunk. "The dust cover! The dust cover! Close your blankety blank dust cover!" I looked at him helplessly, "What is a dust cover?" "Give me that rifle!" he said. I handed him my rifle and he closed the little door over the bolt. "That's the dust cover; where the blank are you from?"

I told him that I had come from Germany and today was the first time I had ever seen a real M-16. He grunted and demanded my orders. I pulled them out of an envelope at the top of my duffle bag. He looked at them for a minute, laid them on his desk, and told me I was being assigned to the second platoon.

"Go across the road and follow that path to the GP medium tents. The second two belong to second platoon. Find an empty cot," he said with a grimace, "there are lots of them. The company won't be back for a few more days. I'll be going out tonight on the resupply chopper and I'll talk to you tomorrow."

"Can't I just go with you and join them tonight?" I asked. "Just do what I said; you have to go to the brigade jungle school before you go anywhere with us." "Yes, first sergeant," I said in my most respectful voice. I picked up my duffle bag and walked out the door. "Don't be in such a hurry;" he said, "you'll soon get more of this shit than you can stand!"

## A Dark and Rainy Night

I hurried out the door and crossed the road before he thought of something for me to do. Following the path, I came to a row of tents in the rubber trees. I found the second platoon tents and walked inside the first one. It was dark and it took a while for my eyes to adjust. There was a narrow path down the center of the tent with a pole at either end holding up a string of lights. On both sides was a row of cots. The lights weren't on and I couldn't see a switch. About half the cots had something on them and the others were empty. I chose an empty one near the entrance and put my things down.

The window flaps were down so I rolled a couple of them and looked around the tent. It was a lethal mess. There were several hand grenades lying in the dirt on the tent's center path. Rifle magazines and individual rounds of ammunition littered the floor. At my feet was a rectangular object and when I bent down I could read "Front Toward Enemy." It was a Claymore mine. Since it was next to my bunk I decided to find another place to sleep. I didn't know anything about Claymores and I didn't want to set it off, killing myself before I got my CIB.

I sat on my new bunk at the other end of the tent and checked the ground around it. I didn't see anything too alarming; I was starting to get use to these wartime rules.

There was a case of C-rations by the door and I decided to eat one of the meals for supper rather than try to find a mess hall. The sun was setting and I didn't want to be wandering around in the dark. It was very quiet in the rubber trees, but I could hear some people talking in one of the other tents nearby. That was a relief because I was a little nervous about sleeping here by myself.

I started to hear a kind of hissing noise in the distance and it seemed to be getting louder. Suddenly, rain was pouring down on my tent and it was really coming down hard. Here was my chance to take a shower in the rain. I smelled bad and this would be a great way to clean up. I stripped off my clothes, found a bar of soap in my shaving kit and walked outside the tent naked, wearing my shower shoes. The rain water was cold compared to the hot air a few minutes before. I started rubbing the bar of soap in my hair and then on my body. The rain was really coming down but I still managed to get soap all over me; and then the rain stopped. I stood there waiting for it to start up again, but no rain.

There was other activity in the air, however. As I stood there hoping that the rain would start again so I could wash off the soap, the mosquitoes found me. They started buzzing around my head. There were multiple high pitched whines as they welcomed me to Vietnam. Then they started landing on my naked body. This was too much. I couldn't stand around waiting for the rain to come back. These bastards would suck every drop of my blood if I didn't start moving.

I ran back inside the tents and the mosquitoes came with me. Sitting down on my cot, I rummaged through my duffle bag for a clean T-shirt and fatigues. I could feel the mosquitoes all over my body. I finally gave up on the clean clothes and put my dirty ones back on. It was pitch-dark in the tent now and I had to find everything by Braille.

Eventually I got my clothes back on and sat on my bunk. The mosquitoes had not gone away and I was starting to feel like a pin cushion. Bumps were rising on my neck and arms and their high pitched whine in my ears was really agitating me. I grabbed a mosquito net that I had seen on the bunk next to mine and pulled it over my head. One or two came in with me but I managed to kill them by squashing them against my face.

I reached for a cigarette in my front pocket and brought my lighter under the net. Taking every precaution, I managed to light my cigarette without setting the net on fire. That would have been the perfect ending to my shower fiasco; running around covered in burning nylon, catching the tent on fire and setting off all the ammunition. I sat there smoking my cigarette and wondered what I had gotten myself into. When I finished my cigarette, I lay down on the cot and went to sleep.

## A New Day

The next morning, I woke up and after finding my way out of the mosquito net, I stepped outside of the tent and looked around. The sun was just up so I grabbed my Norelco battery powered razor from my shaving kit and shaved. That razor was one of the items I bought in the States before I left. It was part of my strategy to maximize my chances of survival and minimize the hassle of living in a war. The razor was a good move. It served me for a year and only needed new batteries about once a month.

Another of my strategic purchases was contact lenses. When I was in Germany, we did a lot of firing of our weapons. I noticed that when I fired my rifle when it was raining, the recoil threw weapons oil and tiny drops of water onto my glasses, making it difficult to see. I reasoned that if I had contact lenses when this happened I would only have to blink and I would be able to see again. This would be useful if the VC were coming toward me to kill me in a rainstorm.

I bought the lenses just before I left and I was trying to follow the eye doctors instructions for breaking them in; but he had never been an infantryman and the conditions I was living in were not optimal for experienced contact lens wearers, much less for the uninitiated. So far I was able to get them in and out but they would not prove to be a good move, like my razor was.

I made myself presentable and went to the orderly room. The first sergeant was there and he wasted no time in giving me my marching orders. "Go to the supply room and draw your field equipment. The brigade jungle school starts tomorrow morning. When you get your equipment squared away, report to the commo bunker and tell the man in charge to put you on the roster for radio watch, got it?" He was looking at my rifle as he spoke, no doubt checking to see if I my dust cover was closed. It was. I realized that he was finished talking to me, so I said, "Roger, First Sergeant," turned on my heel and headed for the supply room.

## The Supply Sergeant (2)

The supply room counter was open. I looked inside but no one was in sight. I knocked on the wall and the supply sergeant came out of the dark background. He didn't have a shirt on and again looked like I had just woken him up. I said that the first sergeant told me to draw my field gear. He grunted and went back into his supply room and turned on a light. I moved to where I could see what he was doing. He approached some large shelves on the wall, grabbed a poncho, opened it, laid it on the floor and began pulling items from the shelves, throwing them onto the poncho.

When he had a small pile of gear, he picked up the poncho by the four corners and threw it on the counter. He turned around, pulled a piece of paper from his desk and said, "Sign here." I took the piece of paper; a standard form used for issuing uniforms and equipment, and started checking off the items on the poncho, throwing them into a duffle bag. "Just sign it, don't you trust me?" he asked. I knew this game so I told him that of course I trusted him, I was just making sure he hadn't given me too many items, which would have messed up his inventory.

Supply accountability was a big thing in the army, even in Vietnam. When a unit had a change of command inventory, the company commander and the supply sergeant might have to pay a lot of their own money to make up the shortages. In Vietnam, where things like equipment inventory could get away from the best of supply sergeants, they had to resort to other methods to keep the books straight. I suspected that this was a possibility and used some tact to keep him friendly, and myself from getting screwed.

The most famous method of inventory reconciliation was the downed helicopter gambit. Helicopters went down quite often in Vietnam and tragically, many times the crew would be killed. There was no place for sentimentality in the supply business. After the crash of a resupply chopper, the unit supply people would turn in a list of their items that were on that chopper. Rumor had that in one case, involving a helicopter from the First Cav, the gross weight of the items alleged to be on board at the time of the crash was five times more than the helicopter could have lifted off the ground.

There were, in fact, several items listed on the form that weren't on the counter. I politely mentioned the discrepancies. Because he had been watching me inventory the gear, he went to the back and got them without an argument. When he came back, he threw them on the counter and asked if that was everything.

I pointed to a stack of rucksacks on the floor and asked if I could have one. He picked one up and threw it on the counter and said, "Anything else, Specialist?" He said specialist like he would say, 'asshole.' "No sergeant," I replied, "that should just about do it; by the way, do you want me to sign for this rifle now?" He grunted again, went to his desk and picked up another piece of paper. He had me read the rifle's serial number and he wrote it on the paper.

I signed for the rifle and thanked him for his help. I could tell he was pissed about being out-flanked on the equipment inventory but we both kept our cool; but he would wait for another opportunity. Some guys are like that in the Army, but I really liked the way President Reagan said it later, "Trust but verify."

## The Commo Bunker

I put away my gear and reported to the commo bunker. The guy in charge was a sergeant from one of the platoons who was in the rear recovering from minor shrapnel wounds. He put me on the roster and told me what time my shift was. Then he began telling me what was required for radio watch. The radios were similar to the ones we had in Germany in our armored personnel carriers. These radios, however, could be configured for carrying on your back.

All the RTO's in the company carried the AN/PRC-25, which weighed twenty-three pounds. It had 920 channels which were easy to access by turning two knobs and reading the frequency numbers in a small window. It was powered by a battery that lasted twenty-four hours and it was a great improvement over the last radio that required the RTO to fine tune it to the correct frequency.

Outside the bunker was a thirty foot tall RC-292 antenna. This gave these radios a much greater range. When we carried them in the field we used a short whip antenna and the RTOs also carried a long whip antenna for greater range.

One of the radios was on the battalion command frequency and the other was on the company frequency. As the sergeant talked on, I was comfortable that I knew what to do, having pulled radio watch in Germany more than a few times. I began to look around the walls of the bunker; above the radios, was some graffiti.

Most of it was typical GI: names of girlfriends, days left in country, proclamations of intent to kick Charlie's ass and so forth. Right in the middle of all this was written, "Dulce et decorum est pro patria mori." I recognized it as Latin from my short stint as an altar boy in the Catholic Church. I interrupted his briefing and asked, "What does that mean," pointing at the writing. "Blank if I know," he replied, "are you getting all this, Specialist?" I assured him that I was and when he finished he dismissed me with a warning not to be late for my shift.

## The Mess Hall

It was getting close to noon so I wandered over to the mess hall. It was next to the orderly room but it wasn't open yet so I walked around in back. There were three Vietnamese women back there cleaning the pots and pans. They had something cooking over a fire near the outdoor sink they were using to wash the pots and pans. There was also a GI with them and his pants were all wet so I figured that he was on KP.

I walked over and started talking to him. He was just out of basic and AIT and was a new guy like me. I asked about chow and he said it would be served at 1130. He too was going to the jungle school, so I told him I would see him tomorrow morning and walked back to the front where several men were standing. The mess hall had opened; no one was taking headcount and I joined the line.

Several cooks were serving the food. One of them was standing over a deep pan of food with a cigarette hanging out of his mouth. I watched and saw a one inch ash fall from his cigarette into the pan. That was pretty bad, but the next guy, serving the stew, had sweat dripping off his nose into the pan.

I took my food to a nearby table and banished the spectacle at the serving line from my mind. I put a table spoon full of stew in my mouth and started to chew. Yuck! Bell peppers! I spit my mouthful onto a free space on my tray. I hated bell peppers and had created many a scene at the family dinner table when I refused to eat them.

"What's wrong?" said a PFC who was sitting at my table. "I hate bell peppers," I said. He started laughing. "Hey man, your shit out of luck. Sergeant Morales, the mess sergeant, he loves them and I swear to God, he puts them in everything." "Great!" I said, "How long does he have till he goes home?" The PFC considered my question for a moment before answering, "He just got here."

## The PX

I couldn't overcome my hatred for bell peppers; they actually made me gag when I tasted one. I picked them out of my stew and ate as much as I could before giving up. I asked the PFC where the PX was. He pointed and said it was a short distance from the company area, so I decided to go there after lunch and get a few things from the snack bar before my radio shift.

When I got to the PX, a small shack made from local materials, I went inside and saw that there wasn't any snack bar here. They had them at the big base camps but this was a forward area and we were lucky to have a PX. The shelves had lots of candy bars; the chocolate ones were melted into goo. There were canned sardines and small canned hams. There were also things like hair spray, which seemed odd, and there was lots of beer.

I grabbed a few snacks, some for now and some for later, and paid with MPCs, funny money that was printed for use by Americans in Vietnam. It was issued to cut down on black market currency transactions and they would change it once in a while. The Vietnamese weren't supposed to use it, but they did and some of them took a financial beating if they had a lot of it when the change came. There were no coins, so the clerk gave me pieces of paper for change.

On the way back to the company I took a closer look at the rubber trees. The bowls that were mounted on the trees were dirty white. They had some water in them from the rain and they hadn't been used for collecting rubber for some time. The French colonialists had created huge rubber plantations that went on for miles. They were still in business in some areas but the small plantation at Lai Khe was inactive.

### The Commo Bunker (2)

I got back to the company area and put my gear together. I fixed up my rucksack and inspected my brand new poncho liner, one of the best things the Army ever issued. It was a light weight blanket, brown on one side and green on the other. I packed what I thought I would need in my rucksack. I was issued two canteens; we still practiced water discipline in those days, but I decided to try and get two more to put in the pouches of my ruck.

When I reported for my shift on radio watch, the man I was relieving was named Peter Clark. He was in the rear recuperating from wounds he received from a booby-trap while on a patrol near Lai Khe. We hit it off right away so he stayed with me in the bunker and we talked. I kept looking at the Latin inscription on the wall and tried to remember my altar boy Latin classes. All my teachers told me to pay attention because some day the information they were putting out would be useful to me. They were right of course, but in my case they were wasting their breath.

Peter had come to the unit in June and fought in the battle of August 25th. I asked him if he knew what the Latin inscription on the wall of the bunker meant. He smiled and told me that he was the one who had written it. "What does it mean?" I asked him. "It is sweet and glorious to die for your country!" he declared with a straight face. I looked at him and he looked at me and when our eyes met we both busted out laughing.

Peter told me that he had enlisted after dropping out of college. He was one of the many young men with an education and an intellectual bent that suddenly found themselves in the Army in those days. They despised the inefficiency and counter intuitiveness of Army life but were determined to be better soldiers than the RA's who wanted to be lifers, like me. A few months later our new CO chose Peter to be one of his RTO's.

After Clark left, I spent the rest of the two hours listening to the rushing noise coming out of two AN/PRC-25 FM radios. After I was relieved from radio watch I looked up the KP who was going to the jungle school with me. I told him to meet me at the orderly room at 0700 and we would walk together to the school. It rained again that night but I didn't try the tropical shower routine. Instead I walked up to the communal shower, got cleaned up, and went to sleep.

### Jungle School

The big plantation house had been taken over by the Army and was now part of the Brigade Headquarters. Near it was a monument to the French soldiers who had been killed in the first Indochina War. Now we were here and I was sure that this time we would win.

I asked around until someone told us where to go for the school. It was nearby and when we got there a sergeant told us to sit in some bleachers facing a stage with a podium. Other troops were showing up so we sat together on a seat near the front and waited. At 0730 the bleachers were almost full.

A captain walked out on the stage and stood behind the podium. He nodded to someone and a loud explosion behind us shook our seats and scared everyone. "Keep your seats!" the captain shouted. "Everything is under control. I want to welcome you to the 3d Brigade Jungle Combat Orientation Course. You need to pay attention to what we are teaching here because it may save your life. If you don't, an explosion like the one you just heard might be the last thing you ever hear in this life. The first class will be on booby-traps and I hope you pay particular attention because there are a lot of booby-traps around Lai Khe!"

For the next hour several sergeants taught us about Viet Cong booby-traps. I paid close attention to this instruction. One of the main things I learned about booby-traps was that they are usually placed around man-made things. The enemy didn't have enough explosives to cover everything so he put them where he thought we might go. The number one place to avoid because of booby-traps was a trail or path in the jungle. Over and over during the class and during practical exercises they hammered home this point. It didn't do much good though, because we still took a lot of casualties on the trails.

I met a staff sergeant who had come from Germany at the same time I did. He had been working on some new techniques while we were going through the course. Over a beer one night at the club he ran one of them by me. He had decided that the way to keep from being hit in the heart by an enemy bullet when walking down a trail was to carry your rifle at port arms all the time.

I tried to interject the main point of the booby-trap class, you don't walk on trails, but he had fallen in love with his great idea and went on and on about how it would save the lives of the men in his squad, because he was going to make sure that they all did it. When I mentioned that the men might get tired of carrying their rifles at port arms all the time, he would have none of it. "They'll get used to it" he said, ending the discussion. I was glad that I wouldn't be in his squad.

There wasn't much the school could tell us about the enemy. His collective name was 'Charlie,' Charles to those who really knew him. They were communists; they wouldn't stand and fight like men, preferring to use mines and booby-traps to inflict casualties. It was clear to the instructors that we could whoop them in a fair fight, whatever that was. When President Kennedy was championing the Green Berets as the answer to the communist guerrilla movements, the Chief of Staff of the Army at that time said that the average U.S. Army infantry soldier was more than a match for a guerrilla. That may or may not have been true and if we could only find them we would find out.[188]

The course was five days long; the last day was a 'long' patrol outside the perimeter. It was long because it took forever to get us organized into squads and platoons. It was long because we kept stopping while someone up front was checking everything for booby-traps. It was long because it took us four hours to move 500 meters. It wasn't a long range patrol, it was a long patrol. We all passed the training course. I wondered if they would send someone who didn't pass back to the states but it wasn't that kind of course. It was, "One hundred men will test today and no matter what, they're gonna stay."

## The Card Game

The supply sergeant had bided his time and approached me a few days after our last encounter. "We're having a friendly little game of poker in the mess hall after chow this evening, wanna play?" "Sure, sergeant," I said without thinking. "OK," he said with a smile, "I'll see you at 2000 in the mess hall."

I had been schooled in the game by some cardsharps while waiting to enlist in the army and though they took me for some of the money I had been saving for a new surfboard, I learned the game and bought a used board. When I was in Germany I played in a few games and held my own so the prospect of going up against the supply sergeant and his buddies was a good antidote for my boredom.

I showed up at the appointed time and the supply sergeant invited me to sit down. He introduced me as the new specialist and I saw that the rest of the players were NCOs. Usually, the NCOs would never play cards with lower ranking enlisted men but they were following wartime rules and I was fair game. Some people might play cards for fun but everyone in that game was there for one thing, my money.

They must have played a lot because they had large stacks of poker chips which cost fifty cents apiece. I looked around the table at each player's stack and bought twenty dollars' worth. One of them asked if that was all the money I had, a rude question in polite circles, which this wasn't. I told them that I had a lot more but I wanted to go easy because I didn't know that much about poker. That brought a quick smile to the supply sergeant's face and he handed me the first of many beers that evening, preparing the way for his plan to soak me.

The cards were dealt, each player calling a game when it was his turn. I stuck with five card draw and stud, simple standard poker games that would not bring me undue attention like some of the games that the sergeants called. I played each hand I was given and won most of the hands that I stayed in for to the end. The supply sergeant wasn't quite so friendly now, and I had to buy the beer if I wanted to continue to drink.

At 2300 a jeep drove into the company area and the supply sergeant, being the senior man went out to see what was up. He returned in a few minutes and said we had to shut it down for the night. He seemed pretty disappointed as he gave me about seventy-five dollars for my chips which I took in an apologetic manner, assuring him that I would be happy to give them a chance to get their money back at the next 'friendly' game.

## Alpha Company Returns

The day after the poker game, the company returned from Operation Danbury. Their return was announced by the sound of trucks with horns blowing and loud diesel engines roaring. Led by a jeep, the small convoy came to a stop in the company street. The troops were standing in the back of each truck and they began to jump off before the drivers lowered the tailgates. With lots of shouting, the sergeants formed the men into a company formation.

*No one serving as a soldier entangles himself with the affairs of this life, that he may please the one who enlisted him.*
*2 Timothy 2:4*

# Chapter 6-September 1966: Part II

### Alpha Company

Alpha Company was commanded by Captain Dennis Howley, the CO. He had been in Vietnam for a year with Special Forces where he had commanded two A-Teams and served as an Intelligence officer on a B-Team. He volunteered for another tour with U.S. troops. The 1st Division assigned him to 3d Brigade and they assigned him to perform aerial observation duties on August 25th. Captain Howley assumed command of Alpha Company after Captain Peter Knight was killed on August 25th.

Alpha Company was supposed to have about 150 men, but seldom did. Casualties, illness and the yearly rotation of individual soldiers who had reached their DEROS, their Date Eligible for Return from Overseas, (or outer space), kept it at about 120.

He stood in front of the company formation in the dirt street. To his left was the first platoon, followed by the second and third platoons. Then came weapons platoon and finally headquarters. He spoke a few words, commending their performance on the operation and then he turned the formation over to the first sergeant who dismissed them.

The first sergeant, who I had already met, was the senior NCO in the company and advised the CO on matters regarding the other NCOs and the enlisted men. He took care of administrative details like the morning report and worked with the XO, coordinating the logistics needs of the troops in the field. The company headquarters included the supply section, the mess sergeant and his cooks, the communications sections and some drivers.

The weapons platoon was the smallest; they were our fire support. They had three 81mm mortars and two 106mm recoilless rifles. Each rifle platoon was assigned a forward observer (FO) from the weapons platoon and his job was to adjust the fire of the mortars.

The three rifle platoons were each supposed to have forty-two men but they were never up to full strength. The platoons were organized into three rifle squads and a weapons squad. They were led by an LT and run by the platoon sergeant.
Each ten man rifle squad was supposed to be led by a staff sergeant. The squad was further divided into two fire-teams, each led by a sergeant. All the men in the squad carried the M-16A1 rifle except the two grenadiers, who carried the M-79 grenade launcher. They also carried a number of M-79 grenades in a vest, and a .45 pistol. The M-79 was gradually being replaced by a grenade launcher that was attached to the M-16. One man carried the squad leader's radio.

The rifleman carried his ammunition and canteens in pouches along with his entrenching tool, a small folding shovel, attached to a heavy belt and held up by suspenders attached to a shoulder harness. We called this our web gear. Each rifleman also carried several fragmentation grenades, a smoke grenade, and a

Claymore mine with a spool of wire and a firing device in a cloth bag with a shoulder strap.

His food, in cans, was stored in socks tied to the yoke of his harness. The sleeping gear, a poncho and poncho liner were tied to his butt-pack; the butt pack, usually full of ammo, was attached to the belt and hung over his rear end, hence the name. The last thing he carried was the wretched gas mask, the M-17A1 Field Protective Mask. It was in a canvas carrier which had a belt that was usually worn around the waist and another strap that wrapped around his thigh.

The weapons squad was made up of two M-60 machine gun crews of three men each and was led by the senior squad leader. A gun crew consisted of a gunner, assistant gunner, and an ammo bearer. The gunner carried the machine gun and a .45 pistol. The assistant gunner and the ammo bearer carried rifles and ammunition for the gun. They all carried most of the same things as the riflemen.

### The Platoon Sergeant

After the formation was dismissed the platoon sergeant sent for me. I found him in a tent that was used by all the sergeants in the platoon. He was an old-timer whose previous assignment had been with the ROTC Department at the University of California at Berkeley. He really liked it there. The anti-war demonstrations didn't bother him, "What do you expect, it's California." When I told him that my grandmother had graduated from Berkeley and that I had learned to swim in the UC Berkeley pool, he considered me a kindred soul and told me stories about his time there.

His favorite story was about Major General Dean, a Medal of Honor recipient of the Korean War. General Dean commanded the 24th Infantry Division during the early days of the war. The North Koreans were over-running his division and he went up to the front to see if he could help. He ended up with a team of soldiers firing a bazooka at T-34 Russian Tanks. He knocked out at least one with a hand grenade before he had to escape and evade until he was captured. He was repatriated after the armistice and retired.

General Dean was an alumnus of UC Berkeley and he would come by to visit the ROTC class. My platoon sergeant knew him well from all the visits and he would try to convince the General to teach a class on the 3.5-inch Rocket Launcher. He said he would tell Dean, "We need a man with experience to teach these youngsters, sir." But, he said that Dean would only laugh and reply, "maybe some other time."

The platoon sergeant asked me what I had done in the Army and I told him about Arizona and Germany. When he asked me if I knew anything about the M-60 Machine Gun, I told him that as a gunner I won a competition for our battalion's organization day activities in Germany. With that he told me that he was assigning me to the weapons squad.

### The Weapons Squad

The weapons squad leader, Sergeant Reeves, told me I was now a machine gunner; my assistant gunner would be Specialist Roland Wilson and my ammo bearer was 'Mac.' I was to draw my machine gun from the supply room and get ammo for it because we would be going out the day after tomorrow.

When I found Wilson, I introduced myself. Roland was a black man from Houston, TX. He had been there for a while and he only had a few months to go. Roland had been in the battle of August 25th. I wondered about what had happened to the man I was replacing but he didn't mention him and I didn't ask.

Roland had an unusual face with a kind of a crafty smile. We hit it off quickly and he took over the task of training me in the ways of a 16th Infantry 'Ranger.' I told him that the squad leader had told me that I was to be the gunner but that I didn't think it was fair since he had been there much longer than me. "I'll be glad to be your assistant gunner," I said. "As a matter of fact, I'll go down there with you right now and we can tell him that you're going to be the gunner."

That crafty smile was on his face when he told me that, no; it was a bad idea to cross the squad leader. He said I would have to be the gunner and he would endure the humiliation of not being assigned the gunner position. "Beside," he said, "I'm black; you know how they treat the brother in the Army." I didn't really know how they treated the brother in the Army; the black guys in my unit in Germany were treated no different than the white and Hispanic guys. As a matter of fact, several black soldiers had been promoted in my company because they were better soldiers than their peers.

I stopped trying to get him to take the gunner job because I could see that he didn't want it. I, however, did. I was remembering the great scene from the movie, "To Hell and Back" when Audie Murphy, playing himself, knocked out a German machine gun nest, took a captured German machine gun, wiped out another machine gun nest and hosed down several German soldiers. For that action, he received the Distinguished Service Cross, second only to the Medal of Honor. My hero fantasies were alive and active when I told Roland that I would be the gunner if he was sure that's what he wanted.[189]

Roland helped me move my things to the weapons squad tent which we shared with third squad. 'Mac' was assigned to be our ammo bearer. Roland introduced him and he shook my hand and said, "Howdy." Then Roland introduced me to some of the other men.

Jose Garcia came to the company in early September, part of a large group of replacements for the casualties of August 25th. He was from Houston, Texas and a good soldier with a quick temper and a sense of humor, dependable and friendly. When he found out I was a backslidden Catholic, he tried to help me get back on track with God but I was a difficult case. He had gotten on the bad side of some of the sergeants and Captain Howley had chewed him out several times for holding, instead of wearing, his steel pot for a moment when he took a break on patrol. Donnie Gunby was a young draftee from Georgia who also saw the humor in most situations. After one of my displays of bravado, he started calling me 'Audie,' as in Audie Murphy, my secret hero; but he wasn't fooled.

Jack Hyland was one of the 'characters' of the company and one of the informal leaders you find in every unit. The sergeant is in charge but when an order is given, the men look to these informal leaders to either affirm what the sergeant says by saying nothing, or requesting clarification.

While he was stationed in Panama, Jack had become argumentative with some older NCOs who he perceived as slackers, hiding in Panama from the war in Vietnam. Rather than marching to the sound of the guns, they decided that he should be the one to leave Panama. There was only one place in the Army at that time for a man like Jack and that was how we happened to meet in this tent on the other side of the world.

Later he became famous in the company when one day, he was overheard by the CO delivering a stinging indictment of the Army to the rest of us while we were waiting for the chow hall to open. The CO, in an unusual lapse of judgment, said, "Well Hyland, just what is it that you don't like about the Army?"

Jack looked at him with his cynical smile and said, "Well, sir, the Army is always handing you a bucket of shit and saying it's a basket of roses." Everyone busted into laughter and hooting, and the CO, seeing that he had stepped in it, left without another word. Jack was one of our heroes because when the time came, he followed the admonition of the day to 'Tell it like it is!'

## The Supply Sergeant (3)

I went to the supply room with Roland. We had to wait in line but eventually we got to the counter. The supply sergeant had an assistant and when he asked us what we wanted, Roland told him we wanted his former gunner's machine gun. "Murry's the new gunner and he needs all the machine gunner's stuff." The supply sergeant told the assistant to get me a machine gun but Roland interrupted and told him we wanted that particular machine gun.

"I don't know which one is which," he said testily. "Look it up!" said Roland. The supply sergeant was a staff sergeant and Roland was a Spec-4, but after a second of looking into Roland's eyes he looked up the name and told the assistant the last four numbers of the machine gun's serial number. The supply sergeant took my rifle and issued me a M-1911A1 .45 caliber pistol with a holster, a magazine pouch, and three magazines. He handed me the machine gun and a bag with an extra barrel, tripod, T+E mechanism, an asbestos glove, and some cleaning gear. He had me sign several pieces of paper, waiting patiently while I checked to see what I was signing for.

## The M-60 Machine Gun

Roland helped me carry the stuff back to our tent and showed me how to rig the machine gun for the field. The M-60 is a gas-operated, air-cooled, belt-fed, automatic machine gun that fires a 7.62x51 mm bullet from the open-bolt position at a rate of 550 rounds per minute with a maximum effective range of 1100 meters. It weighed twenty-three pounds.

Supply didn't have the canvas bag that mounted on the left side of the gun and held one hundred rounds, so Roland told me that I should carry twenty-five rounds in the gun and another 200 in a can in my ruck. "You can forget that Pancho Villa shit around here. We always keep the bullets in the ammo cans; that way they don't get dirty and corroded." "Do we have to carry the gas mask here?" I asked him. "Damn right, you can use it for a pillow at night."

## The Ville

After we squared away my new gear, Roland told me that we were going to the Ville that night for some beer and socializing; then he asked me if I had any money. I told him I did and he said, "Good, you can buy," he paused and looked at the others, "the beer," and they all laughed. As we walked to the Ville I asked him a lot of questions, and eventually I asked him about who had carried the gun before me and when did he DEROS. Roland stopped; so I stopped and turned to look at him. "He didn't;" he said, "he's dead." "What happened?" I asked. "It's a long story;" he said, "I'll tell you about it when we get some beer."

We walked a short distance to the Ville. It was a compound within our brigade's base camp. We had to go through a gate with an MP checking us out as we walked passed.

The Vietnamese had determined that we were tourists, so there were shops that sold souvenirs. Tailor shops did a brisk business. There was loud music blaring out of several large buildings that had a name with the word 'Club' at the end. I followed Roland into one of them and we sat down at one of the tables. I bought a pitcher of beer and paid the young, good looking Vietnamese girl. I tipped her a dollar and she said, "You numbah one, GI!"

Roland and I sat there; we weren't talking about anything in particular. I was drinking as much beer as I could. The music, mostly rhythm and blues and Motown, was loud. I really liked that style of music and was tapping my feet and slapping my hands on the table as I tried to play the drums along with the records.

The club was mainly full of black guys and Roland knew a lot of them. They would come up to him and do the 'dap,' not the full-on production dap that came later in the war but a careful ritual that I tried to follow but couldn't. He would introduce me to some of the guys and they would hold their hands out to do it and I would shake them. They would laugh and Roland would get embarrassed, tell them that I was a rookie, that I had a lot to learn and it was his job to teach me.

There were a lot of young Vietnamese girls in the place. They sat with the GIs at the tables and drank something from small glasses. Several of them approached our table but Roland waved them off. I was pretty drunk by now and really getting into the music. Another Vietnamese girl came up to Roland and sat on his lap; they seemed to know each other. She was teasing him, "Hey GI, how come you never see me, you numbah ten GI." Roland told her, "Well, I'm here now baby, let's go." He turned to me and said, "Wait here, I'll be back."

He lifted her off his lap and they walked together toward the bar. I thought they were going to talk privately, maybe have a drink together, but they walked past the bar and through a door covered with a curtain. Maybe there was a quiet sitting area back there, I thought.

I kept drinking and watching the other GIs getting rowdier. A fight would break out now and then but other guys would stop it and the combatants would soon be laughing and drinking together again. It was really loud and chaotic, my kind of place. Suddenly there was a young Vietnamese girl sitting next to me with her hand on my thigh. She was smiling and I thought she was beautiful. She said, "You like me, GI?"

I didn't know what to say. I never had a girl come up to me and ask me if I liked her. My social skills were primitive at best. I told her that, yes, I did like her, and I was trying to figure out what to say next so she would stay longer when she grabbed my hand and pulled me to my feet. "You come with me," she said and I staggered after her. She walked toward the door with the curtain. Maybe she was taking me to where Roland went, I thought. She led me into a long, dimly lit hallway. There was a door with a number on it every few feet. She stopped and opened one of the doors and led me in. There was a bed and a small table.

When I returned to the bar where Roland was now sitting, I asked him if he wanted another pitcher, but he was ready to go. We were both staggering a little as we walked out. Roland would stop and do the dap with some of his friends while I stood by, swaying. When we got outside where it was a little quieter I said, "Wow! This place is something else!" "Yeah, it sure is" he said as we walked past the MP checkpoint. I asked him if the MPs knew what was going on in there and he laughed. "Fool, the medics inspect these girls once a week; they have to have a card signed by a doctor. The MPs have to check their cards before they can come in. The Brigade runs this place."

## Hearts and Minds

Looking back on that time, I've considered the contrast between Vietnam and Afghanistan. Vietnam was a sexual Disneyland with the short-time girls, the 'boom-boom' parlors and the Saigon Tea. In Afghanistan there was much speculation about the 'Burka Babes,' and we could have a bottle of non-alcoholic 'near beer' after work in the dining facility. Maybe we learned something.

The moral high ground is much more important than the physical in these types of wars. I am amazed at how ignorant our senior military leaders were in Vietnam, but there must have been a lot of this kind of activity in Korea and during WWII. The war for the hearts and minds of the people is won or lost over what seems to be trivial matters like prostitution.

Stuart Herrington, an ARVN advisor wrote, "The American ability to acquire Vietnamese women was a deep source of resentment to virtually all Vietnamese men. To be seen even talking to an American beyond the requirements of one's job was anathema for any Vietnamese women who entertained the idea of marrying a Vietnamese man."[190]

We weren't forcing them to be prostitutes and many of the girls were earning money with their parent's knowledge of what they were doing, but it must have bothered their society as a whole. Of course I had to bear the shame of my own choices; some of our men never went to the Ville.

Later, I used to wonder at the courage of those Viet Cong and North Vietnamese soldiers as they came through our artillery and airstrikes. We were told that they were all on drugs, but I didn't see any evidence of that. Hunted by us, they lived in the jungle, harassed by our artillery and bombed by our B-52's.

Year after year they attacked our infantry positions and they left the bodies of their men occasionally when they couldn't drag them off. These men endured much greater suffering than we did. Their discipline was much stricter than ours. They could be shot for bothering a local girl. We could and did kill them in bunches, year after year, but they kept on coming.

## August 25th

Roland and I walked down the dark road to our company area. I asked him again about the guy who used to be Roland's machine gunner. He told me a little more about the battle on August 25th when they got into a fight with the 'Phu Loi' Battalion. "Who are they?" I asked. He said, "They are some hard corps mo-fo's!" adding that they were VC who came from this area and had some serious grudges with the Saigon government.

"When some other units got into deep shit," he said, "they called for us to come in and help. We did a combat assault into an LZ near the battle and moved on line through the jungle. They opened up on us from bunkers. We couldn't see them; they were up in the trees, in spider holes; some of them were behind us; it was crazy. Captain Knight was killed. It was crazy!"

Roland was pretty agitated, but not knowing any better I pressed on, "So what happened to the gunner?" "I told that fool to stay down, but he had to be a hero." He replied. "What did he do?" I asked. "He spotted a bunker and told me that he was going to take it. I told him not to, but he got up and charged, firing that gun and hollering. He only went a few yards before he fell down."

Roland had stopped in the road and was standing there talking. He wasn't really talking to me; it seemed like he was talking to himself. "I told him to stay down. I told that fool not to do it." I stopped and turned to look at him. There were tears streaming down his face. "I told him, and now I'm telling you; if you want to get through this, you better listen to me. You got it, fool!"

I wanted to learn these things he was talking about, but I was uninitiated and my education would be slow. For the next few weeks, as I got to meet the rest of the platoon, I heard a lot more about August 25th, 1966. It was a bench mark in their lives and a date on a grave marker for the others.

## The Lai Khe Perimeter

There was a perimeter defense line of fighting positions protecting the base camp. Each infantry battalion was responsible for a third of the perimeter. The fighting positions or bunkers had been built when the brigade first came to Lai Khe and now they needed repairs. We spent the next few days down on the perimeter fixing bunkers. The bunkers were five feet high with sandbags for the walls, and the roof which was held up by engineer stakes. There were large openings in the front for observation and shooting.

The sandbags were rotting and had to be replaced. There was a spot nearby where the sandbags were filled by Vietnamese workers and then they were trucked to the various bunkers. It was hard work in the hot sun and nobody was very motivated to get it done.

When I lifted up a rotting sandbag, I found a huge black scorpion lying underneath it and killed it with my entrenching tool. One of the guys said, "It's a good thing that scorpion didn't sting you because you would have been dead in a minute." One of the other guys said, "That's bullshit, it doesn't have any venom." They both stopped working and presented their hearsay evidence to one another until the sergeant at the next bunker yelled at them to "Shut the blank up and get back to work."

I don't know if that was a deadly scorpion or not but I knew that we would be sleeping on the ground in the jungle and I didn't like the idea of one of those things crawling across my face while I slept. I heard one of the other guys say that you should always clear your boots by turning them upside down and hitting the heel and toe against something before you put them on. That seemed like sound advice and I still find myself doing that forty years later.

At night the platoons rotated duty guarding the company sector. Our part of the perimeter overlooked a large open area of abandoned rice paddies terraced on a gradual slope that ended at the river.

**Jose Garcia:** *"Each platoon would pull guard on the company perimeter at night. Captain Howley used to check the lines and take the weapon of anyone he found sleeping. He found my rifle on a bunker. Another guy had borrowed it and fallen asleep. The CO was already on me about wearing my helmet so I didn't relish the idea of having to go up to the company headquarters to get it back. When I told the first sergeant why I was there he smiled and sent me back to the CO's office. When the CO began chewing me out, I started telling him that it wasn't my fault. He soon had me standing at attention and that's when he began to pay close attention to me."*[191]

### The Company Commander

Captain Howley had to rebuild the shattered unit with new replacements and he was dedicated to teaching the company the things he had learned as an airborne infantry and Special Forces officer. Every night the captain was on the prowl after dark. If he found someone sleeping on guard, he would take their weapon and prescribe corrective training for the sleepers when they came to him later to retrieve their weapons.

He insisted that the men wear their steel pots when they were on the bunker line or on patrol. Operation Danbury had been the first large operation for the battalion after August 25th and after observing his command, he was working hard to get the company trained to his standards.

**Jose Garcia:** *"Capt Howley greeted us in the mess-hall. It was right after the battle of August 25th. We were sixteen replacements. Boom! A nearby 155mm howitzer fired and we all hit the floor. He had one foot on the bench and he stood there smiling down at us. "That was outgoing, you'll learn." Boom! It happened again and we were back on the floor. The third time we just flinched and tried to take in what he was saying."*[192]

### Combat After Action Report: Operation Danbury

I didn't hear much about Operation Danbury, but for the purpose of illustrating the standards of reporting, I am including a summary of the 3rd Brigade's Combat After Action Report. The mission was a Search and Destroy operation employing the 'cloverleaf technique' in Binh Duong Province where it was suspected that the VC had logistics bases.

The 2-28 and 1-16 Infantry did airmobile assaults into an area ten kilometers west of Lai Khe, hardly the Cambodian border area that the supply sergeant claimed. The mission was "to kill VC and destroy VC installations and supplies."

The two battalions found old base camps, mine fields, and bicycles. Resistance was light, but slowly increased as the various units began finding large quantities of cached rice and salt. A-1-16 had one man killed by a sniper on 17 September. On the 18th another man from Alpha Company was killed by a claymore aimed at their perimeter. The next day A-1-16 found more rice. On the 19th, A-1-16 continued to find more rice, but at 1200 they were ordered to move to a pickup zone and prepare for an airmobile assault into another area at 1500. By 1600 the entire battalion was in and moving to a new RON.

On the 20th, A-1-16 found large quantities of wheat and rice and they 'apprehended' seventy-one 'old men, women, and children' from XT 699344, a location on the map. The 1968 version of that map shows the village of Ben Lo' at that location with the notation, "abandoned." The people were evacuated to a refugee camp at Ben Cat, a large town south of Lai Khe. On the 21st, 1-16 Infantry was picked up by helicopter and returned to Lai Khe.

The Results section lists four U.S. KIA and forty WIA. The body-count gives the 3d Brigade three VC KIA, by body-count and one VC KIA 'possibly.' It attributes to the artillery; three VC KIA by body-count, ten possibly killed, and three possibly wounded. The Air Force was given credit for three VC KBA (killed by air) and five VC possibly KBA. The totals give the U.S. casualties but leaves a '-' for the VC.

Fire support for the operation was nothing less than spectacular. The artillery fired 11,261 rounds of 105mm and 2,010 rounds of 155mm. The Air Force flew 117 fighter sorties and dropped high explosive bombs and napalm.

Forty-eight tons of rice were captured and removed to a refugee camp. Fifty-nine tons of rice were destroyed along with forty-three houses, 5180 lbs. cement, six tons of salt, 100 lbs. of peanuts, twenty base camps, 118 fox holes, three cubic yards of gravel, eight chickens, nineteen ducks, three small arms rounds, two claymores, two 105mm rounds, one 155mm round, one 175mm round, one 8-Inch round, one 60mm mortar round, four 81mm mortar rounds, nine CBUs, twenty-two bicycles, and one bicycle tire.

I use this as an illustration of the Army's response to the number crunchers at the Pentagon; 'fine, if they want numbers, we'll give em numbers.' The lesson learned was somewhat amusing; "Special techniques found that a claymore mine will collapse a bunker, by firing it face down, it will collapse the bunker." Colonel Sidney M. (Mickey) Marks, the 3d Brigade Commander, said the operation was extremely successful.[193]

## Artillery

In the battle of August 25th, the artillery fired 8,869 rounds of 105mm into a heavy contact. For Operation Danbury, with no real contact, the artillery fired 11,261 rounds of 105mm. Interesting math. General DePuy's thought was, "America is a rich country, and he'd spend that wealth with steel on target to get the job done with minimal risk to the infantry soldier."

During this time, DePuy was ordering the Division to fire 1000 rounds of artillery each night into the jungle, into what were called 'free-fire zones.' This was called H+I or harassing and interdiction fire. The logistics involved are beyond my capacity to understand after twenty-seven years in the army. From manufacturing to transportation across the sea, to movement through contested territory, this was as impressive as the VC logistics, moving supplies on bicycles down the Ho Chi Minh Trail. This firepower extravaganza wasn't appreciated by everyone in General DePuy's chain of command but General Westmoreland liked it so much that it became background noise; the guns firing behind us, the rounds passing over us and exploding somewhere in the jungle ahead. [194]

## The Helicopter War

One morning at formation an announcement was made that we would be receiving airmobile helicopter training. We were told that the training would begin the next morning and we were to bring our web gear, rucksacks, and weapons with all our ammunition, everything we would carry if we were going to the field. The high profile 1st Cavalry Division had been using helicopters successfully, and General DePuy wanted in.

During WWII, troops were dropped behind enemy lines by parachute and glider. Aviation technology advanced with the development of the helicopter. Helicopters were first used by the U.S. in Burma during WWII. During the Korean War, the Marine Corps used them to move a large unit in mountainous terrain. Helicopters were used extensively by the French Army in Algeria, and the U.S. Army took note.

A lot of information had been released in the last few years about the airmobile tests being conducted at Ft Benning during the early sixties. They were doing a lot of wild things with helicopters including such things as rappelling off them and making landing zones on top of trees. The airborne people, mad that they weren't jumping with parachutes, had soldiers jumping out of moving helicopters at ten to twenty feet off the ground. This method was only used once or twice during the test period because of the many broken limbs that resulted.[195]

Eventually, the Vietnam War would become known as the 'helicopter war.' The idea of using helicopters to administratively move large units of troops from one place to another quickly evolved into combat assaults. Armed helicopters gave the infantry close air support at a time when the Air Force was doing everything it could to avoid that mission.

The helicopter enabled us to move heavy artillery quickly so that the infantry was never out of its range. Resupply of the troops in the field by helicopter greatly extended the time they could stay there looking for the enemy. Badly wounded soldiers were evacuated by helicopter from the battlefield, often arriving at fully equipped trauma treatment facilities within an hour of their being wounded.

Command and control changed from the commander moving to the place where he could best influence the action on the ground to the commander moving to the place where he could best see the action on the ground from his helicopter. At 1500 feet above the fighting, with several radios, the battalion commander could explain his actions to the next echelon of command above him, in another helicopter, and transmit his directives to the echelons below him on the ground. Had the fighting been in the desert, this might have been a valid technique, but, nevertheless, air mobility would completely revolutionize the way we fought.

## Air-assault Training: The Troop Ladder (1)

The next morning the company road-marched up to the brigade headquarters. When we arrived I saw a metal troop ladder hanging from the branch of a very tall tree. Another unit was there standing in line in front of the ladder and I watched in horror as each man had to climb that ladder to the top and then climb back down. I hated heights and I couldn't imagine myself doing that.

A sergeant had us sit down and he gave us a quick class on the ladder. It was normally used for troops to climb in and out of a CH-47 Chinook helicopter while it hovered over a small clearing in the jungle. The ladder was a hundred feet long which meant that we might be told to climb down that ladder, or up, carrying all our gear, a hundred feet off the ground. I was really shook. I didn't want the guys to know that I was afraid of heights, but there was no way that I was going to climb that ladder.

I asked Roland if he thought that we could climb the ladder first without our gear and he gave me one of his wicked grins, "You ain't scared to climb that are you?" It hadn't taken him long to cut to the heart of the matter. "No man," I said, "but I never climbed a ladder like that before..." Roland cut me off with a snort and I was afraid now to reveal my weakness to him. Maybe something would happen and we wouldn't have to do it.

The other unit finished and now the first platoon was lining up to climb the ladder. One by one, each man climbed to the top, "You got to touch the limb, touch the limb, you don't come down till you touch the limb!" shouted the sergeant who had briefed us. When you stand in line for something you want, like a pay line, it takes forever. This line, however, seemed like it was moving very fast. I was sweating and took a big drink of water. Then I had to pee. I got permission to use the piss-tube nearby. When I returned to the line I went to the end but Roland was having none of that and insisted that I rejoin him.

Now it was almost my turn. I looked up at the man on the ladder; he was pulling and stepping toward the top. The ladder was swaying a little and it seemed like he was going extremely slow. When he got close to the top he started to come back down and had actually taken one step when the sergeant ordered him to go back up and touch the branch before he came down. The ladder shook a little as he reoriented his body and climbed up two steps and touched the branch. He came down quickly and now it was my turn.

My machine gun was slung, muzzle down across my back. The sling was tight and the gun rested on the back part of my ruck. I could feel the cocking handle digging into my back even though the ruck gave me some protection. The ladder stood before me and there was no way I was going to avoid this. So I grasped the highest rung I could reach and began to climb.

Rung after rung, I kept my eyes straight ahead and placed the forward edge of my boot heels against the rung so they wouldn't slip off. Roland gave me a word of encouragement and the sergeant gave him an "at ease." I just kept climbing. I was starting to breathe hard and my heart was pounding. Sweat was coming down from the leather band in my helmet and going right into my eyes. The sweat in my eyes caused me to lean into the ladder and hook my left arm under a rung to wipe the sweat with my right thumb and index finger. I moved quickly back to a two hand grip and continued to climb.

How much further could it be? That's what I was thinking when the back of my hand hit the tree branch. I made it! Well, that was the hard part. But then I made the mistake of looking over my left shoulder and when I saw how high I was, I felt my whole body cringe. I held on with both hands for a moment and then, looking straight ahead, began climbing down. The biggest danger while going down was getting in a hurry. I didn't put my boot heels against the rungs for several steps and my foot slipped off of a rung. I was able to stay in control, and resume my original foot positions. I was back on the ground quickly and got a slap on the back and a "good job" from somebody.

I walked over and joined the others. We watched the rest of our platoon complete their training task and I felt better. I had been forced to confront my fears and while the Army couldn't make me climb that ladder, I had a stronger need to remain a member of this group of infantrymen than to allow myself to be paralyzed by my fear of heights. I didn't know what they would do with someone who refused to climb, but I didn't want to end up in the 'Mess-Kit Repair Battalion.'[196]

The word was that the ladder climb was to be the extent of our airmobile training and I had completed the task. Now I wondered what we were going to do for the rest of the day. When the company had completed the ladder climb, we road-marched back to the company for chow. I sat in the mess hall, picking out the dehydrated bell peppers from my food, and listening to the other guys talk about how bad it was for them to climb that ladder. That amazed me. I thought I was the only one who was afraid of heights.

We went over to our tent after chow and lay on our bunks. I smoked a cigarette, relieved that climbing that ladder was behind me. Some of the guys were saying that we would never use the ladder because there was always a place to land a chopper in our AO. Then the platoon sergeant came in and told us to fall out with all our gear. "Same equipment as this morning," he said. What are we going to do now? At the formation, the first sergeant said we were going up to the air strip to receive familiarization training with the CH-47.

When we got to the air strip, there was CH-47 Chinook or 'shit hook' as we called it back then, sitting on the ground with its engines off. It had a set of four large blades on top of its fuselage behind the cockpit and another set on its tail. The blades seemed to bend almost to the ground, pulled down by their own weight. The fuselage itself rested on four sets of wheels, two at the front and two at the back.

The CH-47 could carry about 40 troops, combat loaded. It had a back door that opened like the ramp on the back of a C-130. It could carry a large artillery piece hanging underneath it from a hook on the bottom of the fuselage and it could carry the crew for the gun and a lot of ammo inside. The work horses of the Vietnam War, they were always flying back and forth across the sky.

The helicopter was a long way away from where we were told to sit so I leaned against my ruck and watched the activity around the aircraft. The crew and some soldiers were doing something at the rear and underneath it. I had no idea what was going on so I followed the example of those around me and dozed off, stomach full, in the heat of the day on the Lai Khe airstrip.

A loud high pitched whine woke me up and when I focused on the source, I saw the blades beginning to spin on the big helicopter. As they spun faster they drooped less and less until they were as straight as a ruler. Soon, they were spinning so fast that you couldn't see the individual blades. I wondered why they had started the engines. If we were going to get a tour, with the engines running, we wouldn't be able to hear the briefing.

The helicopter began to rise, lifting straight up. As it left the ground, I noticed that hanging down from the rear and the middle were troop ladders. As it continued to rise, the ladders were soon extended to their maximum length.

**The Troop Ladder (2)**

This time we had to climb the ladder hanging from the back ramp into the cargo hold, walk forward to the middle of the aircraft, get on another ladder and climb back down to the ground. Unbelievable, just when I thought it was safe to relax. What was interesting was that I was not near as freaked out this time because of my first trip up the ladder. When it was my turn to climb, a sergeant motioned for me to leave the line and come forward to the ladder. There was a man about a third of the way up and another who had almost reached the top. Hot exhaust fumes filled the air along with a lot of dust and noise.

I began to climb the ladder but this time it was moving a little from the motion and vibration of the helicopter. I continued to climb, a little faster than I had the first time. After a little ways, I took a quick peek down between my feet, and saw the next guy start climbing up below me. I checked my progress several times. The man above me had reached the top and was climbing in. The noise got louder as I got closer to the back ramp.

Looking up again, I saw a man wearing a flight helmet motioning me to come on. When I got to the helicopter ramp, he helped me in and I crawled a few feet before standing up. Midway forward, another crew chief was standing next to an open hole in the floor of the helicopter and the helmet of the man who had been above me on the ladder was disappearing as he began his decent. The crew chief signaled me forward and pointed toward the hole.

This was the worst part for me. I had to get on the ladder and climb down through the hole. I could see the man below me and the man behind me was now inside the aircraft. I was afraid that I would lose my footing or my hand would slip as I tried to get situated on that ladder. I was sweating and my helmet had tilted to an angle where it was almost hanging off the back of my head, held on only by my chin strap around my neck.

I made myself grab that ladder, get my feet on the rungs and I started down. The guy behind me got on the ladder right after me and it looked like he might come down so fast that he would step on my hands. So I picked up speed and made it to the ground pretty fast. As I moved away from the ladder, I turned to see who had been behind me; it was Roland, of course, giving me his wicked grin. "Fool, you better not be taking your sweet-ass time on that ladder, Charlie might be shooting at us if we do this in the bush!"

Repetition is the mother of perfection, but that was the last time I ever climbed a troop ladder hanging from a helicopter; so I knew that I could do it; but I wasn't really proficient. Years later, I had to rappel and face my fear of heights again. That time though, I did a lot of rappelling from a rappel tower with a wall and mock helicopter skids. I learned the Australian rappel. We rappelled off of cliffs at near Ft Hood, and I rappelled out of helicopters many times with all my gear. The more you do something dangerous, the more experienced you become, the more self-confidence you gain, and the more proficient you become. You are able to handle the unexpected which in the case of rappelling, can quickly lead to a life-threatening situation. I would have a few of those years later.

**Ambush Patrol**

One evening, right before chow, Roland and I were notified that we would have ambush patrol that night. This was it: my first chance to deal a death blow to Charlie, save my buddies, and cover myself with glory. Roland noticed my excitement and told me to take a chill pill. "Nothing is going to happen; nothing ever does on these local patrols." Something would happen that night; but it wasn't what I had hoped for or in any way expected.

We assembled after chow. The rifle squad leader who was leading the patrol told us to follow him. "Isn't he going to tell us what's going on or inspect us," I whispered to Roland. "Don't sweat it" was all he said. I followed the guy in front of me as we walked through the rubber trees on our way to the perimeter.

Some of the guys were having what I figured was a last cigarette before we went out. I lit up too, saving an eye from the light. It was almost dark when we reached the perimeter. We walked behind the bunkers for a ways. Then we stopped at one. I could see the squad leader talking to one of the guys on the bunker but I couldn't hear what they were saying.

I figured that they were doing the coordination for our passage of lines. There was a spot in the concertina wire where a patrol could go out, but I thought it was further down the line. We all took a knee while the squad leader talked with the man at the bunker.

Finally, the squad leader motioned to the guy behind him to go. We stood up, one after another, and followed the man in front of us. When I got to the bunker I looked at the guy standing there. I looked back to the guy in front of me and he was gone. I turned right and started to walk toward the wire. Then I heard someone run up behind me and he grabbed my rucksack frame.

"Where the blank are you going?" said Roland. I stopped and turned around. "I can't see the guy in front of me. He must have gone this way because there was no one in front of me after we passed the bunker." "Follow me," he said as he led me back to the bunker. The guys that had been behind Roland were waiting for us.

He kept going straight in the direction of the company area and away from the wire. The column had turned left instead of right and was moving into a small field partially surrounded by bamboo. It was about seventy-five meters behind the bunker line and completely hidden. The rest of the squad was sitting in a circle, waiting for us.

Roland walked up to the squad leader and told him that the new guy, me, had taken a wrong turn. The squad leader didn't say anything about it and told Roland for us to take a position where he was pointing. I was getting over my embarrassment of losing contact with the man in front of me and a new concern was entering my mind. What are we doing here? We were still inside the perimeter. Surely they're not expecting the VC to be moving through here enough to put an ambush patrol. I waited for a while, thinking that maybe we were taking a break. I was dying to ask Roland about what we were doing but I was afraid to after my screw up at the bunker.

Finally, I couldn't take anymore. "What are we doing here," I asked him. "I thought that ambush patrols were outside the perimeter." "Sometimes we do them here." "Why would you do them here," I wanted to know. "Because some nights we're too tired to go outside the perimeter," he said. "What," I whispered, "are you crazy; did the CO tell us to go here for the ambush?"

I heard the sound of someone walking toward us. "What the blank is going on here?" said the squad leader. "Murry is new and I'm explaining the ambush patrol to him," said Roland. I was agitated now and I didn't like what was beginning to become obvious. "What don't you understand about this patrol," he asked.

"I don't understand why we're sitting here when we're supposed to be out there. I came here to fight and I don't understand why we're not going out there where Charlie is." The squad leader was not impressed with my bravado. "How many ambush patrols have you been on." "None, but..." He cut me off.

"I've been on more than one hundred. I've been here for nine months and a few days and I'm tired." "Well, this ain't right sergeant;" said I, "we should be out there where the enemy is." Roland was right behind me telling me to shut up, but I was full of righteous indignation and continued to argue with the squad leader.

Finally he had had enough, "You want to go out of the wire, ok, we'll go out of the wire." He told the squad to saddle up. I could hear the others cursing and asking him what was going on. "The new guy wants to go outside the perimeter, so we're going." "Tell him to shut the blank up and we'll stay here!" they argued. "No," said the sergeant, "you shut the blank up and saddle up, we're moving out!"

The squad leader led us back to the bunker where he talked to the man on guard for a moment. Then he turned left and led us down the road to another bunker. He talked to the man at that bunker before turning to the right, leading us through a gap in the wire and into the dried up rice paddies on the other side.

I was finally in the war. We walked about one hundred meters down the terraced rice paddies. Each one was a little lower than the one before. We were on a slope that went down to a small river that ran through what was a small river valley. On the other side, about 200 meters away, was a tree-line.

The squad leader halted us. He walked back to where I was. "Follow me," he said. I did, and I could hear Roland following me. He took us to the edge of the paddy we were in and told us to set up there. We were to be the point of an inverted 'V' shaped ambush. I could tell that he was pissed so I didn't argue semantics about the ambush formation.

I realized now that I was rapidly making myself the most unpopular guy in the platoon and I had only been here a few weeks. My, I can do anything, Surfer Joe attitude wasn't going to play well with these guys. They had seen the elephant and heard the owl. Most of them only cared about getting out of there alive.

## Stayin' Alive

Winning the war was not the troop's goal in this conflict. The U.S. wasn't going to start a nuclear WW III if it could help it. The 'roll-back' strategy had been changed after the Hungarian Revolt to a 'containment' strategy that would last through the rest of the Cold War. Containment didn't take you 'on to Hanoi' or to Moscow or Beijing for that matter.

During WWII, the U.S. Army started a troop rotation program based on a point system. Most infantrymen never got enough points to walk off the battlefield. They were either carried off or buried there and the veterans were bitter about the system. Korea was more of the same.

When the regular Army went into Vietnam it was announced that everyone's tour would be 365 days. The Marine Corps made their tour thirteen months for the purpose of maintaining their 'warrior' high ground, and other services had their own criteria for the length of the tour.

The Navy SEALs had a six month tour, the Air Force pilots who flew up to North Vietnam had a 100 mission goal, and Navy pilots flew about 120. Everyone knew how long they had to stay here and for most, that became the goal. Charlie and his cousin from the north, Charles, didn't have this view. Their goal was victory or death.

When your goal is to stay alive for the rest of your life, then you must adapt to your environment. The Army tried to help us with this; but their tactics were a mixture of our version of victory or death as practiced during WWII, and death to the enemy by advanced technology. The politicians knew that we couldn't keep losing lots of people so they tried to keep the WWII veterans who were running the war from reverting back to the way they did it back during the 'big one.'

The grunts, mainly young draftees and eager beavers like me came into the war with all the movie scenes rolling through their heads. We wanted to do like our fathers, uncles, and big brothers did in WWII and Korea—come home, maybe with a couple of ribbons on our uniforms (I was hoping for more than a couple) and bask in the praise of our friends and family, the praise that we figured the WWII vets got when they marched in the big parade.

What I'm trying to say is that the men in the squad I was with on this ambush patrol would have followed the squad leader through the wire, across the rice paddies and the river, and continued into the far tree-line to the designated ambush point in the middle of booby-traps and roving VC, if the sergeant had told them to. He chose to sandbag the ambush patrol, remain inside the perimeter with the collusion of some of the men on bunker guard, and send back false situation reports by radio every hour; they were good with that too. What they didn't want was some new guy that they didn't know calling the shots and making them spend the night in a more dangerous environment than their leader had originally chosen.

We stayed there for the rest of the night, and just before dawn, the squad leader called the sergeant on the bunker line behind us on the radio and had him alert the line that we were coming in. No point in getting lit up by our own. We packed up and returned through the wire to the perimeter. Then, as we walked back to the company area the way we came, smoking and joking, no one talked to me and I could tell that Roland was pissed.

## The FNG

When we got back to the tents we dropped our gear off and walked to the chow hall for breakfast. It was closed, so we stood around waiting. I stuck close to Roland, who was shucking and jiving with some of the other 'brothers' in the squad. Still, no one was talking to me and I was feeling pretty lonely. The squad leader was watching me and several times I turned my head and caught him staring at me. When our eyes met, I began to have the thought that he was worried that I might be planning to snitch him off to the platoon sergeant. If I did, it could cost him his stripes or worse. I was already on his shit list and I had a long time to go. I figured it was best to assume a low profile for as long as I could. I wasn't always in control of my mouth or the rest of my body, so who knew how long that would last.

> **Dennis Howley:** *"I knew about the patrol through my own sources. I knew that these kinds of things went on and why. I wanted to fix them by accompanying an ambush patrol now and then but was forbidden by the battalion commander from going out with anything less than a platoon."*[197]

Later in my tour, SSG Magee, my platoon sergeant, told me that when he was a young Marine during the Korean War, he went out on a patrol. They were supposed to cross the valley and recon the forward slopes of a hill on the other side. "My squad leader took us down to the valley and we stayed there all night. The next morning we returned to our lines and he reported that there was nothing on the hill. The next night, the company next to us attacked that hill and was driven back with lots of casualties." My squad leader told me, "If you say anything, I'll kill you." Life in the trenches is not easy and most histories don't include the human failings. For my part, this trench life would little by little expose me and my own weaknesses. For now though I thought I was different than the rest of these guys.

I got Roland to the side when the chow hall opened and the other guys went inside. I told him that I didn't mean to cause so much trouble. He let me know that I had caused a lot of trouble and that I better lay low for a while. I told him that was exactly what I was planning to do; but, I told him, I thought the squad leader was worrying about me reporting our patrol's activities. "Well, are you?" he asked. "No, I'm not going to say anything but I think he was wrong," "Nobody cares what you think," he said, "so shut up, and let's eat."

### The Combat Infantryman's Badge, 3rd Award

We had a company formation and there were some VIPs, including a General. We were called to attention and some soldiers were called to the front. A sergeant from the third platoon was awarded his third Combat Infantryman Badge, a CIB with two stars. He had fought in WWII, Korea, and now he was a squad leader in Vietnam. He must have had some ups and downs in his career because after all those wars he was only a staff sergeant. Still, these men, the veterans, were what held the Army together and as the war dragged on, there were fewer and fewer of them, and slowly the Army began to fall apart.

Roland must have been running interference for me because none of the guys confronted me about the ambush patrol. We went back to the Ville that night. It was the usual riotous activity; drinking, and whoring, then staggering back the on dusty red dirt road through the rubber trees, hollering and laughing. We pulled a night-shift on the perimeter every so often, and went to the Ville any night we were off, carrying on there until the MP's closed it down for the night.

### Booby-traps

We had a class on booby-traps in the company area. Captain Howley was relentless in his efforts to train us to be jungle fighters. The fear of booby-traps had assumed epic proportions in the talk about the jungle surrounding our base camp at Lai Khe. This fear was not unwarranted as there had been a number of people wounded or killed while on patrol there.

> **Dennis Howley:** *"I was big on taking any opportunity to conduct training. A patrol from another platoon had gone out recently and encountered several booby-traps, unnerving the platoon leader to the point where he requested extraction by helicopter. I talked him down and directed him to move his platoon back on foot using their eyes and moving carefully. They made it back without mishap."*[198]

> **Peter Clark:** *"A couple of days after we choppered back to Lai Khe the Second Platoon pulled a day patrol to the north of the company wire. We had a new Lieutenant whose name I forget and a couple of new people. All or most of our non-coms had been wounded on the 25th and I don't remember a lot of sergeants on that patrol, just the Lieutenant and the rest of us.... As far as we could tell, this patrol was for training purposes and based on the notion that if you're throwed you need to get right back up on the horse. At the time I thought it was probably bullshit and just a waste of a day that could be better spent doing nothing, which was pretty much what I was yearning for after the 25th and 26th.*
>
> *As usual, we didn't follow any of the numerous paths or tracks running through the jungle, but steered on a compass azimuth provided by the Lieutenant. The jungle here was not particularly dense, and showed some evidence of cultivation here and there, so the point guy didn't need to use his machete much, and we were making pretty good time. Everybody just wanted to get the hell back to the base camp. About a klick in, the point guy, again I forget his name, stopped cold and hissed "Mine!" He backed up slowly, visibly pale and shaky. "God damn it, I almost walked right through," he kept saying. We all backed up very carefully and put some distance between us and the booby trap, which was a metal cylinder about the size of a beer can taped to the base of a sapling, with a trip wire about six inches off the ground running a meter or [so] through the undergrowth.*
>
> *The Lieutenant and our designated demolition specialist gingerly inspected the device, and decided to blow it in place. The demo guy carefully placed a wad of C4 next to the booby trap and cut a length of fuse.*
>
> *The rest of us went another 20 meters or so back the way we had come, where we hunkered down, most of us lighting up. "Fire in the hole!" The LT and his RTO, and a bit later the demo guy, hustled back down the line of troops. A few seconds later came the whump of a small explosion. After checking out the site, the LT waved us forward. Leaving the scene of the*

*demolition, we were still pretty bunched up. I ended up right behind the point guy, who was walking very slowly and carefully through the low brush.*

*Whump! A flash, nasty little whizzing noises, and a bolus of dirt and debris bloomed a meter or two to my left. I felt like somebody had slapped my leg and thrown sand in my face. The point guy was down, with a bunch of growing red splotches on his side, and four of the guys behind me were down as well. We had been close together as the point guy was going so slowly, and the column was still closed up from our wait for the demo.*

*I stayed on the point after that, with my M-16's safety off, peering into the brush and trying to process the likelihood that Charlie was out there waiting for us, or, worse, coming for us. Behind me the medic worked on the guys. The point man was the worst hurt, but all of them had multiple wounds. The doc had to collect field dressings from us as his got used up. The LT and his RTO located a suitable LZ in a nearby grassy clearing, which we carefully checked for traps, then carried or assisted the wounded guys to it as the dust-off came in.*

*Once the chopper had lifted off, we lined up in the LZ and took a new azimuth. I was on point. Just before we moved out the LT asked me if I was hit. I grinned and held up my left elbow which had been grazed by a piece of shrapnel; my left ear also had been grazed. Other than leaking a little blood on my left thigh I was in great shape, and feeling pretty good about it considering how badly the guys near me had been hit; (The wound on my leg seemed trivial at the time, but became badly infected three or four days later and ended up putting me in the hospital for a couple of days, and kept me out of the field for a couple days longer.)*

*I got the direction from the guy behind with the compass, and headed into the brush. I was being careful and but wasn't particularly concerned, and was probably still high on the survivor's adrenaline rush. After a few uneventful minutes I came to a line of scrubby trees and bushes which bordered an old field of some sort. I stepped between two 6 or 8 foot bushes. I felt OK as I knew I wasn't on a path as the gap was pretty well filled in with branches and leaves and it didn't seem like a traveled way at all. As I lifted the leaves and branches so I could slide through I saw a bright silver braided wire in my hands.*

*In what must have been a fraction of a second but seemed like a couple of minutes, I processed what this shiny wire in the midst of all this vegetation in the middle of this innocuous gap between the bushes signified. Having completed that analytical chore, and reached the most likely conclusion, I then asked myself the next question, which was, have you already triggered the fucking booby trap, in which case you have x seconds to get some distance between you and the explosion. The quickest way to get distance is to keep going forward. But if the booby trap wasn't triggered yet, going forward would certainly do that. But if the booby trap isn't triggered yet, I can back out and with luck it won't go off. Hard to believe, but there was plenty of subjective time to work this out. What I did was take a gentle half step back disengaging from the wire, and then gasp "Mine!" and try to set a new speed record for running backwards.*

*It didn't explode. The LT came and checked it out, and sure enough the trip wire ran through the undergrowth to a metal canister taped to the base of the sapling to my right. Right then I was starting to truly shake with terror. Nothing I had been through up to that point had touched my sense of mortality like the vision of that silver wire in my hand, and nothing that happened since has either. I really hate minefields. At this point the LT called the CO and suggested we should chopper out of the area given the prevalence of booby traps.*

*This seemed like a great idea to me and I am sure the rest of us, but after a brief exchange the idea was nixed; the CO said we had walked into the minefield and we could walk out, or words to that effect. Regardless, we all wanted to get the hell out, but what had been a typical, boring second growth landscape became the literal stuff of nightmares. I was shaky and fearful enough to ask not to take the point, and the LT put our only noncom, a buck sergeant, on point. I felt so ashamed of my cowardice that I took the compass and made a point of staying close enough to the point so that if he hit a trap I'd get hit as well.*

*We didn't blow the trap that I had found, or any of the several more that the point discovered, which we noted and carefully walked around. We just gingerly stepped in each other's tracks and followed the azimuth through an increasing drizzle towards what the LT's map promised was the most direct practical route back to the wire. We really – really – didn't want to try to get through that countryside in the dark, but we had to go so slowly. Anyone who doubts the subjective flexibility of time should spend an afternoon walking through a minefield. Part of me will always be 20 years old, standing in the warm rain, and longing for the impossibly distant horizon just a few hundred meters across that green valley."*[199]

**Dennis Howley:** *"I held a company formation and went over the principals for avoiding and detecting booby traps. Then I introduced the platoon leader of the first platoon. He showed us several ingenious VC inventions including one, a hand grenade on a stake with five or six lengths of thin nylon fishing line attached at one end to the pin and each piece of line had a fish hook at the other end."*[200]

I remembered that class and especially how the LT said, "We found this booby-trap on patrol the other day and were able to bring it back for show and tell. Unfortunately, though, we usually announce the discovery of a booby-trap with the screams of several troops after a loud explosion." I had no way of knowing, but I would soon be going through the same area that Peter Clark described.

*Look therefore carefully how you walk,*
*not as unwise, but as wise*
*Ephesians 5:15*

## Chapter 7-October 1966: Part I

### The Patrol

On the afternoon of 2 October, the platoon sergeant and the platoon leader, a tall young first lieutenant whom I had seen in the company area, but never talked to, came down to the bunker line and called a meeting of the squad leaders. The platoon leader's RTO was there and the word spread from him to the platoon that we had a patrol the next day. Most troops have an insatiable desire to know what coming next. Some learn to develop sources of information so that they can enter into the continual speculative conferences that take place in every fire team, gun crew, and squad. Not everyone is interested and they prefer to sleep through all the discussions about what the future holds. When it gets too loud, they enter the conversation with a "Why don't you all shut the blank up!"

The weapons squad leader told us to meet him in our tent after chow for a warning order. When he came to the tent he brought a map and told us that we would have an all-day patrol the next day. We would be patrolling an area on the west side of the base camp. The area was in front of our section of the perimeter and several 'klicks' (kilometers) west of the river. He told us to carry a basic load of ammo, water, and one C-ration for the noon meal.

After the briefing, Roland came over and told me what to do to get ready. I asked him how late we would be up planning this patrol and he looked at me with a disgusted expression on his face, "Didn't you hear anything? We just did the planning." He asked me some questions about what the sergeant had said and since I knew the information, he assured me that I knew the plan and that now it was time to go to the Ville.

The next morning we were awakened at 0430 and after a C-ration breakfast, we assembled in front of our tents in a platoon formation. Our squad leader checked us out and when the platoon leader arrived he briefed the patrol order. He gave more detail regarding the order of march, and our actions when crossing the river. He wanted the machine guns to cover the crossing. My heart started beating a little faster with the thought that the responsibility for the river crossing rested on us and the other gun crew. He inspected the platoon and made a few on the spot corrections while we waited to move out.

### Some Things We Carried

I was wearing my helmet with the chin straps undone, and looped around the back of the helmet and clipped together. My 'dog tags' were taped together and hung from a chain around my neck. Over my t-shirt I wore an OG-107 jungle fatigue shirt and below the shirt, jungle fatigue pants, with no underpants, and black leather combat boots. Next came the wretched gas mask which hung from my waist on its belt. My web gear came next and consisted of a pistol belt held by suspenders attached to a harness that was draped over my shoulders with a first aid case with a field dressing clipped to my left suspender.

The front of the belt held two ammunition pouches that I used for weapons cleaning equipment and snacks. My holstered .45 was on the right side and two canteens in their pouches hung from the rear. Another pouch with two magazines of .45 ammo occupied the left side of my belt. The canteens in the back were heavier than the things in the front, causing the belt to ride high in the front even when I carried a couple of hand grenades attached to the ammo pouches; this made the web gear a constant source of both physical and mental irritation for the rest of the time I was in the army.

A few months later we were also told to wear flak jackets which brought a chorus of groans from the platoon. They were used in the Korean War and someone sent a bunch of them to the 1st Infantry Division to protect us from booby-trap blasts. After several objections from the guys like, "Why do we got to wear that blankety blank thing sarge, it's too blankety blank hot!" The sergeant told us to "shut the blank up! The brigade commander says all local patrols will wear flak jackets; be happy that he doesn't make us wear them on operations!"

My rucksack and frame hung from my shoulders on a second set of suspenders that rested on top of my web gear harness. In the ruck was a box of 100 rounds of 7.62 ball and tracer linked machine gun ammunition. Beside the ammo, my poncho, some C-ration components, and two more canteens were the only other things I carried in my ruck today. We were going 'lite' because it was only a day-trip.

I carried my machine gun on its left side, balanced on my right shoulder. One of the bipod legs was folded down and I held it with my right hand. It was loaded with a belt of twenty-five rounds which hung from the gun and was draped over my rucksack. As we stood there waiting to go, my fatigue shirt was already soaked with sweat.

Finally we were ready. We each followed the man in front of us on the path to the bunker line and went through the wire at the same place that we went out on the ambush patrol a few nights earlier. We were pretty quiet, and I was impressed by the way that everyone seemed to know what to do. Roland told me earlier to make sure I followed the guy in front of me and stayed on his path; I concentrated on doing this. The booby-trap classes at the brigade school and the one in the company, plus all the talk about booby-traps, made me take his word seriously.

I kept my eyes sweeping the sides of the path through the low grass, looking for fish hooks. Every now and then I looked up to check on the guy in front of me. This was a part of the process whereby a trained infantry soldier becomes an experienced soldier, and eventually, an animal.

A year later, Jimi Hendrix said it all when he asked, "But first, are you experienced, have you ever been experienced?" He had been a paratrooper with the 101st Airborne Division in the early sixties, and while his experiences as a rock star took him to places much different than the place we were in, his words had the ring of truth.[201]

We made it to the river and halted. It didn't look like much, just a large creek after a heavy rain. To cross it seemed a simple task. It was narrow and it didn't look very deep; but the current beneath the surface was very swift. You could cross it standing up and the water would only come up to your armpits at most crossing points; but, if you tripped on something, stepped in a hole, or lost your balance while fighting the current, you could be swept away in a heartbeat.

We lost several men to that river while I was there. They were swept away and eventually they drowned, exhausted by their struggle and unable to get rid of the equipment that was weighing them down. Von Clausewitz said that in war, everything is simple, but the simplest thing is difficult.

**Jose Garcia:** *"The first time I crossed the river, they told us that the Vietnamese had dug some deep holes in the river bed. They used these holes for water storage for their rice paddies during the dry season. We were told to stay on the right side of the rope when we crossed. The guy ahead of me moved too far to the left and stepped into one of those holes. He disappeared underwater for a moment and then came up waving his arms before he went down again. I moved over to help him and stepped into the same hole and down I went.*

*"I must have gone down 10 feet before I touched the bottom and pushed off which helped me get to the surface where I took a breath. Captain Howley was sitting on the bank watching me with a smile as I went down again. I managed to push off the bottom this time toward the bank and when I came up, I grabbed a bush. When the other guy came up again, I held my rifle barrel out to him. He grabbed it and I pulled him over to the bank where some of the others helped us get out. I looked up at Captain Howley. He had a slight smile and asked me, "where's your helmet, Garcia?"*[202]

The platoon leader pointed at me and then pointed to a position to the right of the platoon where he wanted me to set up my gun to cover the crossing; a fire team from the last squad set up to our right. We moved and set up the gun where he had directed. Roland attached a 100 round belt to my twenty-five round starter and lay to my left with a can of ammunition at the ready, aiming his rifle at the tree-line across the river. Mac was on his left.

The first squad sent a guy across with his web gear, rifle, and a rope around his waist. When he reached the other side, he tied the rope to a big bush and the rest of the platoon began to cross by squad. The other gun went across with the LT and his RTO after the first squad and set up on the other side to cover the men still crossing. Soon it was our turn. Roland secured his belt of ammo and I got up, folded my right bipod leg, put the gun on my shoulder, and moved toward the rope safety line.

When I slid down the bank and stepped into the murky water, I let myself drop until my feet touched the bottom. I was almost turned on my side by the current. My helmet shifted to the rear of my head and I thought it was going to fall off. I should have fastened my chin strap, but except for climbing the troop ladder, we never wore the chin strap fastened when we were moving, because of some legend that had been passed down through the ranks from WWII.

According to the story that was told to me, a soldier in that war had fastened his chin strap and when a mortar shell landed next to him, the upward blast caught his helmet and took his head off. Whether he would have survived the blast and shrapnel if his chin strap was unfastened was never explained, but everyone left their chin strap unfastened in WWII, Korea, and Vietnam. The Kevlar helmet that I wore in Afghanistan had somehow been engineered to resist the explosive power of these near misses, and we always wore the chin strap fastened, always.

I held on to the rope with my left hand while trying to balance the machine gun on my right shoulder, shaking my head, trying to reposition my helmet to its normal position. The water was up to the middle of my chest as I slid my feet along the bottom. The current pushed me against the rope, so I tried to lean to the right; I moved as quickly as possible to get to the other side. When I got to the far side, a man was standing there with his hand reaching out. I gave him my left hand and he pulled me up the bank. I moved to a position that the LT was pointing at and Roland joined me there a moment later. The last man in the platoon came across with the rope tied around his waist, and the LT directed the lead squad to move out.

### How We Navigated

The point man and the squad leader worked with each other making sure that the platoon was going in the right direction. In front of us about 200 meters away was a wall of green vegetation, the tree-line. Once we entered the tree-line we were enveloped in a world of jungle green. The ground in our part of Vietnam was basically flat, and except for the occasional streams, open areas, roads and other manmade objects, the terrain was featureless; so we had to navigate using a technique called 'dead reckoning.'

Dead reckoning in the jungle is similar to navigation on the ocean. You use the compass to determine direction and instead of time and the stars to find your location, you measure the distance you have traveled from a known point designated on the map. The distance is measured by pace-count. Two men in the platoon were assigned the duty of keeping count. Every time their left foot hit the ground they would add one to their count. Their count would be added together, and divided by two for the average number of meters, a few inches more than a yard, that the patrol had moved from the last known point.

In preparing for this patrol the LT and the platoon sergeant had taken the information from the patrol order given by the company commander. This information included the grid coordinates of the various places that battalion wanted looked at. Joined by a forward observer or FO sergeant from the weapons platoon, but attached to us, the LT and the platoon sergeant plotted these points on a map of the area. Our maps were quite good. They used contour lines to define the terrain features and symbols for manmade objects such as roads, trails, and villages. The maps were 1:50,000 scale, which meant that one inch on the map represented 50,000 inches on the ground.

Sometimes we were given a Pictomap. These were made from aerial photographs using the information from older maps and combining it with what could be seen in the photo. They were 1:25,000 scale. Occasionally we would get a Pictomap with an area that was all white, marked 'cloud.'

It was always a special time when we went into a 'cloud' because we had no way of knowing what might be there. The guys would speculate on the various possibilities; everything from a village of American 'round eye' high school girls, to the headquarters of the Viet Cong, the infamous COSVN Headquarters that we were always trying to find.

After the points were plotted, the routes were determined. In the jungle, the route was usually a straight line between Point A and Point B, unless other factors dictated changes in direction, such as: suspected enemy concentrations, impassible or difficult terrain, or the need to investigate certain locations that were generally between point A and point B.

Once the routes were determined, a protractor was used to determine the azimuth or compass direction of each leg of the route. There is a difference between a magnetic azimuth from a compass and a grid azimuth on the map, but in Vietnam the difference was so small that there was no need for conversion, which was a good thing, because azimuth conversions were confusing and always caused problems with inexperienced soldiers.

Checkpoints along the way were established at distinguishable points on the map such as a point where you would cross a trail, road, or water obstacle such as a creek or stream. An open area, ruins, anything that could be seen on the ground and was on the map could be used as a checkpoint. Route planning incorporated these checkpoints so that navigation could be verified and the progress of the patrol could be communicated back to the company and battalion.

Route planning was complete when the patrol leader had calculated the distance in meters for every leg of the route. This, along with checkpoints, azimuths for each leg, and any other pertinent information would be recorded in their notebooks and a route overlay would be prepared and left with the company commander before the patrol departed.

It was critical that the patrol knew where they were at all times. The checkpoints would be given code words and could be used as target reference points for describing your location or for calling for fire support. If the patrol made contact with a superior enemy force, its only chance for survival would be the fire support that could be provided by the company's 81mm mortars, the 4.2-inch mortars at battalion, and the various types of artillery available from brigade and higher echelons.

Without an accurate understanding of the patrol's position on the map, it would be difficult if not impossible to bring fire on the enemy before the patrol was overrun. If you had an improper understanding of your location, it was also possible to bring fire on your own position as was depicted in the movie, 'Platoon,' which by the way, accurately depicted many aspects of infantry life.[203]

## How We Moved

In the jungle we moved on the azimuth maintained by the compass man, usually the squad leader. The point man carried a machete and cut a thin path through the vines and other vegetation that blocked our path. Many times the point man would try to go around a clump of brush rather than cut through it. If he went right around a clump, the next time he came to clump he would go to the left.

The squad leader would direct him and the platoon leader would consult his own compass from time to time to make sure that the lead element was on azimuth. To the left and right, about ten or more meters, from the column were the flankers, one or two men who stayed in sight of the main body, while watching for enemy ambushes.

This was my first daylight patrol in combat and I was pretty tense. The guy in front of me seemed to be very casual, gliding through the brush, avoiding the vines; and when he got snared, not fighting, but moving backwards to disentangle himself, and then continuing to move.

I was having my first encounters with the infamous, 'wait-a-minute' vines. This was a thin green vine covered with small, sharp thorns. When you got caught by one, the thorns would first snag your clothing. Feeling the tug you might be tempted to try and break though. If you did, you would soon feel the thorns stab into your skin. The harder you struggled in this way the more pain you felt. The 'wait-a-minute' vines would tear your clothes, tear your skin, and in the end you would have to cut yourself out of them before you could continue. They were one of the many environmental challenges we faced every time we entered the jungle.

There was an oft quoted book about jungle warfare called "The Jungle is Neutral." I always felt that the jungle was against me. You had to learn its ways, but it was never neutral, certainly, never your friend. Among the troublesome inhabitants were the leeches and ants in the trees and on the ground along with the snakes, scorpions, and bugs. By remaining outdoors most of the time we became accustomed to the heat, cold, rain, dust, and humidity, all the while moving through the seemingly aggressive vegetation. All these things made the jungle a bad place to be.[204]

The best thing to do when you sensed a 'wait a minute vine' was to stop, assess the situation and then carefully move whatever limb was in contact with the vine in the opposite direction from the contact. If the thorns got into your clothing, you would have to grasp the vine between the thumb and forefinger, in a space between the thorns, and gently pull the vine away from your clothing, in slow smooth motions.

At the same time you had to keep an eye on the person in front of you so you didn't break contact with the column. I was learning to function as an infantryman in the jungle by the OJT or 'on-the-job' training method: following the man in front of me while trying to slide my six-foot four-inch body through this vegetation, carrying a machine gun on my shoulder and carrying another fifty pounds in my ruck and on my belt. Carrying this load in the ninety-plus degree heat with high humidity was an ordeal on this first patrol, but as time went on, it would become the norm and fade into the background as I learned to focus on the main problem: finding and killing other men before they killed us.

As the file made its way toward our next checkpoint, we would halt for a moment every so often. The soldiers would go down on one knee and face in the opposite direction as the person in front of them. When the column started up again, we would stand up and continue to follow the person in front of us. You wanted to stay as far apart from the person in front of you as you could and still maintain visual contact with him so you could follow his trail and see his hand and arm signals.

The reason we stayed as far apart from each other as we could was to minimize the number of casualties from mines and booby-traps and to prevent ourselves from presenting a target rich environment to any hidden enemy controlling a command detonated explosive device such as a Chinese Claymore. Those things were much more powerful than our Claymores and could take out everyone in a large area if you were bunched up.

As I walked along, the sweat was pouring into my eyes. My shoulders ached from the unaccustomed weight and my thighs were struggling to lift me and the load I was carrying from a kneeling position to a standing position and back to a kneeling position every time the column stopped. The starting and stopping was kicking my ass.

About two hours after we entered the jungle, we stopped for a moment. I was so tired that instead of taking a knee, I just bent over to get a lower profile and waited. The sweat from my forehead streamed into my eyes bringing some tiny debris with it. I was wearing my contact lenses and the debris caused an enormous irritation in my right eye. As I attempted to blink the debris out, the contact lens fell out onto the jungle floor, disappearing in the leaves and decaying vegetation.

I took a knee now, energized by this disaster which had befallen me. These contacts had cost me a hundred or more dollars and they were the only pair I had. I put the gun on the ground beside me and bent over, on both knees now, and tried to find my contact. I kept alert to the sound of the guy in front of me but he was quiet. I wanted to find it before anyone knew what happened.

I was frantically searching the ground where I was sure it fell, when Roland noticed that he couldn't see me and walked up behind me. I was starting to panic because I couldn't find the lens. "What the blank are you doing," said Roland in a harsh whisper. "I lost my contact," I told him. "Well, hurry up and find it before the column moves out." "I'm trying to," I said as I began lifting up leaves to see if it was under one of them.

"Oh, oh, the column is moving," Roland said. "I've got to find my contact," I groaned. Roland made a quick decision and moved around me to catch the guy in front of me. When he did he told him to hold up. That guy told the person in front of him to stop and soon the whole column was stopped and taking a knee. I was still searching furiously when the platoon sergeant came walking up from the rear and asked me what I was doing. I told him and a disgusted smile came to his face.

The platoon leader, who was just ahead of me, showed up and he too made an inquiry as to why I was down on both knees picking up leaves and looking at them. Occasionally men did strange things in the jungle when they got too hot and the stress of knowing that other men might be waiting to kill them on the other side of the next tree, finally got to them. The platoon sergeant and the LT waited for another minute to see if I would find it so we could move out.

I was feeling the pressure as my situation was causing thirty other people to have to remain on one knee and wonder why we were stopped. Finally I heard the platoon sergeant advise the LT to form a long halt perimeter where everyone moved a meter off the trail on either side, and sat down. This left the trail clear for the leaders to move to the LT's position for a quick meeting.

While I was frantically trying to find the contact lens, the thought came to me about the contrast between us and the enemy. They were living in the jungle eating rice and we were worrying about our contact lens. The irony of the situation helped to calm me down. I wasn't that worried about the recriminations I was sure to receive from Roland and the members of the platoon. I was an experienced screw-up and was sure I would survive their ragging. Anyway, most of them thought it was pretty funny and took advantage of the break.

Finally, I found it! The LT called the squad leaders on the radio and told them to get ready to move. I licked all the debris from the lens and put it back on my eyeball. Roland was looking at me with his sly smile and shaking his head. We moved out again and after another couple of hours, we reached the farthest point of the patrol. The LT set up a platoon perimeter in an area that was mostly open, but with clumps of bushes, some trees and grass about two feet high. The platoon sergeant passed the word for us to eat.

Roland, Mac and I took turns eating while the others watched. About the time we finished eating, a bird began making a loud call nearby. The platoon sergeant alerted the perimeter to be at one hundred percent alert. Guys, who were taking a quick nap, were shaken awake by their buddy and everyone prepared for a fight. My squad leader was right behind our position with the LT and I heard him tell the LT that the battle of August 25th had started right after the same bird call. He was sure that the call was actually a VC signal, and we were about to be attacked. Everyone was tense.

Roland opened one of his ammo cans and prepared a hundred round belt for the machine gun. We were straining to hear the sound of VC crawling through the grass. It was like one of those old war movies where the sailors in a submarine are straining to hear the sound of a destroyer approaching to drop depth charges on them. The seconds ticked by on our analog watches; they turned into minutes.

Nobody moved, and nobody heard a sound until the bird called again, it was closer now. It called again, then there was the flapping of wings and it flew away. The LT was smiling and the platoon sergeant was wiping the sweat off his brow. We stayed in our positions for ten more minutes and then we were told to saddle-up. I stood up and adjusted my ruck straps, hoisted the gun to my shoulder and when the guy to my left started moving, I followed him and the patrol resumed.

### Almost Home

When the patrol started we were going in a west-north-westerly direction. Now we were going south. When we reached our southernmost checkpoint, we turned back to the east and headed back toward the Lai Khe perimeter, close to where we started from. Major Rodger's Ranger rules taught us that we should never use the same route twice and we all carried a copy of them in our wallets.

The vegetation was fairly thin for a good part of the way on the final leg of the patrol, but when we were within 500 meters of the tree-line by the river it got really thick again. The going was slow. It was about 1500 and the heat was oppressive. The humidity was high and everyone was hurting. This was the most dangerous time of a patrol. We were close to home and safety and we were exhausted and thirsty. Most of us had finished our water and were going on grit at this point. We stopped a lot because the point man was having trouble trying to cut through the thicket.

**Jose Garcia:** *"I was on point and the team leader told the flank man to move faster. The guy on flank made excuses so his team leader took over."*[205]

I was leaning on the butt plate and I heard the guy on my right as he moved through the brush, walking flank. Suddenly, everything was quiet. We stopped again. I lowered the gun from my shoulder and rested the muzzle on my boot. Then I heard a sound like an empty canteen being struck by something metal. I was trying to identify the sound, it sounded like... 'Ka-Blaaam!' There was a dull red flash to my right, where the flank man had been, followed immediately by a black cloud of smoke and a shower of dirt, then came the screaming. We had found a booby-trap the old fashioned way, again.

> **Jose Garcia:** *"The blast knocked me down. I was hit with mud and brush but no metal."*[206]

The flank man's squad leader came running through the brush with the medic right behind him. I picked up my gun to move toward the site of the explosion so I could provide security for them while they helped the wounded man who continued to scream.

As I moved to the right, I crossed a trail and saw the wounded man lying in the middle of it writhing and screaming, as the squad leader and Don (Doc) Gilliland, the medic, tried to determine the extent of his injuries. The smell of explosives hung heavily in the air and there was another smell that I wasn't able to identify until later: the smell of blood.

Roland and I set up a few meters past where the wounded man was being worked on. His screams of agony had turned into pleas. "Don't let me die in the jungle; don't leave me in the jungle!" He said this over and over again, yelling as loud as he could.

Doc patched him up and prepared a litter to carry him the rest of the way to the open area where we could bring in a 'Dust-Off,' a medical evacuation or MEDEVAC helicopter. The LT was already on the radio requesting it, and when the medic had prepared the wounded man for movement, four riflemen from his squad picked up the litter and carried him into the column. There were two men on point now, cutting a wider path for the litter. The wounded man was still hollering for us not to let him die in the jungle, but morphine was kicking in and his cries were getting quieter.

> **Jose Garcia:** *"A few days before, I told that team leader about church service. He cussed me and said he didn't believe in that stuff. Then he hit the booby-trap and he was calling on God when they carried him. Once we sent a new guy to walk point and he asked me to put my hand over his mouth if he got hit so he wouldn't scream."*[207]

## Dust-Off

After about fifteen minutes we broke through the tree-line, and moved into the open area. We stayed on the edge of the tree-line and formed a wide horse-shoe type defensive formation facing the jungle with the open end behind us. Soon we heard the beating of the Huey rotor blades against the afternoon sky.

The LT directed someone to throw smoke; the smoke grenade popped and began to hiss as the smoke billowed from the canister. I heard the LT verify purple smoke to the Dust-Off bird as the sound of it grew louder. One of the men stood out in the open area with a VS-17 panel spread out at his feet; holding his rifle over his head with both hands, he brought the helicopter in for a landing. The noise was extremely loud as it landed, blowing grass and leaves everywhere.

A medic carrying a stretcher ran from the helicopter to the wounded man and our medic. They lifted him onto the stretcher, carried him to the helicopter and slid the stretcher onto the floor of the bird. The Dust-Off medic climbed aboard and the helicopter lifted off the ground slightly, rotated 180 degrees, lowered its nose and flew down the gentile slope toward the river, gathering speed as it went. It began gaining altitude rapidly and turned toward the south in the direction of the 93d Evac Hospital in Long Binh.

The LT directed us to move toward the river and we crossed it the same way we did going out. We climbed up the rice paddy terraces until we came to the opening in the concertina wire and entered the perimeter. Moving in a single file, we followed the dirt road behind the bunkers toward the rubber trees and our company area. Several guys on the bunkers asked us who got hit and someone told them the wounded man's name. Nobody on the bunker line knew him because he was one of the replacements to come to the unit after the battle of August 25th.

The wounded man was a Spec-5 and had served in the Army four years as a helicopter mechanic. Vietnam was the helicopter war and the need for mechanics was intense. He had just arrived in country and was waiting at the 90th Replacement Battalion for his assignment to an aviation unit, but when several infantry units walked into the meat grinder on August 25th, the people in the replacement pool were swept up, handed a rifle and sent into combat as riflemen.

He had received basic training and attended the Brigade Jungle School where everyone was repeatedly told to stay off the trails. When he took a walk on that trail, his boot hit a thin string stretched across a trail that happened to be going the same way as he was, a short distance from the open area and safety. The string pulled the pin from a hand grenade that exploded at his feet.

## Home

After walking through the rubber trees, we came to our tents. We fell into a platoon formation and the platoon sergeant checked for accountability of men and equipment. The LT left and we were dismissed. I dumped my gun and the rest of my gear on my cot and joined the rush to the 'water buffalo' where we filled our canteens from one of the spouts. I drank two canteens while I stood there waiting in line for a chance to fill them again.

When we finished re-hydrating we went back to our tents and cleaned our weapons. Then we stripped off our clothes and walked up to the shower point with towels wrapped around our waists. There were the usual conversations, but the mood of the men was subdued. We were thinking about a helicopter mechanic who had fallen into the infantry and was now being pulled off a helicopter at the 93d Evac Hospital.

After chow, we went to the Ville, as usual. I got really drunk as usual and found myself sitting next to the sergeant who had led our sandbagged ambush patrol a few nights before. He had been behind the point man today when the flank man hit the booby-trap. The sergeant said that we had stopped because he had fallen to the ground, vomiting and shitting in his pants at the same time. The medics told him he had dysentery and had given him some APCs or all-purpose-capsules, the standard Army treatment for everything that ailed you in 1966.

He didn't act like he was still mad at me about the ambush patrol, so I told him that several seconds before the booby-trap exploded, I had heard a sound like a canteen being hit by something metal. "Do you think that if I had known what the sound was, I could have yelled to the guy and he would have been able to hit the ground before it went off?"

"Maybe," he said, "but probably not. That happened so fast that even if you had known what the sound was, and yelled at him, he wouldn't have known what to do; he was a mechanic and they don't move that fast." I did feel somewhat guilty though and I could still hear the wounded man screaming, "Don't let me die in the jungle!" I was relieved though, that the veteran sergeant didn't think that it was my fault. I was also worried that my contact lens incident would keep me on the platoon 'dumb ass' list, but he didn't even mention it.

The next morning, we had a formation. The company commander told us we would be going out on a road clearance operation on Highway 13, north of Lai Khe near Bau Bang. There were some gasps of surprise that rippled through the ranks. We would be out for a long time and to use the rest of the day to get ready.

He turned to walk away, and then, remembering something, he turned back and faced the company. He looked at us, the second platoon, for a moment and then spoke. "The man from second platoon who was wounded yesterday by a booby-trap," he paused for a moment, "died in the helicopter on the way to the hospital." When the company was dismissed, the platoon sergeant told the dead man's squad leader to gather all of his personal belongings and bring them to the supply sergeant. Then he dismissed us.

We walked back to the tents; everyone was quiet as they remembered the events of yesterday. A number of the guys gathered around Don Gilliland, the platoon medic, and asked him to describe the dead man's injuries. Don was saying that his injuries weren't that bad and he couldn't understand why he had died. "Must have been shock, hey doc?" said one of the guys. "Yeah, it could have been shock," said the medic, ending the discussion.

The guys went back to their tents but the medic's word hadn't comforted them. The Dust-Off helicopter medical evacuation plan was one of the comforting things that the Army liked to tell the troops. If you could hang on until the chopper got there, then you were going to make it.

There were a number of men in the platoon who had multiple scars, some of them long and jagged, all over their bodies. We could see them when we took showers. These were confirmation of the fact that as long as you got on the chopper alive you would stay alive. This was why the man's death hit everyone so hard; the doc said his wounds weren't that bad and we got him on the chopper pretty soon after he had been hit. What happened?

### Operation Tulsa

Operation Tulsa was a road clearance mission on Highway 13, Thunder Road. It was important to keep this highway open for civilian traffic and the military convoys that brought supplies to the various bases north of Lai Khe. Roland was looking down as we walked back to the tents so I asked him what was wrong. "We're going to Bau Bang" he said, "It's a bad place. There was a battle there in November of '65 and Charlie was bringing smoke on the dudes from the Cav." I asked him where it was and he said it was just a few klicks north of Lai Khe.

We went to the tent and got our gear ready for the next day. Then we had to go down and work on bunkers for a few hours that afternoon until the major work had been completed. One of the guys decided to cool off in a stream that ran through our bunker line and when he came out he had several leeches hanging on his body. They had sucked a lot of blood and were about three inches long.

When he saw one of them he freaked out and started hollering for someone to get them off him. One of the sergeants told him to stop moving and squirted some mosquito repellent on them and they fell off. Leeches were the most disgusting of the creatures that tormented us on a regular basis. We hated mosquitoes, cursed the red and black ants, and feared the snakes; but we loathed the leeches. Most of the places we encountered leeches were wet. I didn't know it then, but there were also places where they lived in the trees.

After noon chow we were released for the rest of the day. We were given six meals of C-rations for the operation. They issued them face down so we couldn't try and get our favorites. There were a number of different meals and they were categorized into B-1, B-2, and B-3 units. We took them back to our tents. Everyone was trading meals. Many of the items like peaches and pound cake were very popular and if you didn't get them in your own issue you probably weren't going to get them. Trading was basically done in two ways; you either traded the complete meal box or individual components.

Some of the main entrees were in small cans and some were in large. To open them, we each carried our own 'P-38' can opener on our dog-tag chain. Some genius invented it and it had been in use since at least WWII.

The large cans were usually a little meat mixed with a lot of starch. The small cans were usually pure meat except for 'Ham and Eggs Chopped,' one of my personal favorites after a long night of drinking beer. I had gotten on a 'Ham and Lima Beans' kick and tried to eat them for every meal. That wasn't hard to do because nobody else wanted them. That kick lasted for about a month and then one day I couldn't stand the thought of eating another bite of ham and lima beans. I never did eat another one and rather than eat one, would skip the meal.

When the trading was done, everyone took their cans and accessory packs out of the boxes and stored them. The cans went into boot socks which we tied onto our web gear harnesses or the top part of our rucksack frames. The candy and accessory pouches went into our butt-packs or rucksacks. When we were in the field and issued 'Cs,' some guys would heat them by burning the box with the can inside. Most of us used C4 plastic explosive to heat our meals.

C4 won't explode when you light it with a match, it burns. As long as you don't stomp on it (it will explode) while it's burning, you can use it to quickly heat a can of food. There was so much C4 being used to heat our chow that some months later, the Army stopped issuing it to the infantry and substituted an explosive called Flex-X, which wouldn't burn slow enough to cook on.

Roland and I went to the PX and later we went to the Ville. We knew we would be out in the field for a long time so we got good and drunk at the bar that was popular with the black soldiers. The black guys saw me there so often that they decided that I was a 'blue eyed' soul brother and always made me feel welcome. I really liked being in their company because of their quick wit and ways of describing events and situations that always made you laugh. Things were bad here but you had the choice of laughing or crying about it; my black brothers chose to have a good laugh.

### Bau Bang

The next morning we were awakened at 0430. We cleaned up, ate, and were ready to move by 0530. We moved by truck up to the airstrip that ran alongside Highway 13. There was a long line of Hueys sitting there silently waiting for something to do. We were broken down into groups of seven men; we sat on the ground near our helicopter and waited. I could see that the nose of each Huey had a piece of art and the words 'Robin Hoods' written above it. They were stationed at Lai Khe and I would get a lot of rides from them, but this time would be my first ride in a helicopter.

I looked at the passenger compartment and noticed that there were no seats. Behind the passenger compartment there were small seats facing out with M-60 Machine Guns on mounts pointing down. I wanted to inspect the entire aircraft, but activity was starting to pick up along the flight line.

Trucks were driving down the road and dropping off four people at each aircraft. The flight crews carried their helmet bags, maps and individual weapons. As soon as they found their aircraft they started their preflight activities. When they finished, the pilots took their seats and the crew-chief and the door gunner stood by.

Before long, I heard a noise like a whine that kept getting higher in pitch, then another and another. The large blades on top of the helicopters began to slowly turn. The small vertical blade in the back started to turn also. The troops on the side of the road started standing up. The noise from the helicopters grew and grew until you had to shout when you tried to talk to a person two feet away from you. Then the helicopters were all ready to go and we were signaled by the crew chief to get on board.

Roland pushed me and I moved toward the helicopter. Even though I saw how high the blades were above the ground, I was almost bent over double when I approached it. I put the machine gun on the floor and then crawled onto the floor of the helicopter. Everyone found a place to sit; I was in the middle with my back against the wall facing forward.

The noise was a very loud, high pitched whine coming from the engine and transmission right behind me. The floor was vibrating and the adrenaline was surging through my body. We sat there for what seemed like a very long time. I was holding my gun, muzzle down. The pilots' heads were covered by their flight helmets. They were flipping switches and turning knobs while they talked to each other on the intercom. The other guys were sitting there, occasionally yelling something to their neighbor. I could only hear a word every so often and had no idea what was being said.

Eventually though, one of the pilots looked back to check on us in the back and then the sound of the helicopter changed while at the same time it began to lift off the ground. I watched as we started moving slowly forward and rising off the ground at the same time. The nose dropped down and suddenly I could see the tail rotor of the helicopter in front of us, then a long line of helicopters, each one a little higher than us, slowly gaining speed and altitude. I looked to my left and saw that we were over the tops of the trees. Then I saw the Ville as we flew by. I was looking for our company area but it was behind us. We were flying over the rubber trees and following Hwy. 13 north. The rubber trees stopped and we flew over the bunker line of the unit next to us. We were on our way to Bau Bang.

It was a short flight and after 10 minutes we descended. The helicopters landed on the highway and Roland pulled my sleeve and yelled for me to follow him. We jumped to the ground and ran down the shoulder of the highway and out into an open area that ran alongside the road. The helicopters took off and headed back to Lai Khe.

We halted and got down facing the tree-line 100 meters away. I set up the gun and Roland lay to my left with the ammo. After a few minutes, the LT signaled the squad leaders to assemble and I followed the man in front of me. Our column linked up with rest of the company and we moved several hundred meters to a large open area on the west side of the highway.

The company formed part of a circular battalion perimeter called an RON or 'rest overnight.' This term would soon be changed to NDP or 'night defensive position,' because there was no 'rest' in a 1st Infantry Division field position. The second platoon had from 8 o'clock to 10 o'clock using the clock method of illustrating our part of the circle.

The LT came by with the weapons squad leader and moved us to where he thought was a likely avenue of approach. We were told to dig in and so we did. We had to dig a U shaped hole that was deep enough for us to stand in with our armpits level with surface of the ground. We were to fill enough sandbags to make a two foot wall on either side. The walls would support three engineer stakes about 6 feet long that would be laid across the top of the hole supported by the walls. Then we would fill more sandbags and place them on the engineer stakes for overhead cover. The rest of the guys, the riflemen, dug the DePuy Foxhole.

*And the salvation of the righteous is from Jehovah;*
*He is their stronghold in a time of distress.*
*Psalms 37:39*

# Chapter 8-October 1966: Part II

### The 1st Infantry Division Strategy

Somehow I had the impression that jungle warfare would be stealthy units moving silently through the dense vegetation. When they stopped for the night, they would lie on the ground, weapons ready, and then, before first light, they would be up and moving again as they sought their prey. We weren't exactly sneaking up on Charlie so what was our strategy?

One of the guys was talking to an artilleryman in the Ville who said that we were 'target acquisition.' In other words, we were being dangled out here like bait to tempt Charlie into attacking us while we were dug in; this was so that the Division could cover the battlefield with artillery shells and airstrikes which could kill large numbers of enemy soldiers quickly. It had been effective in the past, but Charlie learned quickly and picked his attacks carefully.

General DePuy had decided that the Big Red One would defeat the VC with firepower, killing them while holding down our own losses until they quit, a strategy called attrition. After the first Ia Drang battle in 1965 where the NVA attacked a U.S. perimeter and were decimated by supporting fires, the strategists like DePuy must have determined that this approach would be the right one.

Taking a page from Orde Wingate's 1944 Chindit operations in Burma, the helicopters would quickly put us in close proximity to suspected enemy locations, hoping to lure large VC units to attack. When they did, we would destroy them with artillery and airstrikes, producing a 10-to-1 kill ratio by body-count for a statistical victory. We would have to defend ourselves until the supporting fires could be brought to bear.

### The Enemy Strategy

The enemy strategy was similar to ours and these strategies would become a battle of the wills that would be played out in Hanoi and Washington D.C. The 9th VC Division, reinforced by the 101st NVA Regiment was our main adversary in the III Corps Tactical Zone. They had generally had their way in every fight with the South Vietnamese Army which was the main reason for the introduction of U.S. combat troops to the war.

From November of 1965, they had tasted some real pain every time they attacked a defensive position of the 1st Infantry Division. Their goal, I believe, was to overrun and annihilate a battalion sized element for propaganda purposes, and so far their tactics had not worked. Pressure from their own chain of command must have been at the root of these failed attempts. The 9th tried to ambush a Cav troop on Highway 13 in June of 66 and the 272 Regiment was hammered again.

The Phu Loi Battalion bloodied us on August 25th, but we wouldn't be assaulting dug-in enemy positions in the jungle again anytime soon, so they were casting around for a way to kill more Americans while we were trying to perfect

General DePuy's offensive defense. From an assault landing until we were dug in; we were most vulnerable when we were on the move. For them, being at the right place at the right time was very difficult and their goal wouldn't be achieved until October of 1967.

## The DePuy Fighting Position

General DePuy gave our perimeter defense a lot of thought and invented a fighting position for it that we called the 'DePuy Hole.' It was designed for two men. The hole itself was rectangular in shape, about six feet wide. It was two feet from front to back, and five feet deep. There was a small hole called a grenade sump in the center of the front wall at the bottom where a soldier could kick an enemy grenade if one fell in his hole.[208]

The dirt from the hole was piled in front making a parapet that protected the occupants from enemy fire. There were two firing ports, at forty-five degree angles, on either side of the parapet. The firing ports were to be the width of an entrenching tool blade inside at the firing point, double the width of the blade at the opening and covered with sandbags.

It took approximately seventy sandbags to complete the position. After finishing the firing ports, overhead cover was added, and finally, a sleeping area behind the hole. These positions were built to exacting standards. If General DePuy inspected them, which he did with terrifying frequency, and found a major deficiency, he would relieve the officer and bust the sergeant.

The soldiers in these holes couldn't see or fire directly to their front. Instead, they fired at the flanks of the enemy soldiers attacking the foxholes of their buddies to the left and right of their position. The attacking enemy soldiers were unable to fire into these positions because of the parapet so they were unable to suppress the defenders fire.

The position was camouflaged when completed and two Claymores were placed in front of each hole along with trip flares. The positions were placed ten to twenty meters apart and sometimes there would be a second line of foxholes behind the first. The interlocking fields of fire made it a difficult proposition for an attacking force; as a last resort, we had an FPL or final protective line in front of each platoon provided by one or both machine guns.

Machine guns were the VC's primary target, and they would try to locate them during their recon phase prior to an attack. If they couldn't, they would try and provoke our machine gunners to fire by probing the perimeter at night. The CO hammered in this point; our guns would remain silent until the signal was given, and when it was, the gunner would fire long bursts of grazing fire on a line that crossed the entire front of the platoon's positions, into the legs of the attacking wave of enemy fighters.

When the whole unit was dug-in with these holes, the VC would be hard pressed to overrun a position like this quickly, if at all. This defense allowed time for the artillery and airstrikes to be brought to bear and any attackers above ground were quickly neutralized.

If we stayed longer than one night, which was rare, in these positions, we would continue to improve our defense: phony positions would be made to deceive the enemy, Concertina wire would be laid and trenches would be dug.

## Resupply

While we were digging in, the resupply choppers would come with sandbags, engineer stakes, and a few D-handled shovels. I would try to get one because, it seemed like the digging went faster. They also brought hot chow in mermite cans and large trashcans of iced beer and soda.

There was mail, if you were lucky, and a sundry pack with plenty of cigarettes, toothpaste, stationary, razor blades and tropical chocolate candy bars. We were busy eating, digging, pulling guard, filling sandbags, and getting ready to send out listening posts and ambush patrols. Many of the guys smoked, including me. There would always be a contention for the filtered cigarettes; the white guys wanted the Marlboros and Winstons; and the black guys all wanted the Kools. That left a lot of Pall Malls, which became my brand.

## Digging In

It took at least four hours to complete a foxhole, usually longer, depending on the condition of the soil and the motivation of the men. We would start digging at 1800 and would finish by 2200 or later. Then we would pull one hour guard shifts on each hole until 0500, when we would have 100 percent 'Stand-To' with everyone standing in their position, ready to fight off an early morning enemy attack. This gave us an average of three hours of interrupted sleep each night.

## Filling In

If we were moving that day, after sunrise, we would empty our sandbags and fill in our holes. Choppers would come in and pick-up the mermite cans, sandbags, engineer stakes, and shovels and we would saddle up and begin the cycle again. This routine became my way of life until it was time to go home a year later. Combat air-assault, a walk in the woods, dig in each night or go on ambush, fill in the holes the next morning, and start all over again.

A few months later, our new battalion commander decreed that we would put a small mound of earth on top of the hole, so that when the soil settled, it would not leave a depression, thereby 'marring' the landscape of Vietnam. This early example of ecologically sound thinking would become very popular in the Army in the 1980's, but Lt. Col. Lazzell was ahead of his time. Whenever we dug in near a B-52 strike, where there were 100 craters, thirty feet wide and twenty feet deep, we wondered why our mound of earth was so important.

## Adjusting and Readjusting the Lines

While we were digging in that night, the company commander came down the bunker line inspecting our positions. He was looking at their placement and the fields of fire. We were about three feet down on our hole, when He called our platoon leader on the radio and the two of them met behind our hole.

Roland took an interest in this meeting and told me to take a break. He must have had a premonition, because he told me, "They're going to adjust the line." The discussion ended with the LT saying, "Yes, sir," to the CO, who moved on, while the LT called the platoon sergeant and the squad leaders for a meeting. Our squad leader came to our hole when it was over and told us to fill it in because we were going to adjust the line to be better tied-in with the next company. "Blankety blank, blank, blank," was heard on the perimeter as the men got the word. Roland smirked and said, "I told you so."

The line was moved about thirty meters forward of our old positions, and we started digging again. We had dug about two feet down when Roland said, "Oh no, here comes 'Big Six.'" "Who's that?" I asked him. "Big Six, the battalion commander," he said.

"What's the problem?" I asked, but he didn't say anything. 'Big Six' had stopped and was talking on the radio and soon our CO and the LT were running to his location. After their meeting, we got the word, fill in the holes, we're moving back twenty meters. The cursing and moaning reached a noise level that was tactically poor, even in the daytime, and potentially embarrassing for the CO. He needn't worry this time, because the battalion commander moved all the bunkers in the battalion and everyone was bitching.

## Road Clearance

The purpose of our being in Bau Bang was to conduct road clearance operations. This meant that there were going to be some large convoys moving material on Highway 13 to bases farther north. We had to clear the road before the convoys rolled, because they would be a tempting target for ambush; so the next morning we cleared the road.

This required us to get on-line and sweep both sides of the road out to the tree-line. We looked for enemy troops, and wires used for command detonated mines, currently known as improvised explosive devices (IEDs). After we swept our section of the road, we were placed in two or three man outposts in the tree-line on both sides of the road. These outposts would be about one hundred meters apart. It was considered a pretty good deal, because you got to sit in the shade for most of the day after the sweep.

Once the outposts were in place, the engineers would drive a bulldozer with a curved steel blade dragging in the ground behind it on each side of the road. This blade would cut any wires that were below the ground. When this was done, engineers with mine detectors would walk down the middle of the road sweeping for mines. This took a while because there was so much shrapnel on the road from the previous battle eleven months before. When the mine sweeping was completed, the convoys would roll down the road as fast as they could go.

Roland and I were placed in a position in the wood-line where we had some shade. We took turns watching while the other one slept or read. Roland read and I decided to find some other books to carry in my ruck for such times. I had one book, a paperback copy of Caesar's Commentaries, which during a particularly oppressive delusion of grandeur, I bought before I left the States. I had read that General Patton had carried one during WWII. It was a boring book for a high school dropout, and although I did finally finish it, I wasn't cut out for a scholarly study of classic military history.

The day passed slowly. A convoy would drive past our location every hour or so. I went down close to the road to watch one and all the trucks had "Orient

Express" written on their bumpers. Too bad they hadn't heard of the famous "Red Ball Express" which carried the supplies to the front in France in 1944. It would have been a much better name.

At about 1600 we were told to prepare to move back to the perimeter. We assembled in a file as the farthest elements moved toward the perimeter, picking up the outposts one by one. We entered the perimeter at 1700. We had no sooner put our things down, when the weapons squad leader told us we had ambush patrol that night.

**Ambush Patrol**

This began a one night on ambush, and one night on perimeter guard for the rest of the time I was a machine gunner. Each platoon was required to send out an ambush patrol every night. Because there were three rifle squads in a platoon, a rifle squad would go out every third night. The ambush patrol would always take a machine gun and there were only two in the platoon, so we had to do it every other night. They also took a medic, and since there was only one attached to our platoon, guess what? He was on ambush every night.

The ambush patrol that night was uneventful; we set up on the other side of Highway 13. There was an abandoned railway grade about 100 meters from the highway and we set up on the grade facing east. Our platoon medic got the night off because another medic wanted to go on an ambush. Nobody knew where he came from; he said he was a Special Forces medic and was on his second tour.
We put out our Claymores on the other side of the railroad grade and the medic put out two of his own. He set up right next to us and I watched him dig a little shelf into the railroad grade and put the Claymore firing devices or 'clackers' on the shelf with the safety wires removed.

When I asked him what he was doing he said that he would be able to fire his rifle and detonate a Claymore with his foot at the same time. Wow, a genuine Special Forces technique. I couldn't wait to try it myself, but Roland wasn't about to let me do that because he could envision my forgetting about them and stepping on one by accident.

Nothing happened that night. The medic was appalled by the fact that some of the men smoked in the ambush position. They would light up by holding their hands under their helmet and lighting the match. Then they would stick the cigarette under the helmet and light it. There was never any light seen but you could smell the smoke.

We didn't always smoke on ambush but that was the patrol leader's call. The rationale for smoking on this particular patrol was the fact that we were 200 meters from a battalion perimeter. The helicopters had been flying in and out all day. Civilian buses had passed by numerous times. Even Ray Charles could have seen that the Americans were set up in Bau Bang.

We returned to the perimeter before daylight, shaved, ate a C-ration and prepared to go back out on the road mission. Our squad leader told us we weren't going on road clearance; there were no convoys that day. Instead, our company would be moving to the next big open area to the north, on the same side of the highway. There we would form a company perimeter to operate from. Since another unit was taking our position, we didn't have to fill in our holes. We would however, have to dig new ones for our new perimeter.

We packed up and the company moved out in a column. We arrived at our new home at noon. The CO assigned the platoons to the perimeter defense. We had from 10 till 2, facing north. The three of us dug a new position and were done before dark. One of the squads went out on ambush and took the other gun crew. That night Roland, Mac and I took turns guarding our part of the line. There was some moon light, and the ground was open for hundreds of meters to our front. We pulled an hour on and two hours off until 0500. Then everyone was up on their weapons for 'stand to,' ready to fight.

### Another Patrol

That morning we were told we had a long, company sized patrol to the east of the highway. Roland went back to Lai Khe for some medical problem, so Mac and I were a two man gun crew. We moved out with the understanding that we would be extracted by helicopter that afternoon.

Our Company Commander, Captain Howley, was cooking up something, but he was playing his cards close to his chest. The men liked him. We knew he had a Special Forces background because he wore a Special Forces patch on his right shoulder. He wanted to close with and kill the enemy, but I'm sure he was a bit frustrated by the conventional methods we were using.

The Special Forces considered Vietnam their war. I never felt that Captain Howley looked down on us, but he did get hot when someone got lost on a patrol or screwed up a simple task. He was also a teacher. He took every opportunity that presented itself during our operations to make teaching points of our mistakes. Me and my ammo bearer were about to become famous in the company as one of his teaching points.

We stopped for chow at noon. Mac and I ate our 'Cs' and waited to move. Captain Howley came along the column and stopped by us. He bent down and picked up a round white paper from the C-rations that Mac had left lying on the ground. He turned to me and said, "I want to see both of you when we get back." He moved on without another word and left us in fear and trembling. Mac and I didn't have any time to speculate on our fate, because the column moved out.

### Ants

We were moving through scattered brush with some trees, but it was not really jungle. When we came to a branch that hadn't been cut, we would push through it, and then turn and let the next guy know to stop while you let it go; that is, if you observed trail courtesy. The guy in front of me had lost touch with his manners in the heat of the afternoon.

He let go of a branch that he had pushed past. I was turning to the rear to check on my ammo bearer and with perfect timing, turned back just in time to receive the full force of the branch on my helmet and the leaves in my face. The impact stung, but didn't cause any damage other than a few small scratches. I thanked him for the gesture and he immediately apologized. He took a step closer to me and looked at my face. Then he opened his mouth and said, "Ants."

At the same time I felt a strange sensation on my face, ears, neck, and inside the front of my fatigue shirt. It was like these areas were covered with crawling creatures, which, in fact, they were. The branch that hit me in the face was the home of a nest of red ants made of several large leaves the ants had somehow bound together. That nest had hit me square in the face and now, there were hundreds of red ants all over the upper half of my body, on my skin and in my clothes; they were not happy.

This called for immediate action, but I had to make up the drill on the spot. I stepped back away from the tree into a small open area behind me, put the machine gun down on the ground, and dropped my helmet. The man in front of me signaled up the column and called for a halt. I put my index fingers together across my throat, and resting my thumbs under my ears, slid my hands up, and wiped most of the ants off my face. By this time, they had begun their counter-attack and were stinging me in a hundred places.

I repeated my face wiping procedure and then dropped my ruck and pulled off my web gear. I wiped each arm where the ants had turned my sleeves bright red. My shirt and t-shirt came off next. By this time Mac was brushing ants off the back of my head and back. Fortunately for me, they hadn't been able to get to my crotch, because my belt was tight around my waist. Several people were helping me now, and together, we had defeated the main attack.

But now there were hundreds of ants scurrying around on the ground at our feet; climbing on our boots and reentering the fray. Mac picked up the gun and moved it out of the battle space. Then he moved my ruck and web gear. I grabbed my shirt and t-shirt and stepped away from the ants. Then I shook out my t-shirt, put it on and did the same with my fatigue shirt. I inspected my web gear and rucksack and put them on, picked up my gun and signaled I was ready to go. The main event had lasted about seven minutes, but I continued to find individual ants crawling on me for the rest of the day.

### The Phony Extraction

Late in the afternoon, we moved to the helicopter pick up zone (PZ), and prepared for extraction. The Captain called for a meeting with the platoon leaders. Five minutes later the word was passed that it would be a phony extraction. Shortly after that, the helicopters came in; we watched as they landed. There were several men lying on the floor of each aircraft; they sat up, and after a moment, the helicopters took off and flew toward the highway.

The LT called for a meeting of the squad leaders; we soon found out that we would be moving some distance away, to set up a platoon ambush on one of the trails we had seen earlier that day. We moved out and walked to a position several hundred meters from the trail. There we waited until dusk before moving to the trail and setting up our ambush.

The wait produced a big concern among the platoon. What were we going to eat for dinner? The guys hadn't connected the dots until now, but slowly, it become clear to everyone that there was not going to be a chow resupply; we had only brought enough C-rations for our noon meal. The bitching began but it was very softly whispered, because we didn't want to alert the enemy to our plight, and have him laugh at us after he ambushed us.

I thanked God that I had opted for the ruck when I came to the company. In it were my emergency rations. I had a can of ham slices, a particular delicacy, and a number of candy bars. The LT had given us a third man for our position, so I shared the ham slices with the other two. I gave them each a candy bar which they saved for later. When we moved out to the ambush site, the guns were placed on either end of the ambush, and there was a squad in the rear for security. We put out a number of Claymores and waited.

Suddenly, there was a bright light to our right where another platoon had set up. We found out later that a man was putting out a trip flare and set it off accidentally. We didn't use trip flares on ambush patrols, so I guess that the guy who screwed up had failed to grasp the commander's intent: a false helicopter extraction and a 'sneaky pete' SF ambush. The CO wasn't impressed with that platoon's skill in the woods. The night passed without incident and we blamed the trip flare incident for the lack of enemy contact.

### The Six-by-Six-by-Six

The fellow who caused the trip flare incident was a good scapegoat. On the other hand he had endangered the mission with his incompetence, just like I had done in the past. The army understands that men make mistakes. These are the meat for lessons learned; it is expected that we won't make the same mistake twice, and that the others will learn from our mistakes.

This was proven several days later, when we were told that we would be going out on another company day patrol and be back before dark. Before the LT could finish his briefing, the whole platoon broke ranks, ran to the ration issue point, and pushing aside the PFC who was responsible for issuing the rations, began grabbing cases of C's and bringing them back to the platoon area. The LT was laughing so hard at the spontaneous response of his men, that he didn't get angry at our violation of good order and discipline. We too had learned a lesson.

Another more painful teaching point emerged from the same mission. When we got back to the perimeter, Mac and I went to see the CO. When he saw us he got right to the point: "You don't leave paper wrappers on the trail for Charlie to find. You could have told him when we had been there by the condition of that paper. You carry everything out or bury it. I want you to bury this paper!"

He showed Mac the piece of round white paper he had picked up on the trail. "This paper will be buried in a six-by-six-by-six," he said. My ammo bearer was fairly new to the Army so he asked him, "What's that, sir?" The Captain didn't blink, "Six feet square and six feet deep," he said. "Murry, you will supervise. Come and get me when he finishes digging the hole. He'll dig another one if it's filled in before I inspect!"

I decided to make a counter proposal which I was sure he would accept. "Sir, why don't you let Mac and I go out tonight as a two man ambush patrol; that way the other guys can take a break and we will have paid for our sins?" He looked at me like the idiot that I was and said, "Don't fill it in until I inspect, got it?" Oh, yes sir, we got it all right, I thought, but it wouldn't be wise to say anything other than, "Yes sir!"

Six-by-six-by-six foot holes were definitely old army, but in the combat zone? Pruitt had to dig one in Hawaii in 'From Here to Eternity' but that was the pre-Pearl Harbor Army. The CO was definitely hard-corps. We spent much of the night messing with that hole. I decided to help Mac because it was a huge job. When we finished around 0200, Captain Howley was walking the line and happened to be there, when I determined we were done. He gave the hole a good look and pronounced it completed.[209]

Then he pulled the offending piece of paper from a notebook in his pocket, dropped it in the hole and said, "Bury it," as he walked off without looking back. We had a few visitors from other platoons while we were digging that hole, and our labors had the effect that the CO desired. No one in Alpha Company ever dropped paper on the trail again.

> **Dennis Howley:** *"To the best of my knowledge once you guys buried it and I had explained the why of leaving NOTHING behind for Charlie to the company, no one left anything again. The American GI is the best in world IF he understands and is kicked in butt to insure he complies.*[210]

**Incoming!**

We continued the road clearance operation. Mac and I were in our outpost when the faint noise of a distant explosion disturbed my concentration on nothing in particular. Then, an increasingly loud noise captured my full attention, until an errant 8-Inch artillery shell slammed into the ground a few hundred meters away with a very loud explosion.

A large black cloud formed around the area of the crater, as the dirt and dust returned to the earth. I looked toward the next outpost where one of the guys was standing, and watched as he took a LAW rocket and extended it to its firing configuration, before placing it on his shoulder and aiming it toward the road.

I looked in that direction but couldn't see anything. The faint noise of another distant explosion now had our complete attention and shouts of "incoming" sounded up and down the road. Then another shell came shrieking in and exploded. It just didn't make sense to me, being the first time I was under fire from such heavy ordinance. It was a lot bigger than the mortars that the VC used, and we hadn't been told that they had any heavy artillery in this area.

I looked back at the soldier with the LAW and he was still holding it, but he was squatting now and looking for the source like the rest of us. Another shell came blasting in and then it was quiet. The next thing we heard was a dust-off chopper coming in, and it took Jose Garcia to the 93d Evac Hospital for twenty-six stitches to his face.[211]

That evening when we got back to the perimeter, we found out that an 8-Inch artillery unit was shooting 180 degrees off its target line. How that could happen is hard to comprehend, but accidents were a major source of injuries and death in this war, and every other one I've studied since.

These kinds of accidents were the basis of a cottage industry that grew in the post-Vietnam army, until it dominated military planning. It was called Risk Management, and while reducing some accidents, artillery shells still get lost on occasion, and every soldier has to wear a bright yellow reflector belt to cross the street.[212]

## Ambush Patrol at Bau Bang
### (Another WTF Moment)

We returned to road clearing the next day, but there was no enemy action. Roland had come back, and that night was our turn for ambush. We went out right after dark, walked about 500 meters north of our perimeter, and set up. It wasn't really an ambush, more like a squad sized listening post. We set up in a V-shape, with the machine gun and me, Roland and Mac on the point of the 'V.'

We had just finished putting out our Claymores and settled in, when Roland told me that there was someone out in front of us. It was very dark and I couldn't see anything. He was acting very nervous and kept whispering, "Do you see them, do you see them?" The next thing I knew, he grabbed the Claymore firing device and yelling, "Claymore!" blew ours, 'Ka-boom!' A second later, several others blew their Claymores and the rest fired their rifles.

There was no incoming fire, so I continued to look to the front, and waited for the squad leader to give us an order. Then Roland jumped up, hollered "Retreat" and started running toward the perimeter, taking Mac with him. Several other members of the squad followed.

I had been told that if we did have to pull back in an engagement, it would be my job to act as rear guard, and hold off the enemy as the rest moved. I was on one knee, holding my machine gun and straining my eyes into the darkness, trying to see the enemy that Roland had seen.

I heard someone behind me and said, "Who's that?" "It's Mac," he said. This was another 'Mac', a rifleman. He was trying to find a piece of his equipment and had been left behind. Then I heard a thud very close to us and told him, "Grenade, get down!" as I threw myself on the ground about 5 feet away from him.

'WHAM!' The grenade went off between us. I was flat on the ground and the shrapnel went over me. He was still on his elbows and knees so the force of the explosion and shrapnel hit him in the side, moving him several feet. He hollered that he was hit, and I moved over to him.

It was very dark and I couldn't see the extent of his injuries, so I told him that he would be ok and to hang on. Holding my machine gun in my right hand and holding his hand with my left, I continued to look to the front for the enemy. When I still couldn't see or hear any enemy activity, I began to suspect that the grenade was one of ours.

After what seemed like several hours, I heard rustling behind me and a voice whispering, "Murry." It was Peter Clark. I whispered back, and he followed the sound of my voice and found us. The medic was with him and he began to work on Mac. Others showed up and formed a perimeter. One of the guys told me I had done a good job staying with Mac.

Eventually, Mac was put on a stretcher and we moved back to the perimeter. The CO questioned members of the squad, and was pissed off at what he found. He got the rest of us together, put us under the command of another sergeant, and sent us back out to finish the night. We went out a little further and passed the rest of the night without incident.

Roland and I never talked about what happened that night. It was really crazy, and I cannot imagine what he was thinking about when he did what he did. One of the other guys admitted throwing a grenade over his shoulder as he ran. He couldn't explain why he had done it, and his squad leader told him to never throw another grenade without looking to see where it was going.

We returned to Lai Khe after several more days of road clearance. Mac was dusted-off, and was gone for a month. When he returned he thanked me for staying with him. Because he was still recuperating from his wounds, he was assigned to work in company supply at the base camp.

Sometime later the Platoon Sergeant told me that I would have gotten a medal for my actions, but the CO would have had to court-martial some others on the patrol. So they forgot about the whole thing. Roland was given an in-country R+R, and a few days later, he was reassigned as the weapons squad leader.

### Demo Man

Our squad leader, Sergeant Reeves had been the unofficial 'Demo Man' for our company. I was always interested in his activities with explosives. He carried some C4 plastic explosive, blasting caps, and time fuse in his ruck, and when someone actually detected a booby-trap, or a unexploded grenade or mortar shell, he would blow it up.

I asked him questions, and after a while he taught me how to carefully crimp a blasting cap onto a length of fuse with my teeth. Then he told me to place the C4 next to the object to be destroyed and alert the others by calling, 'Fire in the hole,' three times before lighting the fuse.

I paid close attention, and continued to show interest so one day he let me crimp a blasting cap onto a fuse. This could be dangerous if you were to forcefully push the fuse too far into the blasting cap. Crimping with your teeth presented little danger, as long as you did the crimp at the tip of the open end of the cap; bite down near the other end, and you would blow your jaw off.

### The 'New' Demo Man

We were out on a patrol near a village. The word had been put out that if we were shot at, we were not allowed to return fire into a village. The VC would try to provoke us to shoot into villages that were resisting their efforts to control them, thereby helping the villagers to see that we were not their friends. These rules of engagement were part of the hearts and minds program that was mentioned now and then. Now we were moving down an overgrown road near one of these villages, when there was an explosion up at the front of the platoon. We put out security and waited.

After about ten minutes, the medic came, leading the LT and Sergeant Reeves. They both had bandages on their faces, and the LT had one covering one of his eyes. They walked past us to an open area and were dusted off. The platoon sergeant took over and directed us to get on line and move toward the village.

There were several Vietnamese working in the rice paddies between us and the village. He made them walk in front of us, in case there were more booby-traps. We looked around the village but didn't find anything, so eventually we moved on. Sergeant Reeve's ruck was still with the medics. I took his explosives and put them in my ruck; that's how I became a 'demo man.'

## 'New' Tactics, Techniques, and Procedures

During a short rest in Lai Khe, we were given a class on some new movement techniques to be used when looking for the enemy. The basic concepts were called 'Overwatch' and 'Cloverleafing.' General DePuy claimed credit for devising these infantry tactics. 'Overwatch' came to him after watching tank training.

He taught two overwatch techniques: 'Traveling Overwatch and Bounding Overwatch.' Traveling Overwatch was used when moving squads or platoons in areas he described as, 'relatively' safe. The lead element, a fire team or a squad, advances, with the next element trailing and prepared to support the lead element by maneuvering left or right to flank the enemy.

Bounding Overwatch was to be used when contact was imminent. One element took up a position from which they could provide immediate fire support to the moving element, for example, on a hill with a view of both the friendly element and where the enemy was likely to be found. This could have had an application when we were skirting an open area, but I don't remember using it.[213] The training for these new techniques took place in the rubber trees near our company area, where it was possible to see some distance when you were standing up. There were, however, problems with these techniques.

Usually the terrain (no hills), and the vegetation (no long-distance visibility), and the incessant urging of someone in a helicopter overhead to move faster, made this movement technique useless for our purposes. We were usually in thick jungle, where it was everything you could do just to keep a decent interval and maintain visual contact with the man in front of you. This was done so as not to present a lucrative target to a VC with a claymore, and so as not to become separated thereby causing a delay as the two elements tried to get reconnected.

Breaks in contact usually occurred when we went over an obstacle like a fallen tree. Once the point man got over it, he would move at the normal pace, and the man behind him would have to hustle to keep up, so as to not lose sight of the point man or his trail. When a machine gunner or radio operator crossed the obstacle, they would sometimes take longer to get the additional weight and bulk over, and contact could be broken.

In order to increase the search area, we were taught the other technique which was called 'Cloverleafing.' Cloverleafing was directed in order to put eyes on more area as we searched for the VC. A single file, with flank security out, could search up to a 40 meter wide path through the jungle area fairly well; a column of two files could search a somewhat larger path. When moving through an area, the platoon, company, or battalion column would stop, and the fire team on point would make a short patrol to the front. At the same time, a fire team from each platoon would move several hundred meters in a kind of (in theory) cloverleaf shaped route from both flanks of the column. They would return after 'searching' along the way for any sign of the VC. General Alexander Haig gave credit to DePuy for 'inventing the cloverleaf,' but Dennis Howley begs to differ: [214]

**Dennis Howley:** *"CLOVER LEAF not from Gen DePuy – a recon road clear technique we used in 82nd, when I was a recon platoon leader, to move, search and move…without losing time…at point called by me, the lead squad went right 100 yards, 2nd squad in line went left 100 yards, 3rd squad* *continued original direction....Weapons squad stopped at depart point as lead returned and became 2nd in line and 2nd became 3rd in line—we moved...repeat...never stop moving and searching."*[215]

## On Point

Walking point was always dangerous, while at the same time prestigious to those who imagined themselves special. "When you walk point, everyone else is 'rear echelon," my platoon sergeant in Germany used to say. He fought with the 2d Infantry Division in Korea, so I guess he knew what he was talking about. When I walked point in Vietnam, I understood that if I encountered the enemy, it would depend on who saw or who heard who first. Since we usually hacked a trail through the bush, it was a moot-point.

Later, when I walked point, while I did look for the enemy, I watched more carefully for booby-trap wires, while moving as fast as I could, being prodded by the compass man, usually a sergeant, who was being prodded by a lieutenant, who was being prodded by a Captain, who was being prodded by an LTC, usually in a helicopter above us, where, in the cool air at 1500 feet, he could wonder what was taking so long down there. A skillful enemy would let the point element pass by and nail the larger element that followed, but not everyone in the bush, on either side, was skillful.

It took a lot of coordination just to keep the unit together when moving through the jungle. So I'm afraid that General DePuy's movement techniques were not very useful to tired, sweaty men who hoped, that by breaking brush rather than walking on trails, the enemy would be someplace else.

Years later, when I trained the recon teams of the Long Range Surveillance units, we used the wedge formation, which would fold into a single file when in thick brush, and expand back to a wedge formation in open areas. Of course we usually only moved through open areas at night, and no one was shooting at us.

As for cloverleafing in Vietnam, we used this often, but I don't remember any big discoveries. I do remember waiting for some lost fire team to return, providing us with a break, while they figured out their back azimuth.

## Wake Up Call

We were back in Lai Khe for a short break, and one night the company CP didn't receive the regular hourly SITREP from an ambush patrol. I was in the commo bunker on other business, and heard the RTO saying "Alpha Three-Three, this is Alpha Six Romeo, if your situation is negative, break squelch twice." The RTO repeated this litany every couple of minutes. Captain Howley was advised that we had lost contact with the patrol, and shortly after, he showed up at the commo bunker.

The RTO told him that we hadn't been able to contact the ambush patrol for their SITREP and he said, "They're asleep, give me the handset." He opened up the map he was carrying. The RTO stepped away from the table, gave the captain his chair, and laid the handset on the table. The CO pulled out his note book, consulted it, and looked at the map. He wrote something in his notebook. I looked at the RTO and mouthed the words, "What the blank, over." He shrugged his shoulders.

The CO picked up the handset, squeezed the push to talk button, and called the mortar section. "Alpha Four-One this is Alpha Six, fire mission, over." "This is Alpha Four-One," they replied, "send your mission, over." "One round HE," he said and gave them the grid coordinates of the target. The mortar crew was about fifty meters away and we could hear them preparing to fire. 'Toook,' the mortar round was on its way. We stood there silently waiting. Eventually we heard the faint sound of an explosion. "Now try them," said the CO.

"Alpha Three-Three, this is Alpha Six Romeo, if your situation is negative, break squelch twice." As soon as the RTO released the transmit button, we heard the rushing noise for a second, and then the squelch broke twice. "That got their attention," said the CO, as he picked up his notebook and map, "Let me know if you have any more problems; I'm going to bed."

After he left, we checked the grid coordinates that he had given to the mortar platoon. They were about two hundred meters past the ambush patrol's designated position, and one hundred meters to the left of their line of travel. I guess he reasoned that they would have least likely gone past their planned location. More likely, they stopped short of where they were supposed to be, either by design or because we tend to take smaller steps in the dark, thereby not traveling as far as our pace count tells us. "The CO don't screw around, do he?" said one of the other commo guys who had been sleeping on a cot. "No he don't" said the RTO, and we went on about our business.

### The New Machine Gunner

When Jose Garcia returned from the hospital, he was told to take the other machine gun. Donnie Gunby was assigned as his assistant gunner. Other men came and went, but after settling their differences, the two of them gradually formed a bond. Jose, a warrior from the barrio of Houston, Texas, and Donnie, the redneck country boy from the red clay of Georgia, had decidedly different views on most subjects. But they realized that if they were to have a chance of getting out of Vietnam alive, it would be because they were a team.

*For I also am a man under authority, having soldiers under me.*
*And I say to this one, Go, and he goes; and to another,*
*Come, and he comes...*
*Matthew 8:9*

# Chapter 9-November 1966

### Bait

At the beginning of November we were sent out to a Special Forces camp, for some unspoken reason, where we dug in.

> **Dennis Howley:** *"We were put next to an SF camp as bait, but Charlie was well aware of that and did not bite. During one incident a machine gunner got spooked and fired. I "corrected" the team and explained that Charlie would recon before an attack to locate and eliminate MG positions; 'don't fire unless you have target or one day you'll eat a grenade!' No more incidents. Later on while in a logger, in our fox holes, A-1-16 took something like 10 maybe 20 grenades into our position by Charlie who had crept past our forward OP. No one fired. Charlie was probably scared themselves and moved to the next company where they were rewarded by a fire power demonstration. I was never so proud of the troops as then; they learned, they understood, they did!!!"*[216]

### Hail and Farewell

After a few days we went back to Lai Khe. We had been out for twenty days and everyone was in their tents, packing their gear and preparing to move into the wooden huts that had been built for us to use as barracks. As we were moving, the word was passed that Captain Howley had emergency leave and wouldn't be coming back. The Army was sure to send him back to Special Forces duty. We were shocked. Most of us had come to like him and we were secretly proud that we had a 'Sneaky Pete' for a CO.

He had taken a shattered company and rebuilt it. Because of his training, we had become a much better infantry company then we were when I arrived. I was hoping that we would have more opportunities for him to use the special tricks, like the phony extraction, that we were sure every Special Forces soldier possessed. The fact that he was going home on emergency leave now, dealt a death blow to my fantasy of his turning the Alpha Rangers into Howley's Howling Commandos, an elite strike force available for every kind of secret special mission.

The officers and senior NCOs decided that we would have a going away party for him that night, because he would be flying to Division tomorrow and then back to the world. The Mess Sergeant was out making the rounds with a jeep and trailer, scrounging, trading, and stealing the things we needed for a barbecue. We also needed a lot of beer and he had a good sum of money from the collection that had been made in all the platoons. Each platoon was directed to prepare some entertainment for the party: some songs, a skit, whatever the talented members of each platoon could come up with.

There were only a few hours to prepare, and we still had to move all our things from the tents to the huts. The whole company worked with a will that afternoon because we all wanted to give the Captain a good send-off. While taking a break, the men of second platoon sat down for a short while on the ground in one of our new huts, and discussed what entertainment our platoon could provide. Some of the brothers wanted to sing some Mo-Town hits, but we could hear some of the guys in 1st Platoon rehearsing several of the songs that we had considered. "Why don't we do a skit?" someone suggested. "Yeah, a skit," some of the other guys chimed in. Ok, we would do a skit. Everyone was throwing in ideas; ideas that were thrown out as soon as they were spoken. Then one of the guys said, "Why don't we do a skit about when we were digging in up in Bau Bang, and they kept making us fill in our holes and move our positions back and forth?"

Everyone was delighted with this idea, and no one could talk as everyone was telling everyone else how the skit should go. The talking turned to shouting as everyone tried to get their great ideas incorporated into the skit. There was laughter and shouting; we probably sounded like the bird exhibit at a zoo, featuring a bunch of angry magpies.

Finally, the platoon sergeant had enough. "At ease," he shouted. Some of the other NCOs shouted the same thing. We all shut up and listened as the platoon sergeant turned chaos into order. He assigned the man who had the original idea to work with several other guys that he designated to come up with the basic skit. The rest of us were to continue moving our belongings from the tents to the huts. We also had to take down the tents and we had to work fast, he told us. "I want everybody back here at 1700; we will learn our parts and do a rehearsal before the party."

Roger that; we all moved out on our missions. As we moved our cots and gear from the tents, guys started finding things that they had lost in the dirt under their cots. When we took down the tents, many more items were found. One guy found a Zippo lighter with the name of one of the KIA's from August 25th. The old timers stopped for a minute, remembering their fallen comrade, before discussing what to do with the lighter. They decided to turn it in to the first sergeant, so he could send it home to the guy's family.

### Combat Losses

One of the least pleasant tasks that an infantryman has to perform is gathering his dead buddy's personal belongings and preparing them to be shipped back to the man's family. What do you send home, what do you keep, and what do you get rid of? Some guys made arrangements with their buddies regarding the distribution of some or all of their personal possessions in the event of their death. Of course, secretly, most of us didn't really expect to die, so these were verbal contracts, usually with no witnesses. The rule was: all the dead man's personal possessions and his equipment were turned into supply as soon as possible after a man was killed.

Nobody was going to send home somebody's skin mags and books, if the dead man had any. Those were redistributed in his squad. Cheap souvenirs like copulating elephants carved out of wood and sold to the GI's on R+R in Thailand were also kept in country. Occasionally, a person's belongings, dead or alive, were stolen while we were out on operations. Some of the guys bought expensive reel to reel tape recorders with speakers, because they were much less expensive in Hong Kong or other R+R destinations around the Far East.

Once, the company commander received an inquiry from Division regarding a letter from the parents of a dead soldier. When the family received his personal belongings, the stereo system that their son was so proud of, the one that he had described in precise detail, was not among his things. Whether the family wanted that stereo because it was such a good one, or because of the sentimental value they attached to it, something that their son had really liked in the last days of his life, I'll never know.

What I do know, is that the problem rolled down hill into the CO's hands and he was forced to order a search of the company area, in a futile effort to recover the missing property which was never found. There was a rumor going around that one of the guys who had gone home recently had stolen the stereo and sold it to someone in another unit. Then he took the money down to the Ville and spent it on women and whiskey. He had been in the rear, recovering from a circumcision surgery, while we were in the field; when they took the stitches out, I guess he had to see if everything still worked.

I don't know what the CO eventually wrote to the parents of the dead man and the investigating officer at Division. None of us would have been disappointed with his position as the ethical standard bearer of our company, if he had chosen to declare it a combat loss. We reasoned that everything bad that happened over here fell into that category. After all, if we weren't here in combat then there wouldn't be any combat losses. The dead man was a combat loss, and since we couldn't come up with his stuff, why not make his missing stuff part of the loss.

If his parents were hoping to get a piece of sentimentality to remember their son by, surely they would take comfort in the fact that their son had died in a place where nothing was safe as he stood with his companions, the young men of his generation, who were sacrificing themselves to preserve the freedom of our great nation, and that of the people of South Vietnam. How would they feel about their son's death if they were told that, well, what actually happened to Johnny's stereo was, well, actually, Johnny's buddies stole it, while Johnny was out in the field getting killed? They sold it, and used the money to buy some beer and female companionship down at the Ville; sorry about that.

## The Skit

When we completed the moving tasks, we reassembled in our new hut and rehearsed our assignments for the skit. The whole platoon would participate, a regular Cecil B. DeMille Production. We broke up into two man teams, and every second man had his entrenching tool. When it was our turn, we would spread out on the dirt road that ran through the company area and scratch at the dirt, pretending to dig foxholes. The guys with speaking roles would do the talking, and we would follow their lead. They practiced their lines and ran through them for us so we would know what was going on. The skit seemed kind of goofy, but I was glad we had something for the Captain's send-off.

There was a Company formation before dinner, and everyone was invited to have a beer or two while we waited our turn to get a barbecued steak. We had a few non-drinkers and they drank soda pop. Everyone was smoking and joking and the Captain was passing through the crowd talking with the men. The guys were laughing and joking with him and making suggestions about what his first act would be when he got back to his wife. It was a special time; one of those times that old soldiers like me like to remember, because these times were the pleasant part of the ancient tradition of soldiering. Without times like these, war would be unbearable.

Most of us were young, and we would never be anymore engaged with our life's situations than we were right then. Everyone seemed smarter, funnier, more handsome, and generally a much more impressive person, than they would ever appear to be, when and if they got back to the world.

Here we could say what we meant and mean what we said; the only political correctness requirement was that we wouldn't publicly throw in with Uncle Ho and the NLF. We could make recommendations and object to orders we thought were stupid, but which of course had to be obeyed in the end, or we wouldn't be an army. The skit we planned to do would be a great illustration of this camaraderie in action.

The 1st Platoon entertained us with their songs. They put together a singing group of brothers with a few blue-eyed souls to help. These guys sang together whenever we were in the rear, and so it wasn't hard for them to sing songs like "Tracks of my tears", a Smokey Robinson and the Miracles hit, just like in the movie 'Platoon,' and "Baby, oh Baby, I love to hear you call me baby," by Carla Thomas. Everyone joined in on the choruses. We weren't smoking dope in a bunker; we were drinking beer together and having fun.

It was our turn next. Peter Clark had been chosen to play our Captain. He told one of the other guys playing the LT, to have us dig in on a line that he drew in the street. We all lined up on that line and pantomimed digging and filling sandbags. One of the guys said, "Well, we're almost done."

Peter, playing the Captain, walked up and looked down the line, "Lieutenant, I told you to have the men tie in with the other platoon, move these holes two feet forward." "Yes sir, three bags full sir," said the man playing the LT, as the rest of us threw down our entrenching tools, cursing and shouting things, like 'Blankety blank, and blankety blank Special Forces don't know blank,' etc. The whole Company, including the Captain, was laughing. The captain's face was slightly red, but he seemed to think it was funny. We went through the same routine several times, and finally ended it with Clark at the bottom of a mass pile-on. The Third platoon and Weapons gave us their entertainment, and by now we were all pretty drunk.

Finally, the first sergeant thanked him for his leadership, especially during the day's right after August 25th. The Captain gave us a short speech and told us that he would be wearing the Big Red One patch on his right shoulder when he went back to Ft Bragg and the Special Forces. The guys gave him a big hand, hooting, and hollering. We didn't say hooah in those days, we said things like, 'Right on! Blanking-A and, Tell it like it is!'

Everyone was smiling, laughing, and having fun. The morale was the highest I'd seen it since I joined the Company two months before. It was the first and last time we would have a company party. Things had been busy for the last two months, but we hadn't seen nothin yet. And we sure wouldn't see much of our Company area in the months to come.

### Change of Command

Captain Howley left, and Captain Bill Williamson took over. Tall and slim, with a Ranger tab on his shoulder, Airborne wings and a Pathfinder Badge on his chest, he came to us from battalion headquarters where he had been the S4 (Supply and Logistics) officer. Before coming to Vietnam, he had served as a rifle and recon platoon leader with the 82d Airborne Division. He also did a tour in Iran where he assisted in the forming of the Iranian Special Forces.

The rumor mill had it that he was a West Pointer. He didn't make any sudden changes in the unit, and we didn't see that much of him as he familiarized himself with his new command.

The company commander position was and is a milestone in an officer's career. It is also a milestone in the unit. The 'old man' sets the tone in the unit, and we were waiting to see what that tone might be. There is more opportunity for a company commander to make big changes in peacetime than there is in wartime. Unless there is a glaring problem, the unit is too busy keeping up with the demands of the higher headquarters for the CO to do much more than lead his company and take us where he is told to go.

We didn't stay in Lai Khe long. The day after the party, we were down on the airstrip early in the morning, getting on the choppers of the Robin Hood Aerial Transportation system, and flying into Operation Attleboro. With Attleboro, the OPTEMPO began to increase to the point where we only went back to Lai Khe for a day every few months. A Third Brigade helicopter crashed, killing the Brigade Sergeant Major. Our first sergeant was chosen to replace him, and we got a new first sergeant. He was originally from the Philippines and seemed a little aloof.

### Operation Attleboro

Operation Attleboro was the first large multi-division operation of the Vietnam War. The 199th Light Infantry Brigade and several battalions of the 25th Infantry Division were in heavy contact with a large enemy force. A 5th Special Forces Group Mobile Strike, or Mike Force, unit had been overrun. Units from the 1st Infantry Division were called in to help out, and General DePuy was directed to take command of the operation. The operation was called Battle Creek, initially, and then changed to Attleboro.

We were flown into Dau Tieng, designated the 2d Brigade's ready reaction force, and assigned to guard part of the perimeter. Dau Tieng was part of the Michelin Rubber Plantation, and there was a large airfield. There had been a fight there just before we arrived, and I saw an M-113 Armored Personnel Carrier, just like the one I used to ride around in when I was in Germany. It had been hit by a rocket propelled grenade (RPG) or a recoilless rifle and burned after the fuel exploded. There was a dead man's body in the back, and we helped to get it out. The body only weighed about ten pounds.[217]

## The VC Air Force

After a few days of guarding the perimeter, we moved out on a battalion search and destroy mission. After leaving the perimeter, we walked through the rubber trees north from Dau Tieng. Then we moved into the bush. When it was noon, we stopped and set up for a long halt, and began to open our C-rations.

There had been a lot of unusual airplane activity above us that morning. Instead of the usual jet-engine sound, it was the sound of propellers. They were Vietnamese A-1 Skyraiders, a single engine, propeller driven fighter-bomber that was used earlier in Korea, and now in Vietnam. I could hear them flying around and earlier I had seen one through a break in the jungle canopy above us.

I was half-way through my can of Spaghetti and Meatballs, when I heard a faint whistling noise in the air above coming towards us. Before I could process the implications of the unfamiliar sound; 'Boom!' a bomb exploded close by and suddenly we were in a world of dirt. My open mouth, my half-empty can, the front and back of my neck, and my machine gun were full of moist black dirt.

"Throw smoke, throw smoke!" came shouts throughout the column. Everyone who had smoke grenades threw them and we all waited for the next bomb, now that they had our exact location. The plane continued to circle our location.

I was spitting the dirt out of my mouth and listening for another bomb coming our way. Either it was a mistake or the pilot was out of bombs. The plane flew away and we cleaned up as best we could. Miraculously, no one was injured; and if anyone had to change his underpants, he did it at the next halt.

## The Hills

We continued north into some of the only hills in that part of III Corps. At a certain point, we were actually rock climbing to get to the top. It was hot; it was always hot, except for when the sun set right after a heavy rain; then it was cold.

The men on my gun crew were smoked, carrying all their gear plus 400 rounds of 7.62 ball ammunition linked with tracer. I had to encourage, exhort, and curse them up that hill. I was carrying a pretty good load myself, with the gun and extra demo, but for some reason, it seemed to me, that whatever you were doing was easier when you were in charge.

We finally made it to the top and formed a perimeter. My gun's position was about 10 meters from the edge of the hill we were on. The ground dropped away quickly; it was hard to imagine anyone assaulting up a hill that was so steep. They would have to pull themselves up by grabbing the trees that were growing on the side. A sergeant from the squad I was supporting told me that if we were attacked, to move my gun to the edge of the drop off.

The ground was solid rock, so there was no way we could dig in. We gathered up rocks to build a small parapet in front of the gun and walls on the side. My assistant gunner was sleeping, the ammo bearer was on watch, and I was working, when our new CO came along to check our positions.

I had taken my helmet off to work, and he told me to put it on. That made me angry, but I did. Then I walked over to the sleeping man and kicked his feet. He jerked up to a sitting position and I told him to put his helmet on. The CO was standing there watching this, but he didn't say anything. Then he moved on. We remained in those hills for several days and then returned to Dau Tieng.

### More Combat Losses

We guarded part of the perimeter again and generally had a quiet time. There wasn't a beer club for us, but there was beer. The Air Force was selling it by the pallet down on the airstrip. A C-123 or C-130 would fly in and sell the beer right off the tailgate. Our company NCO's took up a collection and we got two pallets. You could buy ice nearby, and so we were able to sit around the company area in the rubber trees in the evening and get drunk.

There was an officer's club somewhere on the other side of the airfield. One evening, two of our intrepid lieutenants took a jeep and drove to the club. When the club closed it was dark and there was a blackout on the airfield, so they drove back as carefully as they could, being drunk, and all.

They found a large crater in the ground and managed to drive their jeep into it. Neither one of them was hurt, but now, they had a problem: how to get the jeep out of the hole? It was nose down, almost straight up and down. As they stood there considering solutions to their dilemma, a small fire started under the hood. I guess some gas spilled out of the fuel system and caught fire on the exhaust. This was a bigger problem, and the lieutenants were trying to muster some solution from their collective training and experiences as first lieutenants.

The fire grew larger, and now, they felt that they should seek help because the situation was getting out of their control. They turned back across the airfield, and began walking along the side, looking for someone who could help them put out the fire and pull their jeep out of the ditch, before their superiors found out about their misdemeanors.

Meanwhile, the fire continued to grow. Eventually, it reached the back seat area of the jeep and the case of hand grenades that was stored there. The grenades exploded as one, and completely destroyed the jeep. It all started out as a fun trip to the O club, and now, the lieutenants were looking at making some serious cash donations every month until they paid for the jeep.

There was some talk that they were going to have to pay for it, but others said that it would be a combat loss. I too destroyed some government property while drunk at the airfield; I stepped on my glasses and broke them.

### Saigon

When we got back to Lai Khe, I was talking to one of the old timers in the platoon, and asked him if we ever got to go to Saigon. He laughed, and said that the only way to go anywhere beside the bush was R+R, and medical appointments. "What kind of medical appointments?" I asked him. He looked at my face and said, "If you break your glasses, you can go to Saigon for another pair. How many pairs do you have?" Not wanting to burden him with the truth, I lied and said, "None."

I went to my squad leader and said that I had to get a pair of glasses because my old pair was broken. He sent me to the battalion sick call. Battalion didn't even blink, and told me to go to a place in Saigon where there was an eye doctor and the machine to figure out lens prescriptions.

I went down to the helipad and signed up for a flight to Saigon. There were none going then, but there was one the next morning and I was told to be back at 0700. I went back to the company area; that night I joined the rest of the platoon at the Ville. The squad leader, who I'd angered on the sandbagged ambush patrol, came up to me and said he had heard I was going to Saigon in the morning. When I confirmed this, he said that he and another member of the platoon were also going.

I asked what I should take and he advised me to take my .45 and a smoke grenade, along with my shaving kit. I had been told that no weapons were to be carried in Saigon and I told him. He looked at me like I was stupid, so I decided I would take the pistol and smoke grenade after all. I did ask him why I needed a smoke grenade. "You throw the smoke grenade after you shoot someone, a robber or VC, to break contact and discourage pursuit by the cops," he said.

The next morning the three of us went down to the chopper pad and caught a ride to Tan Son Nhut Airport in Saigon. We took a taxi to a small hotel and agreed to meet there that night. I found a taxi driver who knew the address of the eye doctor and he took me there. The eye exam took until mid-afternoon, and when I returned to the hotel, the clerk told me that my friends were in the bar next door.

The sergeant and the other man were sitting at a table in the bar, but it was so dark it took a while for me to find them. That task was made more difficult by the two females sitting on their laps, making them appear to have two heads, in the smoky room. They were buying the girls 'whiskey,' which was actually tea, but known as Saigon Tea, while they were drinking beer.

### Room Service

We stayed in the bar for a while and then they took me to a place where we got some food. By this time I was so drunk I didn't care what I ate. Then we got a cab to Cholon, the Chinese part of town and went to some bar that they said was special. When we got there, I passed out and the next thing I knew they were pushing me into a cab and sending me back to the hotel. When I got there, I went up to my room and crashed.

Crash!!! Indeed! I woke up with a start and saw my room door bounce against the wall. The light came on, and a man in civilian clothes with a .45 in his hand came into the room in a rush with several people behind him. He was yelling for me to freeze, which I did, because I couldn't think of any other response. If these guys were VC, I was dead.

Even if they weren't, I could still be dead, because the lead guy had his pistol pointed right in my face, finger on the trigger, the muzzle about six inches away from my nose. I put my hands up and sat there on my bed. The other guys, in uniform, with MP armbands, checked around the room, looking under the bed and going through my clothes. When they were done, the guy with the gun said, "Who are you and what are you doing in Saigon?"

I gave him my name and told him that I was here getting glasses. "What unit are you from?" he asked me and I told him. One of the men with him picked up my medical records on the table by my bed and looked in them. "Yeah, he's got an appointment for glasses." The man with the pistol raised it away from my face and I heard him safe it with a click. They hadn't found my own pistol which was under my pillow and I was hoping that they wouldn't. "There's a lot of deserters in Saigon," the man with the gun said. "We got a tip that there were some here. If I were you, I would stay at the transit billets at Camp Alpha, places like this aren't safe." No kidding, I thought. He looked at the others and said, "Let's go, we'll check the other rooms." He looked at the door, "I guess you'll have to move your bed against the door, the lock is broken," he said, looking at the door knob, "Sorry about that."

I waited until they were out of the room before I got up, went to the door and shut it. Moving the bed across the floor, I pushed it against the door to hold it shut. I was still jacked up from the midnight visit from the MP's, so I lay there listening. A few minutes later I heard a loud crash and someone was shouting "Freeze!" I waited for some shooting, but everything was quiet, so eventually, I turned off the light and went back to sleep.

I met the sergeant and the other man from my platoon the next morning. They were staying in town for another night and asked me what I was going to do. I told them I would be picking up my glasses later that morning and heading back to Lai Khe that afternoon. When I told them about the MP's they laughed and said I should have stayed with them in Cholon. We went our separate ways and I returned to the unit that night. I made it to Saigon two more times before my tour was over, and had some more adventures in the Pearl of the Orient; but I never stayed at that hotel again.

## Battalion Change of Command

On 28 November, LTC Rufus Lazzell replaced LTC George Wallace as battalion commander. Colonel Lazzell had been the battalion commander before Wallace and according to rumor, had been wounded in the elbow, by a .51 caliber round in a firefight. He asked to be returned to his command when his wound was healed, and he was, somewhat unusual for the time, because of the long line of infantry officers trying to get a battalion command. He returned to the battalion wearing a brace on his elbow. He was a Korean War infantry veteran and a paratrooper with a Ranger tab.

## Operation Healdsburg

On the morning of 29 November we made an assault landing into an LZ to the east of Lai Khe for Operation Healdsburg. This was very close to where the August 25th battle took place. While we were in the air, we could see the LZ being hit with airstrikes and artillery; just before we landed, helicopter gunships lit up the tree-line.

As we got close to the ground, we climbed out onto the skids of our helicopter, holding on with one hand to whatever was available. The Huey had almost touched the ground, when the crew chief shouted, "Go!" We jumped off the skids and moved forward about fifty feet and took a knee.

I looked to the left and right rear and saw the line of Huey's moving with their noses down and their tails up as they took off. We formed into a line and moved toward the tree-line, firing at suspected enemy locations. We didn't receive any enemy fire; if they were in the area when the airstrikes and artillery started, they were long gone now. We moved into the jungle in a company column formation, with each file about twenty-five meters apart. The Platoon Leader had a map, and periodically he would ask for the pace-count, which he used to calculate our location on the map. The FO, who traveled with the CO, called for an artillery round every so often. They hit a few hundred meters in front of the lead element. This was supposed to break up any enemy ambushes ahead and also served to keep the artillery pointed in our general direction.

We stopped and made our cloverleaf patrols; after the usual all day movement we rejoined the rest of the battalion and formed a battalion perimeter. We dug our fighting positions, sent out an ambush patrol, and settled in to a fifty percent alert perimeter. Recon platoon spotted three VC and shot at them, but they got away.

The next morning someone was wounded by a 'short round' from one of our mortars and dusted off. We moved out again; Alpha Company was separated from the rest of the battalion for the day and we patrolled south. Bravo Company went north and was fired on by an automatic weapon. After the usual fireworks: artillery and mortars plus every rifle, M-79, and machine gun that could be brought to bear—they continued on, and found a recently used, empty VC base camp later that afternoon. That evening we rejoined the rest of the battalion and dug in, again. The next day we continued our company sweep to the southeast, and again rejoined the rest of the battalion in the evening, and dug-in our NDP. That night the VC blew a Chinese claymore that killed one and wounded three from Charlie Company.

### A 'Mad' Minute

The next morning, we were told to 'Stand To' as usual but this time was different. During the battle of LZ X-Ray in the Ia Drang Valley, the commander of 1-7 Cavalry, LTC Hal Moore, added a new element to 'Stand To.' It became known in our outfit as the 'mad minute.'

When the order was given, everybody in the unit fired their weapons simultaneously into the jungle in front of their positions. If the enemy had slipped up close during the night and was poised to attack at BMNT—Begin Morning Nautical Twilight, that is, the point in time when there is just enough light for the attacking force to see where they are going—one way of defusing the enemy's surprise advantage of firing the first shots, is to fire the first shots yourself.

From time to time, our commanders would order us to conduct a 'mad minute,' to preempt a possible surprise attack on our NDP. Word would be passed from position to position, 'Mad Minute' at 0500. When 0500 came, every rifleman would fire twenty rounds; every machine gunner would fire a hundred rounds; and every M-79 man would fire two rounds.

One morning, the word came down the line that a mad minute would begin in two minutes. It was past 0500, already light, and the troops had already stood down. They were going about their morning chores. We knew we were going to move, so a few of the guys were already out retrieving their trip flares and pulling in their Claymores. The word was passed, but as in all military operations, someone always fails to get the word.

## Rodney Walks on Water

I lit a cigarette and left it hanging out of my mouth as I stood there with my machine gun. A one hundred round belt was hanging over a C-ration can clipped to the left side of my gun. The vegetation was pretty thick in front of our positions, and I planned to do a little trimming that morning.

The sun was coming up behind me and I could see the lush green colors of the vegetation in the peaceful light of the pink tinted dawn. Firing broke out to my right, so I pulled the trigger and sent five or six rounds into the jungle in front of me. Then I heard someone shouting to my left, "Murry! Cease fire, cease fire!"

I looked over at the next position, about fifteen meters away. The guy that was shouting at me was pointing to the front of his position and yelling, "Rodney! Rodney!" I looked where he was pointing and saw Rodney running toward the perimeter. He had been busy that morning, recovering his trip flares. He had put them quite a ways out, and now he was trying to cover the distance between the flares and safety.

"Hey Rodney," I yelled. He looked over at me standing there holding a machine gun at the hip with a cigarette hanging out of my mouth. I aimed the gun to a point ten feet to his right and fired 50 rounds in several bursts. I could see the tracers flying past him and I was laughing like crazy.

Out of the corner of my eye, I could see Rodney's buddy standing there with a look of total horror on his face. He was holding the sides of his head and screaming, "Stop shooting, stop shooting!" I could barely hear him as I kept control of the gun while firing long bursts. Rodney saw the machine gun flashing and smoking and heard the sound of the bullets cracking past him blended with the sounds of the muzzle blast, and he put on a burst of speed toward the perimeter. There was a large pool of water in front of his position and I swear he ran across its surface as he sprinted the last few yards to safety.

His foxhole buddy was sitting on the ground sobbing with his head in his hands. He must have been convinced in his own mind that I was shooting Rodney, just because I could. He had been wound pretty tight anyway, and news had come yesterday that his brother had disappeared from a troopship in the middle of the Pacific Ocean and was feared lost overboard, an apparent suicide. He was due to be lifted out on the next resupply chopper for emergency leave back to the states.

Fortunately for me, Rodney saw the humor in the situation and it became a kind of bonding experience. We stuck together quite a bit and I'm sure he determined by now that I was crazy. This incident confirmed his suspicions, but what was he going to do. Everyone needed a buddy and Rodney was mine. Though nothing was said to me about the mad minute, the platoon leader must have seen my need for a career change, and I was reassigned as a fire team leader in the third squad.

I scratched my legs somewhere during Operation Attleboro. The main scratches were on the shins, half way between my knees and my feet. At first they were just like any other scratch, but then they began turning red and swelling a little around the scratch. I didn't see them that often because we were on the move for much of November and December.

*But when you see Jerusalem surrounded by armies,*
*then know that her desolation has drawn near*
*Luke 21:20*

# Chapter 10-December 1966

### Operation Healdsburg (2)

On December 1st, we made a company sized combat air-assault and walked around through the bush looking for Charlie. That night we set up company perimeters and sent out ambush patrols. One of the Bravo Company patrols ambushed a group of VC and killed two. The VC returned later that night and fired M-79 rounds at them, wounding eleven. The next morning Alpha Company spotted three VC and fired at them but they got away. We continued to patrol south and that evening, set up a company NDP.

The next day we continued to sweep south. That afternoon one of the platoons made contact with twelve VC and lit them up. We got artillery support and helicopter gunships, but the only result was one of our guys being wounded by a gunship. The next day we filled in our holes and continued to move south, this time with the rest of the battalion. On the evening of the 3 December, we moved into a perimeter with the rest of the battalion. We were preparing for the usual routine when we were told not to dig in; that was strange.

### Cordon and Search

After the evening meal, we received a warning order to prepare for a night march that would take the whole battalion to a Vietnamese village, where we would conduct a cordon and search operation. We would be the cordon around the village, and the South Vietnamese Army would be the search element. Usually, the only time we moved at night was on the squad sized ambush patrols. For the whole battalion to move a long distance through the dark was something like what Darby's Rangers did in WWII, and I thought it sounded pretty exciting.

When it got dark, we turned to the right and followed the man in front of us. The battalion was in column. The files were very close to each other, and as we moved, we could see the other file on our right. We would walk for a while; the column would stop for a short while; then, we would go again. It was warm, but it was a lot cooler than it would have been in the daytime. We were a tempting target for an ambush, but our security was good. If some of the people who watched us walk by were the enemy, and it was highly likely that some of them were, I'm sure they were disappointed that their intelligence people had failed to detect this operation.

The ground was basically flat, with a few very low hills, a lot of dry rice paddies, and clumps of vegetation every so often. Around 0200 we stopped for a long halt. We had been walking for about five hours. Just as we were starting to get comfortable, there was a big flash and a loud explosion down the hill to our left. It must have been some kind of claymore, but no one was hit. The LT told me to take some men and find the people who had been responsible for the attack. I took four men and we moved slowly down the hill. The whole area was under some large rubber trees, so it was dark, and I felt fairly safe.

We came to a fence with a fence corner post to our left. It seemed like the device had been fired from this area. I decided to cross the fence to check out a clump of vegetation on the other side. The fence had only two strands of wire, and I was able to step through them onto the other side. When I did, I stepped into the moonlight and it was like being on a stage. I decided that I didn't want to go any farther. The other guys agreed that we didn't want to offer ourselves to the enemy for night shooting practice, so we turned around and rejoined our company.

I told the LT that we couldn't find anyone, and we agreed that, whoever fired the device didn't wait around to see the results. The LT reported our patrol's negative results to the CO, and about that time, the column stood up and took off. We marched through the dark across the land, in a hurry now, and we didn't stop until we reached our objective. The two files split off: we went around the left side of the village, and the other file went around to the right.

Eventually, the two files met on the other side of the village, and we formed a perimeter. Part of the perimeter was to watch in toward the village, and part was to watch out from the village to keep the enemy from attacking our rear. We made small positions and sat down to wait. The village dogs barked a lot when we were moving, but after we stopped, it stopped and the dogs began to settle down.

Just before dawn, the ARVNs entered the village to search for VC and draft dodgers. We didn't find out about the draft dodger part until after the operation was over. The ARVNs had a portable loudspeaker with them, and when they started talking, the place came unglued. The dogs began howling, and we could hear some shouting in the village.

All of a sudden, I heard American voices shouting, "Halt, Halt!" I turned to my left and saw a GI standing, a silhouette in the moonlight, holding his M-16 with his right hand, arm fully extended away from his shoulder. He was looking in the opposite direction from where his rifle was pointing, as he fired a shot. Then he quickly took a more conventional firing position and fired two or three more shots into the dark.

People were scrambling to get a glimpse of the enemy, and I heard someone shout, "There goes another one!" A few more shots were fired and then, it was quiet. A few moments later we heard someone whispering for Doc Don, the medic, to come over to their location. The word was passed that we had shot one of the Vietnamese who was running out of the village with a small group of men.

The young Vietnamese man was beyond help, and he died shortly after our medic had bandaged his wounds. It was now daylight, and we got the word to saddle up and prepare to move. I looked over to where the body of the dead man lay. There was an older woman kneeling over the body, silently weeping. She was caressing the face of the young man who lay there with a bandage wrapped around his chest. I was pretty sure that the woman was his mother, and I saw that the conventional wisdom was wrong about the Vietnamese people, not having any value for human life.

Later that morning we left the village and began a battalion sweep to the east. Around noon, one of the Alpha Company platoons was hit with a number of rifle grenades that killed one man and wounded two others. That afternoon, I was told that my squad would be dropped off for an ambush patrol, while the rest of the battalion moved into the NDP. Jose Garcia's machine gun crew was added, along with Doc Don the medic. When we got to the designated point, the LT gave me the signal, and we moved into some brush and settled down to wait for dark.[218]

## Puff the Magic Dragon

When it was dusk, we set up a linear ambush on a well-used trail that went to a nearby village and passed through our perimeter. It was possible that local VC from the village would use this trail to approach our perimeter, for the purpose of placing booby-traps or conducting harassment operations. After the claymores were in place and rear security established, we went on fifty percent alert for another long night.

We were on a slight hill overlooking the trail. On the other side of the trail was a thin wall of vegetation and beyond that, terraced rice paddies. Across the rice paddies, about 1000 meters, away was a wood-line. The sky was red where the sun had gone down, and I was thinking that it looked like another no contact ambush patrol, when there was a loud explosion in the direction of the perimeter.

After a moment, we could hear rifle and machine gun fire coming from the direction of the perimeter. A Chinese Claymore had been detonated from the rice paddies in front of Bravo Company's positions. A lieutenant and a platoon sergeant, sitting on top of a bunker talking, were killed instantly. Several others nearby were wounded. When the shooting stopped, I asked the RTO, who was monitoring the company net, what was going on, and he said that battalion was requesting a Medevac. Then I got a radio message asking if we were able to see or hear anything in our area. I told the RTO to give a negative reply to the question.

After about fifteen minutes, we heard the sound of an aircraft approaching, and it wasn't a helicopter. Then the RTO got a call from Captain Williamson who wanted to talk to me. I rogered, and the CO said that Puff the Magic Dragon was inbound. Puff was a C-47 twin engine transport first used before WWII. It was armed with three 7.62 mm Gatling guns which were capable of firing 6000 rounds per minute at the ground, a veritable wall of lead. He wanted me to direct its fire on suspected enemy locations. Since I had never received any training on air to ground fire adjustment, I was pretty tense.

I couldn't see any enemy locations, and told him so. He said that he wanted the plane to hose down the terraced rice paddies from the suspected location of the claymore, in hopes of catching the fleeing guerrillas before they got back to the safety of their village. He wanted me to bring the fire as close as I could to the edge of the wood-line, just past where we were set up. He figured the VC would stay as close as they could to the U.S. positions, so that we would not risk hitting our own troops while trying to get them.

We didn't have a strobe light so that the aircraft could see where we were. I knew that once they began firing, a hiccup on the part of the pilot could mark the end of our tour in an instant. The CO said he wanted me to direct their firing by sound. I was to tell the aircraft: to come closer to the tree-line; move farther away; or stay where they were and continue to fire. It was my call. Then the CO gave me the call sign and radio frequency of Puff, and told me to call him.

The RTO changed the channels, and soon I was telling the pilot where I was in relation to the perimeter and the tree-line at the edge of the rice paddies. They fired a long burst into the paddies to my right. The noise was incredible. It didn't sound like a firearm, like a real fast machine gun, it sounded like an electric saw cutting through something hard. I couldn't hear the rounds striking and I couldn't see the tracers because of the trees. I sure didn't want to find out the hard way, that they were too close; so I told them that they were close enough.

We were all tensed up, as they say, when the plane passed overhead. The 'Braaag' sound of the mini-guns was really intense. When they had finished their work, we thanked them and got off their push and back to ours. The CO released them, and they flew away. The rest of the night passed without incident, and we returned to the perimeter the next morning at first light.

### Flyboy Games

We were getting ready to move on, when the Air Force showed up again; this time it was a FAC, a small single engine plane like a Piper Cub. The Forward Air Controllers would find the enemy or suspected enemy positions and mark them with white phosphorous rockets. Then, the fast movers, the jet fighter bombers, would come in and drop their ordinance on the area marked by the white smoke. We watched the FAC drift slowly over the distant tree-line across the rice paddies from our positions. Suddenly he fired a rocket off the wing of the plane; 'whooosh' it flew into the jungle below.

The next thing we knew, a jet came roaring out of the sky and dropped a cluster bomb over the spot. The bomb burst open in the air, scattering hundreds of small bombs into the jungle below, where they went off like a string of big firecrackers. A second plane came in right behind the first, and dropped two canisters of napalm which tumbled end over end into the jungle, and burst into fiery red flames that quickly turned into boiling black smoke.

The guys on the perimeter cheered. This was a great show. The third and fourth planes flew in behind the first two and dropped more cluster bombs and napalm. The planes were now in orbit over us, as they came in a second time, one after another, dropping napalm and cluster bombs. Then they came back again, and each one strafed the area with their 20mm cannon. When they were finished, they flew off into the sky and disappeared.

The FAC flew over the strike area a few more times and then flew off at a low altitude over the jungle and disappeared. We all were impressed by the firepower display and were talking about it, when a loud noise came from above us and got louder and louder, so fast it was almost like an explosion.

Everyone was on the ground, some rolled up in a ball, waiting to see what degree of hell the enemy was bringing on us. The sound suddenly separated into four sources, as four supersonic jets finished their dive over the center of our perimeter and flew off in different directions on afterburner. We were stunned. Nobody moved for a moment, and then there was a chorus of cursing, laughing, and groaning as we recovered from a slick trick by the boys in blue.

### Bouncing Betty

We moved out and continued looking for Charlie. There was a large open area to cross, which was nice, because it was a lot easier than busting brush. The air was still cool, but the rising sun would change all that. The nearest tree-line was several hundred meters in the distance, so we didn't have to worry about a near ambush. It just seemed like a nice day for a walk, when the guy behind me exclaimed, "Hold it, I just stepped on a mine!" I turned and asked him, "What did you say?" He said that he had felt a kind of crunch and heard a 'click' under his foot; he was sure he had stepped on a 'Bouncing Betty' mine.

"Don't move," I said as I backed away. Then I remembered the term, 'mine field.' I stopped and shouted "freeze, mines." The word went up and down the line for everyone to stay where they were. Eventually, the platoon sergeant came up the column slowly, scanning the ground carefully, as he looked for the three prongs of a Bouncing Betty or any other possible disturbance of the earth that might indicate a mine. He told our squad to stand fast while rest of the company moved away carefully and set up a perimeter. The platoon sergeant took the man's rifle and web gear and told him to stand fast.

Rumors had been going around that the VC had captured a bunch of Bouncing Betty's from the ARVNs recently and there had been some discussion about them in a booby-trap class. The word was that when you stepped on one, you would hear a 'click,' and once you lifted your foot, the mine would fire a small canister of explosives and shrapnel about four feet in the air, where it would explode, sending hot metal into everyone within thirty meters of the explosion.

By now the platoon leader had informed the CO who then informed battalion. The word came back that an explosives expert from the engineers was on the way. After what seemed like hours, a small 'bubble chopper' landed nearby, and a man walked slowly, scanning the ground, towards us.

He carried a flak jacket which he handed to the man standing on the mine. Then he had some of us fill sandbags, which he placed around the man's foot. By this time we had moved a safe distance away and were in the prone, watching this drama before us. The explosives guy told our man that after he put on the flak jacket, he should throw himself on the ground to escape the blast of metal that would fly above him.

The man standing on the mine wondered if there wasn't something else that could be done to disarm the mine, but the engineer told him this was the only way, other than to stand there until the mine's mechanism rusted solid. These were the last words of the engineer other than to tell him, "Wait until I say go and make sure to go flat on the ground."

We watched as the engineer moved away and then lay on the ground. "Go," he shouted, but our guy didn't move. The sweat was running down his face as he must have been considering many things. "Go," shouted the engineer. "Go! Go!" As he dove to the ground, I buried my face in the earth and waited for the explosion—and waited, and waited.

Finally, I looked up and saw him lying on the ground, holding his helmet on his head. Nothing happened. Then, after about five minutes, the engineer got up and moved back to the sandbagged piece of ground and peered in to check the mine. He couldn't see anything, so he carefully moved some of the sandbags and inspected the ground. There was a broken twig on the ground, but to make sure he pulled out a knife and gently probed the earth where the mine would have been, but found nothing. He said some unkind words to our guy, who then got to his feet with a relieved look on his face, and the war moved on.

## Healdsburg Results

The next morning, one of the men in another platoon was shot and wounded by a sniper. We continued to sweep through our assigned areas. Charlie Company found a base camp and had two men wounded by a booby-trap. That night, the VC fired two M-79 rounds into our perimeter, but no one was hit. The next day, we continued patrolling. Charlie Company found a tunnel complex and three Chicom grenades, twenty-eight rifle grenades, one typewriter, three Bouncing Betty mines, four pair of VC sandals, and several documents.

The battalion was picked up by helicopter and flown to Lai Khe on the afternoon of 6 December. The artillery seemed a bit restrained on this one; we only fired 2312 rounds of 105mm, 659 rounds of 155mm, 128 rounds of 8-Inch, 154 rounds of 175mm, and 437 rounds of 4.2-inch mortar. The U.S. lost four men KIA and the VC lost seven, by body count.[219]

## The M-16 Rifle

When we got back to Lai Khe, I asked the soldier why he fired the first round the way he did the morning we surrounded the village. He said it was because he hadn't cleaned his rifle in such a long time that he was afraid that it would blow up in his face. We had been told that the M-16 didn't need much cleaning and that was why they only issued one cleaning rod per squad. Why anyone considered that statement at all logical boggles the mind. Weapon cleaning is a daily requirement, regardless which weapon. When I was in Germany, we each had our own complete cleaning kit with cleaning rod, brushes, patches and oil.

The rifle had been receiving a lot of bad publicity. There were stories coming out in the news of jammed rifles found in the hands of dead soldiers and Marines. We had been visited by some representatives of Colt Arms, the company that manufactured the rifle. They came to our company and inspected the rifles. Soon after that, all the bolts that were coated with chrome were replaced with dull gray metal bolts.

I didn't find out until much later, after the war, that there had been a really big problem with the rifle, more specifically, with its ammunition. The bean counters under the influence of the chief bean counter, Robert McNamara, had used a different kind of powder, of which they had an excessive amount, rather than the powder the specs called for, to make our bullets. This increased the cyclic rate of fire from 750 rounds a minute to 1000. It was a cost effective decision for someone that saved a lot of money on gun powder, but the savings at the back end were swallowed up by personnel losses.[220]

## Tennis Shoes

Colonel Lazzell came up with a good idea. In a battalion formation, when he told us that he had gone down to Saigon and procured almost a thousand pair of tennis shoes, one of the wise guys said, "Now we're going to play tennis with Charlie?" The colonel told us that each one of us would be issued a pair, and every night, when we pulled into our night defensive positions, we would take off our boots and put on a pair of dry socks and the tennis shoes. This, he said, would cut down on the trench foot cases that were sapping our fighting strength. We all got our tennis shoes and did as he said. It worked!

### The Bulletin Board!

I checked the bulletin board every day when we were in the company area. This was a habit I had developed in Germany. There was a letter requesting volunteers for the Division's Long Range Reconnaissance Patrols. That really appealed to me, and I read it again, and remembered the sergeant at the replacement battalion who helped me get assigned to the Division. He was so cool. He had that monkey on his shoulder and his huge mustache that was almost a goatee. You had to have a CIB and be an experienced combat infantryman. Well, maybe not now I thought, but in a few months I might be ready for that.

The company had sent a man from our platoon to something called Recondo School. He came back without graduating and all he told us was that everyone had to carry a full sandbag in their ruck, along with everything else. I was hoping to get sent to that school, but they never again sent anyone from our company.

I read the rest of the notices and saw a message about helicopter medevac procedures using a Stokes Litter. This was a stretcher that could be lowered on a winch to pick up an injured person in an area where the helicopter couldn't land. The message said that you had to request it when you called for a medevac. I made a mental note and moved on to other things.

### Things Deteriorate

The scratches on my legs had not healed. Going through the brush, climbing the rocks outside of Dau Tieng, walking through the rice paddies, basically living like an animal, tended to wear you down. Our uniforms wore out quickly, and the 'wait a minute' vines would rip a sleeve like a knife. Most of us were wearing the jungle fatigues uniform, and they went down pretty quickly.

The leather combat boots we had were falling apart, the upper part separating from the sole. Many guys had commo wire wrapped around the toe of their boots to hold the sole on. They had told us at Division when I arrived in Vietnam, that we would get our jungle boots at our unit. Two months later we were issued jungle boots in late November.

The Rear Echelon Military Forces (REMFs) were between us and the docks in Saigon, where all the supplies were unloaded. With all the black marketeering going on, it's likely that some of Charlie's guys got jungle boots before we did, but probably not before his own support troops.

### Operation Santa Cruz

On 19 December, we started Operation Santa Cruz. We moved out of Lai Khe by truck and after dismounting, we entered the bush and patrolled for the rest of the day. That evening we set up a perimeter, dug in, and sent out our LP/OPs and squad sized ambush patrols. The next day, we surrounded a village and searched it with no results so we moved back into the bush and continued to "trip-dick around," as Roland put it, until dusk, when we followed the same routine.

I started to feel pain that day in both my legs. I dropped my pants when we stopped for the night and took a look at the scratches. They had turned into open sores. They weren't too bad, but I asked the medic to look at them, and he said I had some badly infected, ulcerated sores. He put some antiseptic in them and told me to keep them clean.

We both laughed at that one, because we had been walking through rice paddies all day and we would be back in them tomorrow. The word was that we would be going back to Lai Khe the day after tomorrow, and he told me to go on battalion sick call when we got back.

I could feel my legs getting worse the next day, as we waded through the rice paddies which were fertilized with Vietnamese 'night soil.' That night I showed my sores to the medic again. He agreed that they did look worse and once again told me to go on sick call when we got back.

On the 21st of December we did a combat air-assault along the Saigon River where we set up a blocking position. That night, the tide came up and we all woke up floating and sputtering. Now I could see why they called it Operation Santa Cruz; there must have been a surfer with a sense of humor in the headquarters.

The next day, we were picked up by the Robin Hoods; it was true this time that the choppers were on the way. They dropped us off on the airstrip, a place we were seeing more and more, and we were driven by truck back to our company area. When we rode in the trucks, we rode standing up to save room, and this time, the bouncing of the truck as we rolled down the rutted dirt road, really caused my legs to hurt.[221]

## Sick Call

I went on sick call that afternoon at the Battalion Aid Station. Doctor P was there with his headquarters medics. I waited for my turn, and told a medic my problems when he asked. He told me to take my pants and boots off, and he gave me a poncho, so I wouldn't have to sit around naked while they worked on their other patients.

When it was my turn, the doctor took a look at my sores and prescribed an antibiotic. There were some other areas on my ankles that were swollen, and he told me that they needed to be lanced. He told his senior corpsman to lance them and got up to move to his next patient. There were quite a few patients, but I stopped him and asked what would happen after they lanced the swollen areas. He said I would be returned to regular duty.

"Regular duty, sir?" I said, "I am in a lot of pain when I walk and it's getting worse. We might be going out again tomorrow, and I don't think I could keep up if we're going to do the same thing we've been doing." He knew that the battalion was indeed going out the next day and he said, "I understand, but you can go with your unit and when you hit the ground, you can walk this off."

"You're kidding me, right sir?" "No I'm not. The colonel has ordered me to send every man to the field if he can walk. My hands are tied; you have to return to regular duty." He didn't look happy as he said these things, and I might have been a little sympathetic towards his position if my legs didn't hurt so much.

## "To Conserve Fighting Strength"
### Medical Corps Motto

The rumors were flying that there was a big operation coming, bigger than anything before it. That might account for all the people on sick call that afternoon. The colonel was a Korean War veteran and this was his second time commanding this battalion in Vietnam. He knew that men burn out; let their fears get the best of them, etc. He also knew that he had to hold a hard line, because if he didn't, his battalion would begin to melt away, as soon as men saw other soldiers getting out of the field for minor medical problems, and pulling safe duty in the rear.

The senior medic took me to a stretcher on stands at the rear of the aid station. He told me to sit down and began examining the swollen areas on my left leg. He placed my left foot on a stool and stepped over to a table nearby. My left leg was starting to throb now, and I sat there wishing that he would do something to relieve the pain in my legs, and the overall sick feeling in my stomach.

He came back with a throw-away scalpel and an aerosol can. He positioned my leg were he could see the swollen area on my ankle, and sprayed something from the can on it. Before I could ask him what he was doing, he stabbed that scalpel into the area he had sprayed.

I felt a very sharp pain where he stabbed me and looked at the spot. Some blood was coming out, but that's all. The doctor had said that the swollen areas were pockets of puss and they need to be drained. I didn't see any puss coming out of the cut he had put in my ankle. "I guessed I missed it," he said, spraying the area for an even longer time.

"What's that?" I asked him. "A local anesthetic," he said, "it kills the pain." "No it doesn't," says I, "that hurt like a son of a bitch!" "Don't worry," he said soothingly, "I used a lot more this time; I don't think you'll feel a thing." "I hope not," I said, "because if it hurts as much this time as it did last time, you can forget about using me to practice medicine."

He gave the area another good spray, and stuck the scalpel into my leg again. This time it really hurt; there was more blood but no puss. I jumped off the stretcher and backed into the table against the wall. I grabbed a flashlight from the table and yelled, "That's it, mother-blank!" "You're not touching me again with that knife!" I was feeling dizzy, and thought I might throw up, but I was prepared to smash that flashlight over his head if he moved toward me.

I saw him turn his head and look at the doc. I expected them to call the MPs, but the doc made a motion with his head as if to say, 'Get him out of here.' The medic told me to get dressed and go back to my company. "Give me some band aids for those stab wounds that you gave me," I demanded. He put some band aids on the stretcher I had been sitting on, and backed away from me a few steps, before turning and walking to the other end of the aid station, where he busied himself with other things.

### Returned to Regular Duty

I dressed and caught a ride back to the company area. When I reported to the platoon sergeant, he took one look and asked what was wrong with me. I told him the story of my trip to the Battalion aid station and what the doctor had told me about the colonel's order. "That quack, he's scared of his own shadow," he said.

The platoon sergeant then began to list a series of questionable medical diagnoses made by our battalion surgeon. I was feeling really faint and asked him if he would mind if I lay down. He told me that he didn't, but warned me about getting too comfortable, "You've got bunker guard tonight." "Bunker guard? I said, "I feel like shit and you're going to put me on guard?" "Got to, the sick slip says you are returned to regular duty; besides you can lie down there and rest."

That evening I got a ride to the bunker line with the rest of the guys who had guard duty. I told the sergeant in charge, a fire team leader from another platoon, that I was feeling pretty bad and might not be able to do too much. He seemed to be distracted and didn't pay much attention to what I said. Maybe he was practicing how to ignore problems that he couldn't solve. They dropped me off at a bunker with another man. There were people occupying the nearest bunkers on my left and on my right. When I tried to walk my legs began to throb and I felt a great deal of pain.

One of my favorite military heroes, Orde Wingate, said that if a man isn't his own physician by the time he is thirty, he is a fool. Well, I was only twenty but I was pretty sure that I was in bad shape and that if I didn't get to a competent medical professional soon, I was going to have serious problems. Serious medical problems in Vietnam always included the possibility of terminal complications, but I refused to contemplate any such thing. I was a surfer from Corona del Mar and I could do anything.

As I considered my thoughts, I realized that I was getting delirious. I felt like I was burning up, even though there was a cool breeze blowing down the line from the North. I staggered over to the next bunker, and told the guys there that I was really sick; that I was going to lie down before I fell down, and would they keep an eye on my sector. They were happy to, and asked me if they could do anything for me.

I staggered back to my bunker without answering. I told the other guy to join forces with the bunker on our right, and collapsed on the ground. I laid my rifle on the ground and using a rolled up poncho liner for a pillow, I went to sleep. The sergeant of the guard shook me awake at about 0600. He had a medic from his platoon with him, and the medic told me he wanted to take my temperature. I tried to hold the thermometer in my mouth, but he had to help me. When he took it out, he shined his flash light on it and let out a soft whistle, "No shit, 105, we've got to get him to a doctor." "Don't take me to Dr. P." I groaned and he said, "We've got to go through battalion, but I'm sure when we get you to Brigade, they'll know what to do."

## A Second Opinion

They helped me gather my things. Because I couldn't walk, they carried me to the Weapons Carrier and drove me to the Battalion aid station. The senior medic saw me, looked away and started talking to Dr. P, who then walked over to look at me. "He has to go to the field, I told him that yesterday. The colonel wants everyone to go to the field!"

Our medic said, "Sir, he's got a temperature of 105." "Are you sure about that?" P said. "Yes sir," said the medic. I butted in, "Sir, I feel like shit; I want a second opinion; there's no way I'm going to walk this off; I can't even walk." The medic added, "That's right sir, we had to carry him to the vehicle, and from the vehicle to here." The doctor stood there for a moment thinking, "Ok, you can take him to Brigade sick call, but I bet they'll send him right back here."

The medic drove me over to the medical facility at brigade headquarters. He parked and got a stretcher. Someone helped him get me on it and they carried me inside. The medics there saw my legs, took my temperature, and gave my vital signs to a doctor. When the doctor finished checking me out he said to them, "Do you see those red lines going up his legs toward his groin? If he doesn't get to a field hospital and some serious antibiotics he's going to lose his legs or worse. Those lines are blood poisoning!" The doctor told the medic that they were admitting me to the brigade dispensary until they could get me on a Medevac helicopter to the 93d Evac Hospital in Long Binh.

### Merry Christmas

I lay there marveling at army medicine; in the same morning, on the same base, one doctor was telling me that I should go to the field and walk it out and another doctor was sending me to a hospital to try to save my legs. The medics helped me out of my filthy uniform, gave me a hospital gown and put me in a bunk. I lay there burning up. Then the medics brought in some bags of ice and laid them on my chest, stomach, and groin. They gave me some pills and made me drink water and fruit juice.

I spent the morning lying on my back and watching a ceiling fan spin around. I must have dozed off, because the next thing I knew, there was a man wearing a Santa Claus hat and a red jacket, open in the front, leaning over my bed saying "Merry Christmas, Merry Christmas." I tried to focus on his face, and eventually saw that it was an older man, and he was wearing a star on each lapel of his shirt. Either the stars were part of his costume, or this was a brigadier general. My eyes traveled down, and I saw that on his jungle fatigues, he had US Army and a name that read, Hollingsworth.

BG Hollingsworth was the assistant division commander. It took me a while to work this out, because of the Santa Claus hat and my physical condition. "Merry Christmas, sir," I said, with as much cheer as I could muster. I hadn't even thought about Christmas, and now a general dressed like Santa was leaning over my bed and shaking my hand. It had indeed been a strange day.

Later that afternoon, after the general moved on to spread holiday cheer to other troops, the medics came in and told me that I was getting on a chopper to go to the hospital. I tried to sit up, but they told me to relax; that they would take care of everything. They put my things in a brown paper bag and placed the bag on my stomach. Then they got on either end of the stretcher and picked me up.

I was carried to a nearby helipad, where a Huey Medevac bird with big Red Crosses sat with its blades turning. They loaded me on. I lay there listening to the engine, trying to detect any change in the sound that would tell me when the helicopter was going to take off. When it finally did, we skimmed down the runway, gradually picking up speed. I knew what we were doing because by now I was a veteran helicopter passenger. Usually I would be rubbernecking and looking for familiar sights but that day I just stared at the ceiling of the compartment.

## 93d Evac Hospital

It was a long flight to the helipad at the 93d Evacuation Hospital in Long Binh. When we landed, there were soldiers waiting to unload me and I was being examined by a nurse within minutes of arriving. Years later, I found out that I was being triaged.

The triage nurse makes a quick but thorough assessment of a person's injuries and puts them in categories of need. The ones that look hopeless are put out of the way. It didn't mean that they were forgotten; it just meant that the medical staff wouldn't commit to any lengthy procedures if there were others who could apparently be saved if they were treated right away.

Colonel Charlie Beckwith told me about his experience with a triage nurse after he had been hit by a .51 caliber machine gun bullet. He had to convince her and the doctors that they had to help him, which they did.[222]

## More Opinions

After I was triaged, a doctor came by, looked at my legs, and read my chart. He told the orderlies to move me to another room where they put more ice on me. Later, two doctors came to my bedside. They lifted the sheet off me and looked me over from my groin to my feet. I listened while they talked. I was trying to figure out what they were saying, and I did hear the word Japan once.

When they were finished writing on my chart, I asked them what they thought about my legs. They looked at each other, and then one of them told me that my condition was serious. I had blood poisoning and there was a possibility that my legs would have to be amputated. They were debating whether to send me to Japan now, or wait to see how I would respond to massive doses of antibiotics.

I told them that I had only been in-country for a little more than three months, and that I would like to finish my tour. They seemed to like my reply and assured me that they would do everything they could to get me back on my feet. That sounded good to me because if they cut off my legs, I wouldn't have any feet.

A few minutes after the doctors left, a nurse showed up pushing a cart. She smiled and said, "Time for your shot, roll over." She gave me the first of many shots of penicillin, right in my buttock. I took these shots three times a day, every day. They were very painful, and I dreaded the sound of the cart and those words.

After a few days, I was moved to a regular ward. My fever had come down and my body was responding to the antibiotics. Most of the other guys were recovering from battle wounds, and I felt bad that my injuries were much less heroic than theirs. Staring at the ceiling was pretty boring, and after a few days I was feeling much better than I had been. Some nice people would come through the wards several times a day and pass out magazines and books. I managed to find a few military history books that were in pretty good condition. Most of the men preferred lighter reading subjects that could take them away from there.

*As it is written,*
*"For Your sake we are being put to death all day long;*
*we have been accounted as sheep for slaughter."*
*Romans 8:36*

## Chapter 11-January 1967

### Ambushed

When I felt better, and was able to sit up in bed, I looked around the ward. On the other side of the room, in the corner bed on the left, was a man with a Big Red One patch on the end of his bed. He was sitting in his bed with his arms in casts when I made eye contact with him.

LT Alfred Carter was an artillery forward observer who had gone out on a platoon patrol with Charlie Company, 1-16 Infantry near Soui Da. The platoon had walked into an open area while pursuing some guerrillas they spotted. Apparently, the guerrillas were there to lure them. When most of the platoon was in the open area, an enemy unit opened fire on them with automatic weapons, killing all but two men and the LT.

We had been at a battalion formation the day we returned from the field, and this was the patrol that our battalion commander, Colonel Lazzell, was talking about when he said that the platoon leader was a criminal. When I was able to start walking again, I used to go over and sit with LT Carter and talk to him. Since he couldn't move his arms, I would spoon feed him and he told me about the patrol. S.L.A. Marshall described the action in his book, 'Ambush,' a series of stories about unit actions during Operation Attleboro and other operations in late 1966. The LT told a slightly different story.[223]

He was with the patrol leader, right up to the time they got hit. The pivotal point in the story was the platoon leader's tactical response to the discovery of three VC. Marshall wrote that they were there to lure the platoon into an ambush. The LT said that the platoon leader had reported the encounter by radio, and had been directed to get them. 'Get them' could be considered synonymous with 'Get some,' in other words, kill them. This was not what the book said. According to Marshall the platoon leader had screwed up, but Carter said that he had been ordered to pursue them. Moving his platoon into the open area was a mistake, but with division's emphasis on results, the point squad's lapse in tactical judgment could have been fueled by the platoon leader's enthusiasm or fear of failure.

Years later, I read the memoirs of a British soldier who served in the 22 Special Air Service Regiment and various units of the Rhodesian Army. He remembered the Principals of War that were taught to him at the senior sergeant's course of the British Army. There were four, and I added a fifth. Using the framework of these Principals of War, we can illustrate their veracity with the story of the ambush:

1. The Slaughter of the Soldier - The platoon from Charlie Company. All but three of those men were killed that day. One of the survivors hung himself later in the Disciplinary Barracks at Fort Leavenworth, the Army's 'Big House.'

2. The Search for Scapegoats - The platoon leader was the logical one to blame. The fact that he wasn't able to give his side of the story, made him a perfect scapegoat.

3. The Punishment of the Innocent - In this case, assuming LT Carter was correct in his knowledge of the facts, the LT would have been punished, but, as fate would have it, he was beyond the code of military justice, and in war, the Army usually considers death as punishment enough for most offenses. If the colonel could have gotten to the LT before the VC did, he, the LT, could have expected to be punished.

4. The Decoration of the Non-Participants-I don't know who received an award after the Charlie Company ambush except for numerous posthumous purple hearts.[224]

5. The Bitter Memories - Don't think anyone who goes to war returns unscathed. Surely in the combat units, the bitter memories are everywhere. From our own actions, where each of us wishes we could rewind back to those days and do things differently, to the actions of others, where we wish that they had been smarter, wiser, more ethical, and more caring. When you consider each person perceiving every event differently, and responding differently to a single event, you start to see why von Clausewitz covered all these things in a 'fog of war.'

> **Jose Garcia:** *"We were on the left flank of a platoon ambush near Soui Da. An Ox cart with 5-6 people rolled by the whole ambush and when it reached us, Gunby blew a claymore. That stopped the cart and wounded the ox. Three people were hit and there were people running past the rest of the ambush and no one opened fire. We threw grenades and I went back to the platoon CP to get more grenades. The LT and Plt Sgt told me to stop making noise. I told them to give me their grenades and they did. Later, the LT got bronze star for directing the fire. These guys were part of the VC unit that ambushed the platoon from Charlie Company the next day."*[225]

### Message from the Home Front

Christmas arrived while I was in the hospital. The general's Santa Claus visit was but a precursor to the attempts by the hospital staff to cheer us and themselves up for the holidays. I received some mail from home at the hospital, including a small reel to reel audio tape; this was before the days of eight track and audio cassettes. It was from my surfing buddies from California.

They had gone to some place back home and made a recording which was mailed to me by my parents. The hospital had a service that brought a tape player around so you could listen to these tapes. They didn't have headphones, however, and so the whole ward could hear your tape. The cart was placed between the beds, and the volume was turned down, but you could still hear someone else's message if you listened.

Since we didn't have anything else to do, when someone's message was played, we would all be quietly listening, looking away from the person who got the message, so that they could feel like they had some privacy. Most of the messages were all-American: mom, wife, children, apple pie, all the good things. Sometimes there would be the voice of a girl friend with some subtle hints about loneliness and reuniting activities. We listened to these with a great deal of interest. A really good one would bring on some ribald responses from the other guys in the room. The message recipient would take these with good humor, sometimes asking us to "Shut the blank up, I'm trying to hear."

When I played my buddy's tape the ward heard a bunch of wild and crazy California surfers using words that sounded like English, but their meaning was totally incomprehensible. My pals were all jacked up, laughing and joking. They used to call me 'future' as in, "I have a future in the Army," something I used to state when we discussed what we were going to do with our lives. 'Future,' as used by them for my nickname could also be used as blanker. They were delighted with their clever play on words and their audio tape was full of 'future' this and 'future' that. I did notice a slight anti-war flavor in the words coming out of the mouths of my friends, as they signed off with "Merry fascist and a happy Nazi."

When their tape had finished, I looked around the ward. Instead of seeing the backs of everyone's head, everyone was staring at me. Nobody said anything, they just stared. Finally, I felt the need to explain what must have been an unusual glimpse into an American sub-culture, a sub-culture that was becoming more and more talked about in mainstream America, thanks to the movie, "The Endless Summer" and the music of the Beach Boys. I just said, "My old surfing buddies from California," as if that could explain everything. The people with the cart gave me back my tape and hurried away. Soon it was time for another shot and the doctors would be making their rounds.

### The Anti-War Movement

The U.S. college campuses became the center of the anti-war movement, thanks to the stupidity of the federal government. The Selective Service Act of 1948 required all men to register for the draft. Initially, married men with children were given a deferment, but in 1953 President Eisenhower ended that deferment for the purpose of equity in the system. President Kennedy restored the deferment for married men, just before I began basic training; there were a lot of bitter men in my company who were married, but missed the change by a few days. Then came student deferments and the rush was on to get an education.[226]

This began a fracturing of our society that continues to this day. WWII had served to blend our nation together and now the Vietnam War was ripping it apart. Many parents, veterans of the earlier wars, saw this war as less than necessary, thanks to Lyndon Johnson and his administration. Johnson was the ultimate politician, painting his administration into a corner because the Asian peasants refused his politics.

The anti-war movement was an umbrella organization that covered a vast spectrum of people. They were motivated by many things including: cowardice, the best intentions of goodwill towards all men, and the International Communist Conspiracy. Eventually it would cover many of the soldiers themselves for a variety of their own reasons.[227]

California was one of the first states to manifest an anti-war movement. Springing up on the University of California campus at Berkeley, it quickly spread to the campuses at Santa Barbara, Los Angeles, Irvine and San Diego. Then it moved to the state teachers colleges, and the private institutions. The anti-war sentiment was hard to argue with. After all, who is for war?

The so-called peaceniks and folk singers were a mild irritant, but some of the hard corps protesters were actually rooting for the other side; we had heard rumors that one of our units had found large amounts of medical supplies in a VC base camp from the 'peace loving students' at the University of California at Berkeley. We discussed this occasionally, and decided that the protesters should come over here first, and see what was going on before talking about 'our' war.

If they weren't willing to come over and walk through the jungles with us, fine. Nobody could fault that. Most of us would have been happy to join our high school friends back home, instead of doing what we had to do here. What we didn't like was anyone talking about the 'Nam' who hadn't been here, and by being here, I mean being in the jungle with the grunts.

I wasn't offended by my friends' jesting in the tape. I figured that they were being their usual wild and crazy selves. I didn't realize that while attending the brand new University of California campus at Irvine, some of them had fallen under the spell of a goateed, shaggy haired English professor. He had opened their minds to the possibility of a world where everyone was equal, everyone had a meaningful job, and everyone was happy, because everyone was a communist.

## The Communists

Communism was the new religion of the industrial age and its apostles were the vanguard of the information age. Its doctrines were as intricate as any of the world's older religions and had great appeal in the colonies of the great powers. While studying in the capitals of their colonial rulers, many of the indigenous people of these colonies were introduced to the philosophy of a German named Karl Marx.

He was raised as a Lutheran and it's likely he developed his philosophy from verses in the book of Acts in the New Testament. Acts 2:44 and 45 say, "And all those who believed were together and had all things common; and they sold their properties and possessions and divided them to all as anyone had need."

Marx saw this as a wonderful thing and decided to revive this 'common' way. He didn't understand that the dynamic salvation of God was being manifested by the new believers in Jerusalem, where the people had been under the yoke of the Jewish religion for centuries.

The experience of the church in Jerusalem lasted only for a short while, and anyone who has received a dynamic salvation from the Lord can tell you that there is an intense 'honeymoon' period after receiving the Lord. Eventually though, we are brought to a more normal situation where we have to seek him every day.

Many have tried to replicate the scene in Acts 2 over the years. They soon found out about the fallen human nature. Marx reasoned that man would need to have his nature re-educated and since men wouldn't like it, they would need to be ruled by some who were able to figure out the best way to establish a paradise on earth. It would be a paradise of workers.

## Wolves in Sheep's Clothing

My friends bought into this theory and were led on by this professor who was like a messiah to them. When I returned from Vietnam, several of them told me that I had to come with them to the University to hear their English professor speak. They had already finished taking his courses, but they went to listen to him so they could get more of his enlightening words.

Going to a college English class was the last thing I wanted to do when I got back, but I went on the off chance that I might meet a college coed like all the ones who were taking off their clothes for Playboy Magazine. I'm sure that the professor knew his stuff. You don't get on with the University of California if you don't, but his lecture that day was way outside my comprehension.

If my friends were hoping that his talking would enlighten me about their new religion, they were wrong. When they introduced me to him after the class and told him I had just returned from Vietnam, he just looked at me and didn't say anything. That told me all I needed to know about him.

## Returned to Duty

After thirty days I was discharged from the hospital. They gave me a new pair of jungle fatigues and jungle boots before telling me to hit the road. I was told to go straight to the flight control center at nearby Bien Hoa Air Base, and from there I could catch a plane or helicopter to Lai Khe.

I had a little money and I stood around the front gate of hospital considering my options. I knew I should do what they said, but after my trip to Saigon to get glasses, I also knew that a day or two in transit wouldn't be questioned. Besides it might take a day or two anyway. I had tried to call my unit as I had been directed to do and tell them that I was out of the hospital, but after several times of going through someone called 'Tiger Switch' and being cut off until I learned to say "Working" when someone said "Working?" I gave up.

A guy walked up to me and asked me where I was going. When I told him I was going to Lai Khe, he happily told me that he was too and that we could go together to the flight control at Bien Hoa. I noticed that he was a sergeant, so I had to make it seem like I was on board with him, but the moment he indicated that he would be happy to go with me to Lai Khe, I decided that I wanted to hang out in Long Binh for a while.

## Hanging Out in Long Binh

There were a lot of places on the road to Bien Hoa Air Base where you could have a beer or two and meet a nice Vietnamese girl to talk with. Since I didn't know what to say to a girl anyway, and the girls only said things like "You buy me Saigon Tea," "You numbah one," or "You numbah ten GI," I thought it would be a perfect way to celebrate getting out of the hospital.

I told the sarge that I would meet him at flight control, after I got a name tag and U.S. Army sewn on my new uniform, thinking that he would leave me alone; but, he needed name tags too. So together we walked out the gate and headed down the road to Bien Hoa Air Base.

There were many tailor shops mixed in with the bars. I found one, and they told us that they could do the tapes in an hour. They also had a subdued version of the Big Red One patch that we wore on our left shoulder. This was the first time I had seen one, so I told them to sew one on for me.

We gave them our shirts, but now we were standing around out on the street in our t-shirts. The tailor shop lady told us, "You go there," pointing at the bar next to the tailor shop, "I fini, I bring," she said pointing to the bar, to us, and to the shirts, using hand and arm signals that helped us to understand what she meant. "You go now, GI, many MPs. You go now!"

I moved toward the door of the bar. When I opened it, music blared out. It was American popular music. I walked in and my new traveling companion stepped in right behind me. It was so dark inside that we had to stand by the door for a minute to get some amount of night vision before we could proceed. There could have been a platoon of VC in there partying, and we wouldn't have noticed until we tripped over one of their rifles. As it turned out, it was full of a joint combined force of U.S. soldiers, airmen and allies of our cause.

We made our way to a table and sat down. A waitress came and took our order for beer. She asked if we wanted girls but, the sergeant said no, so we took our beers. I chugged mine down and ordered another before she had finished giving us our change. The sergeant decided to do that too, and did. This set the tone for our visit to the bar, and we proceeded to get very drunk in short order.

## Took 'Dinky Dau'

I made several trips to the restroom, and on one of them, a Vietnamese man asked me if I wanted to buy cigarettes. "Took dinky dau, took dinky dau," he kept saying. I was intrigued. I knew that dinky dau meant crazy but I didn't know what "took" meant. "I buy cigarettes," I told him. "Took dinky dau, took dinky dau," he said smiling.

Grabbing my arm he said, "You come, you come," and I followed him toward the front door. When I passed the table I told my pal that I was going outside to check on my shirt and that I would be right back. He had a girl sitting on his lap and waved me on, so I followed the man out the door.

We walked between the buildings to the back. He led me down a narrow path between some Banyan trees. We crossed a small footbridge over a ditch with some stagnant water in it and came to a building. He led me inside a small room. A young woman was sitting there and she had a number of cigarette packs in front of her on the table. I looked at them. They were called 'Park Lane' cigarettes. The Vietnamese man was pointing at them, "Took dinky dau, took dinky dau."

The lady handed me a cigarette and lit it with a Zippo lighter. I took a puff and inhaled. It smelled like tobacco, but it tasted different than any cigarette I had smoked before. After I took another puff, she reached over and took the cigarette from my hand and made motions like she was puffing on it. Then she inhaled, and held it for a long time, before handing the cigarette back to me.

The implied task was to imitate her, and I did several times. My head started feeling strange, and then I remembered that time with my buddies, when they gave me a hand rolled cigarette, and told me to smoke it while I drove their car down the freeway late one night. Soon after smoking it, I was driving at twenty miles an hour on the Riverside Freeway, and feeling like I needed to slow down.

Pot! I was smoking pot and I was really stoned. The Vietnamese weed was making me feel like I was in a different world. I sat there looking around and pulling on the cigarette. The women stepped through another door covered by a cloth curtain and talked to someone in the next room while holding the curtain open. I could see several young girls working at a table. One girl was gently pulling the tobacco out of a commercial cigarette, while another girl was stuffing tobacco and marijuana into the empty paper tube of another cigarette.

### A Business Proposition

Park Lane cigarettes had filters, and the mix of tobacco and marijuana was such that only a well-trained cop would notice the marijuana smell. The woman was talking to me, "You like took dinky dau, GI?" "Oh Yeah, momma san," I said, "took dinky dau, numbah one." "Numbah one, GI, you numbah one," she replied and I said "you numbah one, momma san."

Her demeanor changed and with a serious look on her face she said, "GI," while looking around the room like she wanted to make sure that no one else could hear her, "GI, you sell took dinky dau to GI, Bien Hoa?" Slowly, it came to me that she was trying to make a business proposition. I was never any good at business and I never could play, 'Let's make a deal' with anyone. I had bought high and sold low so many times that I had resolved not to do any more business with anyone. That's why I joined the Army, to soldier: I wasn't from the merchant class; I was from the warrior class.

It would take a while longer for me to figure out that many soldiers were business men. As a matter of fact, there were quite a few senior NCOs and officers who were doing big business not too far from here. Our Division Sergeant Major was a businessman.

Anyway, I wasn't interested in becoming a dope dealer but I didn't tell mamma san. I led her to believe that I would sell some cigarettes for her. She was happy but shrewd. She made me pay full price for a pack of Park Lanes. She told me that when I sold them and came back, she would sell me some more.

We shook hands and I stumbled out of the place and followed the trail back to the bar. I stopped at the tailor shop. Our shirts were ready, so I paid for both of them and walked into the bar. While my eyes adjusted to the dark, I stood there swaying and realized that I was really messed up. I had lost track of time and I wasn't really sure where I was, other than that I was in the bar where my buddy was. It came back to me slowly, as I mentally backtracked to the hospital and then back to the bar.

My buddy wasn't at the table. I sat down figuring he was in the restroom. He was, and when he came out, he was staggering. A smile showed his white teeth in the dim light of the bar as he recognized me and plopped down at the table. I gave him his shirt and he paid me back for the work.

"Where did you go?" he wanted to know. "I went to get some cigarettes," I said. "Did you get some?" he asked. I told him that I did. "Give me one," he demanded. "I thought you didn't smoke," I said, trying to avoid explaining the Vietnamese cigarettes. "I don't, but now I feel like smoking. Give me a cigarette!" I told him that I wasn't going to give him a cigarette and get him started down the road to nicotine addiction but he was drunk and having none of it. "Give me a blanking cigarette, specialist!"

This was the first time he had insinuated his rank into our relationship, and it made me mad. "Sure sarge. Wait a minute," I said as I opened the pack of Park Lane's. "What kind of cigarettes are those?" he slurred. "They're Vietnamese. It's all they had." "Ok. Give me one," and give him one I did, the SOB.

Here, I had just picked up his shirt for him, and he returned the favor by pulling rank on me. I didn't mind the fact that we were in the army where a rank structure exists, but I didn't like it when people used their rank to get their way in non-military situations. I tried to prevent him from becoming addicted to nicotine, like I was, and at the same time spare him from a life of degradation and sorrow as a pot head and drug addict, but he pissed me off, and he was sitting there like his stripes should mean something to me in this situation.

"Here," I said handing him a cigarette. I flipped my Zippo open and lit it. He leaned over and dueled with the flame for a moment, as he tried to focus and get the end of the cigarette in contact with the flame. I wasn't very steady myself, but eventually he got it lit. He puffed on it a few times and said, "What's the big deal about smoking?"

"You have to inhale to find out." He did, and started coughing. He took a swallow of beer and continued to smoke, inhaling a little now, and alternating smoke with beer. I was kind of interested to see how he would act when he started to feel the effects of 'took dinky dau.' I looked around the bar; it was still full of GI's. I wanted to see if anyone was noticing any strange smells, but everyone was fully engaged in beer drinking, smoking, and chatting to the girls, so I continued to drink as time passed.

This was the second time I had smoked this stuff and my mind was producing a mass of conflicting thoughts. I could hear every instrument of the band that was playing the song on the record being played. I had the urge to laugh now and then but then I worried that the people around me would notice that I was acting weird.

Suddenly the sarge busted out laughing. I looked at him and he was sitting there looking at his hand that was holding the cigarette. He was staring at his fingers and laughing like crazy. Looking over at me he said, "Look," and held his hand that was holding the cigarette in front of my face; "Look at my fingers!" I looked at his hand. His fingers were pretty thin and long. I looked back at him and laughed, "Yeah," was all I said. That cracked him up, "Yeah man, yeah," he laughed as he continued to look at his fingers.

I ordered a couple of more beers because my mouth was really dry. By the way the sarge drank, his must have been dry also. We sat there for an undetermined amount of time. He was watching his fingers and giggling, and I was spaced out and staring into the darkness at the other end of the room. One of the girls came and sat down. She put her hand on my thigh.

This was like a Lai Khe handshake at the Ville. She looked at the sarge who was still looking at his hand and giggling. "He beau-coup dinky dau," she said with a smile. "You lonely, GI?" That led to a thirty minute interlude in an upstairs room of the building on the other side of the bar from the tailor shop. As I was coming down the stairs, I passed three lieutenants going up and saluted them with loud and thunderous "Alpha Rangers, sir!" They all looked pretty embarrassed to be seen by one of the enlisted swine in such a place.

When I returned to the bar, I was hoping that the sarge was gone, but there he was passed out with his head on his happy hand. I shook his shoulder and he woke up. "Hey man, where you been? I'm hungry," he said. "How's your hand?" I asked him. He looked confused and then he said "it's fine." I'm sure he had no idea what I was talking about, but it had been a different kind of afternoon for him, and he was still trying to deal with many things. "I'm hungry too;" I really was. "Let's go find something to eat." It was dark now and when we walked outside our eyes were adjusted for night operations.

## Bien Hoa Airbase

We walked down the road until the shuttle bus came along. He waved it down and the driver took us to the airbase. We found the PX snack bar and got something to eat. There we met an Air Force first sergeant who invited us to eat at his table. He could see that we were pretty messed up, and when we told him that we had just gotten out of the hospital, he offered to put us up in his barracks.

That sounded good to us, so when we were through eating, we followed him a short distance to some buildings, and he led us to an open bay with double decker bunks. "Everybody stays in town, so there's always plenty of room." He gave us each a bunk that he was sure would not be claimed this night. The bunks had mattresses that must have been five or six inches thick. He showed us where the showers were, gave us a couple of towels and told us he would wake us in the morning for breakfast. Top was a real NCO and black man by birth. Like so many men I met over the years who showed kindness to me, me who only deserved to be shot, I wish I could see him again and say "Thank you and God Bless you!"

## Operation Cedar Falls

The sarge and I caught a chopper back to Lai Khe the next day. A big operation was on, called Cedar Falls, and I was excited to go back to the field. Maybe this time, we would kick Charlie's ass. The 25th Division and several other units had formed a large blocking force and the 3d Brigade of the 1st Infantry Division, the 11th Armored Cavalry Regiment, and the 173d Airborne Brigade were pushing through the Iron Triangle on S+D operations.

Operation Cedar Falls began for Alpha Company 1-16 Infantry with a combat air-assault into the Iron Triangle on 9 January while I was in the hospital. There was some shooting on the LZ and our platoon sergeant was wounded in the hand. After I rejoined the company, one of the guys told me that he was last seen running for the dust-off chopper with the medic chasing him with a field dressing. He got on and flew away. We never saw him again.

SSG Willie Magee, a former Marine and Korean War veteran, became the platoon sergeant. For the next six days they were on the move. On the 10th, Alpha Company found and destroyed twenty-five tons of rice. Other units nearby made some big scores of weapons, ammunition, and lots more rice. The company found a large hospital tunnel complex on the 12th and captured a wounded VC.

## Beer for the Pilot

On the morning of the 12th, I reported into the company area, drew a rifle and gathered up my gear. The first sergeant was there, and when he saw my subdued Division patch he lit into me and his final words after ripping it off my shoulder were, "This is the Big Red One not the big black one!"

The resupply chopper was going out that afternoon. I helped the mess sergeant load the mermite cans full of food, and trash cans full of iced beer and soda. We usually had a dinner meal of hot food flown to us in the field, and everyone got a cold beer or soda.

It seems kind of strange, looking back to the years when they would fly cold beer to you in the field, from when I was in Afghanistan in 2004, where you could get a court-martial for drinking a beer on a secured base. It was especially strange on one of the bases where the Canadians and the Germans, their grandfathers' deadly enemies sixty years before, sat drinking beer together every night.

I jumped on the chopper and we flew into the Iron Triangle. One of the pilots told me to hand him a beer. I did and watched him open it, drink it in one pour and ask for another. I knew we always had a few extra beers, so I gave him another, which he drank just as fast. He drank four beers while we flew to the battalion LZ, and when we landed, as I helped unload the food and beer, he reached around and punched me on the arm, and gave me a thumbs up; a different army, different time.

## Accidents

I moved away from the helicopter and asked a man standing nearby where my company was, but he didn't know. He told me to wait with a group of soldiers who were standing a short distance away. I went over and found out that they were waiting to join their units when they came to pick up their supplies. There was a blown up APC nearby, so I walked over to take a look at it.

There were some men nearby, and I asked if they knew what happened to the APC, "Did it hit a mine?" "No," one of them said, but didn't elaborate. I realized that they weren't real talkative, but I pressed on and asked them what they did. "We're engineers," one of them said. "Really, I'm a demo man myself," I proclaimed proudly. "A demo man?" said one of them sarcastically.

I could tell from the way he said it that they didn't believe me, probably because there was no such thing as a 'demo man' in the army. "Yeah, well I'm not really a 'demo man;' I just blow up dud rounds and booby-traps for my company." They were good with that explanation, and became a little friendlier.

After we talked for a few more minutes, I asked them if they had any spare crimpers. The guys didn't have any in the field, but they did have some back at their base camp, and I could get a pair if I came by their unit in Lai Khe. I asked if they had any spare C-4, and that's when they told me what happened to the APC.

They didn't have any C-4 because the destroyed APC had been carrying their C-4 in the back. There was a box of blasting caps lying on top of the C-4. One of the guys who had been riding on top, jumped through the large hatch behind the turret and landed on the box of caps. End of story.

I rejoined my company that afternoon. The platoon leader told me that I was acting squad leader, and would run second squad until the squad leader returned from R+R.

## Friday the 13th

The next morning, my squad was on point for the company. We also had to put a man out on each flank. All of my men were tired, so against my better judgment, I put a new guy on the left flank. He was supposed to walk within sight of the column and watch for ambushes and other enemy activity. Fifteen minutes later, as we were walking through some bomb craters, there was an explosion to the left front. The new guy was walking on a trail through the craters and tripped a booby-trap, probably a grenade on a string. I ran up to his location and found him lying on his back and bleeding heavily from his legs.

The medic arrived right behind me, and I helped him treat the wounded man. He had two broken femurs, and as I helped the medic put splints on his legs, I could feel and hear crepitus, the broken bones grinding together in his legs. The LT had formed a perimeter and told the men to start cutting down the small trees, so that a helicopter could land to pick up the wounded man. There were a lot of trees, and it looked like it would take an hour of very hard work by everyone in the platoon, before we could clear an LZ.

I remembered the message on the bulletin board and told the LT to request a Stokes Litter with the Medevac chopper. He looked at me like I was stupid, and asked me what I was talking about. I told him again to request a Stokes Litter and told him what it was. He looked like he didn't believe me, but went ahead and asked for the litter.

Twenty minutes later, the dust-off chopper showed up, hovered over the injured man, and lowered a litter on a steel cable attached to a winch. We put him and all his equipment on the litter. They winched him up and flew away. The new guy had come to the company early that morning, got wounded before noon, and was on his way back to the states that afternoon. I never knew his name.

After the medevac, the platoon moved out and entered the jungle. About 100 meters into the bush, we found a huge enemy base camp. It was empty, but there was plenty of evidence that the enemy had been there recently. The exploding booby-trap may have warned them away.

There was a deep trench surrounding the camp with numerous fighting positions attached to the trench. The positions were well built and everything had a neat appearance. We moved into the camp slowly, and found a large number of huts. It looked like Charlie had gone out the back door as we came in the front. The guys were finding bowls of food on the tables in the huts. I sat down on a log to take a break.

I watched Sergeant Magee as he looked around, and when I saw him backing away from a hut, I felt something was wrong and told him, "Hey, Sergeant Magee, if I were you I wouldn't take another step." I said this in a casual way, but he froze where he was. I walked over to where he was standing, reached down, and turned over a leaf on the ground.

There was a CBU Butterfly Bomb buried nose up under the leaf. He would have stepped on it if I hadn't stopped him. Would it have gone off if he had stepped on it? I don't know, but we were all happy that we didn't find out. We left the camp shortly after this, and returned to our perimeter. That bit of good luck would have been better appreciated, had we known about the not so 'friendly fire' incident that afternoon, when a battalion TOT of eighteen 105mm artillery rounds landed on a company of the 1-28 Infantry nearby, killing nine and wounding forty-four.

The next day was more of the same, with patrols around the perimeter. Our ambush patrols went out that night, as usual, and the next morning one of them blew a claymore when they heard some noise. They nailed one VC and got his pistol. The next day was more patrolling, and after we returned to the perimeter that afternoon, we were told that we were going back to Lai Khe in the morning.

### Goin' to Lima Kilo-Amen

Some of the brothers started singing their version of a popular spiritual song by Curtis Mayfield and the Impressions, "Amen." The verses were made up on the spot and the one I remember was, "goin to Lima Kilo (Lai Khe), A-men, goin to have a party, A-men, the first sergeant said so, A-men, Amen, Amen!"[228]

The choppers did show up the next morning, and we did go back to Lima Kilo, where we finished off the month of January, making quick trips to the bush, and partying in between while filling sandbags and burning our shit. Towards the end of the month, I spent the night of my 21st birthday on ambush patrol, and I remember being pretty proud of myself for living so long.

### STATS

Operation Cedar Falls was the largest, and first deliberately planned, multi-division offensive operation of the Vietnam War. The II Field Force, commanded by our former Division Commander LTG Jonathan Seaman, put twenty battalions of infantry, supported by ten or more artillery battalions, into what was called the Iron Triangle. General DePuy called it a 'decisive turning point' in III Corps.

This was a large scale operation designed to defeat any main force VC units that threatened Saigon, and to destroy their logistical bases, but the VC units weren't there. We forcibly resettled the 6000 people of the village of Ben Suc, and several other villages nearby, to refugee camps near Lai Khe, before the engineers destroyed their villages.[229]

Of course there was the usual firepower extravaganza. The total for the Division was over the top with: 215,319 rounds of artillery, all calibers, and 1,358 close air support sorties which dropped 798 tons of bombs, 721 tons of napalm, 74 Cluster Bomb Units, 1445 3-inch rockets, 153,810 rounds of 20mm, and 12,000 rounds of .50 caliber. They also dropped a ton of white phosphorus, which I believe was used to try and start a fire that would burn down the rest of the jungle in the Triangle. But it rained pretty heavily shortly after they dropped it.[230]

Enemy casualties were put at 750 KIA, body-count, naturally, 250 POWs, and 540 Chieu Hoi. Weapons captured included twenty-three crew served weapons, 590 individual weapons along with 60,000 rounds of small arms ammo. Most of the weapons and ammo were discovered in hidden caches. There were 7,500 uniforms captured and 3,700 tons of rice. Many base camps and tunnel complexes were destroyed. Over 500,000 pages of enemy documents were also captured, giving the Intel people a job of work getting them translated.[231]

Allied casualties were reported as eighty-three KIA and 345 WIA. Equipment losses included one tank and three APCs. The U.S. employed an appropriately named bulldozer, the Rome Plow, to clear eleven square kilometers of jungle. Since there was nothing of importance to prevent it, they also bulldozed a large 1st Infantry Division patch into the jungle, for the visual delight of those flying over the area. Since the VC didn't have any aircraft, they were unaware of our claiming that area and reoccupied it soon after we left.[232]

## Target Practice

We had a few days in Lai Khe. One afternoon we had rifle marksmanship instruction and some target practice. We were shooting at silhouette targets between the bunkers on our part of the perimeter, when I noticed that my ejected cartridges were landing close behind one of the squad leaders that I didn't like. He was a typical young white southern racist, and I couldn't understand why he hadn't embraced the freedom that had been given to us in the army to judge one another on performance instead of race.

I moved my position slightly, and after a few adjustments, I was putting hot cartridges down the back of his neck. He was wiggling around, trying to get them away from his skin as he continued to fire his rifle at the targets. I continued to pay much more attention to the strike of my empty brass, than I did to my bullet placement.

I got Rodney's attention and showed him what I was doing, which amused him but the CO noticed my tormenting of one of his sergeants, and shouted at me, ordering me to stop. The sergeant never did snap to what was going on, and continued to try and hit some targets, although now he didn't have the added training value of my hot brass attacks on the back of his neck to overcome.

That night we were down at our new beer club. Rodney and I got in an argument with my target. His racism was a source of irritation to some of the black guys in the platoon, and after a few beers, we were ready to school him on the desegregation order of President Truman, and any other thing that came to our minds that would help him understand that we didn't like him and his racist ways.

After the club closed, we continued our harangue, sitting on the front steps of our hooch. He was pretty drunk too, and argued back that we didn't know anything about the issue, which by then, had become somewhat obscure in our alcoholic fog. It had gotten personal, and since there were two of us and he knew he couldn't beat both of us in a fight, he continued to argue until all of a sudden, he burst into tears.

Now he was sobbing with his head on his arms, and we were laughing and taunting him until Sergeant Magee came over and told us all to knock it off and go to bed. A few days later, I was talking to Magee about something, and he looked at me kind of funny and said, "Murry, you're blacker than I am." I never knew if that was a compliment or a complaint.

*Watch therefore, for you do not know the day nor the hour*
*Matthew 25:13*

# Chapter 12-February 1967

### Operation Vietnam

When we returned to Lai Khe after Cedar Falls, we continued to go out on S+D operations so often that I wondered why they chose to try and delineate any particular time by giving it a name. We were on Operation Vietnam, and it never ended until you got to go home. Nevertheless, the next operation, Operation Williston, took place from 1 to 12 February 1967. Our company had been assigned to the 1-4 Cav, to conduct road clearing on Hwy. 13 near Bau Bang.[233]

### Operation Williston

This time period coincided with the Vietnamese New Year, which they called Tet. A deal had been cut and a cease fire would be in effect from the 8th to the 12th of February. During that period, nobody was supposed to take any offensive actions, so we had to stay in our perimeter and only send out LP/OPs and ambush patrols during the night.

We started with an airlift to a secure LZ. After digging in, we sent out the usual LPs and ambush patrols. Each day we cleared the road, set up our outposts, and took a break. In the afternoon we were re-supplied by helicopter. On the third day the platoon sergeant told us that one of our NCOs was killed on an ambush patrol at a laterite pit south of Lai Khe, where the engineers went each day for road building material. There was an ambush patrol placed there every night, and the routine caught up with him.

### Routines

I was taking a nap while my partner was watching. He woke me up by shaking my arm and, when my eyes opened, he was holding his finger to his lips and hissing quietly. "What's up?" I asked him. "There's been some shooting over there," he said, pointing to his right. We were both up and ready to fight, when the squad leader came running by. "Stay there and keep your eyes open," he ordered and continued on his way.

We waited, and after a while, the platoon sergeant came by and told us that three guys from one of our platoon's machine gun crews had been shot by a VC. "They were all laying down reading the funny papers, when a VC and a young boy walked into their position. The VC had an AK. He hosed them with it and took off. Sergeant Smith went into the bush by himself looking for them."

Staff Sergeant Smith, our squad leader, was a veteran of the Dominican Republic operation where he was a recipient of the Silver Star for his actions with the 82d Airborne Division. He was a country boy from Alabama and at home in the woods. I watched the area to our right, and after a while, Smith came out of the tree-line. He came out near our location, so I waved at him and he came over.

He told us, "I followed their tracks, but they looked like they were made by people who were running, and I didn't want to get too far out there by myself."

I really admired his courage to go out there by himself for any distance, and told him so. He just laughed and told us to keep our eyes open, as he moved back to the area where the men were hit. By that time a dust-off chopper had arrived and medevac'd the three wounded men to the hospital in Bien Hoa. They all survived, but we never saw two of them again. The third guy came back a few months later, and told us he was laying there reading the Stars and Stripes when he heard a noise. He looked up and saw a Vietnamese man standing there with a small boy standing next to him. "He aimed the AK from his hip and started shooting. We all got hit and he hauled ass."

## The Races

I tried to get to know Sergeant Smith. He was a likeable NCO with a sense of humor for most things, but he was hard on you if you screwed up. From Alabama, he complied with the integration policies of the Armed Forces that were ordered by President Truman. But every time we were back at the base camp, he showed how he felt about it by requesting a song from the Lai Khe radio station that he would dedicate to the 82d Airborne Division, "Papa Oom Mow Mow," by the Rivingtons. When I asked him about his musical tastes, figuring that he would be a country music fan like the rest of the NCO Corps, he told me that there were a lot of black soldiers in the 82d but that was all he would say.[234]

As I look back, I remember that there were a lot of black paratroopers in those days. The anti-war people were complaining that the black people were being sent into combat at a higher percentage than the whites, but actually, the paratroops were always a volunteer outfit. So why were so many black soldiers in the airborne infantry? I'd say it was because the civil rights movement had shown that if you could fight for your country, you should have the same rights as the rest of the country.

The younger soldiers like me were very susceptible to the mystique of the elite forces, and I too hoped to jump out of airplanes someday. So I can understand why even a freak like Jimi Hendrix ended up in the airborne when he was in the Army. Nowadays it is difficult to find many black soldiers in combat arms. I think their parents must have told them that the older generation paid the price; so if you're going into the service, get a safe job.

## The Tet Truce

Tet is the Vietnamese New Year and it is the most important cultural event of the year, like our Christmas and New Year. Just like we do, everyone in Vietnam tried to get home for Tet, including the VC.

The truce, as it was explained to us, required us to stay in our perimeters and not conduct offensive operations, that is, search and destroy. The VC were supposed to stay put, but many of them had families near their bases, so probably some went home while other VC/NVA units took the opportunity to move to a different location.

**Bill Williamson:** *"Even though it was the TET Truce, a safety radius was drawn around the positions of the U.S. units that would allow them to protect themselves in case a VC unit was beginning to position itself to attack the U.S. unit. To further that protection night ambush patrols were placed within that circle."*[235]

### Ambush Patrol

On the first day of the truce, I was moved to another squad as a fire team leader, and that night it was my squad's turn for ambush patrol. A sergeant, just arrived from the States, had been assigned to the platoon and he was our new squad leader. I walked point and the new squad leader walked right behind me. The plan was to set up on a trail about 700 meters south of our perimeter. We took off just as it was getting dark and walked along the edge of the wood-line towards the trail. I stopped every so often to listen and check the area in front of us. On one of these stops I noticed that my squad leader's M-16 rifle was set on full-auto.

I told him, very quietly, to put his weapon on safe like everyone else. "I'm the only one who keeps his weapon on fire and I don't want someone walking behind me with an unsafed weapon." He didn't like the fact that I was giving him orders, but he did as I said and motioned for me to move out. A little ways further he stopped us and said that this is where we would set up. I thought we should have gone a little farther and told him, but he insisted that we were in the right place and told us to set up here. The squad set up on a line, about ten feet between positions. The men put out their Claymores and we settled in to wait.

It was dark now and we couldn't see a thing. I was on the right side of the ambush and the squad leader was on the left. I had a radio near me and I took turns monitoring it with the RTO. About an hour after we set up, I began to hear noises to our right front. I could hear people walking and talking and what sounded like bicycles rattling. I alerted the men near me and called the squad leader on the radio.

When I began talking, it alerted the company HQ. When I stopped, I heard Captain Williamson alerting the mortar crews to be ready to fire. The sound of the movement to our front increased and I waited for the squad leader to order us to open fire. He never did, and we sat there listening to what must have been a battalion of VC move past us. They had crossed Hwy. 13 and were continuing east for the holidays. The next morning, the CO sent patrols out and determined that the trail used by the enemy was the one we were supposed to ambush. The squad leader was reassigned, and I became squad leader.

### 3d Platoon Ambush Patrol

The next night, the 3d Platoon sent out an ambush patrol, this time to the west, on the other side of the highway. Soon after they left the perimeter we heard some firing and looked that way. Red tracers were flying through the brush, and green tracers were arching into the sky. After the shooting started, a Duster cranked up and roared out of the perimeter.

The Duster was a twin barreled 40mm Anti-Aircraft Gun mounted on a tank chassis. It crossed the road and the crew started firing to the southwest. There was a large open area just to the south of where the ambush patrol had made contact, and the VC were fleeing across it. The Duster fired a slew of 40mm, and when the crew couldn't see any more VC, they returned to the perimeter.

**Bill Williamson:** *"Since several ambush patrols were out that night, the plan was to keep two dusters in the Company NDP with them on alert to immediately move to reinforce any ambush patrol that made contact. When the 3d Platoon patrol made contact, the two dusters zipped down Highway 13 to the point opposite the contact and opened direct fire into the area where the VC were providing murderous covering fire for the ambush patrol."*

**Jose Garcia:** *"I turned 22 that day and my gun crew was celebrating my birthday. They held me down and slugged my arm 22 times. Someone made a C-ration dessert and we had cold drinks from the resupply. Roland Wilson told me I would get killed. When the shooting started across the road, I opened fire in the same direction as the twin 40's."*[236]

**Bill Williamson:** *"The high rate of fire typical of an anti-aircraft weapon and the "super-quick' fuses on their individual rounds created havoc among the VC unit. The super quick fuses were so sensitive that leaves and small tree limbs would detonate the individual rounds. This resulted in a shower of shell fragments impacting on the VC unit and a high rate of casualties for them."*[237]

The next morning the 3d Platoon ambush patrol returned to the perimeter and we eventually heard part of the story of what had happened. Years later, I heard the rest of the story.

On their way out, they were walking parallel to the road, when the point man of a VC element on a trail that crossed the road, bumped into the machine gunner in the middle of the squad. "Who are you?" the machine gunner said. "Choi oi!" was the reply, and the machine gunner opened fire down the trail with a long burst. The VC point man was a female armed with an AK-47. He took her out with the long burst we had heard, along with several other VC that were behind her. The green tracers came from one of them.[238]

The medic ran up to the front because he thought one of our guys got hit. He found the female VC and thinking that she was one of ours, began to frantically work on her. He was reciting her injuries as he found them, "He's hit in the stomach, in the chest, in the head, oh my God, he's hit everywhere." After the others determined that everyone was ok, they started laughing at the medic, which made him mad, as he tried to save the life of his 'comrade.' The rest of the company got a good laugh when one of the guys told the story.

### Picking up the Pieces

That morning, our platoon was directed to make a sweep through that open area to see if the Duster had hit anyone. As I was walking along I noticed what looked like a bundle of rags lying on the ground. Maybe the enemy dropped something in their haste. I walked over to it for a closer look. There was an SKS rifle lying underneath the bundle so I reached down to pick it up. It wasn't a bundle of rags, because rags don't bleed. It was part of a body, but it looked very strange. I prodded the body part with my rifle, and in doing so caused it to roll over and now, I was looking at something that resembled a rolled pastry.

The dead man's head was in the middle, and his body was rolled backwards around his head all the way to his feet. One or two of the guys came over when they saw I had found something. We all stood there staring at a really strange example of death from a high powered weapon. The 40mm round hit him but didn't explode was my guess. We weren't doing autopsies on our enemies in those days, so we policed up the rifle and continued the sweep. A general flew out to the perimeter that afternoon and decorated several members of the ambush patrol.

**Bill Williamson:** *"The search of the ambush site the next morning revealed that the VC unit did contain a number of women and they were also carrying rucksacks filled with ink and printing materials. We also found parts that we thought were appropriate for printing presses. All of this caused us to conclude that the unit was a psychological warfare unit that was being repositioned under the cover of the TET Truce. There were also several dozen dead VC (both men and women) that were badly chewed up by the duster's rounds."*[239]

## Village Cordon and Search

A few hours later, we were told to saddle up and get on some tanks and APCs belonging to the 1-4 Cavalry. We hauled ass north on Hwy. 13 for a few miles until we saw a small village ahead on the right. The lead tank and several APCs pulled off the highway and moved east around the south end of the small collection of huts; the other vehicles continued north and went around the north side. We jumped off and formed a line facing north. The platoon leader told us to move forward and search the village.

We had never done a village search; usually, we just cordoned off the village and the ARVNs did the searching. I was carrying a machine gun and went into the first hut in front of me. It was kind of strange just walking into someone's house carrying a machine gun. If the enemy or an armed homeowner had been inside, I would have been dead. I pulled open the door and stepped inside. There was an old woman on the other side of room. She looked as scared as I felt.

I made a threatening gesture with my M-60 and she gritted her teeth and closed her eyes in preparation for the pain that comes with bullets going through the body. Even I could see that I'd frightened her, so I attempted to calm her with English language phrases like, "Don't worry mama san, we're just looking for VC." Then I asked her if she had seen any VC. She just stared at me, so I looked around the hut. There was a small hole in one of the walls that could have been a peephole, so I pointed at it and said, "VC, mama san, VC?" Once again she clenched up, waiting for me to shoot her. Then I heard a loud explosion nearby.

**Jose Garcia:** *"LT Menton was wounded while talking to a woman when Charlie blew a claymore. A piece of shrapnel hit him in the belt buckle and he was medevaced."*[240]

I left the old woman and joined the others in the center of the village. The medics treated LT Menton, moved him to an open area where a dust-off chopper landed, and took him away. After the medevac left, a jeep pulled up. All the men that were found in the village had been gathered into a group. There was a man in the back of the jeep with a sandbag over his head. Eye holes were cut in it. The man stood in the back of the jeep, and the village men were paraded in front of him. He pointed out the VC to an ARVN officer.

I remembered reading about a similar practice used by the German Army in France during WWII. The problem was that the French would take the opportunity to get revenge for long standing feuds. We were told to get on the vehicles and, that was the last time I participated in a village search. I can still see the face of that old woman when I pointed my machine gun at her.

## Claymore Ambush

SSG Klutts, the only 'Ranger' qualified sergeant in the company, was a squad leader in our platoon. He wasn't well liked and we thought his last name pretty well described his abilities, but he showed us a trick. After our experience with a large element of VC walking past us while we were on ambush, and the meeting engagement on the trail by the ambush patrol from 3d Platoon, the CO ordered us to patrol more aggressively.

One afternoon, after a long patrol, our platoon was returning to the perimeter when we stopped near a trail for about 15 minutes, while something was going on up at the front of the column. When we began to move again, I came upon Sergeant Klutts doing something to a tree on the side of the trail. When I got close to him, the column stopped and I asked him what he was doing.

He showed me a C-ration spoon and a clothes pin with some metal pieces on the ends of the clothes pin. He had some wires attached to the pieces of metal on the clothes pin. The spoon had a hole in it and a piece of string was tied to it. He said, "I'm going to put a Claymore in this bush and sight it down the trail. Then I'm going to cut the positive blasting cap wire in half and attach each end to a metal piece on the clothes pin. I will separate the metal pieces with the handle of the spoon and run the string across the trail. I'll put the other ends of the blasting cap wire in these holes on this old radio battery. When Charlie comes down the trail and hits the string, he's gonna wish he skipped this holiday."

The column started moving again, so I asked him if he needed any help, wanting to see more. He said that he was almost done, so I moved with the column and a few minutes later we were inside the perimeter. We had just started eating chow when we heard an explosion in the direction of the Claymore. "Saddle up," shouted the platoon sergeant. We formed up quickly and moved back to the area of the Claymore. The odor of the explosive and another smell, blood, were heavy in the dusk.

There were several bodies lying in the trail, and one of them was moving. One of our guys ran up to the one who was moving and fired a 20 round magazine at him on full auto and then started yelling, "I got one, I got one;" but he hadn't hit him at all. The man's legs were shredded by the Claymore and he was bleeding out fast. A squad leader, Sergeant Aloha, walked over to him, looked at him for a moment, and then shot him in the head with his rifle. The CO showed up and told me to take rearguard and withdraw my squad back to the perimeter last. I bounded the men by fire team back to the road and had one team cover the rest until we all crossed the road and reentered the perimeter. Sergeant Klutts was pleased, and we were impressed with the success of his Claymore ambush.

### A Failure to Communicate

After Tet, we went back to road clearance operations near Bau Bang. We were set up near where we had been the first time I came here, on the west side of the road. I received a radio message telling me to take my squad down to where a checkpoint had been established on Highway 13 and relieve the squad that was there. There was a lot of civilian traffic on the road: buses, large trucks, and small open trucks that carried people. Alpha Six, Captain Williamson, called me on the radio.

My RTO gave me the handset and I gave my call sign and waited. "This is Alpha Six, I want you to expedite the traffic to the South, over." "Expedite the traffic?" I said out loud. The squad was looking at me but no one spoke. I called him back, "Alpha Six, this is Alpha two-three, say again, over." "This is Alpha Six, I say again, expedite the traffic to the South, over." That time I clearly heard the word, 'expedite,' so I said "Alpha Six, this is Alpha two-three, roger, over." "This is Alpha Six, out." I looked at the other guys, "What in the hell does expedite mean?" I asked. No one said a thing.

This was bad. The CO had ordered me to do something, and I was too proud to call him back and ask him what 'expedite' meant. The guys were standing there looking at me, so I began to work the problem verbally. "Let me see, 'expedite,' hmmm, 'expedite.'" I hemmed and hawed for a while and then it came to me.

"Expedite, it's got an 'X' in it, like the 'X' at a railroad crossing, right?" The guys all nodded their heads. "Yeah, it's got an 'X' in it like a railroad crossing. That means that he wants us to stop the traffic going south, 'expedite' means to stop."

"I wish he'd learn to speak English," one of the guys said, but everyone was relieved that I had translated the CO's message. I stepped out onto the road and held my hand out like I was a cop directing traffic back home. A bus was coming, and when the driver saw me, he began to slow down. I didn't move so the bus came to a stop, and the driver started talking to me in Vietnamese. He appeared to be agitated, as he spewed out a stream in the sing-song language of Vietnam. I just smiled and made a gesture which in the U.S. meant 'calm down, chill out.' Who knows what it meant in his culture.

### Communication Breakdown

I had only recently found out that the Vietnamese hand signal for 'come here' was almost the exact opposite as the one we used. When you wanted someone to come to you in Vietnam, you held your fore-arm parallel to the ground, and waved your hand up and down with your wrist, at the person you wanted to come to you. When we want someone to come to us, we extend our fore-arm and bring the palm of our hand up toward us. Many times I saw Vietnamese peasants out in the rice paddies stand and stare at us when we waved for them to come to us. We didn't know if they were afraid or they didn't like us. They would just stare at us until we walked over to them.

Meanwhile, the traffic was backing up at our checkpoint. Vietnamese drivers tried to persuade me to let them pass, but I 'expedited' each one. Suddenly, one of the guys called out, "Convoy coming!" I looked to the north and saw black smoke above the highway. This is weird, I thought. Why would the Captain stop the traffic going south if a convoy was going south? Why indeed?

The RTO came running up to me holding out the handset, "It's Six, man, and he sounds pissed!" "This is Alpha two-three over," I said. He came back with, "Why has the southbound traffic stopped?" "Because you told me to stop it, over," I replied. "I told you to expedite the traffic to the south; that means to make it go fast to the south." (I'm sure he would have added, "You idiot," but he was a gentleman to his troops). Thanks for the vocabulary lesson, I thought, "Roger, Alpha Six, I will make sure that happens, over." "This is Alpha Six, out!"

## Change of Command-Division

On 10 February, Major General William DePuy finished his tour and Major General John Hay took command of the division. Everybody hoped that things would slow down after General DePuy's manic pursuit of the VC, but that was not to be. General Hay made a few minor adjustments to our foxholes, now they were called the 'Hay Hole,' and if anything, our optempo increased.

## Sick Call, Again

Two days later, we had guard duty on the bunker line at Lai Khe. This time we were covering our sector and the sector next to ours that belonged to a company from the 2-28 Infantry. The water pump for the Lai Khe base was here, and our position was right behind the Vietnamese village in the middle of the base camp. During the early morning hours, the VD agents infiltrated our positions and we availed ourselves of the services they provided.

I was with one of the girls, lying on my poncho liner, when a helicopter flew over us, coming in from the west to land on the airstrip. One of the pilots must have seen us through the Plexiglas at his feet because, the next thing I knew, they were circling above our position and one of the door gunners was leaning out, taking pictures while the others waved.

It was all fun and games until three days later, when I experienced a great deal of pain when I tried to urinate. I went to our medic and told him about it and he started laughing. "Gone, gone, gone, gone, gonna, gonorrhea," he sang, a parody of the chorus of a popular song of the day. He sent me on sick call where I got my first shot of penicillin.

The doctor wasn't very nice. He diagnosed me with gonorrhea, just like our medic said, and ordered me to take the first of three penicillin shots. "You're gonna hafta get a shot or you know it's gonna rot, gone gone," went the rest of the chorus of the song that our medic sang to me as he was preparing the injection. Man, did that shot hurt!

When I returned to the company area, met the CO on the way back to my hooch. I saluted him and he returned it. We passed each other, and I was hoping to get into my hooch when I heard him call my name. I stopped and turned around.

"I see from the sick call report that you had a medical problem this morning. Everything ok?" he asked, toying with me a little. "Yes sir, the medics took care of everything." "I hope it wasn't anything serious." "No sir," I said. "I understand you were having a lot of pain when you were urinating." "Yes sir," I knew I was done for now.

"Did the battalion surgeon tell you what the problem was?" "Well, yes sir, he said that I needed three penicillin shots and that that would take care of it." "Take care of what?" "My medical problem, sir." "What did he call your problem, Murry?" This was the signal that he was done toying with me. "The clap, sir." He looked at me for a moment, "How did you get that?" "It must have been down at the Ville, sir." He knew that it was unlikely that I had been infected in the Ville, but didn't choose to pursue it. He turned and left. I was back on multiple shit-lists, and I had six months to go.

## Operation Tucson D

The next operation took place in the Long Nguyen Secret Zone, a place so secret that I never heard of it until I read the after action reports forty years later. This 'secret zone' was just west of Lai Khe and extended to the north. We spent a lot of time there trying to discover its 'secrets.'

The operation started on 14 February with an air-assault into an area north of Lai Khe. There was an intensive prep of the LZ, and we went in hot. Charlie must have taken off, because we made it to the tree-line standing up. Each company took off on its own course into the jungle for what turned out to be the great rice hunt. That afternoon we found 20,000 pounds of rice. The other units of 1-16 and 2-28 Infantry were finding rice also. By the end of the day, we had taken 408 tons of rice from the VC.

While the higher ups were happy, we were pissed. We had to carry the bags of rice out to a larger trail, so the Cav unit could drive it out to the highway. The VC weren't happy either, and the small elements, charged with guarding the rice, were busy laying mines and booby-traps and sniping when they could. Shortly after midnight they mortared the battalion perimeter, and eight men from Bravo Company were wounded. I slept through the entire event.[241]

> **Jose Garcia:** *"One night, we heard mortar rounds leaving a tube and ten or twelve rounds landed nearby. After a check for accountability, Murry was missing. People were looking everywhere and finally found him, wrapped up in a poncho, sleeping. One night, from the position next to mine, Burris shot at me then apologized next morning. The next night, I woke up in front of our position after sleepwalking past perimeter. I decided to low crawl back to keep from getting shot but everyone was sleeping."*[242]

## The VC Hornets

We were on a company sized search and destroy mission. We had been finding small rice caches all over the place. The rice was stored on small platforms a few feet off the ground. The last squad in the file was setting them on fire with any dry brush in the area. They would stack it beneath the platforms and light it on fire. This would set the platforms on fire, and eventually, the rice that wasn't burned would spill onto the jungle floor, and with time become unusable. The VC might recover some, but we didn't care. This method was better than us having to carry the rice to a road or an LZ, so it could be transported out of there.

As we continued moving through this area, we found more and more caches. Some of the drier vegetation had caught fire, and the smoke and flames were creating a dark curtain behind us. Eventually there was quite a conflagration. We were walking into what little wind there was, so there wasn't any real danger of the fire advancing toward us, but we were in a hurry to get out of there. I was with my squad, and we were moving quickly through the thin brush, when we heard a shout from the lead platoon. Everyone took a knee. I prepared to shoot and I could hear safeties clicking on the rifles around me.

Someone started screaming up in front, then several more. "What the ..?" All of a sudden someone up there started yelling, "Retreat, retreat!" Then I heard the sounds of a large number of soldiers crashing through the brush to our right front. We moved slightly off the trail, and then I heard someone moving quickly up the trail from behind us. I turned to see who it was and saw the first sergeant.

He had a determined look on his face and he was talking to himself as he passed us. "What the hell is going on up there? I'll straighten this shit out!" he muttered as he stormed ahead. By now we figured that something bad was going on up front. Since there were no bullets or grenades involved, and it didn't include anyone from our platoon, we took the opportunity to make ourselves comfortable, We remained ready to move into action if need be, while we waited for the first sergeant to 'straighten things out' up ahead.

There was more shouting, then screaming from the front of the column, and then we saw the first sergeant running down the trail toward us. His helmet was gone; he had his rifle in one hand and with his other, he was swatting all around his head and the back of his neck. He flew past us back down the trail.

One of the guys said, "I don't think top straightened anything out up there." Then there was stirring from the men ahead of us. "Don't move!" "Look out!" "Stay still!" I looked up the trail from where I was sitting. There was a formation of very big hornets flying slowly down the trail toward me, about two and a half feet above the ground. It seems that the point man had cut their home in half with his machete, and now they were out for some payback.

They would stop at each man and look at him. Everyone was frozen. They came to me, and out of the corner of my eye, I could see them staring at me. The noise of their wings was deafening. They hovered there for a very long minute. I could feel them looking me over to see if I wanted some of what they had given to those people up front. Usually, we all stood up for each other in bar room brawls and fire-fights with the enemy; but this was different.

I tried to send a telepathic message to the lead hornet telling him that I was very sorry about the disgusting behavior of those other people. I wanted to tell him that we had just met these other people, and that if we had known what they were going to do to piss you hornets off, we wouldn't have had anything to do with them. I had told my parents the same thing many times.

My message seemed to satisfy the lead hornet, and he moved on to the guys behind me. I joined the chorus of recommendations, "Don't move, don't look at them, stay still, etc." Eventually the hornets grew tired of their sport and moved on to find a new place for a home, or maybe they flew back to COSVN Headquarters where their VC handlers gave them new orders.

The company began to regroup. All of the weapons and most of the equipment were recovered. When all the platoon leaders had accounted for their personnel and equipment, they notified the CO, who ordered our platoon to take the point position and continue the sweep. I'm sure that the man on point was very careful about where he swung his machete.

The 16th Infantry Regiment had a glorious history. Some said that the men of the regiment had fought like Rangers at Omaha Beach during the D-Day invasion of Europe in 1944. Yes, we had a proud tradition and each one of us tried, within our own abilities, some beyond their abilities, some even beyond the call of duty, to uphold the honor and glory of the 16th Infantry. But that day, we suffered one of the regiment's most ignominious defeats, the day the Rangers met the Hornets.

### A Shot in the Dark

The battalion moved to a new perimeter; on the way, we came to a large clearing. We skirted along the tree-line until we reached the southern end of the clearing, which had narrowed into a small open area about twenty meters wide. The going was slow, but we got to our destination several hours before dark.

The company dug-in as usual, but my squad, was alerted for the ambush patrol. The ambush location was about halfway back towards the clearing. We moved there through the dark and set up on a trail.

At about 0500, we heard a mortar firing nearby. The sound was coming from the direction of the clearing we had passed on the way to the new NDP. The CP called us on the radio and told us to send an azimuth on the direction of the mortar. The squad leader had the compass, but he couldn't read it in the dark. Taking flashlights on ambush was forbidden due to some incident in the past, and now, we couldn't read the compass.

The squad leader was straining his eyes, the mortar tube kept spitting out rounds that were landing in our perimeter, and the CP pressed us for an azimuth. "Tell him that they are being fired from the south end of the clearing we passed yesterday morning," I told him. "How do you know?" he said. "Just tell them," I whispered, "that the mortar is in the south end of the clearing."

He didn't have any other options, so he told them what I said. A few moments later I heard mortar rounds leaving the tubes from our Company's position, and soon, they started landing in the direction of that clearing. They must have fired twenty rounds, and then they stopped. The enemy mortar had also stopped firing. The rest of the night passed without incident, and the next morning, a patrol was sent back to the clearing to check on the effectiveness of our rounds. They found a base plate for an 82mm mortar right where I told them the firing was coming from. There were a number of fresh craters around the clearing, so it looked like they just grabbed their tube and ran.

## Operation Tucson D: Results

The artillery fired 7,267 rounds of 105mm, mostly for LZ prep and the typical shooting that went on here and there throughout all our operations. The Air Force flew seventy-one sorties of close air support. The butcher bill was low unless you happened to be on it.

The brigade lost three men KIA and thirty men WIA. We also lost one APC destroyed and three tanks damaged. There were no known enemy losses. There was 1,622.2 tons of rice discovered. Of that, 1482.2 tons were destroyed and 140 tons were extracted. That's 2800 bags of rice weighing, 100 pounds apiece, that had to be carried at least 50 and up to 200 meters from the cache, to a road or trail big enough for the APCs to carry it out.

According to my wife, a serving of rice weighs 35 grams, which comes out to 42,047,424 servings, which, by my calculations, is enough rice for three meals a day for 38,399 men for a year. We also destroyed 27 tons of salt; what's life without a little salt?[243]

If an army travels on its stomach, the VC in that area were going to be moving slow on half-rations for a while. This operation was a part of a build up to Operation Junction City, which would be the largest operation of the Vietnam War. The army was interested in body-count, not rice count. Maybe we got all the rice in the area, and that's why we encountered so few VC later; maybe there was a lot more rice nearby. If we got all the rice, maybe the VC would have had to give up their 'large unit' war, and we could have gone home.

## Meanwhile, Back at the Ranch
### Lessons in Leadership

The first sergeant called for a meeting of the NCOs, and those like me who were filling NCO positions. He told us to sit down on the cots in one of the huts while he spoke to us about leadership; 'guts' leadership was what he called it. He wanted us to lead our squads and platoons from the front with our 'guts.' He didn't have much more to say about the subject, but he managed to stretch the session out for thirty minutes. No one openly disagreed with him, but the atmosphere in the hut was tense. The older NCOs had their own opinions about the first sergeant and his 'guts' leadership style; it looked like the words that were meant to inspire us before the next 'big push,' were falling on deaf ears.

## Weapons Squad Leader

Sergeant Magee took me aside after the first sergeant's exhortation and told me that I was now the weapons squad leader. Roland had gone home along with some of the older sergeants. Most of the replacements we were getting now were men who had just finished basic and AIT. The Army had stripped the units in Germany of the NCOs in 1965 to cadre the units being sent to Vietnam, and now, more and more of the fire team and squad leader positions were being filled by Spec-4s like me and PFCs.

I went back to the weapons squad hooch and had a meeting with the gunners outside. Jose had been leading his crew for some time. Donnie, his faithful companion, was his assistant gunner and Howard was the ammo bearer. The other gun crew was led by Robert, a draftee from Philadelphia. His assistant gunner was Fred from New York and a man from New Jersey. I let them know what I knew about the upcoming operation, which wasn't much, and told them to get ready for more of the same stuff we had been doing.

The weapons squad was supposed to have two machine gun crews and two recoilless rifle crews. We had the 90mm recoilless rifles, but seldom brought them to the field. I demonstrated their use once to some visiting somebody's, while we were on road clearance in Bau Bang, but that was the only time we used one.

As weapons squad leader, I was to assist the platoon leader with the placement of the machine guns for our night defensive position. The machine guns were usually placed on either the left or right flanks of the platoon, with one of our rifle positions between them, and the next platoon on their left or right. The machine gun was to provide our final protective fire in the case of an enemy onslaught. This meant that the machine gun would fire across the front of the platoon at about eighteen inches above the ground, when a signal was given. Until that signal was given, they were to hold their fire to keep the enemy from determining their position and taking them out with an RPG.

As the platoon leader assigned positions, I would draw them in on a sketch. Then I would shoot an azimuth with my compass and note their left and right limits of fire. On the sketch, I would also note any dead space or man-made features that could affect us or the enemy; finally I would draw the FPL or final protective line for the machine gun.

When we were finished, we would turn this sketch over to the company commander who would incorporate it into the company fire plan. This was done every time we moved. The company and battalion fire plans would include target reference points for mortar and artillery concentrations. All of this preparation, plus our fighting positions, made our perimeters a tough proposition for an attacking force; I don't know of any perimeters like ours that were ever completely overrun.

## The Irish Girls

The next day, in order to dodge the usual work details, I took the two gun crews down to the bunker line for a little shooting practice. We were just going to shoot some bullets at the bushes down by the river, and let the assistant gunners and ammo bearers get a chance to fire the guns, so that they would be ready to take over, if the need should arise. We were just getting ready to shoot when a jeep drove up.

It was Colonel Lazzell, but that's not all. In the back of his jeep were a couple of young, round-eyed, beautiful, young women. He had all our attention until he got out of the jeep and came over to us. The guys were trying to see around him and I had to hiss at them before he got close enough to hear me. "Alpha Rangers, sir!" I bellowed while standing at attention.

We usually didn't salute on the bunker line, because we thought that the officers would appreciate us not announcing their presence to possible enemy snipers. It gave us a kind of perverse thrill, not to salute someone who could have us on charges, if we deliberately failed to salute on any other occasion.

Besides, you could never tell about these things because, I don't think I ever saw a directive telling us not to salute. Some officers were quite taken with the responsibility they bore to uphold military traditions like saluting, and they would rather die from a round through their head, than allow anyone to fritter away a chance to enjoy the privilege of saluting a superior officer.

The colonel graciously acknowledged my acknowledgment of his presence and asked me what we were doing. Wanting to impress him, I told him we were getting ready to conduct some machine gun drills; we never did them here, but I had done them before in Germany. He smiled and told us to get on with it. Then he walked back to the jeep and the girls. I had the two gun crews set up about ten meters apart and told them to get ready. I told Joe that he was alpha gun and Robert that he was bravo gun.

"Alpha gun, Bravo gun, 500 meters, troops in the open, Alpha gun, fire!" Joe fired a burst at some of the bushes we were talking about before the colonel showed up. "Bravo gun, fire!" Robert fired a burst. I continued alternating between the two guns for several more bursts, before shifting fire to another group of bushes that were closer, while increasing the frequency of the bursts.

We continued in this way, until the two guns were starting to smoke, and I called cease fire. I looked back to where the colonel was standing. The two girls were standing up in the back of the jeep; and, since they were wearing shorts, the two assistant gunners were able to see and describe to the others the two most beautiful pairs of legs on the whole planet, or at least on that part of the bunker line at Lai Khe, Vietnam.

They seemed to be impressed with our professionalism because they gave us a round of applause when we stopped shooting. I was hoping the colonel would bring them over and introduce them to us, but he was in a hurry and drove away, leaving only the image of the most beautiful girls in Vietnam, waving slowly to us before disappearing in the cloud of dust stirred up by the jeep's tires, as they sped away. We heard later that the girls were from Ireland and were hitchhiking through Vietnam on their way to somewhere else.

### The Circus Comes to Lai Khe

That afternoon after lunch, a troop of Vietnamese circus performers came to entertain the troops at Lai Khe. We were in the company area so we were ordered to go to the brigade headquarters and be entertained. There was some juggling and tumbling; but to me, the most fascinating act was this guy, who could get all wrapped up around himself and get into a small transparent box made of plastic.

His assistant sealed the box, and an interpreter told us that it was air tight. He stayed in there for about 15 minutes which seemed impossible, while the other acts performed; but the interpreter told us that he was practicing yoga and didn't need to breathe as much as we did.

Finally, after a Vietnamese rock band played a few songs, the man in the box was let out. His act was the subject of much speculation in the 'Ville' that evening when we were practicing our own form of yoga, 'beer yoga,' where we didn't have to think as much as other people.

## Operation Junction City

Operation Junction City was the largest multi-division search and destroy operation of the war. The 1st Infantry Division, the 9th Infantry Division, the 25th Infantry Division, the 173d Airborne Brigade, and the 11th ACR, along with Special Forces and ARVN units, entered War Zone C. They swept through areas where the enemy had built large base camps and logistics facilities, to support the 9th VC Division and elements of the North Vietnamese Army, that were starting to turn up in this area. The operation was initiated by helicopter and airborne assaults along two roads, forming a horseshoe-shaped cordon around the area to be searched.[244]

## Airborne!

The operation started on 22 February, 1967. The airborne assault was conducted by the 2-503 Parachute Infantry of the 173d Airborne Brigade; it was the first combat jump by American paratroops since the Korean War, and the press gave it a lot of coverage. It was rumored that the drop zone was secured by the 11th ACR. One of the paratrooper sergeants in my company laughed and said, "Yeah, they had to get the Cav to surround the DZ, so they could stop the troopers from running back to Bien Hoa to get a gold star sewn on their jump wings."

The airborne mystique was still strong but fading. General Westmoreland, who rode to the top on the coattails of the 'airborne mafia,' had used Junction City as theater, a pageant if you will, and nothing could have been more dramatic than a combat parachute assault, especially on the cover of Life Magazine.

Years later, when a magazine devoted to the Vietnam War printed a story about the 'combat jump,' a member of the 11th ACR wrote to the editor saying, "You characterized this airborne insertion as an actual combat operation into a hot LZ. Nothing could be further from the truth." He then went on to say that the airborne troops had landed on a DZ secured by the 11th ACR of which he was a member, and had taken part in the operation. Life Magazine had photographers on the ground to capture the 'Kodak' moment for the folks back home.[245]

Meanwhile, the rest of the troops were brought in by helicopter, and by nightfall the 'Horseshoe' was in place. From the 20 to 23 February the 1-16 Infantry pulled security at Lai Khe. On 22 February, we were given a warning order to be ready move the next day, and on the afternoon of 23 February, we were airlifted to Soui Da, where we staged for Junction City. Our mission was to clear and hold a stretch of Provincial Route 4, forming the southeastern part of the horseshoe. The mech units attached to the brigade had already entered the area, and eleven armored vehicles had hit mines on the road.[246]

## Suoi Da

When we arrived at Suoi Da, we pulled security at the base. Our battalion occupied the positions of another unit that had deployed that day. We settled in, and things were quiet until 0315 the next morning, when we were heavily mortared. We heard that a captain and several others were killed or wounded.

It was the captain who had been running the Brigade Jungle School when I went through; he had been the one who set off the big explosion that got our attention on the first day. I was shocked to hear he had been killed; he had been so alive and inspiring that first day.

It wasn't until 2012, when I talked to the actual captain who was wounded, not killed, that another of my recollections was cleared up. It was not the captain who had run the brigade's jungle school but the CO of Bravo Company, Captain Lou Murray, whose wounds took him to Japan and out of the war.[247]

During the mortar attack, I was laying on my stomach with several others in a sleeping area consisting of a wall of sandbags, three bags high around us. I saw one of the old timers lying on his back with his arms and his legs in the air during the attack. I asked him why he did that, and he said that he was hoping to get hit by a piece of shrapnel so he wouldn't have to go on the operation. The next day we marched down to the airstrip where we were picked up by Hueys and dropped off in War Zone C.

### Combat Air-assault

A battalion-sized air-assault was a sight to see. The planning for these extravaganzas must have started months before, at least for the logistical aspects. For us, it started when we were put into groups, usually seven or eight, sometimes less, depending on the heat and other factors that the aviators had to deal with. There might be up to 100 Hueys lined up, fifty on each side of the air strip. There we would sit and wait until it was time to go.

The pilots would start the engines. They would whine and the blades would slowly start to spin. The spinning and the noise would increase, until there was a very loud whine and the chopping sound of the blades. There was a lot of dust at some of these places, and it would take a moment until most of it was dispersed.
We sat waiting until the crew chief motioned to mount up. If there were no seats, we would crawl onto the floor of the aircraft and claim a space. Soon the helicopter would be vibrating, almost like it was raring to go. Inside the troop compartment the whine of the turbine was extremely loud, the complete opposite of most war movies where you hear the sound of the blades and not the turbine. It seemed like it took forever, but finally, we could feel the bird shudder a little, then slowly lift, tilting forward and starting to move.

If you sat up a little you could see the tail and bottoms of the choppers in front of you, a long line of them, gradually gaining altitude. When you looked out the side door, you would see the a chopper next to you, part of the line of them that were on the other side of the strip; if you looked the other way, you could see the trees flashing by until you were above them.

The whole line would continue to gain altitude until we reached 1500 feet, which was considered above the range of small arms fire. The temperature was noticeably cooler up there, and that was one of the pleasant aspects of the flight. The pilots kept the formation tight, too tight for me. Sometimes these young eagles would get so close to the bird next to them that the main rotor blades would overlap. They would get all excited when they did that, but I was not impressed; actually, it would scare the crap out of me.

The fire support plan for an assault landing, as we called them, was a masterpiece of joint operations. The Air Force fast movers would be screaming in and dropping their ordinance on the area surrounding the landing zone. When they were done, the artillery would take over, and finally, as we were coming in to land, the helicopter gunships (usually C-Model Hueys and later the Huey Cobra) would be firing machine guns, rockets, and 40mm grenades into the tree-lines around the landing zone.

Now we would be losing altitude, and most of us would slide on our butts across the floor to the edge of the troop compartment and sit with our legs dangling out the door. As the ground got closer, we would step down and stand on the skid, holding on to whatever we could. The door gunner would be firing long bursts into the tree-line that we were going to assault. The first birds in front of us were on the ground and from the skids we could see men moving toward the tree-line, firing their weapons.

Now it was our turn. Jumping off the skids, we hit the ground and moved out just past the blades and waited for a moment until the helicopter took off again. The guys on the other side of the bird ran under the line of Hueys flying over their heads. We formed a line and began moving quickly toward the tree-line in front of us, firing our weapons toward the ground just inside the tree-line.

The Air Force was orbiting over the LZ, striking trails, road junctions and other suspected enemy locations out past the tree-line. The artillery was hammering other areas around the LZ. The noise was unbelievable, especially when an F-4 Phantom jet flew over in one of those slow orbits. They were the loudest airplanes I ever heard.

We moved into the wood-line. There were enemy bunkers everywhere. Thank God they were empty; they hadn't been touched by the artillery and airstrikes. It would have been a bad place to be, out on that flat open field, nowhere to go but forward, with a determined enemy in these bunkers, covering the landing zone with automatic weapons, RPGs, and mortars.

We formed up as a platoon, tied in with the other platoons and moved along the tree-line toward our company's assigned position. There we formed our perimeter around an open area south of where we had landed, about seventy-five meters from the road we were to secure. Bravo Company and the battalion headquarters continued south and set up another perimeter about 700 meters from ours. Charlie Company had gone into another LZ even farther south, and set up a third perimeter.

As soon as we were assigned our part of the perimeter, we started digging in. There were a number of enemy bunkers and a few of them were in a location that supported our own defenses. They were modified to meet our bunker standards. Even though it was almost as much work as digging a new position, the ones who used the enemy positions got a small amount of satisfaction, knowing that their enemies had helped in the digging of our holes.

### Ambush Patrol Ambushed

The ground was soft and we completed our positions by 2200. Each platoon sent out an ambush patrol and listening posts. The first platoon sent out their ambush patrol to the south just after sunset, and they were ambushed shortly after they left the perimeter. One man was killed and several were wounded. The rest of the company was on stand-to while the first platoon went out and recovered their comrades.

When the survivors returned to the perimeter, Captain Williamson directed the 1st Platoon LT to send out another squad to conduct the ambush, and sent the survivors from the first element with them. One of the men refused to go out. I'm sure he was shook up by what happened, and the CO tried to reason with him, but to no avail. After several attempts to coax the man into doing his duty, the Captain informed the soldier that if he didn't go he would be court-martialed and sent to Leavenworth for 10 years. The man wouldn't budge, so the CO told him he was under arrest and had him restrained under guard until he could be taken to the rear the next day.

I stood near the CP with several others and heard the exchange. We went back to our platoon CP and discussed what had happened. We were sympathetic with the soldier and also with the CO. The soldier had lost his nerve, and by this time, I realized that doing so was a real possibility with everyone at some point or another. The CO was responsible for the mission and for taking care of the men. It is critical that the commander creates a climate where it is difficult for the members of his command to give in to their weaknesses.

We were faced with a dangerous situation, and many, if not all of the men would have gladly let themselves be flown out of there, if there was an honorable way to do so. If the CO would have let this man slide, the rest of the company, starting with the weakest members, would be looking for ways to go backwards rather than forwards. If this continues, you don't have an army anymore. The next morning the man was flown out, and he did indeed get ten years.

### Demo Work

The next day we went out and swept the sides of the road and out-posted it. In most places the vegetation came right to the edge of the road. One of the squads from another platoon found a 105mm artillery round and about ten 40mm M-79 rounds. They were close to the road, and I was called to go and blow them up. I placed a charge with double fuses and requested permission to blow the explosives. When permission was given, I gave a 'fire in the hole' call on the radio and shouted the warning three times as loud as I could.

After I lit the fuses, I walked across the road with the RTO, and we lay in the ditch and waited for the charge to explode. When it did, I walked back across the road to check if anything remained of the ordinance, but all I found there was a smoking crater and vegetation that was starting to wilt. The RTO came up and said that the CO was calling for a dust-off; someone had been injured back at the perimeter. I wondered what happened, but there was no way of knowing until we got back that evening. Eventually, in the late afternoon, we pulled in the outposts and returned to our perimeter.

### Hot Chow

The resupply chopper landed with our food, water, mail, etc. While I was standing in the chow line, the first sergeant came up and congratulated me for almost killing the commo sergeant. Apparently the good sergeant was lying on top of the CP bunker, getting a sun tan while monitoring the company net, when I called and asked permission to blow my demo charge. He gave me permission and even relayed the 'fire in the hole' warning to the rest of the company; then he went back to sunbathing rather than taking cover. When the charge went off, a piece of shrapnel, probably from the artillery shell, came down out of the sky and hit him in the torso. The medic who worked on him told me he would be ok, but he was out of the war. Most of the guys thought it was funny, but I don't think the CO was happy about losing his commo sergeant in such a stupid way.

After I got my chow, I ate it in my usual way. They used to serve the hot meals on paper plates. That night, I ate the piece of steak they served, a special treat, with my hands. That took a couple of minutes. Then, after picking out as many of the bell peppers that I could find, I folded the plate in half, held one end of the fold to my mouth, and shook the rest of the food in, chewing as fast as I could until it was gone. I could finish my entire meal in less than three minutes.

### After Dinner Talk

After dinner, I was sitting with Sergeant Magee, and he was considering the first sergeant's ways. "You know, Murry, the first pig, he a rotten muthablanker. He gives us this big talk about 'guts leadership' and he's getting a bottle of whiskey sent to him in the field with the resupply, every night." "How do you know?" I asked him. "The mess sergeant told me, he replied."

I didn't see how anybody could drink a fifth of whiskey a day but those were hard drinking days in the Army for many of the old soldiers. "Besides," I said, "maybe he's sharing it with someone." "He ain't sharing with me," said Magee, "it's like I said, that first pig, he a rotten muthablanker." I sat there considering this new name for a first sergeant. I didn't share his concern about the use or possible distribution of the whiskey; it had kicked my ass so bad in high school that the very odor of it made me gag.

I had heard names like the 'first shirt,' 'top sergeant,' and 'top kick,' but I had never heard of the 'first pig.' Sergeant Magee was a former Marine, and I figured that it was a Marine term. Rodney came up to join in the conversation, so I tried out the new term on him, "Rodney, you know that first pig, he a rotten muthablanker." Rodney cracked up, and we started a series of sentences using 'first pig.' Sergeant Magee was amused, and it helped us all pass a few more minutes in the Nam.

The LT came over to join in the merriment. He wanted to be one of the boys and he was big enough to intimidate most of the platoon without having to get official all the time. We were wary of him and already had one occasion to doubt his capacity for cognitive reasoning, when he asked us to listen to his great idea.

He proposed that if we got in a firefight, one of us should climb a tree and tell him where the enemy was, so he could maneuver the platoon, having the advantage of an aerial observer. Perhaps he was envious of the higher ranking officers in their helicopters. Rodney quickly put an end to that notion by saying, "I ain't climbing no blanking tree in a firefight."

The LT joined the conversation with a statement directed at Rodney and me, "Murry and Rodney, if you had been in Miami Beach in 1964 you would have heard of Dinky Menton and his brother..." There was the slightest of pauses and Rodney, with perfect timing, inserted "Dum-Dum," before the LT could say his last name. That really cracked up Sergeant Magee and me. "Dum-Dum Menton, Dum-Dum Menton," I said it over and over. The LT was looking daggers at me, and at the same time, he was smiling a little because he knew he had been had by one of the fastest mouths in Vietnam, and there was nothing he could do about it.

## Friendly Fire

He was trying to come up with a verbal retaliation, when we heard the sound of armor coming down the road to the west. I looked across the perimeter just past the mortar pits to see if I could see the vehicles. There were still a number of guys in the chow line, and the mess sergeant was sitting on an empty mermite can, dishing out the meat. The armor was making a lot of noise, at least one of them was a tank and the rest were probably APCs.

'Crackity, crackity crackity crack' went a string of bullets just over our heads. A split second later, I saw a flash and puffs of smoke on both sides of one of the mortar tubes about thirty meters away. The last thing I saw, while swan diving into the large VC bunker we were using for our platoon CP, was several of the mortar crew diving over the sandbag wall around the mortar tube that had been struck.

No one knew what happened. Were we under attack? Had the enemy ambushed the armor column from across the road from our perimeter? What was going on? There were several more bursts of fire cracking across the perimeter. Meanwhile, Sergeant Magee, Dum Dum, Rodney and I were trying to get untangled from one another in the VC bunker. Magee and I had actually bumped heads while diving into that bunker from opposite entrances. It's a good thing we were both wearing our helmets, as per SOP, or we might have had some serious headaches.

> ***Jose Garcia:*** *"Me and Gunby raced to the hole, dove in and got stuck. Shrek pulled me and Ward pulled Donnie in."*[248]

One of my gun crews had opened fire toward the north, and other positions on the perimeter had opened fire. After a minute or so, we heard someone yelling to cease fire. The word was passed, and soon it was quiet again. We climbed out of the bunker and I went over to the gun crew that had opened fire to see if they were ok. They were, but they had started a fire in the grass in front of them, so I helped them put it out.

When I went back to the CP, I heard the mess sergeant cursing and laughing, so I went over to see what was up. "Those chow-hound sons-a-bitches," he said. "I dove into a hole when that fire was coming in, and some of those guys from your platoon crawled over while there was still shooting, and stole a bunch of these steaks." He was laughing and cursing, showing his admiration for these men who obviously liked his cooking enough to risk their lives for seconds.

## Incoming

The next two days passed without any significant enemy contact. We went out every day and secured our part of the road. At night, we sent out ambush patrols and improved our positions. One night, just after dark, we heard a mortar round leave the tube somewhere to the southeast of us. The LT shot an azimuth as did several other company elements. The round passed over our perimeter and landed on the other side of the road.

Several more followed with the same results. Eventually, the FDC section of our company mortars worked out a firing solution and sent a few rounds out to where they believed the enemy mortar to be. The intersecting azimuths must have helped because, after several of our own rounds landed, the enemy mortar stopped firing, and it was quiet on our perimeter for the rest of the night.

## The General Took a Look

We had a visitor, a general, who flew into our company perimeter, and after talking to the CO, came and inspected our positions. Much of our section of the perimeter was facing thick jungle, and when we first got there, we had to clear fields of fire for our final protective lines.

The general was interested in these lines and got into the machine gun positions so he could check them. I watched as he inspected Robert's position and was happy to see that he was pleased with its construction. When he got in to check the FPL, he paused, looked again and just stood there. Oh, oh, I thought, this doesn't look good.

He bent down and looked again. Then he turned to Robert and said, "Show me your final protective line." He moved out of the way, and Robert got in the hole. He had a stake set for his left limit which was also his FPL. He looked, and then looked again. "It was right here sir!" he told the general.

"Well it's not here now," the general replied. "Yes sir, I don't know what happened, it was there before." The general got out of the hole and moved on. After I told Robert to fix the problem, I followed the general's entourage. The inspection of the rest of our platoon's positions went smoothly, and he moved on to the next platoon.

I went back to the machine gun position and found Robert and his ammo bearer out in front of the position next to theirs. They were digging away at a mound that happened to be in the middle of their FPL. The mound was the home of a termite colony and they were squeezing streams of insect repellant into the small holes as they dug. The termites had created this mound within hours of their original mound being damaged after the gun crew first cleared their field of fire. The jungle had violated its neutrality again.

That afternoon, without fanfare, LT 'Dum-Dum' Menton was reassigned to the XO position, and we introduced ourselves to our new LT, Jules Sermuskis. He was of Lithuanian parents, and Rodney set the tone for the leadership challenges he faced by asking him, "Sir, what's the smallest book in the world?" The LT had no idea and foolishly asked for the answer. "The Book of Lithuanian War Heroes," said Rodney, ending our first meeting with our new platoon leader.

## The Battle of Prek Klok I

The next morning, the 28th, we cleared the road as usual and settled down to pass another hopefully uneventful day. At around 1100 we heard artillery shells landing to the southeast. Then the Air Force showed up, and the airstrikes joined the sound of the artillery. Soon after the shooting started, the CO alerted the company, and we were told to return to our perimeter immediately. When we got there, we were told that Bravo Company had hit the shit, and we were going in to help them. They were on a company-sized patrol and walked into a horseshoe shaped ambush.

Helicopters flew in shortly after this, picked us up, and we were flown to an LZ near the fight. The second platoon went first and I was in the first helicopter with the new LT, his RTO and several riflemen. We jumped off shooting; the LT led the way. He even critiqued my bullet placement as we ran, "Too high," he said. As we moved, we continued to fire until we secured the tree-line.

There had been a few VC on the LZ when we came in, and one man was shot while he was getting off the bird. His buddies threw him back on the chopper which flew him to the medics. The rest of the company flew in, and we established a perimeter. As soon as our company perimeter was established, another company from a different battalion was flown in to go help Bravo Company. Why they didn't leave them to guard the perimeter and let us go in to help a company from our own battalion, I don't know.

All that night the artillery fired high explosive rounds into the jungle, and parachute flares lit the sky over the battle area and our perimeter. The survivors of Bravo Company were brought back to the perimeter, and some of our guys asked them what had happened.

They told a story of heavy automatic weapons fire coming from every direction and snipers in the trees. One story we heard was about a sergeant who was found sitting with his back against a tree. When the relief forces got to him, he looked at them and said, "Those mothers are good," and died. According to the reports, Bravo Company lost twenty-five KIA and twenty-eight WIA. Division claimed that they killed 167 VC by 'body-count.' One of the platoon sergeants, Matthew Leonard, was later awarded the Medal of Honor posthumously for his actions on that day.[249]

*Be sober; watch. Your adversary, the devil,*
*as a roaring lion, walks about,*
*seeking someone to devour*
*1 Peter 5:8*

# Chapter 13-March 1967

### Body Parts

The next morning, after filling in our holes, we moved through the battle area. There were few enemy bodies lying around. We passed one, and I looked at a sight seldom seen—a dead enemy. He had one of the sun helmets that the hard-corps regular NVA and VC forces wore and a clean khaki uniform. Apart from the fact that he was dead, he otherwise looked very healthy. He was well fed, and the expression on his face didn't reveal any last minute regrets for his choices in life. He had no visible wounds, but I didn't feel like turning him over to find out what killed him, what with the possibility of booby-traps and all.

A little farther down, I saw a leather holster lying on the trail. It was a lighter color than our holsters, so there was a good chance that it was an enemy holster and a nice light souvenir. Why someone ahead of me hadn't picked it up, never occurred to me. I bent over to carefully inspect it for booby-traps; I looked at it closely and I noticed that one end of it appeared to be damaged and discolored.

Upon further inspection, I realized that I was looking at a foot that had been severed from its leg and the rest of somebody somewhere. The man in front of me noticed my interest in the foot, and told me that there was a dead body in the tree above me, and it was missing a foot. I never turned my head to look because the column moved out; as we made our way through the battlefield, I was wondering about the holster that turned into a foot.

### New NDP

Alpha Company continued to move through the jungle, and eventually, we walked into the battalion perimeter where Bravo Company had been staying before the fight. They had been flown back to Lai Khe to reorganize and be reconstituted. We moved into their positions to guard the battalion perimeter. The second platoon positions started on the northwest side of the road that ran through the center of the perimeter and curved around to the west. I was directed to put one of my machine guns in the first hole next to the road.

Now a few nights before, we had been lit up by an armored unit that was running up and down this same road doing 'Thunder Runs.' They were trying to disrupt the activities of the 'Mad Bomber,' a VC operation that was burying command-detonated mines in the road every night, the same kind of activity that currently goes on in Iraq and Afghanistan, only now they call them IEDs.

I told the LT that the position was too close to the road, but he insisted that we had to put a gun there. We went back and forth a few times until he gave me a direct order. After watching the CO send one of our guys back to face 10 years for combat refusal, I didn't want to find out what you could get for disobeying a direct order; so I did as he said. I told the guys that they had to be extra alert when the armor came rolling through because of their proximity to the road. The next few days were occupied with the routine duties of perimeter defense, local patrols, ambush patrols, and LP/OPs. The new platoon leader was asserting himself a little more under Sergeant Magee's tutelage. I usually went with the LT when he checked our positions if the platoon sergeant was busy with logistics issues.

### The 'Random' Claymore

One night the LT told me to pick a position on the perimeter, and at 2100, tell them to fire a claymore. This was something we had started doing about a month before; we called it the 'Random Claymore.' We fired a claymore every few hours at different parts of the perimeter, the theory being that Charlie wouldn't come around our perimeter if he knew there was a chance he might be hit by one of these claymores. The way Charlie fought, if he felt like coming around our perimeter, the random claymore plan wasn't going to be a deterrent.

The LT joined me at the hole, and at 2100, I told the soldier on watch to fire a claymore. He seemed a little reluctant, but when I insisted he do so immediately, he picked up the clacker. The LT and I took cover behind his position, on the off chance that Charlie had crawled up and turned the claymore around, in hopes of sending those pellets into our perimeter instead of his face.

The soldier hollered "Claymore, claymore, claymore," and squeezed the clacker. 'Pop' went the claymore. When I say 'pop,' I mean 'pop' like a .22 rifle, not 'Ka-blamm!' like one and half pounds of C4. It sounded to me like only the blasting cap went off, and I was pretty sure I knew why. In order to keep from drawing the battalion staff's scrutiny to the problem, I told him to fire the other Claymore, this time we had a satisfactory explosion. The LT was curious about what happened, so I told him I would investigate and let him know.

I told the soldier to come with me, and we followed the wire out to the remains of the claymore. The right side, near the blasting cap well, was gone. We took it back to his bunker. The LT had left by the time we got back, so I looked at it with a flashlight under a poncho. The plastic case was shattered, and I could see the metal frame that held the ball bearings, but otherwise, the case was empty.

"What happened to the C4?" I asked him. He fidgeted for a moment, and then told me that he had been pinching it out a little at a time and using it to heat his C-rations. "I guess you know that is going to stop!" He assured me that it had. I went back to the platoon CP and told the LT that the claymore had malfunctioned and left it at that. It had been a long day, and his desire for sleep had overcome his curiosity, so we settled in for the night.

### Thunder Runs

About 0100 in the morning, I was on radio watch. I was extremely tired, and as I sat there listening to the hypnotic rushing sound of the radio, I must have dozed off. I could vaguely hear the sound of tracked vehicles coming down the road, and then screaming. The LT called my name, and we ran through the trees and brush toward the sound of the screaming which was coming from our right flank position. When we came out of the trees, I could see an M-48 tank stopped on the side of the road near where our machine gun position had been. As I got closer, I was looking for the position, but I couldn't find it. The tank was jammed up against a tree trunk and was idling in gear. Some people were on the front of the tank, and they were pulling a body out of the driver's hatch.

As I looked around, I realized that the tank was stopped on top of the machine gun position. The screams I had heard were from the gun crew. I found two of the men on the other side of the tank away from the road. Robert was slightly injured, and the other was more serious, but looked like he would make it. I asked Robert where the third man was and he pointed toward the tank, "He's under there."

I went over to the tank. It was still running and making a lot of noise. One of the crew had climbed in and put it in neutral, but for some reason, had left it running. The battalion commander, the CO, the LT, the medics and the battalion surgeon were all there conversing. I went up to the LT and told him that one of our guys was under the tank, and that we had to get him out.

The LT said that they, pointing to the command group, were discussing the situation. I know the LT was feeling bad due to our argument about the position that was now a parking lot for a tank. I stood there wanting to do something, when I saw the battalion commander tell the surgeon to crawl under the tank and check the man underneath. The doctor didn't look very happy about crawling under a tank at 0100 while it was running, on the side of the road in Vietnam, to check on a man who had probably been crushed to death instantly.

I followed the doctor and watched as he crawled under the tank. He found the soldier and looked him over with a flash light. He put his hand somewhere on the soldier's body, waited another minute, and then crawled back out saying, "He's beyond help." I wasn't sure if he meant that the man was dead or that he was still alive but couldn't be helped.

I went to the LT and the CO and asked if we couldn't get some jacks flown in so we could lift the tank off our man in hopes that he could be taken to the hospital and saved. The CO didn't think that was going to happen, and at that moment, the battalion commander ordered the tank crew to drive the tank off the position. I stood there helplessly while the driver revved the tank's engine once and put it in reverse. The tank seemed to drop straight down off the tree trunk, and bounce once, before it rolled backwards out onto the road then clanked forward to the other end of the perimeter, where it joined the other vehicles.

Later we found out that the tank was coming down the road toward our perimeter with its main gun facing to the right. As it approached the perimeter, the driver allowed the tank to drift a little too far to the right, causing the main gun to strike a tree on the side of the road. This caused the turret to spin around, striking the driver in the back of the head and knocking him out.

The tank continued to roll forward right over our machine gun. The man on guard tried to wake the others and get them to move, but the whole thing happened so quickly that one of them never moved, and the tank drove over him. There was no mention of this in the reports afterward. According to the Brigade AAR, the night of the 5-6 March passed without incident.[250]

The next day Sergeant Magee and I worked on reconstituting the decimated gun crew. Robert, the gunner was able to drive on. Carl, a new guy from Texas, was added to Robert's crew along with David, a draftee from New York. Robert asked Jose if he would trade John from Chicago for David from New York. Robert and Carl were black and so was John from Chicago. Robert told us he would like to be the 'soul gun.' Jose and I laughed, and since Jose didn't have any objections, I said ok. They went back to their crews and made the swap.

We continued to sweep a portion of Highway 4 each day. Occasionally there would be a platoon patrol or a company sweep, but no contact with the VC or the COSVN HQ. Other elements of our battalion and brigade were finding base camps and small amounts of supplies; so the VC were still around. At 2200 on the 10 March, about six clicks north of us at Prek Klok, after a heavy mortar attack, Artillery Base II, guarded by the 2-2 Infantry, was hit with two ground attacks. They held their positions, and the enemy forces were driven off by air and artillery support. According to the report, there were 197 VC KIAs (BC) and five VC POWs. Our losses were one KIA and thirty-one WIA. On 12 March, we were picked up and flown back to Soui Da. The next day, the rest of the battalion was flown back to Lai Khe, but we were flown to Phuoc Vinh.[251]

### Operation Junction City: A Pause

Junction City would continue, and we would be back. The 3d Brigade AAR listed these statistics: There were 59,312 rounds of 105mm and 19,417 rounds of 155mm fired in support of the 3rd Brigade. The Air Force flew 338 close air support sorties. Our casualties amounted to thirty-five KIA and 147 WIA, and we claimed 414 VC KIA and eight WIA. The 'Mad Bomber' and his boys accounted for three APCs, a tank dozer and a truck destroyed, and eighteen tanks, one artillery howitzer, four APCs, and eight trucks damaged. There were a total of fifty-five enemy weapons captured including a twelve gauge shotgun and three AK-47's.[252]

### Operation Lam Son-67

On 17 March, the brigade started Operation Lam Son-67. This was the Revolutionary Development mission, 'Winning the hearts and minds of the people.' The 1-26 Infantry was based in Phuoc Vinh. Since they were out, we remained in Phuoc Vinh, guarding the perimeter while the rest of the brigade was spreading goodwill in the division AO. We had the usual platoon-sized day patrols and squad ambush patrols at night. Occasionally we had a night off which we used to drink as much beer as we could before passing out around our positions.

One night, our whole platoon went to the beer club run by our hosts. My buddies and I bought a case of beer and sat at a table drinking. I could tell that the sergeant who was running the club didn't like our behavior. We were loud and rowdy and we were all teasing the cute Vietnamese girl who was waiting on our tables. I went outside to pee, and not finding the rest room, began peeing off the back porch. Several of our guys were doing the same thing. The girl came outside for something, and when she saw us she giggled and went inside. The sergeant who ran the club came out a minute later and started yelling at us, calling us rude, ugly Americans.

One of the guys asked what the problem was, and he went off about how we were all waving our weenies at the girl. Someone speculated that maybe she enjoyed the show, and that pushed the sergeant over the edge. "That's it, the club is closed. I'm calling the MPs." We went back inside and joined our buddies at the table. The sergeant came in yelling for us all to get out; the club was closed, and the MP's were on the way.

Figuring it was time to leave, we managed to get everyone moving toward the door, saying goodnight to the little mama san who was smiling at us as we left. We staggered down the road yelling and laughing. Some of the guys became entangled in the concertina wire, and our medic had to rally a few of the less drunk NCOs to help him pull them out, so he could bandage their wounds. Eventually Sergeant Magee accounted for everyone, and we went to sleep.

## Stoned

We were patrolling outside the perimeter one day and took a long break. I still had the 'dinky dau' cigarettes from when I got out of the hospital. We were on our way back to the perimeter, so I figured I could smoke one safely and see what it felt like to be stoned on patrol. I asked Rodney if he had ever gotten high, and he said no, but seemed interested. I told him to come with me, and we stepped around a couple of bushes and both had a couple of deep puffs on one of those cigarettes.

In a short time, we were wasted. I had a hard time holding it together when the break was over and we started moving. Then the lead squad halted, and we all took a knee, waiting. The word came back for me to go forward. I went up to the front, and the LT told me that the point man had found a booby-trap, and for me to blow it. I was messed up enough as it was, and now I had to blow a booby-trap?

I followed the point man, and when he stopped and pointed, I saw it and told him to go back. It was a Russian or Chinese hand grenade, and there was a vine wrapped around the safety lever. The grenade was lying in the grass in a natural open area between two large clumps of vegetation, a good place to put one. The vine was attached to a small tree trunk on the edge of one of the clumps of vegetation. I got on my hands and knees to look at the grenade and noticed that the vine was moving. I jumped back and lay flat on the ground waiting for it to go off and hoping that I was far enough away to avoid the shrapnel.

After a few moments, I realized that it wasn't going to go off, so I raised my head and looked at it again. It was still tied to the vine. I turned and looked in the direction of the patrol and saw the point man lying on the ground, staring at me. I gave him a smile, a thumbs-up and went back to the grenade. The vine was moving around that grenade like a snake. Now I knew what the sarge was staring at in the bar the first time he smoked this shit.

I prepared a demo charge, but I was freaking out. The hallucinations were continuing, and the LT wanted me to hurry up. When I put the charge next to the grenade, I gave myself a couple of extra inches in case that vine moved again. The charge went off and blew the grenade. That was the last time I smoked any of that shit in Vietnam, where in 1967 we were just starting to feel the effects of the great rebellion back in the states.

## R+R

I got a slot for R+R while we were in Phuoc Vinh. My parents sent me $200.00 in a personal check and I had about a hundred dollars of my own. We continued patrolling the area during the day and drinking beer in the club at night.

I lost my wallet with the check the night before I was supposed to leave. After I raised much hell in the company area, someone responded to my drunken cursing of the person who stole my wallet, and the cursing of his family unto the tenth generation, and returned it to my platoon sergeant.

I was hoping to go to Australia and get some waves, but when all they offered me was Hong Kong, I took it, just to get out of Vietnam. I caught a chopper back to Lai Khe, put on my khaki uniform, grabbed my AWOL bag and caught another chopper to Di-An, where we were given our travel orders and sent to Bien Hoa.

The Air Force flew us to Hong Kong in a C-47, and when it came in for a landing, I thought we were crash landing in the water until I saw the runway that sticks out into the bay. The airport had a large room where an American Army captain gave us a briefing about the rules for behavior in Hong Kong. Most of the rules that he announced brought roars of laughter from the troops, and this made him mad. He struggled through the briefing and ended it with the big rule—we had to be at the airport at 0800 five days from now, or else. The 'or else' came out of his mouth like the crack of doom. It caused all the clerks and jerks, and all but the most irreverent of the grunts, to stop joking and pay attention.

### "Do You Take a Check?"

He gave us a list of hotels. Some were near the airport, and the others were across the bay. As soon as he dismissed us, we streamed out of the briefing room, and I found a hotel near the Star Ferry. I checked in and asked the clerk if he would cash my parents' check but he wouldn't. The desk clerk recommended that I try one of the many tailor shops nearby. A lot of GIs talked about the great deals you could get on a suit in Hong Kong; I heard a number of them say that they were going to buy two, some even said three.

Why somebody would want to buy a suit, much less two or three of them, made absolutely no sense to me; but, since I didn't have any other prospects for getting my check cashed, I decided to give the tailors a try. I found one who was willing to cash my check if I bought a suit. I told him that I didn't want a suit. He did his best to convince me to buy one, showing me different kinds of material, and telling me how good it would look on me. I passed. Finally he offered to make me a pair of pants for $30.00, and we made the bargain. He measured me, cashed my check, and I paid him.

### The Welsh Regiment

Hong Kong is a beautiful place. A British Crown Colony at the time, it was clean and orderly. There were some beautiful sights, but I don't know if I saw any of them. I entered the first bar I saw and began drinking. There I met some soldiers from the British Army, the Welsh Regiment, who took me under their wing, as I tried to uphold the honor of Her Majesties Colonial Rebel Forces.

The Taffs, as they called themselves, were a rowdy bunch and were able to overlook my lack of manners and uncivilized behavior. They seemed to understand that I was only hours away from the combat zone and determined to think about something else. They had the curious custom of drinking their beer at room temperature and dropping a shot of lemon juice in it. Remembering a slogan I had heard years ago, 'when in Rome…,' I followed suit and put away a few.

I hung out with these guys until the bar closed, and they kicked us out. They weren't willing to let me wander off in my condition, so they took me back to their barracks with them and gave me the bunk of one of their buddies who was on leave. I passed out, and the next thing I knew, someone was shaking my shoulder. I jumped up not knowing where or what I was, and saw two men in uniform. One appeared to be an officer and the other, I couldn't tell.

They were smiling, and one of them, the officer, said "Yes. Well, Jones Ten told us there was a Yank here, and we just wanted to see if you were getting on." He introduced himself as Major__, the company commander, and the other man, the company sergeant major. I snapped to attention as best I could and rendered my best RAF salute, which brought another smile to their faces. The major told me to make myself comfortable and said something about appreciating what we were going through 'out there.' I thanked them for their hospitality, shook hands with both of them, and they left.

### Dumb-Ass!

The last night before I was to return to Vietnam, I went out and got hammered. When I woke up the next morning, I checked my watch. I had less than an hour to get to the plane. I was in an alcoholic fog as I tried to get dressed and pack my things. I raced out of the hotel and ran to the Star Ferry. I knew that it was going to be close, as I willed the ferry to go faster. The sea breeze revived me, and I regretted that I didn't find out if there were any beaches in Hong Kong.

When we finally got to the other side, I ran to the taxi stand, jumped in the first cab and told the driver to take me to the airport. He said that he couldn't. I could tell that his English was limited, and he could tell I had some limitations of my own. I was starting to get excited and I told him to take me to the #%*^! Airport! This caused him to get excited and he made it clear that he wouldn't. I jumped out of the cab and went to the next one, same response. What the hell was going on?

Nobody wanted to take me to the airport. The first driver came back with a man who told me that no one would take me to the airport because it was on the other side of the bay. Duh, in my drunken stupor I had forgotten where I was. I ran back to the ferry just in time to get on one going back. This didn't look good.

When the ferry docked, I ran to the taxi stand, and this time the first driver I met was all too happy to take me to the airport. I told him to drive fast and gave him more money. We had an exciting ride through the crowded streets of Hong Kong. The driver said we were almost there, and I was looking for signs when I saw a C-47 rising over the rooftops ahead of us, winging its way back to Vietnam.

### Under Arrest

Now I'd done it. I broke the number one rule for R+R in Hong Kong. There wasn't anything else to do but go to the airport. Maybe that wasn't my plane; maybe there was another one leaving soon; I wouldn't know until I checked in with the R+R center. I walked in and saw the same officer who briefed us when we arrived. There was another man, a Marine, sitting near the captain's desk looking discouraged. The captain looked at me and said, "Well, I see you've decided to join us." I started to offer a lame excuse, but he cut me off.

"You're under arrest at this time. You will be confined to a room in a nearby hotel until tomorrow morning when the next flight leaves for Vietnam. You are not to drink any alcoholic beverages or leave the room. I don't have to remind you that you are both in deep shit and I advise you not to make things worse for yourselves: got it?"

He looked at me. "Yes, sir" was all I could say, and the Marine, who looked like he was going to cry, said the same thing. The captain drove us to the hotel and checked us in. He told the desk clerk that we were not allowed to leave or to have any alcohol or visitors, and, "You know what I mean when I say no visitors," he said to the clerk who let a brief smile pass over his face.

The captain dismissed us, and we were taken to our room on the second floor. We each had a double bed, and there was a TV. It was better than a jail cell, which I'm sure the captain would have put us in, if he had had one available. I looked out the window and saw the captain's car driving away. At the same time, a young man called up from the sidewalk and said, "American, you in trouble?" I nodded. "This happen all the time, you want beer?" I nodded again. "You lower sheets and I get you beer." I went back in the room. The Marine was sitting on his bed with his head in his hands.

I pulled the sheets off my bed and tied them together. The Marine gave me a puzzled look. I walked over to the window and looked down. "How much," I asked. He gave me a price. I'm sure that I could have gotten a better price down on the street, but that wasn't an option. He told me to put the money in the sheet and lower it. "How do I know you won't take off and keep my money?" I asked.

He was a little offended. "American, I do this all the time. Send down the money, I no rip-off." He was familiar with the current GI talk, so I decided to trust him. He took the money and returned shortly with two six packs of cold bottled beer. He tied them onto the end of the sheet, and I pulled them into the room. When I turned around with a six pack in each hand, I saw that the Marine had a look of horror on his face.

"What are you doing?" He moaned. "Didn't you hear that captain order us not to drink any alcohol?" "That wasn't an order; it was a suggestion." I told him, "Nobody orders a soldier not to drink on R+R." I handed him a beer which he refused until I pushed it into his hand. I sat down on my bed facing him and asked him what was wrong. He told me that he was sure that he was in deep shit when he got back to his company. I asked him what he did, and he said he was a grunt. I told him that I was too and reminded him that we were already in deeper shit as infantrymen in Vietnam, than these R+R people could comprehend.

"Think about it." I told him, "What are they going to do? Send us to Vietnam and put us in the infantry? they already did that. Now, anything they do to us could only be an improvement, right?" A small smile came to his face. "Right!" I said again. "Blanking A!" he said and reached for the bottle opener.

We drank the beer and got some more; later, the desk clerk brought us some visitors, and we finished up our R+R. The next morning, we were picked up by the captain and taken to the airport. I'm sure he smelled the beer on our breath, but chose not to say anything. He said that we wouldn't be able to get on the plane unless some other dumb GIs missed their flight; but apparently missing flights was a fairly common occurrence, because four people missed theirs that morning and we were soon on our way back to Vietnam. The plane landed in Da Nang, and I said goodbye to my Marine buddy. I wonder if he made it home.

When I returned to Lai Khe, I caught the afternoon resupply chopper and was soon back with the 2nd Platoon. When I asked what I'd missed, one of the guys said that they had been rocketed with 122mm Katyushas. When they saw the expression of surprise on my face, another guy busted out laughing and said they were bullshitting me. The first guy must have been a prophet, because Charlie would bring smoke on Lai Khe and other bases with those rockets a little later in the war. On the afternoon of the 31 March, we were picked up and flown back to Lai Khe for a rest.

### Operation Junction City II: Combat Air-Assault

After we cleaned up, we were making plans for a trip to the 'Ville,' when, twenty minutes later, in typical Big Red One fashion, the rest was over. At 1600 we were alerted for a mission. Another unit, the 1-26 Infantry, commanded by LTC Alexander Haig, had made contact and was heavily engaged with a large enemy force near the Cambodian border. Haig's helicopter had been shot down, and a number of his men were killed or wounded. Rations were issued and we were trucked back to the airstrip.

We loaded onto helicopters and flew west. As we approached the landing zone, we could see jet fighter-bombers circling the LZ. One by one they would peel off and go in low and fast. They were hitting the tree-lines around the LZ with napalm and high-drag 500 pounders. The bombs had built in air brakes which popped open when they were released and slowed their descent, allowing the plane to fly past before the bombs exploded.

The smoke was billowing up in columns, and it looked like we were flying into a hornet's nest. Just before we landed, the door gunners began firing long bursts into the wood-line on our right. We were out on the skids when the crew chief shouted "Go!" Jumping to the ground, we began to move toward the tree-line, firing our rifles as we moved. Fortunately there were no enemy forces, or we would have had a hard time.

### Incoming!

We formed up by platoon, spread out, and began to move across a large open area to a distant tree-line. It appeared that things were not as bad as they seemed when we were coming in. We had gone about 500 meters and we had about 500 more to go, when I heard the sound of many mortar rounds leaving tubes somewhere off to our right. We didn't know who was firing, so we continued on our way.

Then I heard the hissing sound of about ten incoming mortar rounds which went off in quick succession around us a moment later. This was the first time I had come under mortar fire this close to me in daylight. Everyone hit the ground but the CO who told us to get up and move on the run toward our objective.

We were up and running when I heard the hissing announcement of more rounds coming in. The enemy had us under observation and adjusted his fire. I hit the ground along with those around me. As soon as the rounds exploded, we were up again; running toward our objective. This happened two or three more times before the Air Force drew a bead on the mortar locations and silenced their fire.

## Losses

We stopped at the thin tree-line and began to form a perimeter with Bravo Company. My squad was facing out across the large open area we had just traversed. I went out in front of our position to check some equipment that was lying on the ground. I found a helmet with a bullet hole through it and some blood on the inside. There was a picture of a young woman with a couple of smiling children taped inside the helmet liner. It belonged to one of the men from the 1-26 Infantry who had been part of the initial fight that morning.

A man walked up to my side and was looking at the helmet as I held it in my hand. It was Colonel Lazzell, the battalion commander. I said something about it being a shame that the soldier with a wife and children had been badly wounded or killed. Although I was a Spec-4 and he was a colonel, we were both touched by the apparent loss of a soldier and the sorrow that was heading toward a new widow and her children via Western Union.

After a moment, he told me I was doing a good job and said goodbye. It may have been that he appreciated the moment with another soldier who wasn't intimidated by his rank and shared a sentiment with him. I returned to my position, and with Maguire, a fellow Californian, took turns digging and filling sandbags. Some of the guys nearby had hit rock about three feet down. They asked me to use some C4 to blow up the rocks. I tried, but the rock was too large so eventually they moved the hole, and we all continued to dig in.

No one could say what was going to happen next, but that wasn't an issue. Every position was built to the exacting standards of our SOP, and no one rested until their hole had a berm in front, 45 degree firing ports, sandbags for overhead cover, camouflage, and claymores out front.

**Jose Garcia, Machine Gunner,**
**2d Platoon, A-1-16 Infantry**
(Jose Garcia)

**Donnie Gunby, Assistant Machine Gunner,**
**2d Platoon, A-1-16 Infantry**
(Jose Garcia)

**'Ghost'- David Ward - Jose Garcia,**
**2d Platoon, A-1-16 Infantry**
(Jose Garcia)

**Robert Pointer (standing) Machine Gunner,**
**2d Platoon, A-1-16 Infantry**
(Jose Garcia)

**Carl Johnson, Assistant Machine Gunner,**
**2d Platoon, A-1-16 Infantry**
(Jose Garcia)

**Alan Roese, Squad Leader,**
**2d Platoon, A-1-16 Infantry**
(Jose Garcia)

**Jose Garcia at the battle of LZ X-Ray (Xom Bo II).**
**Peter Clark made this sketch while recovering from wounds he received in the same battle.**
(Peter Clark)

**Jose Garcia**
(Jose Garcia)

**Rodney Floutz, Squad Leader,**
**2d Platoon, A-1-16 Infantry**
(Jose Garcia)

**2d Platoon, A-1-16 Infantry**
**C-130, gonna take a little trip**
(Jose Garcia)

**2d Platoon-Catching Z's**
(Jose Garcia)

**Captain Dennis Howley**
(Peter Howley)

**Airmobile!**
**UH-1B Iroquois (Huey)**
(Jose Garcia)

**Troop Extraction**
(Jose Garcia)

**LTC Lazzell Explains Something to General Westmoreland**
(U.S. Army)

**The 'Ville'**
(Jose Garcia)

Donnie Gunby, Greg Murry, and Jose Garcia
2014
(Greg Murry)

Ed Christiansen, Greg Murry, Bill Williamson
2014
(Greg Murry)

**Author-En route to Vietnam**
(Greg Murry)

**Don and John Gilliland**
(Don Gilliland)

***"You'll get over it, Joe. Oncet I was gonna write a book exposin' the army after th' war myself."***
(Bill Mauldin)

*...and he cried out with a loud voice, saying to all the birds that fly in mid-heaven,*
*Come here; gather yourselves to the great dinner of God*
*Revelation 19:17*

# Chapter 14-April 1967

### The Battle of Ap Gu

It took me and McGuire until 2300 to complete our hole. It was very dark that night, and I was exhausted. Maguire and I began pulling one hour shifts; I went first. Nothing was going on; it was very quiet. At 0300 after he woke me up, I looked to my front across the large open area and saw nothing. Sentry duty was a struggle, and we were constantly nodding off. We had to stand up, kneel down and smoke cigarettes without allowing the light to be seen; it wasn't fun.

### Incoming!

I finished my turn and woke Maguire. He got up, and as soon as I saw that he was really awake, I lay down and started to slide into sleep. I heard some faint explosions in the distance, and then someone behind us said 'stand-to,' but I was going down fast.

'Ka-Blaamm!' a mortar round landed close by. Wide awake now, I could hear more coming in as I dove into the foxhole. We were being shelled, and the rounds were coming in hot and fast.

I found myself upside down on top of Maguire who had done the same thing a second before me. He was hollering for me to get off him, and I was telling him to shut up. I managed to roll off his back to the right and sat in the bottom of the hole, holding my helmet on my head. Explosions hammered our ears, the ground was shaking like an earthquake, and dirt was falling into the hole, covering us.

The enemy barrage was extremely accurate. There were a lot of rounds landing very close to our foxhole. I was sure that one of them was going to land right on the overhead cover and nail us. Maguire wasn't saying anything, so I asked him if he was ok and if he had his weapon and ammunition. He said that he did. I didn't have mine so I told him that as soon as the mortar fire had shifted or stopped, I was going to stand up and grab my rifle and web gear which were laying right outside our hole.

The rounds were still coming in, so we waited in silence. I had an overwhelming need to pee, so I got on my knees and peed in the corner of my side of the hole. The mortar rounds began to slow down, and I could hear the sound of rifle fire. I stood up in a crouch, stuck my head out of the entrance of the foxhole, and grabbed my rifle and web gear. Maguire had also stood up and was manning his firing port; I did the same.

### A Series of Malfunctions

I could hear the bullets cracking as they passed over our hole. I couldn't see anything, but since the guys on our left and right were firing, I took my rifle off safe and fired a round into the darkness. A round, because when it fired, the cartridge did not eject. I had a malfunction called a 'failure to extract' with the cartridge case remaining in the firing chamber of my rifle. I didn't have a cleaning rod to clear it, so I couldn't shoot. To our left I could hear my squad leader shouting, "Here they come; we're going to be overrun." Thinking that it was claymore time, I grabbed my clacker and squeezed. Nothing happened. The mortar rounds must have cut the wire.

Great, I thought, no rifle and the Claymore is a dud. I still had my grenades so I told Maguire that my rifle was jammed and that I wouldn't leave him but I needed to get a cleaning rod. I climbed out of the hole, my hand reaching for the ground to steady myself but it found no ground, and I fell a short ways into a hole in our sleeping area that hadn't been there before.

It was a crater from a mortar round and it was a big one. All my equipment was shredded including a five gallon water can that was full of holes. The enemy had come very close to taking us out.

Sergeant Smith was still hollering and Maguire chose that moment to fire a twenty round burst of tracer ammunition into the dark, where, as it turned out, the enemy was. I threw a grenade as far as I could to my front, still believing that we were being overrun, but it didn't explode.

So far, my combat career was going nowhere. My rifle was jammed and my Claymore was a dud along with my grenade. I still had another one and I decided to save it until I actually saw an enemy. I ducked behind our bunker and called to the next position over, a machine gun position manned by Robert's gun crew, and asked for a cleaning rod. One of them shouted something, but I couldn't hear what he said because a storm of bullets blew through the branches of the tree that was right behind our position. It was like a hundred bullwhips cracking at once, and small branches and leaves began falling on top of me and our position.

I had seen the stream of tracers fired by Bob, and so had the enemy. Tracers are a two-way street. They let you see where your bullets are going, but they also let the enemy see where your bullets are coming from. Now we were the center of attention for the entire enemy force. Long bursts of machine gun fire cracked over my head and into the trees behind me, dropping more branches and leaves on me and our position. I yelled at Maguire to stop shooting tracer. The sky was just starting to lighten when I heard movement to my left.

### Squad Leader Again

It was Sergeant Smith, crawling down the line. He had been wounded. I asked about his condition and he said that his wound was not real serious but he needed medical attention. When I asked him if he needed any help, he said no, and to stay where I was. I saw he was carrying his rifle and asked him if he would trade with me, suggesting that he wouldn't need one at the aid station. He gave me his rifle, took mine and crawled off down the line. The sky was getting lighter. There was a lot of firing across the field where the other battalion had their perimeter.

The 1-26 Infantry, commanded by LTC Haig, later to be Secretary of State under President Reagan, was under heavy attack by a regiment of the 9th VC Division. The enemy breached the perimeter and attacked the battalion CP before they were repulsed and the perimeter was reestablished.

Meanwhile, it was now light enough to see. The Air Force showed up and began bombing the enemy forces on the far side of the open area. F-4 Phantoms came in very low and dropped high-drag bombs and napalm. Puff the Magic Dragon showed up and poured a thick stream of red tracer fire on enemy forces below them. All of a sudden, I saw a string of green tracers coming up from the ground and going toward the plane. This was a serious fight. The enemy had heavy mortars and anti-aircraft guns.

Sergeant Magee came by to check on us and stayed for a while. Dum-Dum also showed up. He was lying behind a foxhole like the rest of us and trying to get a better view of the action when an airstrike came in. Sergeant Magee told him to get down but he continued to rubberneck. I saw a bomb go off and a piece of shrapnel came skipping across the field like a flat rock skipping across a pond.

Before anyone could say something, the piece of metal struck him in the side and stuck there. The medics came and bandaged him. He was all right but needed a dust-off. This meant that we would be getting a new XO. Later, I was directed to write recommendations for both of them for Bronze Star Medals. Apparently my way with words made a big impression on the clerks and jerks in the rear, because they upgraded the recommendations and gave them Silver Stars.

## Mopping Up

Unbeknownst to us, the enemy force in front of us had crawled across the huge open area to our front while it was dark. They managed to dig shallow fighting positions, and when the mortar fire ended they opened fire on us. We later determined that their mission was to pin us down and prevent us from maneuvering on their buddies who were making the main effort.

Now, the enemy soldiers in front of us were either dead or wounded. Sergeant Magee and I were watching the area when one of them started crawling across our front. We began to fire at him because it looked like he was crawling toward a machine gun near him. I don't know if any of my bullets hit him, but he suddenly stopped crawling and thrust one of his legs into the air, all most straight up, where it remained for a moment and then came down slowly to rest on the ground.

One of the other squad leaders was told to take his squad and check the enemy bodies to see if any of them were alive for the medics. Airstrikes and artillery continued in the distance and helicopters began landing nearby. Some of them were dust-off choppers and some were bringing resupply.

I surveyed the area around my foxhole and was amazed by the number of mortar near misses. I counted four large craters within five feet of our hole and a larger number of 82mm mortar craters. It was later determined that the large craters were made by 120mm mortar rounds. They were the equivalent of a 105mm artillery round. There were quite a few of these craters around our platoon's positions.

My canteens were full of holes and the top half of my rucksack was shredded, but my pistol belt, ammo pouches and shoulder harness, though damaged, still functioned. I was considering how I was going to carry water, when a helicopter landed about a hundred meters to the right front of my position.

In the distance I saw the squad leader approaching a body. Suddenly he began backing up and firing his rifle with one hand. Puffs of dust appeared around the enemy soldier as the squad leader continued to back up and fire his rifle. Then he stopped, brought the rifle to his shoulder and fired several rounds before walking back toward the enemy soldier. When he was close, he stopped and looked at him, then put his rifle muzzle to the man's head, and looking away, fired a round into his head.

None of this could be heard from where we were because of the helicopter noise. The squad leader later told me that when he walked up to the enemy soldier the first time, the man snarled at him and grabbed at a hand grenade on his belt, so he shot him several times. When he checked him again and saw that he was still alive, he took no more chances and shot him again, in the head.

The battle at Ap Gu was one of the most lop-sided victories of the Vietnam War. We had one man wounded, and there were about forty enemy dead in front of our positions. The Blue Spaders lost ten KIA in the battle and it was reported afterward that 609 enemy bodies were found in front of the battalion positions. That was a kill ratio of unprecedented proportions, and the higher commands were impressed. LTC Haig received the Distinguished Service Cross and was given command of the 2d Brigade after its commander was wounded. This battle was a total validation of the defensive positions envisioned by General DePuy.[253]

### The VC Try to Fly

Jose's machine gun crew had returned. They had been out on ambush when the mortaring started. He said that they packed up and were heading back to the perimeter, when they heard someone trying to start the helicopter that had been shot down while carrying LTC Haig the day before. If the VC had pilots with them who could fly American helicopters, we had greatly underestimated their capability and sophistication.

### Pursuit

> **Bill Williamson:** *"The next morning the 1-16th received orders to pursue the enemy unit. LTC Lazzell decided that A Company would lead the pursuit and directed me to go up in an H-13 and conduct an aerial recon that would assist our movement. As the H-13 reached the far side of the open area, I could look down on the enemy activity as they were recovering their killed and wounded. I was surprised to see them using grappling hooks and ropes to pull the bodies to collection points where they were being stacked up like logs. There were oxcarts near the stacks of bodies and the bodies were being loaded onto the oxcarts for movement north to Cambodia which was only a half dozen or so miles away. Further along I could see the oxcart trail and oxcarts loaded with bodies moving along it. There were easily 70 or 80 bodies visible at that time."*

When the CO returned from his recon, we moved to the north to sweep through the area that hid the enemy bases. We entered the tree-line near a sign in English that warned us not to go any farther. The vegetation had taken a real pounding from the airstrikes and artillery. As we moved through the devastation, the point platoon stopped and sent back word that there was an enemy force ahead. We all tensed up as we took a knee and waited. Nothing happened, and after ten minutes we moved out again.

Suddenly, a sergeant who had recently joined us, yelled, "Hit it!" and we all dove to the ground facing out, looking for a target—once again, nothing. We lay there until the CO came up through the column and asked who gave the alarm. The sergeant told him, and the CO asked him what he saw. The sergeant hadn't seen anything, but he thought he had heard something. The CO wasn't happy and told us to move out.

> **Bill Williamson:** *"After nothing further developed, A Company resumed its advance and then there was more noise ahead of us. We halted again and waited only to see American soldiers emerge from the jungle. I went forward and identified them as members of the 1-2 Infantry and the Company was commanded by a classmate of mine from West Point and a fellow platoon leader from our days in the 82d Airborne Division, CPT Pete Boylan. 1-2 Infantry had the same mission that was given to us, pursue the retreating enemy. 1-2 Infantry was approaching the area from a different direction. Fortunately, cool heads prevailed and no rounds were exchanged. It had the potential to be a serious friendly fire incident. After further searching, no enemy units were found. They had all withdrawn into Cambodia and we did not pursue them beyond the border."*

## Strange Days

That afternoon, we found an enemy base camp. It was the usual camp, just like all the other ones we had been finding. It had a deep trench around it's perimeter with fighting positions every few meters. The positions all had overhead cover and were so well concealed that you had to see into the trench before you could see that there was anything man-made. Inside the camp, about fifty meters from the perimeter, were wooden huts with tables and benches.

Our platoon was searching the camp, while the others secured the area. As we swept through the middle of the camp, I came upon a well. Several of us were looking at it, when the CO walked up and said that it might be an entrance to a tunnel. He told us to lower a man on a rope to check it out.

Sergeant Magee asked for volunteers, and one of the men from a rifle squad stepped forward. He was helped by a sergeant to make a Swiss seat. The rope was tied onto it and he was lowered into the well. It was pretty deep and he was hard to see when all of a sudden he began shouting, "Pull me up, pull me up, there's a guy down here!"

We pulled him up as fast as we could. When he got to the top he told us that there was a hole in the wall at the waterline and a man was standing there who tried to grab him. Wow, there was an enemy right below our feet. The CO asked him a few questions, and then he told me to throw a grenade into the well, which I did. I heard it hit the water and several seconds later it exploded. A pillar of water, the same dimensions as the diameter of the well, came out of the hole, and when it was no longer constrained by the hole, collapsed, soaking us from the waist down.

We waited, peering into the darkness for some sign of the man in the well. After a few minutes the CO told our guy to go back down again and check it out.

This time he carried a pistol and a flashlight, both of which were tied with cords to his belt. We lowered him in again, slowly. He went deeper and deeper, and we waited for him to shoot or say something.

We couldn't really see him in the dark, and then "There's blood and guts all over the place down here," came his voice from deep in the well. After a minute, the CO called down to him and asked him what he was seeing now. No reply. Then the CO asked him if he was all right. No reply. "Pull him up," he ordered. We were all pulling on the rope again and when he got to the top of the hole, he was unconscious—very strange.

The LT and some others got him out of the Swiss seat, and someone else called for the medic. The man was lying on his back, not moving. The medic checked him out for a moment and then stepped back, as bewildered as we were. The CO leaned over him, calling his name and shaking his shoulder.

All of a sudden, the man sat up, shouted, and grabbed the CO around the throat with both hands. He was frantically trying to strangle him and would have done so, if several of us who were standing around, hadn't jumped on him and pried his fingers off the CO's neck. We were really in the twilight zone now. We continued to hold him down, and he struggled with all of us, wild eyed, turning his head from side to side. This went on a few more minutes until he finally relaxed.

Everyone was shaken by what had happened. The CO told us to disarm the man and tie his hands together until the medics could check him out. We wrapped up our search of the base camp and started back toward the LZ.

I didn't learn the lesson about grenades in wells until long after the war, when I found an article written by a lieutenant who told the story of the death of one of his soldiers. They had found a well, thrown a grenade inside, and lowered their man in to check it out. They left him down there for a while before realizing that he was in trouble.

When he failed to respond to their shaking the rope and then shouting, they pulled him up unconscious. They called the medic just like we did, but that time the man was dead. The man writing the story was as mystified as we were, and sometime later, he told the story to an engineer officer. The officer explained to him that when the grenade went off underwater, it burned all the oxygen right out of the well.

### Demo Work

After a quick search of the base camp, we moved on, and after several more hours of struggling through bombed-out trees, we came back into the large open area to the east from where we'd entered the jungle. We were moving along the edge of the tree-line when we came upon the enemy mortar positions. The firing points were in deep holes dug in the ground. They were deep enough for the tubes to be below the surface which reduced their noise and flash signatures. When we heard them coming out of the tubes during the early morning darkness, no one saw where they were coming from.

From this location, I could see our positions on the other side of the large open area. The tall tree that gave my own position some shade must have been used by them as an aiming point, Of course, after the first rounds landed on our lines, no one was up looking to see where they were coming from. We were all in the bottom of our holes, except for the few LPs and ambush patrols trying to get back to the perimeter in the dark, and they were more worried about who might be out there with them.

The mortars were gone, but there were quite a few mortar rounds lying around. There were more at the bottom of one of the holes. They were Chinese made 82mm shells. The CO told Sergeant Magee to have me destroy them. I picked up all the ones lying on the ground and carefully placed them in one of the holes. I made a charge of C4 and placed it on top of the shells. The company moved out and I waited by the hole until the last man was 100 meters away before I lit both fuses. We were almost back to our perimeter when the charge went off, destroying the mortar rounds.

> **Bill Williamson:** *"As A Company moved through the open area back to our defensive positions of the night before, we encountered a row of stakes about five or six feet tall, spaced ten to twelve feet apart. As we got closer to them, we could see that explosives were attached to the top of the stakes and these explosives on the stakes were connected by wire or Det-Cord that would allow them to be simultaneously detonated. However, the air and artillery of that morning had broken the connecting wires/cord and they were now inert. To me, these devices were not part of the morning attack, but rather were a part of a landing zone ambush that was intended to destroy the helicopters participating in the air-assault by the 1-26 Infantry or by us on March 31st. Fortunately, neither air-assault landed near the stakes with the attached explosives."*

We returned to our old positions. I found a map left by some staff officer on top of my bunker, and saw that the area we were occupying was named LZ George. I thought the map would come in handy, but then we were told that we would be flying out on Chinooks in two days. I was glad to hear that.

We spent two nights in our positions. I still didn't have any canteens and was extremely thirsty. I went up to the company mortar pits and drank some of their coffee because it was the only fluid available. The next day I took one of the dead VC's canteens and used it for the rest of the operation. Their bodies were still out in front of our positions, but no one was interested in burying them. We had enough digging to do as it was.

There was no mistaking the smell of decomposing flesh, the smell of death. The human body is a wonderful thing, housing a human spirit. When the spirit leaves the body, it begins to decompose and in decomposing it begins to smell. There had been more than 600 men killed within a half a mile of where we were. The bodies of the enemy dead were swollen and turning black. The stench from 600 dead bodies lying in the sun was incredible. The sky was full of buzzards circling the dinner table.

On the last day, Sergeant Magee told me that he had a demo job that he was sure I would like. I followed him down our line of foxholes about fifty meters from my position. There, lying on the ground, about fifty feet from the nearest foxhole, was a 500 pound USAF bomb. It had been dropped during the first day's fight and had failed to go off. It had been in our perimeter through the mortaring and incoming small arms fire and was undisturbed, thank God. This was something special. I sat down for once and gave it some thought. I only had a small amount of demo left and told Sergeant Magee. He said he'd be back and took off toward our platoon CP.

Roland Wilson had told me that sometimes the Air Force dropped bombs with a timer which would detonate it a few days later. This was in hopes of nailing the VC who would have hauled it to a jungle camp to saw it in half and take out the explosives for their mines and booby-traps. He also mentioned some anti-tampering devices, so I decided not to try and move anything. While I was musing over the many deadly possibilities, Sergeant Magee returned, carrying an enemy backpack with some kind of demo, and told me I could use it for the job.

I decided to dig a small hole under one side of the bomb, near the center, for all the explosives. I reasoned that by doing this I would increase the force of the blast and hopefully detonate the bomb. After I stuffed the explosives in the hole, so that they were touching the bottom side of the bomb, I cut four fuses and crimped the blasting caps to them with my teeth, as usual. The fuses were long, and the plan was that I would light them and leave on the last bird. While we were waiting for the birds, I had become a little more familiar with my bomb now, and someone took a picture of me sitting on it.

The extraction finally began, and when the last bird was loaded and ready to go, the crew chief gave me a wave. I lit the four fuses and walked quickly to the helicopter. It took off and I tried to keep my bomb in sight. I really wanted to see my crowning achievement in the world of explosive ordinance disposal. The bomb got smaller and smaller as we flew away. There was still five minutes to go when I lost sight of it. When the time was up, the helicopter had turned, and I never saw it go off.

### The Hawaiian Comes For a Visit

We were flown back to Quan Loi on 4 April, 1967 to spend the night. We had just moved to the area where we would RON, when I noticed a helicopter landing about 200 meters away. As soon as it touched down, a man wearing a Hawaiian shirt stepped out and walked in a crouch from under the blades which were still turning, and then stood there looking at his watch. A soldier ran up to him, then suddenly braced and rendered a sharp salute.

The man in the Hawaiian shirt returned it, spoke to him for a moment, and then the soldier ran back to where he came from. The man in the Hawaiian shirt seemed a little familiar, but I had no idea who he was. From the left side of my vision, I saw our company commander running across the field, his two RTOs right behind him, heads down, elbows pumping, trying to keep up. The CO was a tall man with long legs, but I never saw him get very excited and I never saw him run like this. Who was the guy in the Hawaiian shirt?

The CO reached the Hawaiian, stood at attention and saluted. It was returned, and as he stood at attention, the Hawaiian seemed to be doing all the talking. Their meeting only lasted about two minutes; then the Hawaiian shook his hand, they saluted, and the Hawaiian moved at a crouch back to the helicopter, which had kept its motor running the entire time. He jumped in and the helicopter took off, nose down as it picked up speed, disappearing over the rubber trees of the Michelin Plantation.

The Hawaiian was General Westmoreland. He had flown in to congratulate us for our part in the battle of Ap Gu. Since we weren't in the main event, we didn't rate a full stop, but he was kind enough to stop by and let Captain Williamson know how much he appreciated our efforts. The guy who had run up to General Westmoreland when he first landed told us later, that the General said to him, "I've been here thirty seconds and I don't see anybody moving!"

**AAR Summary**

As good as our enemy was at ambushes, booby-traps, and other aspects of guerrilla warfare, when it came to conventional assaults by their main force units on our positions, they had not yet figured out the way to overcome General DePuy's defensive tactics, that were behind the design of our perimeter defense.

They were as old school as we were, utilizing their mortars to soften up our positions before crossing the open field in orderly ranks, in an attempt to overrun the 1-26 Infantry positions. A few of them did manage to get into the perimeter and make it to the battalion CP before they were killed along with 600 of their comrades, who were now becoming a feast for the birds of the air and the ants. This was in comparison to a total of ten KIA and sixty-four WIA for the U.S. forces. It was a close run thing, but once the artillery shells started landing among them, they had run out of time.

They would have done a lot more damage and possibly defeated a unit like ours if they had done what the enemy unit in front of us had done. They managed to get forty men and their equipment to within 100 meters of our positions without us detecting them. If they would have crawled forward until the U.S. troops saw them and then jumped up and run in amongst them, they would have been able to kill a lot of us in what would have been total confusion in the dark. Yes, they would have lost a lot of men, maybe, but they lost a lot of men the way they did do it and gained nothing.

My own lessons were less insightful. This was the first serious combat I had been in. Alpha Company only had a few wounded, none seriously, and we had killed all the enemy troops in front of our positions with our own small arms. My rifle had jammed, so I made a mental note to beg, borrow or steal a cleaning rod of my own. The non-firing claymore and non-exploding grenade were bad luck, right? and the multiple near-misses of the enemy mortar shells were good luck. I gave no thought to any intervention by a higher power and figured that combat wasn't so bad after all. Unfortunately, it wouldn't always go this way.

The 2d Brigade report on lessons learned included the following entries. I wonder if these were written by a young LT or by a sleep-deprived operations officer. I suppose that context is everything, but since the writer failed to provide the backdrop, some of the entries were quite amusing:

"2. *Landing Zones must be thoroughly checked for possible explosive devices. These consist of mines buried and on top of the ground.*"

Yes but the landing zones that are utilized for combat air-assaults are not available prior to the landing for mine sweeping and EOD work because presumably they are in enemy territory.

"3. *(C) To get captured documents and materials evacuated rapidly. S-2s should have a length of rope with a sand bag so these items can be lifted by LOH through the trees."*

Unless the 2nd Brigade provided helicopters to the S2s, I wonder how the S2 on the ground was expected to get the other end of the rope up to the chopper hovering above the trees.

"8. *(C) A-22 bags containing ammunition required by the maneuver elements should not exceed 800 lbs. or the UH-1D cannot lift them."*

The 2nd Brigade had been in Vietnam since July of 1965. This lesson was learned over and over again as troops were rotated or became casualties.[254]

## Operation Harvest Moon

After a day at Quan Loi, we were flown by C-130 to Song Be and flown from there by Chinooks to a place called Bunard in the northern part of III Corps. It was an abandoned French rubber plantation near Highway 14. The Nha Trang Mike Force, a 5th Special Forces Group unit, had parachuted into the area in what was touted as the first Special Forces combat jump of the war.[255]

There was a lot of publicity at the time about how the brave fighting soldiers from the sky had parachuted behind enemy lines to seize this strategic location from the enemy. The intention was to establish a Special Forces camp at Bunard, and to do so they needed to buy some time while they built it. The Nha Trang Mike Force was apparently needed elsewhere, so the Green Berets of the Bunard SF camp asked the legs of the 1st Infantry Division to patrol their AO while they built their camp.

## Special Forces

I was enthralled by the Special Forces. There had been some small articles in magazines and a few paperback books about them in the 1950s. It wasn't until President Kennedy visited Ft Bragg, NC in October of 1961 and was treated to a Dog and Pony show that is still talked about to this day, that they were introduced to the American People. The people of this country were told that there was now a special group of soldiers that could take on the communist supported guerrillas in a dozen different 'Brush Fire' wars that were springing up all over the world.

The Special Forces were a continuation of the OSS Special Operations units of WWII. The Operational Groups (OGs), the Jedburgh Teams, Detachment 101 in Burma, and, although not OSS, the stay-behind guerrilla leaders in the Philippines, all served to organize the resistance forces of countries occupied by an invader. Resurrected by veterans of these units during the Korean War, using slots that became available when the Army disbanded the Airborne Ranger Companies, the new Special Forces came on the scene, prepared to play a role in the U.S. strategy of Roll-back, the eventual pushing back of the Soviet Union's forces in Eastern Europe.[256]

The Special Forces learned the languages of the various Eastern European countries and prepared to be inserted into those countries when the time was right. There they would organize resistance movements like those in World War II. These forces could either support conventional operations like they did in France during and after D-Day, or hopefully, they could have such an impact that the masses would rise up and cast off their oppressors, reclaiming their homeland, so that they could be aligned with the West.[257]

The early SF people worked real hard at this. They recruited many displaced persons under the Lodge Act, who were living in Western Europe in the aftermath of WWII. These people were put on teams that targeted the places they came from. As native speakers with many contacts in the targeted denied areas, they would be real assets when the balloon went up.[258]

There had been a number of initiatives by the allied intelligence agencies during this period. Many attempts were made by the Brits and the U.S. to insert agents into Eastern Europe and even into the Soviet Union. Most of these operations were disasters, compromised by traitors such as Kim Philby of the British Secret Intelligence Service, and condemned to failure by the inability of these services to appreciate the efficiency of the internal security apparatuses in these countries. I'm sure that when the rumors of information leaks got to these guys in SF, like they always do, it must have given them some second thoughts about their role in the Roll-back plan.[259]

There was a small revolt in East Berlin in the early fifties, and for a short time the dreamers in CIA and the State Department must have thought that the great day was eminent, but nothing came of it. Then, when the Hungarians really rose up against the Russians, the world held its breath, waiting to see if now was the time to do it, to roll-back communism to the borders of Soviet Russia.[260]

The President at that time was Dwight Eisenhower. He had commanded the Great Crusade in Europe eleven years earlier and he didn't want to go to the mat with the Russians. After what must have been a vigorous debate within the administration, the Roll-back strategy was discarded and a new policy of containment was adopted. The West had gone on the defense.[261]

This was a sea change for the Special Forces. By now they had managed to stand up two Special Forces groups. Since there wasn't going to be a war in Europe anytime soon, they were in desperate need of a mission. As the Eisenhower years came to a close, the Russians were on the offensive all over the world. The Soviet Union's Premier Nikita Khrushchev told the world that the Soviet Union would support the wars of national liberation everywhere. Many insurgent groups took these words for the names of their movements.[262]

When John Kennedy took office, his inaugural speech set the tone for his administration when he told the world that we would support freedom-loving people everywhere, meaning specifically those nations with communist sponsored and supported insurgencies. The U.S. and the Soviet Union then squared off to fight proxy wars. After the Cuban Missile Crisis, any attempt to rally the American People to go to war with the Russians was quickly abandoned.

These wars of national liberation were the answer that the Special Forces were looking for. They reinvented themselves as counter-guerrilla fighters, able to arm, train and lead indigenous forces against the communist infiltrators who were fomenting guerrilla warfare in the third world. By the time John Kennedy showed up at Ft Bragg, the SF proclaimed themselves the force-multipliers from hell.[263]

If they had the proper funding and were allowed to expand, they could probably keep the communists at bay, and the President wouldn't have to send American boys to fight other boys' wars; besides, they had these really cool green berets that must have warmed the Irish blood in the President's veins. He pushed their expansion; made sure they had plenty of money, and looked for opportunities to use these skilled men.

His first opportunity came in Laos. But after a few years, a convention was signed, requiring all foreign troops to leave the country; so Laos became a CIA playground in which they stayed busy until 1975. Fortunately, one of Laos' neighbors was experiencing their own insurgency, and it was here that the Green Berets would attempt to wage their brand of special warfare and keep South Vietnam from falling to the communists.[264]

The first Special Forces teams started arriving in Vietnam in the late fifties. As part of a strategy developed by the CIA, they began establishing camps that were manned by them and their South Vietnamese Special Forces counterparts. There they practiced the 'oil-stain' theory of counterinsurgency and were quite successful in creating local self-defense forces that could defend their own people from the VC.[265]

Teams would come from Ft Bragg and Okinawa on six month TDY deployments where they would live in a camp and meet the locals. Occasionally, they provoked the National Liberation Front, the Viet Cong, to attack them. The first Medal of Honor of the Vietnam War went to a Special Forces captain who led the heroic defense of his A-Camp.[266]

Operation Switchback directed the Special Forces to leave the control of the CIA and come under the control of the Army in Vietnam, part of the blow-back from the Bay of Pigs operation. Eventually all Special Forces in South Vietnam were assigned to the 5th Special Forces Group (Airborne). The group's headquarters was in Nha Trang. Their mission changed and they would no longer practice classic counterinsurgency, but would take the local self-defense forces and convert them into mobile strike forces and border surveillance forces.

The teams would no longer be on TDY, but would have a one year stabilized tour like the rest of the Army. It was now obvious that the Special Forces alone were not going to be able to defeat the communist insurgency; but they had made themselves seemingly indispensable in Vietnam, and as Special Forces expanded, they had to get men to fill their ranks.[267]

The veterans of Korea and WWII provided them with their leadership, but they were going to need thousands of more men, and there weren't enough veterans capable of filling those slots. They began recruiting the best and the brightest, and they got them. Young men from all over the country began to respond to the challenge of the Green Beret.[268]

I listened to Master Sergeant Donald Duncan, one of their best, who was later their first 'traitor,' give a recruiting pitch to my basic training company at Fort Ord. I thought he was the coolest soldier I had ever seen, standing up on that stage in his Levis and turtle neck sweater. I would have signed up right then if I weren't a National Guardsman.[269]

These young men met all the challenges that SF could throw at them. They went Airborne all the way, many attended Ranger training, and for them, it was just like the high school or college football team before they came in the Army. They were awed by some of their leaders' exploits in WWII and Korea. They worked hard, earned their Green Beret, and went to war.

They were still, however, young men. Some of them believed the PR, became arrogant in their estimate of their enemies' capabilities, and like the rest of us, paid for that arrogance in blood. They also became arrogant in their behavior toward their own countrymen who were sent to shore up the dike that they had tried to build.

### Bunard SF Camp

When I got off the Chinook helicopter at Bunard, where my battalion had been sent to provide security for the Special Forces A-Team that was building the camp there, I didn't expect a brass band; but I was expecting them to appreciate their fellow countrymen who were showing up to lend a helping hand. Instead, the first thing I heard out of one of their mouths was, "Hey, Lieutenant Williamson, what are you doing with those legs?"

I looked over at the Mike Force troops who were going to board the helicopters that brought us here. The indigenous troops were looking at us like we were the enemy. I never did see who yelled at our company commander, who was a captain. I figured it was some soldier who had served with him in an airborne unit in the recent past. That remark and the decidedly unfriendly attitude of the team we protected while they built their camp gave me a bad taste in my mouth toward the less professional members of their elite organization.

### Digging It

We marched from the airstrip to our assigned positions around the camp and started to dig in. For the next month, we never stopped digging. First, we finished our primary fighting positions, then we built false positions designed to fool an assaulting enemy force. Sleeping positions with overhead cover were completed, and when we had finally finished putting out concertina wire, Sergeant Magee decided we needed trenches.

I have come to realize over the years that he was absolutely right. An infantryman should continually improve his position. He might start out with a foxhole, but given enough time he should build a castle. Unfortunately, the troops didn't subscribe to any doctrinal publications, so the job of the junior leaders was made greatly more difficult. The guys bitched about everything when we started to dig the trench.

### How I Made Sergeant

After we had succeeded in digging the trench exactly the way the platoon sergeant said, the battalion commander, Colonel Lazzell, inspected our area. I showed him around our positions and he seemed pleased to see me. I guess he remembered our conversation on the battlefield at Ap Gu on the 31 March. "Hey,

Captain Williamson, I want you to put some stripes on this man," he yelled to my CO. Captain Williamson said the only thing he could say in front of the troops when the battalion commander gave him such a public directive, "Yes, sir."

Lazzell moved on with our CO, the LT and Sergeant Magee. They stopped at the next squad's positions and he turned and looked back at the trench. I'm sure that Sergeant Magee was hoping to hear the colonel give the same directive to the CO that he gave about my promotion. Instead he heard the colonel tell the CO that, "Whoever designed that trench didn't know what he was doing. There are no curves in it, an enemy gets in that trench and he can shoot everyone in it." Colonel Lazzell had fought in Korea when the lines were fixed and the fighting resembled WWI in the trenches.

Sergeant Magee was looking gray as the colonel moved on to the next platoon's positions, and the bitching reached a new crescendo on the bunker line. Not only did we have to put curves in a straight line trench, but the company to our right, who had so far resisted the urge to dig a trench, was now ordered to tie in with ours, with curves.

Between digging holes, filling sandbags, and making straight lines crooked in the ground, we also had a full schedule of patrolling activities. We conducted platoon-sized patrols for up to ten kilometers from the camp during the day and squad ambush patrols at night.

### The Fighting Ambush Patrol

One night, I was sitting up with the RTO who was monitoring the company net. The CO came on the radio and directed the mortar platoon to conduct an H+I mission. He gave the grid coordinates of the target and left the net. About a minute later, just before the first round was fired, a voice came on the radio, announcing their call sign and saying "Cease-fire, cease-fire!" The CO told the mortar platoon to standby and called the element that had called cease fire. It was our platoon's ambush patrol. The CO asked the squad leader why he called cease-fire, and the squad leader said that the target grid coordinates were where he was.

The CO checked his map and told the squad leader that he was in the wrong place, and to move his squad to the correct ambush location immediately. The H+I mission was canceled, and everything settled down to normal for the rest of the night, at least in the perimeter. The ambush patrol returned in the morning, and I could see by some of the faces of the men, that they were upset with their squad leader for setting up in an area that was almost mortared by their own company. One of the guys took me aside when I asked him how he was doing, and he told me a story that made the call for mortar fire incidental to the main event that took place afterward.

After the squad leader called cease fire, and they moved out of their position, he and the senior team leader began to argue about something every time they stopped on the way to their new ambush location. Nobody knew exactly what the argument was about because they had it in whispers a little bit away from the rest of the troops. When the squad arrived at their proper location, the two were arguing even more forcefully and their whispers could be heard at the other end of the file. The troops took a knee and waited for the squad leader to direct them in the occupation of the ambush position.

The argument grew louder and now they were cursing and threatening one another. As the troops nervously waited, the two leaders went from verbal to kinetic. One shoved the other, and before anyone could move they were on the ground rolling over and over punching each other. The other team leader made a quick decision and told the rest of the squad to follow him. They moved about twenty-five meters away from the two combatants and lay in the grass, hopefully out of the sight of any enemy forces attracted to the sound, but close enough for the fighters to rejoin them if and when they came to their senses.

My buddy said they fought on the ground for several minutes until one of them got a grip on the other's throat and began to strangle him. The man being strangled groped around on the ground until his hand found his rifle which he unsafed and brought the muzzle in contact with his adversary's chest.

This stopped the fight, and they both rolled away from each other, the man with the rifle staying ready to defend himself if the other made a threatening move with his own rifle. The other team leader got their attention, and they rejoined the rest of the patrol. The squad leader moved to one flank of the patrol and the team leader moved to the other. "This is no shit," he said, "they stayed at opposite ends of the patrol, facing each other instead of the trail for the rest of the night."

## Gooks

There was very little noticeable activity in the Bunard area at that time, but that didn't mean it wasn't dangerous. The battalion recon platoon sergeant, Robert Emro, was killed while on patrol by a VC who was probably hidden in a tunnel or spider hole. The platoon sergeant was the last man in the file and was shot in the back of the head. The platoon searched the area but found nothing. He was an older man on his second war.

On one of our patrols, we were moving through an area where there were some well-used trails, some like dirt roads. We had just crossed one when I heard a man in the trail fire team stuttering, "Goo, goo, goo, gooks!" I ran back and he pointed down the trail. There were a lot of footprints, and one of the other guys said that a large group of men, women, and children had run past them. I told them to follow me, and we took off running following the tracks.

After about fifty meters, running as fast as we could, I stopped everyone to look and listen, but there was no sign of them. Continuing at a walk, we passed several branches of the trail that they might have used to get away from us, but it was like they disappeared from the face of the earth. I found a game snare on one of the trails and decided that it was too risky to continue on because of the possibility of booby-traps or ambush. We returned to the platoon, and I reported what happened to the LT. Later that day, we found a number of small huts clustered together in the brush. They had been used recently and we found a few rounds of 7.62x39mm in one of them.

On another patrol, we found a nice little house in the middle of nowhere, with a steep, A-frame type roof. No one was home. It was in a lovely setting. There was a flowing stream, a small pond in front of the house and everything around it seemed perfect. We left it as we found it, a nice place in the middle of the jungle.

I only had one direct contact with the SF men in the camp. They sat up on their hill bar-b-queuing and running their generator, while we lived in holes and guarded their camp. I went up there one day and asked one of the engineer sergeants if he had an extra pair of blasting cap crimpers. I was tired of crimping them with my teeth. He said he didn't, but I thought he did. That could be because of my suspicion that he wouldn't have given one to a leg, even if he had a hundred. We left Bunard on 25 April, 1967 and returned to Lai Khe.

## Arc-Light

Back in Lai Khe, we had more than a few beers that first night. I went to sleep on my bunk and was sleeping the sleep of a drunken exhausted infantryman. At about 0400, high in the sky over the sleeping countryside, a flight of three BUFF's, B-52s, were releasing the bombs that they had carried all the way from Guam, a small island in the Pacific Ocean, almost 2500 miles away. Eighty-four 500 pound and twenty-four 750 pound bombs dropped away from each aircraft and fell towards the jungle below. Anyone near the target and awake at that time would have heard a rapid series of high pitched "Wooh, wooh, wooh!" as the bombs approached the earth.[270]

A series of flashes in the dark, followed by a continuous string of explosions, shattered the peace of our base camp. The ground began to shake like a major earthquake as the bombs detonated in rapid succession. The shaking didn't wake me, but it did disturb my shotgun that was resting on two nails in the wall above my bed. The shotgun joined the other metal falling from the sky that morning and landed on my head, giving me a slight cut on my forehead and waking me up with a start. I tried to stand up and make sense of what was going on. Later that morning, we waited by the airstrip for another ride back to the war.

## Ambush of the VC Money Man

Toward the end of the month, we returned to Lai Khe. An ambush patrol nailed a small element of VC one night. They killed several of them, and when they searched the bodies, they found several thousand dollars in U.S. currency. The sergeant turned it in to his platoon leader against the advice of the members of his squad, who considered it their just reward for a successful ambush—statistically, a rare event.

The LT sent it up the chain of command, and eventually, the battalion commander was forced to decide what to do with it. After much consideration, I'm supposing here, he decided that the best use for the money was to throw a big party for the battalion officers at the Ville. The only thing that would have pissed off the squad who got the money more, was if he would have had them wait the tables at the party.

*And might release those who because of the fear of death*
*through all their life were held in slavery*
*Hebrews 2:15*

# Chapter 15-May 1967

### Promotion

In May I was promoted to Sergeant E-5. The colonel had ordered our CO to promote me when we were at Bunard, and one day, without ceremony, Sergeant Magee handed me the orders that made it official. There were no education requirements for promotion to sergeant then. Normally, the platoon sergeants and the first sergeant made their recommendations to the CO. They had determined that you knew the basic requirements of an NCO or that you were capable of learning them quickly. The battalion commander superseded that process for reasons known only to him, and I was now a sergeant.

In those days, the platoon sergeant and the squad leaders schooled the new or acting sergeants with on-the-spot corrections and after-hours advice. I had heard about the 7th Army NCO Academy at the Flint Kaserne in Bad Tolz, Bavaria, when I was stationed in Germany; but there were a number of men promoted to sergeant in my unit, and none of them had attended the Academy. Later in the war, the Army would establish a training course for NCOs similar to officer candidate school, or OCS.

The men were chosen to attend if they showed leadership potential during their basic training following induction into the Army. They became known as 'shake and bake' or 'instant NCOs.' Twenty-eight years later I would graduate from a primary leadership development course or PLDC. This course was required for anyone chosen for promotion to sergeant. In the following few years, I would graduate from two more NCO courses, each required before promotion to the next rank. In some ways, they have greatly improved the NCO Corps.

I took my promotion with a light heart, thinking about the extra beer money and never having to pull KP. I had been bearing the responsibilities of a sergeant on and off since AIT at Fort Polk, when I was an acting-jack platoon sergeant and thought I knew it all.

I bought some subdued sergeant stripes in the Ville and had them sewn on a jungle fatigue shirt. The next time I was in Saigon, I bought a set of metal Marine Corps sergeant insignia, bent the cross rifles off, and wore them on my shirt collar, a new practice coming into the Army.

Several months before, I was awarded SP or Special Proficiency pay—fifty dollars a month. This was the last gasp of an old extra pay incentive known as Proficiency or Pro-Pay. Pro-pay had three levels, and there was a yearly examination. It had been done away with a few years before, but SP pay would be around for a while longer.

Normally, to get it, you had to take a yearly examination for your MOS. But in Vietnam, the CO was authorized to waive the exam and award it to NCOs who were proficient in their duties. That he awarded it to me, left me scratching my head; but I decided to let well enough alone and not mention it in case it was a clerical error and I lost it.

## Combat Infantryman Badge (CIB)

The men in the company that had been at LZ George on 1 April were awarded CIB's. Once again, it was without ceremony, and we were given orders authorizing us to wear what has been described as the 'coveted' CIB. Of course, we were happy to be able to wear them on our uniforms like all the other combat soldiers. The soldiers of WWII, when the badge was first awarded, had to endure much harsher conditions and a much more dangerous infantry life, as the casualty figures for that war attest.

I met a man who got his in Korea, and he said they wouldn't give you one until you were seen to kill an enemy soldier. We had met the requirements that have generally held steady through the years which are: that you have an infantry MOS and are assigned to an infantry unit conducting offensive operations against an armed enemy, and that you engage in actual combat with the enemy. I guess, since the fight at LZ George met those criteria, that is why we got them now.

## Flex-X Fiasco

During a road clearance operation, 3d Platoon came across an unexploded butterfly bomb. I was called on the radio and told to take an RTO and meet a sergeant who would show me where it was. We found him and he took me to the butterfly bomb.

I told him that we would take it from there, and he went back to his platoon's area. The butterfly bomb lay in the sand; the area around it was fairly open. I dropped the ruck and removed my explosives. This would be my first opportunity to use the new stuff that was being issued to replace the C4 we had been using in enormous quantities to heat our C-rations.

The new explosive was made by DuPont and it was called M-118 Flex-X. It was issued in rectangular sheets about twelve inches long, three inches wide and a quarter inch thick. There were four sheets in a package. The sheets were olive drab, and on one side there was a piece of plastic that covered a strong adhesive.

The explosives were designed for cutting hard metal objects like pipelines and rails on train tracks. I didn't know anything about this new stuff, but how hard could it be? I opened the package and took out a sheet. I figured out the adhesive feature pretty quickly, so I decided to set up a two blasting cap detonation. I cut the time fuse and crimped it into the blasting caps with my teeth; I still hadn't got my hands on a crimper. I laid the fuses in the sand and pulled the plastic off the adhesive. Then I put the caps on the adhesive, side by side. I pulled the plastic off another sheet, laid the adhesive side on the caps and squeezed the sheets so that they stuck together.

I packed my gear back in my ruck and put it on. The RTO gave me the handset and, listening to the net, I waited until the traffic ceased. When it did, I called company headquarters on the command push. "Alpha Six Romeo, this is two-three, fire in the hole, fire in the hole, fire in the hole, out." I lit the fuses, and we moved to a nearby defilade position and lay down behind a small mound of earth. The explosion would come in about 15 seconds. There was a line of ants going into a hole in the mound, and I watched them while I waited. When the time was almost up, I put my fingers in my ears and opened my mouth; 'Pop,' went the blasting caps.

This was not the desired effect. We waited for several minutes, and then I walked over to the butterfly bomb. The two sheets of Flex-X were blown apart, but hadn't gone off. I was amazed; two blasting caps had exploded in the middle of these two sheets of explosives and hadn't set them off. I went back and called the CP on the radio, told them I had a misfire and to standby.

Then I pulled open two more sheets, and this time, I used two blasting caps with fuses and two more blasting caps next to them to act as boosters. I stuck the two pieces together and called for clearance to fire. They gave it; so I announced 'fire in the hole' and returned to my place behind the mound. This time the 'pop' was louder, but I knew the explosives hadn't gone off and now I was mad. I called the CP and told them I had another misfire. The RTO told me that Six wanted me to hurry up and destroy that butterfly bomb, so that everybody could get back to work. "Roger," said I. I looked at the Flex-X and decided that it must be faulty.

I stood there wondering how I was going to get rid of this butterfly bomb. Then it came to me, just like many of my great ideas that always led to trouble. I looked around for a depression near the bomb and found a set of deep truck tire tracks in the sand about ten feet away. They probably came from the supply or mess truck of a unit pulling road clearance here in the past.

My plan was simple, but risky. I would put all my gear behind the mound nearby and call 'fire in the hole.' Then I would run back here, toss a grenade with great accuracy from about five feet away and dive into the tire tracks. I was sure, based on my experience with the grenade on the ambush patrol, that the explosion and shrapnel would pass over me.

I proceeded ahead with my plan before a more rational thought could intrude. I notified the CP, walked to within five feet of the bomb, pulled the pin on the grenade, made a perfect toss and heard it gently clink against the butterfly bomb as I dove for safety. No pop this time. I was barely in the rut when, with a loud 'Ka blaaam,' the grenade followed, by the bomb blew up. Actually, the bomb and the grenade went off so closely together that it sounded like one explosion. The blast was louder and more powerful than I expected, but the general rule for explosive blasts held fast.

Explosions like to go up and out and don't usually go flat across the ground. They say that there are old demo men and bold demo men, but there are no old, bold, demo men. It's a good thing I didn't stay in demo work after Vietnam, because it's obvious to me that I wouldn't be telling this story now.

## Propaganda

The battle for men's souls was going on at the same time as the battle for the body-count. The 'bullshit bombers,' Air Force planes that dropped leaflets instead of bombs, were littering the landscape with small pieces of paper. The leaflets had cartoons to illustrate the point that all would be forgiven; if the VC would 'Chieu hoi,' they would get a good deal.

Pictures reminding them of B-52s, weeping wives and pleading children, and text that offered these men living in the jungle, money for guns (something that is being tried in the U.S. as this was written) and a chance for a new life. Many of them did come over, and some became 'Kit Carson' scouts; but that was later. In 1967, the VC were short of toilet paper and appreciated the leaflets.

We were asked to assist in this effort by placing leaflets, designed and printed by our own propaganda specialists at Division, on our trails through the jungle. Last year I helped my buddy dig a six-by-six-by-six to bury a small piece of paper, and now they wanted us to drop these as we walked through the jungle.

A two edged sword, they prominently displayed a full color picture of our patch, the Big Red One, and a message in both Vietnamese and English. The message in English was for the VC who hadn't yet learned to read Vietnamese. It said, "You are fighting against the invincible Big Red One. It has never been defeated, and you would do well to surrender," or words to that effect.

The VC had their own propaganda operations which were targeting the American people back in the States. The peace movement, for all the good intentions of many of its members, was undermining the morale of the American people, who for the most part, were trying to remain oblivious to the distant war.

The VC did try to get to us, however. One day while we were clearing the sides of Hwy. 13 again, I found a red piece of paper on the ground near the road. It was printed in English and the message was aimed at the black soldiers. It asked them why they were fighting and dying in Vietnam when the country that sent them here wouldn't let them enjoy the same rights as the white soldiers. It mentioned the lynchings, bombings, and murders that were a regular occurrence in the South during the civil rights struggle that was taking place at this time.

**Loc Ninh and the French Bunker**

We rode to Loc Ninh by helicopter, as usual, and the company set up in an old French Army fort. There were berms around the perimeter of the fort, and at the entrance was an old French two-story concrete bunker. There were several old structures on the other side of the compound that the company CP used, but our platoon was assigned the sector of the camp that included the two-story bunker where the platoon headquarters was established.

There was a village near the camp and a Buddhist temple just on the other side of the berm. One night we saw all of these Vietnamese dressed in the orange yellow robes of the Buddhist religion. I wanted to see what they were doing, more out of religious curiosity than tactical necessity. I found another guy to go with me, and we went over the berm between two positions, and tiptoed up to the temple. We found an open window and peeked in.

There were several hundred people crowded into a large room. A man was waving an incense burner which was billowing out smoke, and there were lots of candles. The whole congregation was chanting quietly. The scene spooked me and I wanted to get out of there fast. The guy with me wanted to stay and watch some more so, we stayed for another minute, and then he started to giggle. I grabbed his arm and pulled him away from the window, and we both tiptoed away toward our camp. We both started to laugh and we started running for the berm before we couldn't contain ourselves any longer.

The next day, we got word that the whole Battalion was moving into the camp. Several of the battalion staff came over and looked at our bunker. They talked to the LT in private, and after a few minutes he came over to us and told us what we already knew; they were taking the bunker, and we had to move somewhere else. He said we had thirty minutes to get our stuff out.

I was mad about this, irrationally so, but mad none the less. Here we finally had a decent place to stay out of the rain, and now these REMFs were taking it from us. Everyone packed their gear and moved out. When the last of our guys left, I decided to leave a welcome message for the staff. I pulled a bottle out of my rucksack and smashed it against the wall.

The bottle contained Nuoc Mam, the fish sauce of Vietnam. I carried it to spice up the rice sold by the locals. "Mama's nookie," was what Rodney called it. The Vietnamese made it by filling large vats with freshly caught fish, salting them and leaving them to rot in the sun. The fish oil and juices were collected as they drained from the bottom of the vats. It had an odor that could only be described as pungent, but no one I knew, who had gotten a good whiff of Nuoc Mam, would ever use that word to describe something that "smelled like shit."

I left the bunker with a happy face and said to one of the staff who was approaching from the distance, "It's all yours, sir," and moved to our new CP location. I got a lot of amusement watching those home wreckers trying to move into their new digs. They piled all their stuff outside and one by one, went in for a few minutes and then came out with very unpleasant looks on their faces.

## Leaving On a Jet Plane

When we returned to Lai Khe from Loc Ninh, one of the old-timers came back from the stockade after serving time for something that had happened before I got there. If you got stockade time it was considered 'dead' time. That meant that once you finished your sentence you had to return to your unit and continue serving until you had completed a year of 'good' time.

We all got drunk in our new club down in the rubber trees near our hooches. When the club closed, we went back to the hooch. The old-timer was pretty pissed off about having to stay past his DEROS date, and the other brothers were laughing at his antics.

He was telling everyone that he was leaving the 'Nam' whether he had a plane ticket or not. "Yeah, fool, how you gonna act?" said one of the guys. "If the man don't give you orders, you ain't going!" The old-timer jumped up, "You don't think I can fly outta here anytime I want, motherblanker?" "Shit no you can't," replied the chorus of brothers, egging him on. The old-timer said, "Watch me, motherblankers!" and taking a step, he jumped up on a bunk and dove like Superman through the screen that covered the windows.

The brothers busted up, howling and laughing, but some of the guys stood up to look, almost as if there might have been a chance that he actually could fly out of there. He had landed in a heap in the dirt between the buildings. Some of the brothers went out and helped him up. He was kind of sobbing now, "Man, I just want to go home."

## Demo Training

I had been the company demo man for a number of months. The CO wanted me to train several other guys to do demo work. Someone must have mentioned some of my foolish methods, and it was decided to get some others trained up in demo work before I blew myself up. Why they would want me to train anybody was a good question, because I could only teach them my foolish ways.

Anyway, we came back to Lai Khe for a one day break. We would be going back out the next morning. Everyone else was going to the Ville that afternoon, and I had to take several new guys and go down to the perimeter and teach them how to blow up duds. I was given a large box of unserviceable explosive devices. There were many hand grenades with the safety lever broken off, 60mm mortar rounds, etc. I didn't really look very deep into the box because I had other ideas.

I grabbed two blocks of C4, about five pounds, several electric blasting caps, and the blasting machine from the ammo tent. Then I got a roll of WD-1 telephone wire from supply. We drove down to the bunker line with the box and my equipment. I had never used electric blasting caps before and I figured now would be a good time to learn.

I had the guys carry the box, and one of them unrolled the wire and followed us. I walked out in front of one of the bunkers and found an old open foxhole. It was about fifty meters from any of the positions. I had the guys put the box in the hole. The top of the box was about a foot below the surface. I lay the two blocks of C4 on top of the grenades. I took one of the electric blasting caps and twisted the wires coming out of it onto the telephone wires; so far so good.

I told the other guys what I was going to do. One of them asked me about their training. "If you blow up all the grenades, what are we supposed blow up?" "That's a good question," I said. "Now go with the others up to where the reel of telephone wire is. No one touch the wire and no one touch the blasting machine, got it?" They assured me they did and hurried up the slope to the bunker line.

I pushed the blasting cap into a hole I made with a pencil in one of the blocks of C4, gave the wires a last check and walked up the slope and joined the others. After telling everyone to get behind the bunker, I attached the blasting machine to the telephone wires that were sticking out of the side of the reel. I called the company on the radio and requested permission to go hot on the demo range. I got permission, and then called them back and gave the 'fire in the hole' warning. "Tell everyone to take cover; this is going to be a big one."

I could hear people shouting "Fire in the hole," up in the company area. I had told everyone on the bunker line to be sure and take cover when we called out the warning. I had all the guys I was training to call in unison facing to the left and right. Then I handed the blasting machine to the guy who asked me what they were going to blow up, and told him, "This is what you get to blow up; now, twist that handle."

He did, and for a split second nothing happened. I had seen this type of machine in movies, and the explosives went off as soon as they twisted the handle. Then it came; a massive explosion, much louder than I had imagined, took place. I was happy; if we had a misfire, we would have had to wait for a long time, and I was ready to go to the Ville.

We returned to the company area, and people were asking me about what I had done on the bunker line, "What the hell did you do? It was raining shrapnel back here. The stuff was coming down on the roofs like a hail storm." "I was teaching a demo class, I said, "they graduated and now it's time to go down to the Ville and celebrate."

## Time to Pray

My squad had ambush. We were to go west from the Lai Khe bunker line, cross the river and go into the jungle on the other side to set up an ambush. I went down to the bunker line that afternoon with a map and planned the route. That evening, we walked through the gap in the wire and headed for the river. The water was low and we crossed without incident. After about two hundred meters, we came to a grove of young rubber trees. It was still barely light; I told the squad to form a small perimeter.

I was tired and scared and considered staying here for the night. I could see no reason to walk into one of the most heavily booby-trapped areas in South Vietnam, in the dark, for the unlikely event that we would ambush the enemy. It seems that I too was susceptible to weakness.

I was seriously considering this, when the enemy intervened and started firing mortars rounds into Lai Khe. We could hear the Lai Khe alert siren start to wail, but we couldn't hear the rounds leaving the tube, so we knew the mortar wasn't near us. The SOP for counter-mortar fire didn't take any of that into account. The artillery batteries started firing pre-plotted concentrations into every open area around the perimeter.

I called the CP and told them that we had not gotten to our ambush site, and for them to contact the artillery and tell them to stop firing into our vicinity. The CO came on the radio and told me to send my grid location. I could see our location on the map, but I couldn't read the numbers. I told him we were in the young rubber trees about 200 meters west of the river. He insisted that I give him the coordinates, so I told him that I didn't have a flashlight and couldn't read the numbers on the map. He came back with, "Then, I suggest that you keep your heads down and pray."

By now, artillery was starting to land nearby. We couldn't see where it was hitting because it was landing in the jungle, but we could hear it screaming in and exploding with loud booms. About that time, one of my guys was starting to freak out. He crawled over to me and said, "Come on sarge, let's go back; if we stay here we're going to get killed." He might be right, I thought; if we got up and ran to the river we might be ok.

Then another consideration came to me, one that brought calmness to my churning mind. Why not stay where we were and keep our heads down and pray? I told the man that we were staying where we were, and for him to calm down and not move. The artillery was still flying into the nearby jungle, making a lot of noise. I knew that since the enemy was long gone, our biggest danger was from our own artillery. I told the rest of the guys in a normal voice that we were staying where we were until the shooting stopped and for them to keep their heads down.

The guy that wanted us to go back was pretty frantic, so I stayed next to him in case he tried to leave on his own. A few seconds later, three large artillery shells roared in and landed about half way between us and where we'd crossed the river. I'm sure that if we had gone back when he wanted to, we would have been right where they landed. Three more shells followed them into the same area. I could hear pieces of shrapnel hitting the trees above our heads.

The second group of three signaled the end of the artillery fire in our area. We lay there for about fifteen minutes and waited. It was dark now, but the moon was up and gave us plenty of light. I told the men to get ready to move. I gave the point man a direction and followed him towards the tree-line. We made our way to the ambush location and passed the rest of the night without incident.

### Operation Dallas

Due to another shifting of battalions, we were tasked with guarding the Phouc Vinh base camp. While we were in Phuoc Vinh we were put up for a few nights in the 1-26 Infantry huts. On 16 May we were alerted for Operation Dallas. The VC had launched some rocket attacks on Bien Hoa Airbase, Phuoc Vinh, and Tan Uyen. The two huts given to our platoon were full, so I stayed in the hut next door. There were several guys from the 26th and myself. I went to chow and asked one of them to watch my rifle. When I came back it was gone. I asked where the man was who said he would watch it, and one of the others just shrugged and said nothing.

I did a search of the area but couldn't find it. I reported the missing rifle to my platoon sergeant, and this started a series of rebukes from everyone above me in my chain of command. I didn't argue; all I wanted to know was where I could get another weapon because we were alerted for the operation the next day. Nobody had an answer, and eventually I began to realize that they were stumped and preferred to rebuke me rather than make arrangements to borrow a weapon from the 1-26 Infantry or another nearby unit.

### Shit Happens

The next morning we had a C-ration breakfast and got ready to go. I still hadn't found my rifle. It looked like I would be going to the field without a weapon. Can they do that—send a man to the field without a weapon? I sat on the edge of my bunk and nursed my hangover while considering my plight. I could hear the rest of the platoon in the next building chattering away, and then there was a loud explosion. I threw myself to the ground thinking that we were under a mortar attack.

Then I heard screaming from next door, and someone yelling for a medic. After a moment, when no more rounds came in, I got up and went next door to see if I could help. The men were coming out of the building. Some were bleeding from wounds and some, though they appeared to be uninjured, were dazed. There were several men seriously injured, and the company medics were gathering to do their work. One of my buddies was standing a ways from the building, so I went up to him and asked what happened. He told a tale that would have been unbelievable anywhere else but here.

One of the sergeants was checking his gear and decided that the four hand grenades that he was carrying were too heavy; so he asked in a loud voice if anyone wanted two hand grenades. Someone at the other end of the room said that he would take them, so the sergeant threw them, underhanded, to the man at the other end of the room. He only caught one and the other landed on the floor and rolled under a bunk.

Some of the men heard the lever fly and the snap of the fuse being ignited. They threw themselves to the ground just before the grenade went off. One man was killed, another blinded, and ten others were wounded. After the wounded were medevaced, Sergeant Magee came up to me and asked, "Do you still need a rifle?" I said I did. "I think we've got some spares; go see the first sergeant."

Later, when we returned to Lai Khe, I had to sign a Statement of Charges for the missing rifle. The government was going to charge me $130.00. Several months later, the XO, LT Ed Christensen, told me that my rifle had turned up, and that I would not be charged for it after all. It seems that one of the men from the 1-26 Infantry had stolen it and tried to send it home in his hold baggage, a duffle bag that we were allowed to send home early. The Customs inspectors had found it, and now he had some big problems of his own.

### Desertion

With the mass casualties in our platoon came yet another rearrangement of the platoon leadership—I was now the fire team leader in another squad. The squad leader was an older sergeant, recently arrived from Germany. We were flown by helicopter to an area south of Phuoc Vinh. The next couple of days were spent looking for VC rocket launchers or anything else that might be useful for their war effort.

While on a company sweep, we stopped for noon chow. The squad leader put me and another man on an OP while the company set up a patrol base. Noon chow was eaten there, and patrols were sent out to search the surrounding area. My partner and I made ourselves comfortable and took turns watching while the other slept or read.

We hadn't been told how long we would be there and we didn't have a radio. The afternoon heat came, but we had some shade. I kept wondering when we would be called in because I had never seen us lay up this long before. The afternoon wore on. There was no sound of anybody moving around us, which was the way it should be, but I was still uneasy.

I was taking a nap when my buddy woke me and told me he could hear a chopper nearby. I sat up and tried to locate it. I could hear it, but I couldn't see it. It kept coming closer but it was too close to the ground for us to see it over the vegetation. Finally it came into view; it was flying low and circling around a point for a moment before moving to another and doing the same thing.

There was a man standing on the skid looking down. This was a slick, so they wouldn't be looking for the enemy this way. I wasn't sure what was going on, but I decided to wave to them as a friendly gesture, before they decided that we were a target of opportunity, and put two more points on the big score board.

I waved my arms at the chopper and so did my buddy. Eventually, someone saw us and the bird came over our position. The man standing on the skid was older and his hair was pure white. He waved to us and yelled to us, but we couldn't hear what he was saying. He gestured to us to get down, so we figured he wanted us to stay where we were.

The chopper gained altitude and continued in a wide orbit over our position. We gathered up our gear because we now realized that we were probably the objects of a search, and the chopper was probably vectoring a ground element to our location.

A few minutes later we heard some thrashing through the tall grass and around a bush came the point man of one of the squads from our platoon. We didn't spend any time chatting, but he told me that we had been left when the company took off after the noon meal. Our squad leader had forgotten to call us in. By the time anybody realized we weren't with column, the company had arrived at the battalion perimeter and was busy preparing their NDP.

When somebody realized we were missing, the alarm was raised. Eventually, the fact that A-1-16 had two MIAs reached Division, and the man who was leaning out of the helicopter that found us was BG Rogers, the assistant division commander. Our buddies were glad to see us and wanted to know what happened. We told them that we didn't know. As it turned out, there were some others in the battalion that wanted to know the same thing.

The platoon sergeant told us to report to the LT, and he told us to go to the CO who ordered us to report to the battalion XO at the CP. When we reported, the XO, a major, told us we were being charged with desertion. Desertion in time of war carries some pretty stiff penalties. "Say again, sir!" I said to the XO. "You are both being charged with desertion; I am going to read you your rights," which he did and then asked if we wanted to make a statement.

I knew this was bullshit and rather than prolong it, I spoke up and told him everything that happened. Since I was the senior man, he wanted to know why I hadn't gone looking for the company after a reasonable amount of time. What's reasonable about any of this I thought? Instead, I explained to him that we were where we were assigned to be, and there was no time limit given that would have caused us to leave our place of assignment. "Besides sir, wandering around unannounced is a good way to get killed." "Do you have anything to add?" he asked my buddy. "No sir, that's what happened," he said. The major dismissed us and we returned to our company. Our squad leader was court-martialed later, and we didn't see him again. On the 21st we were flown back to Lai Khe.

## Inspiration from Colonel Lazzell and the Chaplain

After several days of the usual Lai Khe routine, we were told to assemble as a company in the rubber trees between our hooches and the bunker line. The battalion commander was coming to speak with us. There was a lot of speculation about what he might say. The first time I heard him speak was when he told us about the tennis shoes.

Another time was when the whole battalion was assembled in front of the Battalion Headquarters on the other side of Highway 13. We had returned to our base camp after being out in the bush for a little more than two months. He looked quite happy, standing there on this platform that elevated him above the assembled troops. "Men," he crowed, "you'll be proud to know that during the last operation we broke the USARV record for continuous time in the field."

He stood there smiling, waiting for the cheers to ring out. He hadn't done the research regarding his target audience though. Instead of cheers, the only thing I heard was a very low muttering from several hundred lips, words like 'son of a bitch,' and 'mother blank' and some terrible threats about what might happen if he attempted to break our new 'record.' He stood there for a minute, and finally decided to do what many experienced officers and NCOs do under the same circumstances; he acted like nothing had happened and dismissed the battalion.

The last time he spoke to us was when the platoon from Charlie Company got wiped out. He had called the platoon leader a criminal for getting his platoon wiped out by 'bandits.' It was a good thing that the LT was dead, because the way the colonel said criminal, if the lieutenant were still alive, he would have been in deep shit, instead of a deep hole back home.

As we assembled under the rubber trees, we saw the battalion commander and another man standing off at a distance, talking with the company commander. The RTOs were standing by the jeep that had brought them there. We stood in the ranks waiting for the show to start. The platoon wise guys were vying with one another over who could make the funniest statement to keep the rest of us amused while we waited.

This was the normal way that soldiers dealt with tension resulting from fear of the unknown. Nobody knew what this was all about, but the old timers knew that if the last two speeches by the colonel were any indication, this one could only spell trouble. I couldn't think of anything that we had done wrong that would warrant a production like this. This was a mystery that would soon be revealed to us when the colonel was ready.

As the low level chatter continued in the ranks, the platoon sergeants attempted to cut it off when it got too loud. We technically shouldn't be talking because the last command we had received in this formation was 'at ease,' but we had been standing here for ten minutes and it was unreasonable to expect a group of infantrymen in our condition to stand here like we were at Ft Benning in front of a group of drill sergeants. "At ease, damn it," was heard from time to time but without rancor. The platoon sergeants were also tired of waiting for the axe to fall.

Finally, the group of officers finished their pow-wow, and the company commander ran over to stand in front of the first sergeant who had called us to attention. The chatter had almost, but not quite ceased. Some of the hard core comedians were still trying to get one more offering in before the colonel started. The captain called the platoon leaders to their posts, gave us 'at ease' and introduced the battalion commander.

"Men," he began, "I want to talk to you about a very serious situation involving this battalion." "Oh, shit, here it comes," someone said. "Shut the blank up," came the whispered voice of our platoon sergeant from the rear of the formation. The colonel continued, "Men," he said dramatically, "this battalion has the highest venereal disease rate in the entire 1st Infantry Division." He stood there in silence and let his words sink into our minds. Unlike the last time he spoke to us, this time he was looking for some quiet remorse for this less-than-thrilling proclamation.

It was dead quiet for a moment, and then the company broke out in loud cheers and laughter. There was no way he could have pretended this wasn't happening. Men were giving each other five, the brothers were dapping, and the platoon leaders were looking horrified as they stood in front of their platoons. The Colonel exploded in anger and began cursing.

Everyone shut up as he went off about how we were hurting the war effort. Every time a man got VD he couldn't go out in the field because he had to get shots to cure it. He reminded us that some forms of VD in Vietnam couldn't be cured, and that if we got one, we would be sent to an island in the Philippines where we would be kept until we died. "The girls who have not been checked by the medics are working for the VC. They're not VC agents, they're VD agents!"

This brought a few chuckles, and that helped him to regain his composure. I'm sure that he would have enjoyed seeing us all off on a voyage to that island in the Philippines, but then he wouldn't have a battalion, would he? No more record breaking epics in the jungle, no more chances to repay Charlie for shooting him in the elbow with a .51 caliber bullet and causing him to have to wear a brace on his elbow for his tour. No, the Colonel needed us more than we needed him, so he worked a little to bring the tension down enough so that he could introduce our next speaker, the Brigade Chaplain.

The Chaplain meant well. He was in the minority camp however, in regard to morality among the troops in Vietnam. He tried to appeal to our better nature, reminding us that when our tour was over, and we returned to hearth and home, we would feel ashamed of ourselves. That may be true, we thought, but we had seen a few among us return to hearth and home in a body bag inside an aluminum body carrier.

Eat, drink, and be merry was the philosophy of this Army. Planning on that blessed future event took a back seat to the satisfying of our more immediate carnal needs right now. Buy now, pay later was a popular concept in our society at this time. But here it was live now, pay later and we embraced it for the most logical of reasons, later probably wouldn't come.

The chaplain knew he was playing to a rough audience, but he bravely pushed on, knowing that many of the officers, NCOs, and soldiers would be back in the boom-boom parlors before sunset. Eventually, he ran out of gas. The CO thanked him and he scurried through the rubber back to Brigade. The colonel had left him, having been driven away in the same jeep that brought both of them here thirty minutes earlier. One of the guys noticed him leaving and speculated that he might be going to the Ville to get a jump on the line.

*For also if the trumpet gives an uncertain sound,*
*who will prepare himself for battle?*
*1 Corinthians 14:8*

# Chapter 16-June 1967

## Operation Bluefield

On 5 June, we air-assaulted into an area northeast of Lai Khe and commenced S+D operations. The first day, Alpha Company found a base camp with some large huts used for classrooms and the usual bunkers. Another platoon killed a VC hiding in a well. That night the VC fired a rifle grenade into the perimeter wounding one man. The next day we continued searching for Charlie. Other units found base camps but we found nothing. On the third day, we found another small base camp and some enemy hand grenades and other explosive devices which were destroyed by one of my 'demo man' protege's. That afternoon we found another base camp and more demo work. We dug in that evening and followed the usual routine of LPs, ambush patrols and fifty percent security on the perimeter.

The next day we filled in our holes and moved to a PZ and waited for the helicopters. They arrived, and we air-assaulted into another cold LZ and spent the day rooting through the brush. Charlie Company found a civilian Jeep that someone said had been stolen from USAID. That afternoon, the word was passed that the choppers were on the way, and we got a ride back to the battalion perimeter. The next morning, the 9th, we were extracted by air and returned to Lai Khe for yet another beer fest at the Ville.[271]

The tally for the operation included one VC killed (body-count), 23 weapons and several hundred rounds of ammunition captured. Our losses were one KIA and two WIA. The artillery supported the operation with 6676 rounds of 105mm, and 3513 rounds of 155mm. The Air Force gave us seventy-three close air support sorties, mainly for LZ prep. Colonel Marks summarized the operation by saying that although the mission was to close with the 273d VC Regiment; little damage had been done to the VC. At the same time however, he said that the units involved had gained much needed experience in the preparation for and the conduct of an airmobile assault, resupply operations, and jungle combat operations. Since that was all we had been doing since I came there ten months previously, I suppose his commander's analysis was for another audience.[272]

## Friendly Fire

While we were in Lai Khe, I took an ambush patrol out, and this time I went to where we were sent, a position where we could nail anyone trying to destroy the pump that provided water for the base. It was in front of the 2-28 Infantry section of the perimeter. We checked in with the people on guard at the bunker next to the path through the concertina wire, and told them when we were coming back; they of course, assured us they would watch out for us. We passed through the wire and made our way to the ambush site where we passed the night without incident. Early the next morning, we headed back before sunrise, at the time we arranged with the perimeter guards. As we approached the line, several bullets 'cracked' over our heads.

We hit the ground and I shouted "Friendly troops, cease-fire!" Several more bullets flew by. Again I hollered "Cease-fire, friendly troops!" and they shot a few more. Now I was pissed. "If you don't stop shooting we're going to assault that bunker!" Brave words, but I was mad, and the other guys were game.

"Who are you guys?" said a voice from the perimeter. "We're Alpha Company, 1st of the 16th Infantry, friendly troops!" I shouted. "OK, come on in." I told the guys to stay where they were and walked up to the entrance of the path through the concertina wire to the perimeter. I followed the path and walked over to the bunker. It was starting to get light and I could see that these were not the guys who let us out the night before.

"Why did you shoot at us?" I asked the one who seemed to be in charge. "We thought you were VC," he said sheepishly. "We told your buddies that we would be coming back through here at this time; didn't they tell you?" "They got pulled off last night, and we were sent down here. Nobody told us anything; we're engineers," he said. Then I noticed that he was holding an M-14 rifle which explained the loud crack.

"OK, no sweat. I'm calling the other guys; no shooting, right?" He nodded and I called them. After they came through the wire, I decided to take a little detour and we walked through the village of Lai Khe, home of our bar girls, barbers and the KPs that worked in our mess halls. Most of them were still sleeping, but the few that were up waved at us shyly as we passed through.

### Operation Billings

Operation Billings was the Division's first major effort in War Zone D. Two brigades, including eight infantry battalions, one less than all the infantry battalions in the Division, moved into an area north of Phuoc Vinh. The mission was to find and destroy the 271st VC Regiment, believed to be in this area, and destroy enemy bases threatening Phuoc Vinh, a large Division base camp. The operation started on 11 June, when an infantry battalion was flown to the Chi Linh Special Forces camp, where they established a large perimeter for a battalion of 105mm artillery. The artillery was positioned to support any of the infantry battalions involved in the operation.[273]

On 13 June we air-assaulted into War Zone D, and set up a two battalion perimeter with the 2-28 Infantry at LZ 'Rufe.' Two of the 2-28 Infantry ambush patrols had contact that night. The next day we found an old base camp before noon, and an hour later, Jose's gun crew spotted five VC. Jose let loose, but his M-60 malfunctioned after the first shot and the VC got away, leaving their rucksacks behind. Two hours later, and a klick north of us, Bravo Company made contact with a VC element. They pulled back as per our SOP and directed artillery fire into the area. Then they went back in and made contact with a VC battalion.

### Bravo Company-Xom Bo I

Bravo Company was hit from the front and both flanks; they must have walked into a hasty U shaped ambush. For the next four and a half hours they shot it out with the VC. We heard the shooting as we returned to the perimeter, but Colonel Lazzell didn't change our route. At 1900 that evening, the VC withdrew.

Bravo Company lost six men KIA and coincidentally, the VC lost sixty. That was a remarkable feat of accounting in the jungle after dark. Bravo Company also had sixteen WIA, and they were assisted by Charlie Company in evacuating them. There were two men missing, but they were found several days later at a hospital where they had been medevaced.[274]

## The False LZ

For the next two days, our two battalions conducted company sized patrols around the area. We lucked out on the 15th and guarded the perimeter. On the 16th, we spent the day guarding the engineers while they cut down trees with explosives and chainsaws in a large, generally open area. We were trying to deceive the VC into believing that we were going to use it as a large LZ.

> Peter Clark: *"As my year in country neared its end, I realized I loved Vietnam, the military life, and the infantry in particular. What I didn't like was fighting, at least that part of fighting which posed a serious risk of my violent dismemberment or death. In furtherance of this desire, and as things were quiet in the field, I begged and was granted an in-country leave when my DEROS (Date of Estimated Return from Over Seas) was about three weeks off, to explore the possibility of extending my tour in a slightly less dangerous context...*
>
> *"This leave was extended at the end by a real difficulty in getting a flight from Ton Son Nhut to Lai Khe, but I finally hitched a ride in a two-seat spotter plane and landed in Lai Khe on June 15. I found the company area deserted, except for a handful of troops; the battalion was in the field on an operation. By then it was too late to catch a re-supply chopper, so I spent the night in my bunk. Next afternoon I was on a re-supply chopper to re-join the unit and re-commence humping the battalion radio for the Old Man."*[275]

I was directed to use my demo supplies to blow some large branches that were holding the tree trunks off the ground. The initial demo work that knocked down the trees however, had also stirred up every red ant for miles, and they were converging on the ground around these trees.

When I walked over to the tree to place my charges, the ants climbed on my boots and were attacking my neck before I knew they were there. I dropped my charges and started brushing off the ants on my neck. Then I noticed them on my shirt and pants. As I looked at my boots, I saw lots more ants all over the ground I was standing on. I turned and ran back toward the wood-line until the ground was clear, and continued to brush the ants off me. When they hit the ground, they immediately tried to get back on my boots for another go. I did this several times before I got most of them off me.

Meanwhile people were shouting at me to get my charges ready. An engineer was coming around stringing 'Det Cord' between the various charges, so that they could all be detonated simultaneously. I squirted insect repellant on my boots and hands and re-entered the fray. The ants were waiting for me as I ran back to my charges that were lying on the ground by the tree branch. I picked up the charges and brushed off the ants while running in place. Then I placed the charges on the troublesome branches and continued to run in place until the engineer arrived.

He sneered at my work and took his time wrapping the Det Cord around the first one. Then the ants found some of his flesh and he joined me for a run in place, but now I could leave and did so. He finished his work and walked quickly to the next charge while trying to brush off the ants that were now in a stinging frenzy on him. The ants were all over that field, and no amount of prodding by the officers was going to get us back out there, so the engineers blew the charges and we were done. That afternoon while we were clearing the false LZ, our perimeter at LZ 'Rufe' was hit by thirty or forty mortar rounds, wounding twenty GIs.[276]

> **Peter Clark:** *"At this point I was seriously into the single digits as a short-timer, so another week or so in the field wouldn't have been my first choice of how to make the time go by, but I wasn't seized by any premonitions of dread. The chopper landed, I was given a sack of something or other, and made my way through a battalion RON (Rest Over Night) to the company area. In a short time I was back in my place on the roster, just another day at the office.*
>
> *"Unlike the wild and woolly days gone by, in 1967 we all carried our TOE weapon, in my case a .45, and of course the usual accoutrements of life in the field. In addition, RTO's were treated by their officers as useful beasts of burden, and were hung about with extra smoke grenades, and other useful items, like trees at Christmas. (In classic GI revenge mode, most RTO's carried large numbers of what appeared to be spare batteries, but in fact were empty battery boxes filled with items of comfort and convenience.*
>
> *"The rule was that batteries should be changed every 12 to 24 hours, but a good one would last for days. Some of us were adept at appearing to change a battery while in fact simply removing and replacing the perfectly good one in the radio, or so I have heard. We all did carry at least one spare, but the damn things weighed about 5 pounds and most officers thought four or five looked just right on the back of an RTO."*[277]

### Rodney Gets a Break

This was Rodney's last night in the field. His feet had been giving him a lot of pain, and the doctors said he had 'hammer toes,' which would get him out of the infantry. He was being reassigned to Division Headquarters and was told to get on a resupply helicopter the next day. Some of the guys went to him and discretely inquired as to the best way to get 'hammer toes,' but he said it was a natural development, not man made. We all envied him and wished him farewell.

Later that evening, we received a warning order. In the morning we would be moving a short distance with the 2-28 Infantry, to a new two battalion perimeter called LZ X-Ray. After dark, I heard a mortar round leave a tube a long way from us. A short time later, I heard the round come hissing into our perimeter where it exploded with a loud bang. "Incoming, incoming" was shouted around the perimeter. No kidding, I thought. The enemy FO could complete his registration mission without firing another round and he did.

It was quiet for the rest of the night. At 0500 we had stand to and by 0700 we were moving out on our 'short' walk to the next LZ. We each carried two 81mm mortar rounds in sandbags that were tied together. The string between the bags rested on my shoulder and the weight of those mortar rounds soon caused that string to dig into my skin, cutting off the blood to my arm. It was very painful.

**Peter Clark:** *"So on the morning of June 17 we set out through medium to high jungle, a light rain falling which often failed to penetrate the canopy, the temperature rising into the mid-90s, all in all not a bad start to a day in the field. As usual, the headquarters group consisted of the Old Man, his two faithful Radio Telephone Operators (RTO's), one carrying a radio on the company frequency, which consisted of a radio for each platoon, carried by a platoon RTO for the lieutenant platoon leader, and a radio on the battalion frequency, which I carried.*

*"The battalion net consisted of a radio for each company, likewise carried by an RTO for each company commander, as well as the battalion commander, LTC Lazzell. Lazzell in turn had a radio on the brigade frequency, so orders could move down through the chain of command, and situation reports and other information could move up to the higher echelons.*

*"These radios weighed about 20 pounds; batteries not included, and were pretty reliable. Actual communication went through a telephone handset with a push-to-talk button. While it was possible to change frequencies, as a practical matter each radio was continuously monitoring its assigned frequency.*

*"Each participant in the net had a call sign: mine was Devour Alpha Six Romeo, which identified the 1st Battalion, 16th Infantry (Devour), Company A (Alpha), Commanding Officer (Six), RTO (Romeo). In addition to the RTO's, the company medic, and the artillery forward observer and his RTO were part of the group, and sometimes the company first sergeant, if he wasn't dealing with logistic or administrative crap back in Lai Khe or being a presence elsewhere in the column."*[278]

The column seemed to stop every 50 feet. Everyone would take a knee and face out either left or right and wait for the guy in front of them to stand up and start moving again. We would take the mortar rounds off our shoulder and wait until we had to move before putting the string back on one of our shoulders, usually the opposite from the one we had been using. Of course it was very hot and humid, as usual, and the salty sweat was pouring out of my steel pot into my eyes. This went on for about four hours until we heard that the 1st Platoon had reached the open area that was to be our next patrol base.

**Jose Garcia:** *"During a short halt, about 200 meters before we got to the open area of LZ X-Ray, Gunby said, "I don't like the looks of that trail." He pointed to a trail about 10 feet to our right. I asked him what's wrong with it. He said, "There's no grass or leaves and it has been used a lot recently.*

*"Donnie was a country boy from Georgia and I always paid attention to his observations in the field. I showed the LT and the CO and eventually LTC Lazzell came. When the CO showed him the trail, Lazzell had an aggravated look which gave me the impression that he was concerned that we were behind schedule. He called for an airstrike and one jet dropped two bombs way off to the right of the open area we were approaching. Then Colonel Lazzell said to move out and 200 meters later we hit the open area."*[279]

We came to the edge of the open area from the southern end and started up the right side, staying inside the vegetation that surrounded it. To our right, I could see a wide, well-used trail that was running north and south, and there were freshly dug fighting positions everywhere. Nothing new really, I had seen things like this often enough.

Alpha Company was supposed to take from twelve o'clock to two o'clock on the perimeter with twelve o'clock being at the north end of the open area. Bravo Company had from two o'clock to four. The battalion Recon Platoon took from four to six.

**Peter Clark:** *"So in the usual course of business the Company HQ group followed the point platoon, in this case I think the Second, and was followed by the other rifle platoons and the weapons (mortar) platoon. The clearing itself was slightly depressed relative to the surrounding jungle, mostly knee-high grass, and was spotted with clumps of saplings and brush, but gave pretty good sight lines in all directions up to the tree-lines, which were likewise spotted with smaller vegetation gradually becoming denser until it became serious jungle."*[280]

The 1st Platoon would tie in with the 2-28 Infantry on their left and the 3d Platoon on their right. The 2d Platoon would be in reserve behind them. Bravo Company was to tie in with the 3d Platoon. As we came close to the northern end of the open field, we dropped off our mortar rounds with a sigh of relief and continued on to the north end of the field. The 1st and 3d platoons set up about 20 meters in front of us, and we could hear them rustling around in the bush as they adjusted their positions to cover their front. The 2-28 Infantry had not shown up yet, so our left flank was open.

**Peter Clark:** *"The company moved north along the ragged tree-line on the right, where the point platoon stopped at about the northern-most edge of clearing. The weapons platoon moved into the clearing itself, and set up their 81 mm mortar tubes and the rifle companies slid into the jungle and hunkered down. The Company HQ group was on the edge of the clearing, around 50 meters from the northern end.*

*"We didn't start to dig in because other units were still arriving and our final position in what was going to be a battalion perimeter couldn't be determined until everybody was linked up. Fairly soon after we arrived the company moved north and west so that we covered about half of the northern end of the clearing, the third platoon linking up with Bravo Company which had moved up the other side.*

*"Our first and third platoons were a few meters into the jungle on the right side, and the battalion command post was just to our south, in a small clump of trees on the edge of the clearing. Hueys started coming in with ammunition and other supplies, and one or two Light Observation Helicopters had landed as well. It was hot but not unusually so, and a little hazy. The rain had stopped and, pretty much, things were as good as they got in the field."*[281]

**'Friendly' Troops**

I put both machine gun crews on the ground near the left flank, and we all sat and waited for further instructions. It was now noon time and we began opening our cans of C-rations for lunch. I heard a helicopter in the distance, and the sound was growing louder as it got closer. As the helicopter approached the field behind us, there were several single shots to our left where the 2-28 Infantry was moving, and immediately, several of their troop's hollered "friendly troops!"

**Peter Clark:** *"In the jungle, you hear the battle more than you see it. And every battle starts the same way: one or a couple of shots. Between the time the first shot registers, and whatever happens next, there is ample time to process and interpret your place in the universe. That was a shot, that was an M-16 round. Will there be another, or was that some numb-nuts who stumbled with his safety off? That was another M-16 round. Damn, that was a third M-16 round – reject the clumsy numb-nuts hypothesis. Maybe a point man who thought he saw a VC? Uh oh, that is a second rifle starting up, and a third/fourth/fifth. More than that. Nervous squad, firing up their sector because numb-nuts loosed the first round? Explosion, grenade? New sound, like an AK? That was an AK, one two three oh shit. And at about that point, two seconds into the battle, the lazy short-timer brain goes and hides and something else takes over."*[282]

I didn't think too much of this, figuring like everyone else, that it was the 2-28 Infantry, and one of their point men was shooting at noise being made by our 1st Platoon. I told Jose Garcia to face his gun in the direction of west-northwest, our left flank and told Bob Pointer to face his gun to the northwest. While Bob was setting up his gun, Jose opened fire.

**Jose Garcia**: *"I heard the VC before I saw them. "Listen Junior, I hear Gooks out there and no one is supposed to be there talking Vietnamese." Donnie replied, "I don't hear anything, you are wrong." Donnie was from the Georgia backwoods and could see things I could not but I always felt I could hear better and I had a better sense of direction to sound then he did so we made a good team.*

*As I kept looking in the direction of the voices, I saw a group of VC moving forward into position. I had always been told not to shoot unless I had multiple targets, so I opened fire. Then everyone opened up, so did the VC. I think that by our gun opening up, we forced them to spring their ambush a little early."*[283]

Immediately, after Jose opened fire, several long bursts of automatic weapons fire sent a swarm of bullets cracking through the area where we were sitting, and suddenly, we were in the fight of our lives. Heavy firing broke out to our front and hundreds of bullets were cracking over and around our heads creating a cacophony of extremely loud bullwhips.

"The AK-47, the preferred weapon of our enemies, makes a distinctive sound," said Gunny Highway in the movie "Heartbreak Ridge." The scriptwriter was close, but actually, it is the ballistic 'crack' of the 7.62x39mm bullet fired by the AK-47, traveling at 2300 feet per second, that makes the distinctive sound heard by those who are receiving its fire. The enemy soldiers were so close that the sound of their rifles' muzzle blasts combined with those bullets breaking the sound barrier, cracking past our ears in bursts of ten to fifteen rounds.

There were so many such bursts coming from so many weapons to our left and front that I knew I was going to be killed, so I said a quick prayer. I didn't ask for forgiveness or to be spared, I guess I felt that God was tired of me and I was finally reaping what I had sown. My only prayer was, "Oh God, please make the news of my death easy on my parents."

**Peter Clark:** *"At this point what we were hearing was a small-to-medium firefight a hundred meters or so to our right, as we faced the northern end of the clearing. We couldn't see anything; the rifle platoons were invisible a few meters inside the tree-line, and the shooting was coming from somewhere beyond them. I wasn't hearing any incoming rounds, and while we all knew we were engaged, after the first minute or two it didn't seem so bad.*

*My job was to monitor the battalion net, so I knew when the battalion CO jumped into an observation helicopter and took to the air. What I realize now is that almost all the useful emerging intelligence about the battle was auditory, and the battalion CO had placed himself where he couldn't hear anything that wasn't coming through his radio headphones in a noisy open chopper. At that moment, of course, he was connected by radio to his battalion command post, which had set up a little behind us on the right side of clearing, in the modest shade of a cluster of small trees which extended out from the woodline towards the center of the open space.*

*Within a few minutes gunships and fighter-bombers started making passes over the jungle to our right. The firing had died down to a sporadic rattle. The rhythm of firing was same as the time the platoon from Charlie Company had gotten wiped out when it was lured into a NVA ambush. There wasn't much coming through the battalion net. I had time to feel sorry for the poor bastards out in the jungle and hopeful that the worst was over when a couple of shots to our front and a couple of bullets whining overhead snapped my head around to the north. This time the firing seemed to start slow, and seemed scattered over the northern end of the clearing, a few AK rounds, a couple of 16s, a M-60 opening up with a few short bursts. Instead of the crescendo of a suddenly engaged platoon, the sounds told of a widespread and deliberate exchange of fire by increasing numbers of troops along a wide front. In retrospect it seems like a long, long time between the first bullets going over our heads and the tearing, enveloping roar of colliding battalions, but probably only 30 seconds or so elapsed."*[284]

**Jose Garcia:** *"I kept firing where they went down until my first belt of ammo was gone. Then some VC above and to my left opened up on me and missed me by inches. The bullets mangled some of my ammo belts that the ammo bearers had dropped on my right side. His burst kicked up dirt and rocks that stung my face and eyes, blinding me for a few seconds. I dropped my M-60 and covered my face and eyes out of instinct to protect my face. When I could see again, I turned to my left and looked at Gunby. I could see the bamboo being cut between us and just above our heads as two AK-47s were criss crossing on us.*

*"Gunby was whiter than white. I had never seen him so pale and he was shook up. He had just turned 20, and he had every right to be a little shook up. His words, I will never forget, "Garcia, ain't no way in hell we are going to make it out of this one alive." By the large volume of return fire and the burst from the tree, I knew he was right, but I needed him now more than ever to feed the gun.*

*"Excuse the language but it's what we used at the time, "Blank it Junior, let's see how many of the little bastards we can take with us; give me another belt." Gunby snapped out of it and he slapped the next belt into the feed tray and I slammed the cover shot. Then I started dusting off the trees just to my front left."*[285]

### Brave Men

I was lying in the prone about three feet behind Jose's feet and I could see Bob's crew to my right. Carl and John had left their ammo cans on the other side of a small trail that ran off to the north from the edge of the open area. There was a freshly dug fighting position in the middle of the trail a little north of them.

I told Carl and John to get the ammo and bring it to Bob. He had begun firing at figures moving through the brush in front of him, and they were shooting at him. Carl jumped up into a low crouch and crossed the trail to his ruck frame that carried his 400 rounds of ammo in two cans. He grabbed the ruck frame and dived back across the trail.

As he flew across the trail, he suddenly dropped the ruck and did a half flip, ending up on his back close to Bob and the gun. He got up, grabbed the ammo, took up his position and fed a fresh belt to Bob's now empty gun. John crossed the trail right behind him, grabbed his ruck and returned to Carl's left. After dropping his ammo, he went back to Bob's right side and began firing his rifle to his front.

**Peter Clark:** *"By then I, along with the rest of the Company HQ group, were lying flat on our stomachs. Captain Williamson had the headset for the company net pressed to his ear, even though I was a foot away I barely heard what he was saying. With my earphones I could follow the battalion net, but the ambient noise drowned out the sounds of speech. I did gather that our second platoon was engaged all along its line, and that the adjacent platoon was taking fire as well.*

*"The table of organization (TOE) calls for an RTO to carry a .45 caliber automatic pistol as a personal sidearm. Our previous CO had mandated that every swinging dick in his company had at least an M-16 and a basic load of ammo, but as the brass got more into such things we had been returned to the TOE weapons. When that had happened I was delighted not to have to hump the rifle and 200 or so rounds of 5.56 ammo; now, as the firing increased and green NVA tracers streaming out of the jungle, I felt naked and helpless.*

*"One of the Second Platoon guys emerged from the jungle, heading towards the battalion HQ; he was bareheaded, had no weapon, and was bloody. Shortly afterwards another trooper came out, without web-gear but with helmet, and carrying his M-16. Holy shit, I thought, and pulled out my .45 and chambered a round. Captain Williamson must have heard the slide snapping back, because he turned his head and shouted over the battle noise, "Put that damn thing away before you hurt someone.*

*"OK, so maybe I was over-reacting, and slid the thing back into my holster. I yelled at the withdrawing trooper, another Second Platoon veteran who should have known better, "If you're not going to use that '16, give it to me!" Of course he didn't.*

*"By now the center of the clearing was swept with automatic weapons fire. If our weapons platoon had gotten off a few rounds at the beginning, they weren't getting any more now. The battalion HQ staff on the ground was dead or wounded. The suppressing fire and airstrikes continued, but still to the right and way into the jungle on that side, while the firing was almost completely to our front."*[286]

Jose was blazing away furiously at the enemy soldiers attacking to his front, and they were firing back at him. Donnie was feeding him belt after belt; David and a fourth man 'Ghost' were firing their rifles to the front. Robert's gun was firing burst after burst, and the vegetation was being shredded on the sides and above both positions.

The tempo of incoming enemy rounds increased until it seemed like every gun in the world was shooting at us. My perception of time was another phenomenon; it seemed like it stood still. People were shooting, RPGs were 'shishing' in and exploding, mortar rounds were exploding in the trees above us spraying shrapnel everywhere, and it was like it had been going on my whole life.

I heard someone calling for a medic and I saw Turner, our platoon medic, crawling up to someone a little distance to my right. As he got closer to the body that was lying motionless, a grenade exploded right next to him and threw him about four feet into the air. He came down on his back and lay there unconscious near the person he had been trying to help.

I turned back to observe Jose's situation, when a tremendous volley of fire came through the bamboo and small tree branches in front of his position, throwing vegetation everywhere. One of the bullets struck the handguard of 'Ghost's' M-16, blowing half of it off. 'Ghost' turned back to me with a smile on his face and said with a steady voice, "That was close," before facing back toward the enemy and returning fire.

**Peter Clark:** *"Whether it was because we were exposed to the increasingly heavy fire coming into the clearing, or because he wanted to be closer to the action, Capt. Williamson got to his feet and led us diagonally across the clearing to the northernmost point, directly behind Second Platoon. We went to ground a few meters south of the serious tree-line, the captain, me, the company RTO, and a couple of other troops. Just inside the jungle, Joe Garcia and his M-60, along with several other Second Platoon riflemen, were fully engaged with enemy to our front. I could see Joe whom I recognized, along with Gunby, part of his team, and some other folks here and there in the brush.*

*"After another interval which might have lasted a few minutes or a few hours, mostly spent by me trying to be very, very flat, Captain Williamson jumped up again and took off towards the center of the open space to our rear. "We got to get more machine gun ammo," he shouted. More than anything I wanted to stay hugging the earth, but training took over (after a few shameful seconds in which I wrestled with the possibility of just staying put) and I lurched to my feet, and, staying as close to ground as I could without slowing down, took off after him.*

*"I never did actually catch up, but I homed on the tall, thin figure of the Old Man towing his RTO, with another couple of guys nearby. Re-supply choppers had dropped off some stuff in the center of the clearing before the shooting started, and Captain Williamson grabbed a couple of boxes of 7.62 machine gun ammo from a heap on the ground and turned around. I found a box of 7.62, grabbed it, and ran back to the same spot on the edge of the tree-line. At some point I passed my box up to Captain Williamson, and re-commenced lying very, very flat."*[287]

I saw Jose rise up a little to get a better look and then move forward several feet where the ground rose up slightly. He raised his gun a little higher and began to fire long bursts to his front. David moved forward with his ammo and gave it to Donnie who had moved forward with Jose to continue feeding the ammo.

When David raised his head, he was struck in the right eye by a bullet that exited through the top of his head. Leaving an inch and a half square hole with the scalp anchoring the skull bone at one end, it gave the effect of a trap door that had been left open.

I crawled over to him and saw that he was still alive and conscious. I tried to give him some words of comfort, telling him that he would be ok and that we would get him to medical aid soon. He indicated that he heard me with a slight nod of his head.

**Peter Clark:** *"At some point a guy from the weapons platoon appeared on my left and lay down a few inches from me. Capt. Williamson was prone on my right and slightly ahead of me; my head was around his knees. I think the company RTO was to his right and ahead. Joe Garcia and his team were a few meters into the jungle; the ground was just slightly rising to the north. Beyond Joe was dense foliage and tall trees, classic triple canopy jungle. I was aware of other folks still firing into the jungle, and others lying awfully* *still. Bullets were whickering overhead, it seemed inches above our prone bodies.*

*"The sound of incoming rounds continued to increase, and the higher pitched return fire from our weapons seemed to diminish. Whump! A mortar or RPG round exploded in the clearing a couple of meters behind us, shrapnel whistling over our prone bodies. A few seconds later, another round landed a meter to my left. Dirt and debris flew over me. The blast tore the fatigue shirt and most of the skin and muscle off the weapons guy's back, exposing his ribs, bright white against the blood. He started to get up and I grabbed his arm and pulled him flat. "Stay put, you'll be OK," I shouted into his ear. "That's a million dollar wound, you're going home." "Do you think so?" he asked. "Sure, you'll be fine, I can see it isn't bad," I lied.*

*"Whump! This time the round landed less than a meter to my right. At the same time as the dirt and smoke erupted from the ground, my leg felt like somebody had hit it with a two-by-four. My ears were ringing and the sounds of the battle had faded. I was suddenly aware of how the earth smelled as I pressed my face into it. It smelled alive, rich, sour. It smelled so good. This is what I thought with my face pressed into the damp soil.*

*"My leg is hit. Maybe it is gone. If it is, if I want to live, I will have to get a tourniquet around the stump. To do that, I will have to move at least enough to get my belt off and get it around the leg, and maybe I will get shot doing that. What's left of the leg may be pretty mangled, and it may be a shock to see it. I will have to overcome the shock, overcome the fear of the bullets flying inches over my head, and attend to the leg if it is bad. That will require a lot of effort.*

*"On the other hand, I can do nothing. I can stay with my face in the dirt, and maybe just bleed out, and it will be like going to sleep. So unless I'm going to attend to that leg, there is no point in turning my head. I thought about my options, taking my time to consider them. Nope, I thought, I don't want to die just yet, I'll look at the leg and do what I can to live. Do it. I turned my head to my right, and the sight of a more or less intact fatigue pants leg with a few red holes in it was just about the best thing I'd ever seen, and remained in that position until my oldest daughter was put in my arms following her birth by C-section 13 years later."*[288]

At that moment, several RPGs exploded in the bamboo to my right front, and the enemy fire increased even more. Howard and another rifleman from our platoon had moved into the freshly dug enemy fighting position in the middle of the trail and were under heavy attack from somewhere to their front.

Others saw them using their ruck sack frames to stop the enemy grenades from coming into their hole. The LT was just to their right rear, up on one knee, firing well aimed bursts from his CAR-15 up the trail. Both sides were now firing at one another from about 10 meters distance through the thick vegetation.

**Jose Garcia:** *"Someone was yelling at Howard and Haggerty to get out of the enemy hole and pull back. Haggerty did but Howard remained in the hole where he was killed by enemy grenades."*[289]

**Peter Clark:** *"My next thought was, if I can live through the next couple hours, I'm going home for a while. Forget about any extended tours. Living through the next couple of hours seemed like the immediate problem, though. Captain Williamson had been hit in the left foot and leg by the same round that got me, but he didn't appear to be paying any attention to the injury, just listening and yelling into the company net handset. He had the RTO's headphone held against one ear.*

*"As my hearing started to come back the roar of rifle and machine gun fire ebbed and flowed like surf on a beach, but it sounded like there were a lot more AKs than M-16s firing and the incoming rounds were thicker than ever, seeming to crack by a few inches overhead. I raised my head up a little and could see Joe Garcia hunkered down behind his M-60 and a few other guys to his left and right. As I watched he started firing to his front, short bursts a few seconds apart.*

*"It crossed my mind that maybe somebody should take some more ammo up to him, but as soon as I had the thought, any impulse to actually do it faded away. I put my face back down in the dirt, and thought I was probably going to die, and was sad about that for a couple of seconds.*

*"I could hear Colonel Lazzell over the battalion net; he had been talking to the Bravo company commander. "Now, I want you to prepare to refuse the flank," he said. Bravo Six came back, "Devour 6, refuse my flank, over?" "That's right, refuse your flank. Now, you know what I mean by that, Bravo Six?" "Yes Sir, I know what you mean." This was such bullshit, of course Bravo Six knows what refuse the flank means, "he's a goddam West Point infantry captain," I thought. I know what it means, and I'm a fucking Spec-4."*

*"As I listened more closely, the impression grew that Col. Lazzell was an old man who was out of touch, flying around in his LOH without a clue as to what was happening on the ground, giving random orders because he didn't know what else to do as his command got slaughtered. At some point he started talking about gunships and airstrikes, and I was hopeful that he would get us some help, but the strikes came in on the far right, where the firing had started but long since stopped.*

*"The strikes went where the battle had seemed to be happening when the colonel went up in the chopper and ceased to hear anything coming from the ground, and couldn't see anything under the triple canopy jungle. Damn, I wished somebody would talk to him and tell him what was going on. I pushed the handset at Captain Williamson, and he listened a couple of seconds, maybe said a few words, but quickly thrust the handset back and went back to the company net.*

*"'Since you're gonna die anyway,' I thought, 'what harm can it do to talk to the colonel.' So I pushed the push-to-talk and said, "Devour Six, this is Alpha Six Kilo, those strikes are not where the VC are, they are too far to the right, the VC are in our front." Lazzell answered, "Alpha Six Kilo, put your actual on." I said, "My actual can't go on right now, we need artillery in our front."*

*"Lazzell responded, "I need a casualty report, put Alpha Six on." "This is Alpha Six Kilo, Alpha Six is a casualty, I am a casualty, we are getting overrun and need some help."*

*"The colonel may have responded but the brigade commander (Devil 6) came on the net at that point. "Alpha Six Kilo, what is your situation?" I told him, "We are being overrun from the front, we are low on ammunition, and we need artillery to our front." He came back, "Where do you want artillery?"*

*"God, am I supposed to call in artillery? This was not what RTOs with a live actual were supposed to do without permission. I was going to be in so much trouble if I lived. Captain Williamson was focused on the company net, though. Wot the hell. "Five zero meters north of the tree-line at the north end of the LZ," I said. It seemed just a few seconds later shells were landing to our front, but too far into the woods."*[290]

**The King of the Battlefield**

A new sound came into the bedlam of the battle. To the northwest of us and about five miles away, a battalion of 105mm howitzers, the 2-33 Artillery, began to fire in close support of our defense. The FO, a lieutenant from the field artillery, and his RTO, an artillery sergeant, each with a radio, were adjusting the fires of a multitude of cannons. They were with the CO, about twenty meters behind us, in the open. One of them directed the rounds of the 105mm battalion, and the other was coordinating the fires of the 155mm, 175mm and the massive 8-Inch howitzers. With four radios in one place, they were a tempting target for the snipers to our west; but the snipers were apparently fixated on our mortar crews just past them to the east, who were busily firing those shells we had humped in.

**Peter Clark:** *"Gotta bring it down, closer to the tree-line, two zero meters," I said, and after those rounds landed there was definite lull in the incoming fire, but after a couple seconds it ratcheted back up to a roar. "Bring it right down on the tree-line," I shouted. At about this point Captain Williamson may have noticed I was talking above my pay-grade. "Give me that," and grabbed my hand-set. He seemed annoyed, which meant he was truly pissed. I didn't care at this point if I was going to get court-martialed or whatever, as there had seemed little hope of surviving in any event.*

*The captain was talking on both hand-sets, so there was nothing I needed to do except rest. The howl of the incoming artillery rounds ended in enormous explosions right to our front, the earth shook, and hot, spent shrapnel bounced off my radio and steel helmet. I had never heard a sweeter sound. Again I tried to cover myself with my helmet and the radio, and pressed my face into the dirt, and reveled in the crash and thunder of the incoming rounds, and the peace that came from having nothing left to do. If I had died then, it would have been OK."*[291]

The attacking enemy soldiers had completely overrun the left side of 1st Platoon and were now attempting to do the same to us. We were also under a heavy assault from our left, and it was Jose's and Bob's guns and crews that were holding the entire left flank of the battalion. In the distance, I heard the rumble of eighteen tubes of artillery that were aimed right at us. A second later, I heard what sounded like an extremely fast freight train from hell: whistle shrieking, wheels screeching, and headed straight for us.

I shoved my face in the dirt, as eighteen 105mm artillery rounds landed in a zig-zag line about fifty meters to my front. The explosions were so close together that it was hard to distinguish each round. Dirt was everywhere, tree branches were falling here and there and hot pieces of shrapnel fell onto our backs. Because it rained on and off during the battle, those hot pieces of metal, when they landed on our wet clothing, caused steam to rise from our backs.

> **Bill Williamson:** *"The Artillery Forward Observer was LT Dick Dalton. He did a great job of directing the King of the Battlefield on where to place the Artillery that the Queen of Battle (Infantry) requested. They fired thousands of 105mm rounds in very close support of our defensive positions. Oddly enough when the battle was over, all of the Infantry officers had been wounded and evacuated and Dick Dalton, an Artillery officer became the interim Company Commander and safely extracted the remainder of the Company from the battlefield."*

The firing from both sides slowed down momentarily after that first volley landed, but then it picked up again. The FO called in some adjustments, and a short time later, I heard the rumble of the guns again and the banshee returned. This continued as the enemy force pressed forward. Some more RPGs slammed into the trees above the heads of the guys facing north, and several more were wounded. The automatic weapons fire increased again, as the enemy attempted to overrun the 2d Platoon.

I heard voices shouting, "Throw smoke," and I knew that meant close air support was coming. A short time later, a large white cloud drifted through the vegetation on our right and came right down our firing line. It was tear gas. Some of the guys started yelling "Gas!" and we automatically grabbed for our masks. I put mine on, but I couldn't get any air to come in. The filters were wet, so I took it off quickly and stuck my face in the dirt, hoping that the gas would pass over me and not get into my eyes.

> **Donnie Gunby:** *"When that gas came I figured that one of our guys threw it by accident thinking it was a smoke grenade or an enemy bullet hit someone's tear gas grenade."*[292]

As the tear gas drifted past us, a concentrated barrage of RPGs slammed into the trees above our firing line and grenades began to explode all around us. The LT and the men to the right of him dropped back ten feet. Robert saw that his crew's position was isolated and pulled back so that he was on line with the rest, still facing north. Carl came with him; John was lying face down and not moving on the ground between their old position and me. I told Joe to bring his gun back so we could reform our line.

**Jose Garcia:** *"I was told to pull back twice. The first time only a little. After the tear gas came I was told to pull back again. I told Gunby to pull back with Ward. When I moved, I hit Ward with my feet. Then I grabbed him and yelled at him.*

*"He tried to say medic and then he vomited a thick stream of blood all over my shoulder and face. He had been hit in the eye. I turned away and looked straight ahead and fired a long burst forward. When I looked back at Ward, he was face down in that mess. I turned his face away from it and told him to play dead. "If you move, they will shoot you again so play dead, Ward, help will be here soon." He never responded.*

*"I moved 7-8 feet to my right behind a tree and start firing again. I figured that if I had some cover, I could still protect Ward and what was left of the left flank and draw the attention away from Ward. Then here comes an RPG aimed at me that hit a tree behind me and it rained down shrapnel. It got me on the left arm and temporarily paralyzed my left arm and hand. That was a big problem because I couldn't get the bi-pods back down and the barrel was too hot to handle with one hand. That RPG shrapnel also hit Ward because he groaned at the same time I yelled out from the burning shrapnel."*[293]

I turned around and saw the platoon sergeant and another sergeant with their feet in the open area. We had run out of maneuver room. If we didn't hold here we were through. The bodies of the dead and wounded lay around us and in front of our firing line. The artillery continued to crash into the jungle in front of us, and now we could hear the jets passing over our heads as they struck the suspected enemy troop concentrations to our north with napalm, cluster bombs, and regular bombs. At least they weren't bombing us.

**Jose Garcia:** *"I balanced the M-60 with my right hand and shoulder and kept firing as they kept coming. Over the next hour or so, I got two more RPGs that hit that damn tree behind me and caused me to drop my M-60 two more times to put out the fire. I could see the hole in my clothes and smoke coming out as the hot metal was burning through.*

*"Each time I yelled when I got burned and dropped the 60 to put out the fire. I heard Ward moan and groan again so at least I knew he was still alive. Poor guy, besides the eye, he got hit 3 more times with shrapnel from the same RPGs that I got hit with.*

*"There was a new man from LA. I didn't want to know him. One day he showed me a picture of his family. Two days before the fight, I told him that if fighting broke out, to drop his ammo to my left and then get behind me. He did and was hit and I last saw him face down. He must have survived because his name is not listed with the dead."*[294]

### The Counterattack

When I turned around, I realized that we would have to move our firing line forward in order to secure our dead and wounded. The enemy fire seemed to slow down, so I crawled over to Alan who was a little behind and to the left of me. I told him to get his squad on line and at my signal we would all move forward to regain our positions and get our people.

I passed the word to the right and we began crawling forward. All of a sudden, a number of RPGs crashed into the trees around us and automatic weapons fire swept through our area like a swing blade. Alan was killed with a bullet to the head and several others were wounded or killed. My gunners kept up their fire and with the others, repulsed the enemy's final assault on our position.

**Jose Garcia:** *"I spread and cleaned the ammo for the gun and laid the .45 pistol besides me, hoping we could hold back one more charge. They were so close we could hear the field whistle blow when they coordinated their attacks. When the whistle blew once more, we got ready, but thank God the last few blasts of the whistle we heard was a call for them to retreat. Haggerty and five or six other walking wounded had been to my right flank also firing and hanging on."*[295]

The firing tapered off slowly and finally stopped. Everyone was just lying there in the prone looking to their front, when some medics from the battalion aid station showed up and started treating the wounded. One of the 1st Platoon men was trying to crawl back to the perimeter, but he had been badly injured in his right arm. He lay on his side pushing with his legs and waving his other arm as he tried to move toward us.

The medics were there encouraging him to continue, because no one wanted to go forward of our line for fear of getting shot. I turned my attention to my own squad. I crawled back over to David Ward who was lying nearby. I was sure that he was dead, so when he moaned I grabbed his hand and assured him that he would be OK, before calling for a medic.

**Peter Clark:** *"Time slowly returned to the earth, as the sight and sound and feel and smell of a close artillery bombardment faded. On the underside of the receding sounds of the barrage, the crackle of small arms was diminished, and soon was only random bursts and shots, close but not directed at us. Airstrikes and artillery now seemed to be falling hundreds of meters away from our position. For the first time since the battle started, I heard choppers coming into the LZ.*

*"For some time I followed Captain Williamson as the two of us limped about the battlefield. Seriously hurt folks were being taken to the center of the LZ, where dust-offs were beginning to land. I remember searching for cigarettes, and finding a pack in the thigh pocket of my fatigues, and pulling it out to find it mangled with shrapnel holes and soaked with blood.*

*"At about that point I realized my leg felt slippery and my joints weren't quite right. I got kind of woozy and figured I needed to lie down. "Captain, I don't think I can carry your radio right now," I said. The captain gave me a sharp look, but I guess he figured I wasn't goofing off, and told me to hand off the radio and get myself a dust-off. Somebody helped me back to the aid station where miraculously there was an empty stretcher and I got put on it, along with what seemed like lots of other guys, mostly more bunged up than I was."*[296]

Robert Pointer's crew was in bad shape. Carl Johnson had been hit in the neck at the beginning of the fight and the bullet had severed his jugular vein and resealed it. Carl had continued to feed ammunition to the gun through the entire battle. He was one of the first to be medevaced after the shooting stopped, but we heard later that he had died soon after reaching the hospital. Robert was slightly wounded and was medevaced that evening. John Brantley was dead.

Jose's crew was not much better. Jose had been wounded several times by shrapnel, but would be ok. 'Ghost' was also wounded, but would make it. David Ward had been shot in the head and was medevaced. We heard later that he had lost his eye, but survived the terrible wound and was sent back to the states.

> **Jose Garcia:** *"One thing that is humorous now but not so funny then. The last RPG punched a hole the size of a nickel on my right buttock. Man it burned and I know how those poor steers feel when they are branded. The Lt. Medic came up to me and asked me where I was hit, I said the left arm. He took his scissors and ripped off my left sleeve to put a dressing on my arm.*
>
> *"Where else," he asked, "Behind my right knee." He cut and ripped half my pants leg and put a dressing there. "Where else," he asked. 'That's it, that's it,' I said. I was not going to tell him about the one hole on my right buttock, I felt he might leave me butt-naked. Since screening devices are getting better at the airport. I will have to tell you the story about what a commotion it caused at the airport the last time I flew out of Atlanta."*[297]

## SITREP

I found our LT with the platoon sergeant and reported to them. The LT was wounded, but able to walk, and the platoon sergeant was also wounded in the back, but he didn't know it yet. They told me to report to the company commander and give him our casualty figures and our status. I went into the open field and found Captain Williamson with his RTOs.

The CO had been wounded in the soles of his feet by a mortar round, but was standing when I approached him and gave him the 2d Platoon's status report. "Sir," I said, "The 2d Platoon got hit pretty hard." I gave him the casualty figures: out of forty-two men that walked in that morning, there were eight of us fit for duty. He looked at me and said, "Don't get emotional, Sergeant Murry." I never forgot his response and used it myself in later years. I exchanged a few words with Peter Clark, one of his RTOs, a former member of 2d Platoon who was also wounded, and then I left.

> **Jose Garcia:** *"I had just broke out of the jungle to the LZ with an RPG in my right hand after being ordered for the second time by the LT to leave the field and get on a Dust-Off to get my wounds treated. The LT ordered someone to take my M-60 and .45 and stood there till I left.*
>
> *I had picked up the VC RPG for protection from the jungle floor and started walking towards the clearing. The LT leading the Medic Platoon had just finished tying dressing on two of my wounds and I told him he should take his people another 20 yards or so forward to see if there were anyone*

*else maybe still alive that got left behind when we were ordered to fall back because of artillery coming in closer during the battle.*

*He argued with me and said he would go no further until he had protection. I told him I would give him protection and I picked up my M-60 again. I asked for a volunteer assistant gunner and this guy I had never seen volunteered to go with me.*

*I dropped my M-60 four times that day because of the pain inflicted by those wounds and incidents that day. It's not about how many times you drop your M-60 or weapon but it's about how many times you pick it up again to fire your weapon."*[298]

I went farther south into the open field, looking for some water for our men. Helicopters were landing in trail on the east side of the LZ, but my side was quiet. Suddenly I saw a cloud of black smoke erupt from the ground at the south end of the LZ. Another one erupted twenty-five meters closer to me than the first one.

The enemy was mortaring the LZ in hopes of hitting the incoming troops and possibly a helicopter. I was fascinated by the on-coming black clouds heading straight for me. By measuring the distance between each explosion, I quickly determined that one was going to land very close to, if not on top of me.

The gunner was traversing the LZ in measured increments: dropping a round, traversing, another round, traversing, very methodical and very mechanical. I just knew I was going to get it now. Five rounds had landed, and I was sure the next one would hit me. I put my head down and tensed my body as if that would help stop the hot metal from penetrating my skin and pushing into my vital organs.

I lay there waiting, but nothing happened. The pattern was clear, the timing was predictable, but no round landed. I lifted my head up to look and heard another round hissing in. I ducked and it went off to the north of me, about twenty-five meters away. The explosions continued to march across the field at the same interval and timing. I guess the gunner accidentally turned his traversing mechanism two clicks instead of one.

Shaken by this incident, I returned to the platoon and found the small group of uninjured ones waiting near the edge of the open area. We had started the day with forty-two men, the only time we were ever completely up to the authorized strength for a rifle platoon, and we finished the day with eight men, the size of an under-strength rifle squad.

Donnie was the only uninjured man in the squad beside me. I told him to take Joe's gun and face to the left flank. I helped him gather the remaining machine gun ammo and directed one of the riflemen from Alan's squad to stay with him. I was beginning to feel guilty about something, but the details of my guilt would take a while to surface, because I was just starting to come down from what had to have been the most intense adrenaline rush ever.

**Jose Garcia:** *"I heard my last name called and it was Captain Williamson, asking me "what happened." He was limping around with a radio guy behind him. I just answered, "I tried sir...just couldn't do any more." I am not sure now if that's what he meant or what, but that was the last time I saw him."*[299]

Robert Maguire, the man who had shared a hole with me at LZ George, was sitting down with his back against a large ant hill. He looked very pale. His eyes were open and he was staring at eternity. He had apparently been hit in one of the opening volleys of the fight and had bled to death while leaning on that anthill. One of the guys asked me to close his eyes, and as I was walking over to do so, a medic walked passed me and did it.

> **Peter Clark:** *"I remember waiving off some of the teams picking up stretchers as I felt guilty to be there at all, with only a few holes in my leg, and the battalion chaplain kneeling by my stretcher and taking my hand with tears in his eyes. I remember finally getting put on a dust-off chopper, climbing off my stretcher so I could sit on the floor as the stretcher racks were full. Another not-so-badly shot up GI and I were watching blood drip from the bottom of one of the stretchers, and made eye contact and gave each other a small, rueful, smile, sharing as we were the blessing of the fickle battle goddess and the inseparable mixture of guilt and joy that comes with survival.*
>
> *"At some point I remember being carried at a run from the chopper to a triage point, getting hooked up to an IV line, and a shot of morphine. I started to fade at that point, and the medic shook me hard, saying "stay with me, now." The few seconds of oblivion had felt enormously peaceful and good, and I realized that dying wouldn't have been so bad, or maybe that was just the morphine. But after that it was just the 93d Evacuation Hospital, painless surgery, air-conditioning, clean sheets, and Demerol IM PRN. My tour was over, and a week early, at that."*[300]

Jose's and Robert's guns and crews had been the bulwark of the company's left flank defense, and later, I submitted statements requesting that Jose be given a Silver Star and Robert a Bronze Star for their valor. I found out many years later that Jose's Silver Star was downgraded to a Bronze Star, and I don't know if Robert ever received an award for his actions that day.

A man from 3d Platoon received a Silver Star. He was on an OP with a comrade when the fighting started. Together they managed to kill at least ten enemy soldiers that were rushing toward them down one of the trails that led to the LZ. Then his partner was killed, and he ran out of ammunition. He retrieved one of the enemy weapons and killed at least ten more before they figured that this was a bad trail. He withdrew to the perimeter with his buddy's body and their weapons and joined the main line of resistance.

> **Bill Williamson:** *"The 3rd Platoon OP (Observation Post) was directed to withdraw back into our perimeter due to the enemy advance and the friendly artillery fire creeping towards us. They refused to do that as directed and stayed on to continue their mission and assist in directing mortar and artillery fire. When they were satisfied that there was little more to do, they withdrew. The soldier killed was SP4 (later promoted to SGT) Ed Heyer who was in charge of the OP.*
>
> *"In early 1967, Heyer's Father had died back home in Alabama. Heyer went home on emergency leave for the funeral and was offered the*

*opportunity not to return to Vietnam but he chose to return anyway. To me, this was a testimony to his patriotic spirit and also his commitment to the men in his unit."*

The mortar platoon, which had set up their mortars in the open area, came under fire from VC snipers in the trees to west when the battle started. Almost every one of them was wounded by this fire except the platoon sergeant, a combat veteran of the Korean War. Witnesses saw him fighting like a man with his hair on fire—a one man mortar platoon. He was talking on the radio to the FOs, adjusting the mortars, firing rounds, and shooting at the snipers with his CAR-15.

### Extraction

Eventually, we got the word to move out to the open field where we would be picked up by helicopter and flown to the fire support base at the Chi Linh airstrip. The artillery battalion that had fired support for us was set up there. The uninjured survivors from Alpha Company, including eight from the second platoon, boarded helicopters. As we flew out of that LZ, I was looking down into the jungle, trying to spot the anti-aircraft gun that I was sure was going to shoot us down. I was starting to feel like a fugitive from justice.

We landed at the fire-base just before dark. Someone led us to an area inside the perimeter and told us to bed down for the night. Shortly after that, we were told that we had to send out an ambush patrol. I carried the gun that night, and Donnie carried the ammo. Nothing happened, and we returned to the fire base in the morning.

I talked to some of the infantrymen who had been guarding the artillery during the fight. They told me that they had all been put to work opening the boxes of shells and passing them like a bucket brigade down lines of troops to the guns. While at the airstrip, I was interviewed by a reporter from Newsweek. He said he was going to submit his account of the battle for the weekly 'action' feature in his magazine. He said it would run if another battle in the Mekong Delta didn't trump it, but, it did.

### STATS

Our fire support was spectacular. During the battle that day the artillery fired 7,621 rounds of 105mm, 513 rounds of 155mm, 38 rounds of 175mm, and seventy-eight rounds of 8-Inch. The Air Force flew forty-three sorties and dropped napalm, cluster bombs, 500 and 750 pound bombs, rockets, and 20mm cannon fire. One of the airstrikes hit the 2-28 Infantry and killed two of their men.[287]

Helicopter gunships put rockets and machine gun fire into the jungle around the LZ. The main killer was the artillery. It was so close that both sides were under its fire, but the VC got the worst of it. There were 329 VC reported dead by body-count, of course, and one POW. Our losses were listed at thirty-seven KIA and 147 WIA. Seven Chinese or Russian 7.62mm weapons were recovered.

The fire support for Operation Billings was even more spectacular with a total of 41,655 rounds of 105mm, 3,521 rounds of 155mm, 832 rounds of 175mm and

936 rounds of 8-Inch. The 4.2-inch mortars were busy, firing 5,170 rounds, and the Air Force flew 276 close air support sorties.[301]

## Aftermath

Sergeant Magee had missed the battle because he was home on emergency leave at the time. When he returned, I'm sure he noticed a big change in my disposition. I had become withdrawn and was only talking to Donnie, the only unwounded member of my squad. We received a big influx of replacements that had to be integrated into what was left of 2d Platoon.

Jose came back eventually and so did Robert and some others. We never saw David again. We were sure he was dead, until a chaplain told us he had survived and was back in the states. Robert had some problems with me, but when I tried to talk to him about them, he said, "I don't want to talk about it."

## Battalion Change Of Command

Someone threw a smoke grenade into Colonel Lazzell's sleeping area at Lai Khe, usually a sign of an unresolved conflict with a lower ranked individual. It was a harbinger of things to come. The MPs were sent out to find the culprit, but without success. On 20 June there was a change of command, and LTC Rufus Lazzell passed the guidon to LTC Calvert Benedict. I don't remember if I attended, or even if we were invited.

*Or what king, going to engage another king in war,*
*will not first sit down and deliberate*
*whether he is able with ten thousand*
*to meet the one coming against him with twenty thousand?*
*Luke 14:31*

# Chapter 17-June 17th, 1967-Redux

### After Action Review

The After Action Review is the formal process that is used by the Army to analyze the results of an event. After reviewing what was intended to happen, unit members attempt to articulate what actually happened, why it happened and how it could be done better. The key element was the participation of all unit personnel. Candor is required for the process to work.

If the unit commander had created a climate where this candor was encouraged, many insights were gained, and the unit improved. Evolving from the group interviews conducted by S.L.A. Marshall during WWII, and the 'Performance Critiques' of the peacetime Army during the Cold War era, the AAR came to its own at the National Training Center during the re-building of the Army after Vietnam.

Those who remain in the Army are expected to use their experiences to try and improve the capabilities of their unit. Infantry combat is not like most other human endeavors. One of the problems with trying to logically analyze a combat action such as the one I've just described is that, unlike training, at the end of the battle many of the participants are either dead or have been evacuated for their wounds. Another problem is that a soldier is generally unable to separate himself from the mass of conflicting emotions that result from surviving such an event. It's been said that the only thing worse than a battle won is a battle lost.

Many of the survivors of this battle, on both sides, would spend the rest of their lives trying to sort out these lessons. I am one of them. The enemy had their own version of the AAR that they were reputed to conduct after every combat action. They used a self-criticism model developed by Mao Tse-tung and the Chinese communists. Leaders critiqued their subordinates, then the soldiers critiqued each other, and admissions of fault or failure were expected. The VC surely conducted one of them shortly after 17 June 1967; now it's time for ours.

### I. What was supposed to happen?

The U.S. strategy was one of attrition. The senior leaders believed if they killed enough enemy soldiers, the North Vietnamese and their Viet Cong partners would quit. The battle of Xom Bo II on 17 June came as the result of an aggressive move by the 1st Infantry Division commander, who ordered the 3rd Brigade to seek out and destroy some large formations of the 9th VC Division, that were believed to be in this area. The 3d Brigade inserted its two airmobile infantry battalions by helicopter, where they conducted search and destroy operations, just like they had been doing for the past 18 months.

The NVA/VC strategy, formulated by General Giap, the victor at Dien Bien Phu, was designed to force the U.S. Congress to call for the withdrawal of U.S.

forces after the casualties became unpalatable for the American people. His strategy called for a protracted guerrilla war, designed to wear down the enemy forces, while building up conventional military forces, for a final general offensive. Other members of the North Vietnamese high command felt that the main force units should fight big-unit battles when they had the advantage.[302]

Accordingly, the 271st VC Regiment had their own orders: annihilate an American battalion for propaganda purposes. To do so, they had prepared an LZ ambush. They had already had contact with the Americans the day before, and they considered that this was a likely spot for an assault landing by helicopter.

They dug positions around the LZ with good fields of fire, and then withdrew for several hundred meters from those positions on trails they had made, and there, they waited. Their plan was to stay in their staging areas while we conducted our usual air and artillery strikes in preparation for a combat air-assault by helicopter. As soon as the fires were lifted, and just before the helicopters arrived, they would run down the trails and be in their pre-dug positions waiting for us as we moved from the helicopters toward them.

**II. What Happened**

Whether by design or happenstance, I'm not able to determine from the official documents that I have researched, we didn't air-assault into that place; probably the helicopters weren't available. Instead, we walked in—just another walk in the sun.

> **Bill Williamson:** *"The plan that day was to conduct an air-assault into that open area. I remember COL Marks (Bde Cdr) and MAJ Chikalla (Bde S3) coming to tell LTC Lazzell and MAJ Jezior (Bn S3) that the aircraft that were intended for use in the air-assault had been diverted to another mission. They directed LTC Lazzell to have the battalion walk into the LZ. It was fortunate they did. As bad as that day was, it would have been much worse if the VC/NVA had been allowed to spring their LZ ambush as planned."*[303]

The signs of the enemy's presence were everywhere. Some of the guys pointed out the freshly dug fighting positions and the recently used trail around the LZ; but we had seen these things before, many times. For the past few months, we had searched the jungles of III Corps, finding base camp after base camp. We even found enemy camps with food on the tables, left by the phantoms we could never quite come to grips with.

On 17 June, when we arrived at the northern most point of the LZ, the first and third platoons began forming their part of the perimeter defense and the second platoon took a break behind them. We were supposed to tie-in with an element of the 2-28 Infantry, but they had not arrived. Most of us were preparing our C-rations for a noon meal, when a helicopter approached the LZ behind us. There were several shots in the direction of where the 2-28 Infantry was supposed to be and some shouts of, "friendly troops!" That didn't seem to raise our level of awareness much higher, but we did take some precautions.

The landing of the helicopter must have caused the enemy commander to think that we were making an air-assault without the usual preparations. He ordered his troops to execute the plan. They ran down their trails toward the LZ and must have been startled to see small groups of American soldiers sitting on the ground in front of them. The VC had the initiative though, and they attacked at various locations around the LZ. The Recon Platoon of the 1-16 Infantry put up an epic defense in the southeast part of the perimeter, and there were several attacks in the 2-28th area of responsibility. This review covers the northeast part of the perimeter because that's where I was.

After Jose Garcia opened fire, there was a lot of automatic weapons fire from our front, and the VC went through the 1st Platoon fairly quickly. The resistance made by the 1st Platoon brought just enough time for the 2d Platoon to form a hasty line that held. That line eventually connected with the 3d Platoon, which except for an OP, went unscathed. The main attacks in our sector were stopped by the platoon's machine guns and rifle fire. After the initial assaults, the enemy forces came under intense artillery fire and airstrikes, and after several more attacks, withdrew.

## III. Why Did It Happen?

The questions that need to be discussed are: (1) Why didn't we know the enemy was nearby? (2) How did the enemy achieve tactical surprise? and (3) Why weren't we prepared to defend the perimeter when they attacked?

### Reconnaissance

(1) The answer to the first question seems simple. A reconnaissance of the area by competent scouts should have alerted the leadership to the presence of the enemy, and they would have reported the high probability of enemy contact. There was none of that.

When compared to the enemy's agility and mobility, we looked and acted like lumbering giants. Even with all the LRRPs and battalion recon units, it was a rare occasion when a large enemy unit was located and successfully engaged by infantry. When they were detected by recon: air or artillery were the preferred methods of engagement. The question remains: Why didn't we send the recon platoon from either the 1-16 or the 2-28 Infantry to scout ahead of the main element?

In August 1967, General Hay released a document titled 'Fundamentals of Infantry Tactics. In Section 2 he wrote: "I will expect to find in your command, at the minimum, evidence of your attention to and emphasis upon:

a. Exploiting artillery and air firepower for all missions.

b. Maintaining security and dispersion under all circumstances.

c. Moving to contact with particular care to find the enemy with scouts.

Sub-section c seems clear that this was a lesson we learned the hard way two months before at LZ X-Ray.

### Routine

(2) The second question: Since there was no recon, why was the enemy able to achieve tactical surprise once we arrived in the area of the battle? The signs of their presence were everywhere. We had mostly competent officers and NCO's in

the battalion. They were dedicated to the mission and did their best to take care of us. What things contributed to our inability to read the signs?

In police work there is a term, 'The Deadly Routine.' Our operations had surely taken on the appearance of routine. If the intelligence staff had reliable information that an enemy regiment was waiting near the LZ, I'm sure that our leaders would have emphasized the possibility that we would soon be in contact with a superior enemy force.

Of course, the intel people had no such information, so nothing of the sort was mentioned in the warning order or the operations order before we moved out on our walk in the sun. This was another routine movement from point A to point B like all the others. There was something else though, a contributing factor that had much to do with our inability to read the tea leaves, so to speak.

**The Effects of Sleep Loss**

In the 1990s, I became aware of a field manual, FM 22-9 Soldier Performance in Continuous Operations. It was required for a non-commissioned officer course I was teaching. I thumbed through it, and as I did, I started seeing words like sleep deprivation, efficiency and stress. I stopped thumbing and began reading. It was all there.

The manual sited historical examples and scientific studies done by the British and American armies. In study after historical example, the facts were presented without ambiguity. The less sleep a man has, the less he is able to perform complex and ambiguous tasks. Among the effects of sleep loss the manual listed were: decreased vigilance, reduced attention, slowed perception, increasing omissions, and slowed comprehension.

The manual emphasized that the effects of sleep deprivation were harder on leaders. While the average Joe can continue to carry a heavy load, dig a hole where he is told to dig, watch his sector for an hour at a time, and perform his bodily functions on three to four hours of sleep a day, he can't do much more than that very well. The added stress of leadership responsibilities causes the mental acuity of the leader to deteriorate to a greater extent than that of those without such burdens.

Using the tables in FM 22-9, we can see with hindsight that we were in extreme sleep deficit. Most of us were unable to equate the appearance of freshly dug fighting positions and large recently used trails with the probability of imminent enemy contact. We hadn't 'connected the dots' that the enemy was near: Bravo Company had been in contact with a large enemy unit several days before; our perimeter had been mortared the day before with twenty men wounded, and we had received a mortar registration round the night before the battle. We should have taken added precautions.

According to FM 22-9, sleep deficit is cumulative; you can't make up months of three to four hours of interrupted sleep a night with one night's sleep. Since we never had a good night's sleep unless we were off for a night in Lai Khe, a rare occurrence, most of us were severely degraded in the ability to perform our duties.

The first version of FM 22-9 was published in 1983 and was obviously written with input from combat veterans. It was a stark portrayal of combat and its aftermath. Actually, it was unique among the rest of the dry and antiseptic manuals being produced for the modern army of pre-Desert Storm. It must have struck a nerve with the recruiting command and other sensitive members of the army, because the next version which came out in 1991 had been sanitized. Stories of suicide under heavy bombing and other horror stories were gone. I have found manuals from the pre-WWI army and many different versions of most other manuals; but the FM 22-9 of 1983 seems to have disappeared.

Perhaps these things would have occurred to the colonels and generals who were controlling our optempo, if they had been sharing our living conditions, but thanks to the helicopter, they usually got a good night's sleep in their headquarters. General Hay's quarters in Lai Khe had air conditioning. The scene in the travel trailer in the movie "Apocalypse Now" was not far-fetched.[304]

## Defense

(3) Why weren't we prepared to defend the perimeter when they attacked? By taking into account the matters of routine, and sleep deprivation, I have to conclude that we felt no sense of urgency to move swiftly and deliberately from a cross-country movement into a solid defense.

In the years since that day, I have served with units that prided themselves on battle drill SOPs and rehearsals, but I've never seen a training scenario that addressed moving into a defensive perimeter and steadfastly following the priorities of work, until a basic defense was in place: positions assigned; OP/LPs established; claymores and trip flares emplaced; and everyone working intently to finish before any administrative details were addressed. There are many fine details in planning for such a move, and it seems to me, that it should be a basic part of infantry soldiering.

## The O-O-D-A Loop

John Boyd, an Air Force fighter pilot turned airplane designer and strategist, was a student of Sun Tzu, as was Mao, Ho, and Giap. If John Boyd's O-O-D-A loop is to be believed as the formula for victory on the battlefield, because of our diminished capacity, we were initially unable to perform the first two 'O's: observe and orient. In combat, Boyd said that it's all about who has the initiative and keeps it.

The enemy started out behind the curve when they heard the helicopter land without the usual LZ prep, but because they had already prepared positions and were oriented to the area, the enemy commander was able to regain the initiative with his decision to order his unit to move to the pre-dug positions on the edge of the LZ.

The few shots from the 2-28 Infantry area gave us the time to observe that there was danger to the northwest and to orient our defenses in that direction. The enemy lost the initiative briefly, when Garcia opened fire. At the same time, the enemy troops were momentarily fascinated by the presence of our troops, sitting on the trails that they had expected to run down unimpeded to their fighting positions. Regaining the initiative, the enemy overwhelmed the 1st Platoon with the shock and awe of multiple automatic weapons fired at point-blank range.

The machine gunner's initiation of fire and the brief resistance put up by the 1st Platoon, bought enough time for a hasty defensive line to be formed which held until the artillery bought hell to the attackers.

### Senior Leadership

After WWII, Colonel Charles Hunter, the real leader of Merrill's Marauders, wrote a bitter denunciation of General Joseph Stillwell's apparent lack of situational awareness regarding the physical condition of the Marauders. Many of them died of diseases that they were unable to resist due to exhaustion. He quoted the Army Field Service Regulations of 1923 which stated that the commander was required to know these things. "It is essential that he know from personnel contact the mental, moral, and physical state of his troops. The conditions with which they are confronted..."[305]

If David Hackworth's account of his trip to Vietnam with S.L.A. Marshall is to be believed, these senior leaders were generally unacquainted with the condition of their troops in the field. Yes, they visited the front every day, flying everywhere by helicopter, but I never heard of an American general spending the night in a battalion perimeter or accompanying an ambush patrol. General Moshe Dayan, the famous one-eyed Israeli general, did, and his analysis was that, "The Americans are winning everything but the war."[306]

General William Westmoreland was the commander of the U.S. ground forces in South Vietnam. He was responsible for defining the strategy that dictated the operational decisions made by his subordinate commanders. An artillery officer in Europe during WWII, he transferred to the airborne infantry after that war. He was awarded a CIB for his service as the commander of the only airborne infantry regiment in the Korean War. General Westmoreland had no infantry combat experience at the platoon, company, or battalion level; nor had he ever fought in the jungle; nor had he ever fought guerrillas.

General William DePuy was one of the best and brightest of his generation of Army officers. He recommended many of the operational techniques promoted by General Westmoreland when he served Westmoreland directly as his operations officer. He was awarded the CIB for his service as an operations officer and battalion commander in Europe during WWII. His CIA service during the Korean War appears to have been a qualifier for his position as Director of Counterinsurgency and Special Operations for the Deputy Chief of Staff for Operations at the Pentagon prior to his move to Vietnam.

When given his own command, he was determined to prove his tactics on the battlefield. Twelve days after he took over the division, he published his rules for combat in no uncertain terms. General DePuy regularly relieved commanders who didn't demonstrate an offensive spirit and he also established a zero defects climate in the division. He had no infantry combat experience at the platoon or company level; nor had he ever fought in the jungle; nor had he ever fought guerrillas.[307]

General Hay had recently taken command of the division from General DePuy—a hard act to follow. He was awarded the CIB for service with the 10th Mountain Division in Italy during WWII. He had no infantry combat experience at the platoon or company level; nor had he ever fought in the jungle; nor had he ever fought guerrillas. He was determined to increase the division's score on the big board and at the same time defeat communist aggression in Southeast Asia. While we hoped things might slow down a little after he arrived, if anything, the optempo increased. He did however, query his experienced subordinates and used their input when he published his own rules a few months after he took command.[308]

## IV. How It Can Be Done Better

Besides ensuring that the troops get the proper rest, FM 22-9 emphasizes strict training standards as the most important preparation for sleep loss in combat. When this manual came out, the Army was in the midst of the great post-Vietnam War rebuilding process. Soldier training had greatly improved since the 1960s. During the Vietnam War, the Army's training focus was preparing soldiers to hold the line at the Fulda Gap in Germany, while we lost 58,000 men in a sideshow in Southeast Asia.

### Training for Combat

From the time our first combat troops landed in Vietnam in 1965, it was several years before a theater-specific training plan was developed and implemented for infantry soldiers going to Vietnam. The Army did put its soldiers through an 'Infiltration Course' in basic training. The soldiers would low-crawl one hundred yards while .30 caliber, water-cooled machine guns would chug away at 400 rounds a minute, firing five round bursts at least ten feet above them.

As the trainees crawled under barbed wire entanglements, an occasional demolition charge was detonated in special pits. The trainees went through this three times: once in the daytime with no shooting; once again in the daytime with shooting; and once at night. The general feeling among the trainees afterwards was that they had now experienced something close to combat, telling each other, "It wasn't so bad."

The AK-47 fires at a rate of 600 rounds a minute. Soldiers are taught to fire short bursts, but in a close-range assault, the length of the bursts can increase. The effects of near misses by bullets from Soviet 7.62x39mm automatic weapons on the human body are such that uninitiated can have no comprehension.

The reason the AK-47 is called an assault rifle is because it was designed to produce a shock effect on troops in the defense when assaulted by Soviet troops. The shock effect makes soldiers duck down to avoid being hit by the terrible objects flying past their heads. These objects are making so much high pitched cracking noise that glands in the body of those being shot at are releasing enormous amounts of adrenaline. This 'adrenaline dump' leads to tunnel vision and time perception distortion, none of which is conducive to returning accurate fire in combat.

When I first arrived in Vietnam, I went through the Brigade's one week Jungle School. We had several training events while I was with the 1-16 Infantry during the time of this narrative: 'airmobile' training which consisted of climbing a troop ladder; a few hours practicing 'over-watch' movement techniques; and firing our weapons several times. The total amount of time we spent in formal training was about eight hours.

### V. Train as You Fight

I have looked back on those days and compared the training schemes, then and now. Then, I would have recommended training and rehearsals for several things we did most often, and had the least amount of training for: ambush patrols, establishing a perimeter defense, and shooting.

**The Ambush Patrol:** There are a number of sergeant skills that must be mastered before a sergeant should be allowed to lead an ambush patrol. The most important are: troop leading procedures, night land navigation, calling for fire, and medevac procedures, and understanding the proper employment of claymores and machine guns. These skills must be perfected and demonstrated to competent leaders before he is certified to lead. He must train his squad and rehearse all these procedures, especially the contingencies.

**Perimeter Defense:** Perimeter defense starts with planning. Leaders make plans based on the best information available. The piece of the pie, the interval between positions and who will occupy each one, is a simple planning procedure. The unit should be able to move from a file into a defensive position without stopping. From there the NCOs enforce the priorities of work until a basic defense is in place. That should include OPs, claymores, and a small berm in front of each position, in that order.

**Shooting:** What is needed is a 'combat conditioning,' Train-Fire Range, where the soldier qualifies, firing at pop-up silhouettes while AK-47s using live ammunition are fired past him from twenty-five meters to his front, two feet to his left and right. After he is able to qualify as an expert with his weapon, he should be 'conditioned' for combat on these kind of ranges.

### The Reality

The modern army of the 1980's demanded that soldiers 'train like you fight,' but most training areas will not allow you to dig the same foxhole you would need in combat because of 'environmental concerns.' Live fire combat conditioning exercises like those used by the British Commandos to train Darby's Rangers would get a general court-martial conviction for any commander attempting to use them to prepare his soldiers for combat.

Truly realistic training is beyond the capacity of most units to conduct. Safety regulations and concerns for the 'welfare' of the troops stifle the attempts of the veterans to introduce the uninitiated to the rigors of combat. In most units, strenuous PT events are substituted for real combat training, and physical fitness, although essential, is made the mark of combat readiness.

### When Will They Ever Learn

I tried to use FM 22-9 to educate my commanding officer in a special operations unit where I was serving as the operations supervisor. We were conducting surveillance of drug traffickers using high-tech electronic equipment.

One day I watched a young sergeant trying to figure out how to assemble the many components of our camera monitoring system in the CP after he had been awake for twenty-four hours.

He was one of the smartest young men in the detachment and he stood there for five minutes before he attached a cable to a monitor. Then he stood there with some more cable ends in his hands and stared at them for the same amount of time before attaching another.

That is when I snapped on what I had been reading in the continuous operations manual. When we returned from that operation, I went to my boss and recommended that we rearrange our 'pre' and 'post' deployment schedules in order to better cope with the effects of sleep deprivation. I reminded him of recent incidents where our men had put the wrong cable on the power supply, resulting in a flash of light, blue smoke, and expensive repair bills.

He was a dyed-in-the-wool Ranger and angrily insisted that all these things could be overcome by willpower. The manual disagreed, and so did I, but I was a sergeant and he was a captain, so nothing changed. This is why the lessons learned process is flawed. David Hackworth called it CRS, "Can't remember shit" and Pete Seeger's army service during WWII is probably the source of his lamentative chorus: "When will they ever learn, when will they ever learn?"[309]

*And do not fear those who kill the body, but are not able to kill the soul;*
*but rather fear Him who is able to destroy both soul and body in Gehenna.*
*Matthew 10:28*

# Chapter 18-July, August, September 1967

### On the Road Again

On 1 July, we were flown to Quan Loi. We secured the perimeter and participated in another road clearing operation. We had a number of nights that we were able to find some beer and get drunk. Each day, some elements of the battalion did road clearance while others guarded the perimeter. Robert came back from the hospital during this time, and it was then that we had a drunken talk.

One of the medics chimed in that it was my fault that John had died. I did see him face down on the ground and not moving during the fight, and told the medic that I thought he was dead. But now I had to assume responsibility for all the deaths in my squad and Alan's squad as well. Since there was nothing I could do about the dead men, I continued to withdraw into myself, drinking and thinking.

### Jose Returns

Jose returned from the hospital with his third Purple Heart. Not long after, he went out on an ambush with a new squad leader. During the night, the squad leader heard a noise and threw a hand grenade into Jose's position blowing off his right leg at mid-thigh. The grenade also blew off Donnie's knee cap. According to the others on the patrol, the squad leader went to pieces when he saw what he had done. Jose ended up taking charge of the squad.

He directed the sergeant to pull himself together and set up security. When the medic appeared dismayed at the sight of Jose's bleeding stump, Jose gave him his own belt and directed the medic to use it for a tourniquet. Then he told him to take care of Donnie. Finally he instructed the sergeant on the procedures to call for a dust-off.

Jose is a real hero in my book for the way he behaved during the entire time I served with him. He was a moral man, and if he ever went to the Ville, it was to have a beer and keep an eye on people like me. If anyone deserved the credit for holding the flank of the battalion that day in June, it was him. He was also a practical man. When he was gravely wounded by the errant hand grenade, he saw that if he didn't take charge of the situation he was going to die.

### Losing It

One day, Sergeant Magee and I were walking through the rubber trees toward the bunker line. I was arguing with him about something and suddenly we were both reaching for our rifles. I looked at my rifle as I brought it off my shoulder into a ready position and saw that I had forgotten to put a magazine in it. Sergeant Magee had gotten his CAR-15 off his shoulder and realized that he didn't have a magazine either. We stared at each other for a moment, and then busted out laughing. The next day I was transferred to the 1st Platoon.

Things in the 1st Platoon were about the same. Most of the men I had known were either dead or gone with their wounds. One night after a beer drinking exercise at our club, most of us, including me, were passed out on our racks. The lights were still on, and one of the men still awake noticed a large rat walking on the wooden frame above the window at the other end of the building. Deciding that he had to do something, he fired a twenty round burst from his M-16 over the sleeping men on their bunks.

I jumped up, thinking we were under attack, and hit the light bulb nearest me with my hand, breaking it while yelling at the other men to get the other one. Of course our marksman missed the rat, but the shooting alarmed someone, and soon the brigade alert siren was sounding. As soon as it became clear to my befuddled mind what had actually happened, I returned to my bunk and went unconscious, quickly enough to avoid the commotion when the officers arrived to investigate.

At the end of July, the word came down that there would be an additional company, Delta, added to the battalion. A number of men from Alpha Company were transferred to the new company. We had an influx of new personnel with the attending changes in leadership as PFCs became fire team leaders and Specialists became squad leaders. The new company was given a seventy day training period, which was ten days longer than the basic unit training course given to infantry recruits in 1963.[310]

On 13 August we did a combat air-assault into the Bau Bang area on Hwy. 13. I had been made the field first sergeant and I was to take care of administration and logistics in the field. This meant that I was to make sure that the perimeter positions were squared away and that chow and the supplies were distributed. We had a new company commander, CPT Arnold, but I didn't get to know him very well. During a meeting in his tent, I recommended that we request sling-blades from Lai Khe, so that the troops could clear fields of fire in the tall grass in front of our positions. He took my suggestion and was pleased with the results, so he left me alone.

### Lessons Learned Process

One night, just before I left, I was talking to a lieutenant who had just been assigned to the company. Someone out on the perimeter opened fire with their M-16. The LT was standing there talking to me and he continued to talk for several more words before he noticed that I was in the prone. "That was outgoing fire," he told me. I continued to lie on the ground for another minute, waiting to see if those shots would be followed by the first shots of an enemy attack.

The LT began to chide me about being nervous, and when I got to my feet, I told him that I was indeed nervous. "Sir, I've been here for a while. Bullets fly faster than sound. People don't usually fire their rifles at night. If the VC had been out there, and returned fire, their bullets would be among us before we heard the sound of their rifles being fired."

He wasn't impressed, as many young officers in those days were not with anyone they outranked. I guess they were being told in their basic officer courses that officers should know everything, or act like they did, in front of the sergeants in order to develop their command presence. Whatever the reason, a lot of fine young officers never had a chance to develop their basic combat survival skills, because they were too busy establishing their command presence. They didn't realize that they weren't in charge of the enemy.

### The Mess Sergeant Strikes for the Last Time

I came in from the field two days before I was to go home. I packed my extra things: a bright red smoking jacket that I had had made down at the Ville months before, some photos, my pants from R+R, and my poncho liner. The mess sergeant was leaving around the same time. We agreed to go to the shipping point together and when we got there I was told that I had to have a full duffle bag if I wanted to ship things home.

The mess sergeant offered to put my things in his bag, and he would send them to me when he got home. I'm still waiting for my things. He had made me participate in his Bell Pepper extravaganza for a year, and now, he made me show my appreciation by giving him my only souvenirs of Vietnam. It was just as well that I didn't ever see them again, because when I got home I would be doing everything I could for the next thirteen years to forget about Vietnam.

### 'FIGMO'

I got my orders and saw that I was reassigned to the 1st Battalion, 3d Infantry at Fort Myer, Virginia. I asked one of the older sergeants about the unit and he said that it was called "The Old Guard," the Army's ceremonial honor guard that buried people at Arlington National Cemetery. Great, here I was, a man who was responsible for the deaths of several American soldiers, and I was going to an honor guard. It didn't make any sense.

On the day I left the company, Sergeant Magee came up to me and we shook hands. I apologized to him for my violent response to his orders on the way down to the bunker line a month earlier. I asked him if I could get a 16th Infantry Certificate, and he drove up to battalion and got me one before dropping me off at flight operations. A helicopter landed an hour later, and several of us got on, and I took my last helicopter ride in Vietnam.

I sat on the right hand side, so I could see the company area. As we flew over the rubber trees, I could see our street and my hut. As we flew higher, I could see the bunker line and the river valley in front of it. I kept leaning and looking to the rear of the helicopter to see behind us, but eventually the familiar territory passed, and I leaned back against the back wall of the troop compartment and stared at the backs of the pilots until we landed at Di An.

### The NCO Club Was Closed

Those of us who were going home reported into the Replacement Company on the edge of the perimeter and were assigned tents. We had to go to several places to clear the division. That evening I went to the big NCO club expecting to get drunk. But there was lock on the door and a sign said that the club was closed until further notice pending an investigation. I went to the PX and bought some snacks and went back to my tent. Then I remembered that Rodney was here somewhere. So I asked around at the orderly room, and one of the clerks told me to look for him at the Bob Hope Stage. I walked over to the stage which had been built for the Bob Hope Christmas Show. It was a tradition for the armed forces in WWII, Korea, and now, Vietnam. As usual, the only ones who got to see the show were the rear echelon military forces, but it was a nice gesture on the part of Hollywood.

There were some dressing rooms on the sides of the stage. Rodney had moved into one and was there when I knocked on the door. He had extended, now working as an R+R representative, and was getting ready to do a six month tour in Bangkok, Thailand. We sat around and talked for a few minutes. He offered me one of his SKSs which we were allowed to take home as souvenirs.

I picked up one of them and looked at it while we talked and then gave it back to him and thanked him for his offer. We exchanged addresses and agreed to look each other up when he got back. We sat around drinking beer until it was time to go to bed. I left him there and went back to the tent.

## Awards Ceremony

The next day, was taken up with various administrative details, and the last office was where we were given our tour medals. As we entered the building, a clerk sitting at a desk gave us two small brown cardboard boxes. In one was a U.S. Vietnam Campaign Medal and in the other a medal from the Government of South Vietnam. A year ago I had come to Vietnam for medals and now…

'Clunk…clunk…clunk' came a sound from the other end of the room. As the line moved forward, I could see that most of the soldiers were dropping their medals into a trash can as they walked out the door. I wondered what I would do when I got to the end of the room, and when I did, I dropped my boxes in the trash can. Medals are for heroes, and I wasn't a hero.

## 'Repple Depple' Adieu!

That afternoon, I boarded a bus along with a number of other men, and we rode to the 90th Replacement Battalion to wait for our plane ride home. There were amnesty boxes outside the office that was handling departures. A lieutenant threatened us with all manner of punishments if we were caught with any of the prohibited items listed on the wall next to the large boxes. I didn't have anything on the list, but I looked into a box and saw claymores and grenades among the bags of weed and other items in the box.

The NCO Club was also closed for investigation at the 90th Replacement Battalion. I would have to wait until I got to my next duty station, before I saw the man who was responsible for my not being able to have a beer in the club before I left the country. The first Sergeant Major of the Army, William Wooldridge, former Sergeant Major of the 1st Infantry Division and recipient of two Silver Stars for his actions in WWII, lived across the street from my barracks. He appeared before a Congressional committee and invoked his Fifth Amendment rights a number of times, when they asked about his participation in the so-called Khaki Mafia, a cabal of army sergeants who were skimming the profits from the NCO clubs they ran in Germany and Vietnam.

## Bien Hoa Airbase

I wandered around the place where I had been almost a year ago to the day, then finally went in and lay on my bunk until morning. They called my name the next day, and I rode a bus over to Bien Hoa Airbase where the flights for home were leaving. I remembered when we flew into the same place several months before, before 17 June.

We were in the back of a C-123 and our company's weapons carrier was strapped down in the cargo hold. I was sitting in the seat behind the wheel and pretending that I was steering the plane. The other guys were mildly amused. We landed at Bien Hoa for fuel before flying to Lai Khe. The loadmaster made us get off while they refueled the plane, and the crew took a break. He told us to wait under this large tin roof with no walls. There were many benches, so we lay on them and rested.

An airplane full of replacements from the world pulled up and all these fresh faced privates who were beginning their tour came walking into the waiting area. We had been out in the field for a long time. Our uniforms were filthy, festooned with bandoleers and hand grenades, and we carried our personal weapons. We looked bad, we smelled bad, and under certain circumstances we were bad. The new troops stood there staring at us, until a sergeant came running up and told them to get on the bus.

That was fun then, but I wasn't having fun now. Some of the guys that were with me on 17 June were dead. Most of the rest of them never came back to the company, and I had no idea about what happened to them afterwards. I sat there thinking about the battle and all those guys, thinking, thinking, thinking.

A 707 taxied up, and a large group of new arrivals to Vietnam came down the ramp and walked toward us. Some of the guys who were going home were hooting and making remarks like, "New meat" and "Sorry about that" and "364 days and a wake up, sin loi, GI."

I just sat there waiting for either a rocket to come in and kill me like I deserved, or the command to get on the plane that would surely crash, if the rocket didn't get us before we took off. When they did tell us to start walking for the plane, it was like the scene in the movie, "Platoon" when the veterans pass the new guys at the beginning of the movie. Some of the old guys were saying things like "You'll be sorry," and the new guys either stared at us, or looked straight ahead as we passed each other.[311]

## Going Home?

I climbed the stairs and entered the plane. I took a window seat and looked out, watching for the rockets. The crew was in a hurry to get going because there had been some recent rocket attacks and they didn't want to be in one. When the cabin door was shut, the pilots gave that plane the gas, and we were soon hurtling down the runway.

The troops were chanting, "Go, go, go, go!" When the wheels left the ground, the troops in the cabin all began to cheer. I didn't join them, knowing we were doomed and there was nothing to cheer about. Thirty-seven years later I was sitting in the back of a C-17 hurtling down the runway at Bagram Air Base in

Afghanistan, listening to the children and some grandchildren of the Vietnam era veterans doing the same thing as their fathers and grandfathers had done long before. I didn't cheer that time either, but for different reasons. That time I didn't want to leave.

Somehow we made it to Okinawa, where we stopped for fuel and waited several hours at the air base. I got a hamburger at the snack bar and wondered if I was going to get home alive after all. The next time we took off a few hollered, but most of us just sat there. The flight took a long time, and sometime after dark, we were told to prepare to land at Travis Air Force Base. This time, when the plane touched down, again, everyone cheered but me, although I did smile. I still half expected the plane to blow a tire and crash on the runway.

## Oakland Army Terminal

There were buses waiting that took us to the Oakland Army Terminal for final processing before we were released to go on leave or be discharged. There we were greeted by a sergeant who formed us into a line, of course, and they started taking our sizes for new Class A uniforms. Then, after some recruiters gave the NCOs a pitch about how much the Army needed new blood, they asked if any of us wanted to volunteer to be hometown recruiters.

I couldn't imagine myself trying to talk young men into going through what I had just been through, and I had been lucky. I had enough friendly blood on my head and hands; I didn't want anymore. If someone wanted to be a soldier, that was their business, and while the need for recruiters was obvious, I wasn't going to be one of them.

At the end of the processing, we were given our Class A uniforms. After putting them on, we were free to leave and go home. I was in the dressing room changing when I heard some of the men talking about the big meal that we could get before we left the base. It was a steak dinner with all the trimmings. 'Soul' food had recently been added to the menu, due to some stateside agitation by leaders of the black community, who wanted to make sure that the 'brothers' weren't being left out.

'Soul' food consisted of ham hocks, collard greens and a few other items eaten by low income people of all racial and ethnic groups in the south. One well-meaning white guy was talking to a couple of 'brothers' and said, "I bet you 'soul brothers' can't wait to get to the mess hall and get some of that 'soul' food!" One of the 'brothers' looked at the other, then they both looked at the white guy, "Soul' food, sheeeit! I gettin me a steak!" said the first. The other man chimed in, "Right on!"

*And when you hear of wars and rumors of wars, do not be alarmed;*
*it must happen, but the end is not yet*
*Mark 13:7*

# Chapter 19-October 1967

## Ong Thanh

When I came home, I couldn't help reading the newspaper every day for reports from Vietnam. On the 17th of October, while I was on leave, the 2-28 Infantry, our partners on June 17th, walked into the meat grinder. They went into an area a little north of where we found all the rice during Operation Tucson D in February. 'Intelligence' said that the 271st Regiment of the 9th VC Division was there. This was the same unit we had fought on June 17th.

General Hay, who had replaced General DePuy, continued DePuy's quest for big battles with the VC, hoping to destroy large numbers of them with airstrikes and artillery, while the 'target acquisition' infantry fought them off from defensive positions. The results of the battle of Ap Gu on the 1st of April were what our commanders were dreaming about ever since. But the enemy had learned, and would not be attacking our defensive positions anytime soon.

The 2-28 Infantry had been in the field for 10 days conducting 'search and destroy' operations. On the 17th, the battalion left their NDP in an open area and moved as a column into the same part of the jungle where they had made contact with the VC the day before. As the lead company moved past unseen VC bunkers on their right, the VC moved around the left flank and formed a hasty ambush. When the shooting started, a second company moved forward to reinforce the first. In the battle that ensued, the battalion commander and most of his command group were killed.

Altogether, there were fifty-seven KIA, seventy-five WIA, and two MIA out of the 155 men who started out that morning—basically, the destruction of a U.S. battalion. The battalion commander was LTC Terry Allen Jr., son of Major General Terry de la Mesa Allen, the famous commander of the 1st Infantry Division during WWII. This put the story on the TV news and the front page of newspapers around the country. Once again, like August 25th, the Army portrayed the battle as a victory.

## The History Books: I

Unlike the battle of August 25th, 1966 this one would have extensive press coverage. Two books were written about it, and a documentary was made and shown on Public Television. BG James Shelton wrote one of the books, "The Beast Was Out There," in 2002. Shelton had a tough time writing what was on his heart in the aftermath of that battle.

Like most professional soldiers, he tried to balance the truth with his concern for the families and reputations of the dead, especially Terry Allen and General Hay. In the book he recalls a Big Red One officer's dinner in 1994, when he sat next to General William Rosson. Rosson had been Terry Allen's commander in Germany and had participated in his wedding.[312]

General Rosson complimented Shelton for an article he had written for 'Vietnam Magazine' about the battle. But then he said, "I wish you had provided a little more on the battle itself, including the circumstances attending Terry Allen's death. As it is, I have the image of a worm-like column, two companies in length, making its way slowly (one thousand meters in two hours) through the light jungle of the Long Nguyen Secret Zone. No frontal or flank security. Suddenly the head of the column is hit, and the enemy maneuvered down both flanks of the U.S. column, inflicting massive casualties. Surely there was more to it than that." Shelton later wrote that "those words haunt me to this day because I have found it so difficult to explain the battle in more precise terms."[313]

Anyone planning on serving as a leader in the infantry would do well to read his book. There is real value in Shelton's descriptions of his time as an infantry battalion's operations officer, the S3. "Our aim was to bait the enemy into attacking us. We'd go into this jungle area, dig in, patrol during the day, and wait for the enemy to hit us at night…the tempo of operations in the 1st Infantry Division was phenomenal…

Every time we were scheduled for some rest, an emergency operation would materialize and off we went…there was little or no rest, continuous and changed operations, and a new chain of command (bouncing from brigade to brigade on a continuing basis) every day…'hurry up and wait'… the grueling pace in a demanding environment took its toll on the stamina of all men."

He adds to the real history when he describes the field conditions of the troops. "For men assigned to combat units, sleep normally came from exhaustion; and many nights were as exhausting as the days...one problem we had with LP's [listening posts] was that both soldiers would go to sleep, regardless of the dangers…Exhaustion seemed to be the normal cause of falling asleep in an LP.[314]

Shelton's description of the time they came out of the field after 10 days and were ordered by the battalion commander to do PT the next morning, the only time they had ever done PT, was extraordinary, but believable, army BS. He recounts the time that two battalions, one of them his, surrounded a village and then lit each other up, "The biggest firefight our battalion was to have until the battle of Ong Thanh…"

Short-rounds from the artillery, airstrikes gone wrong, negligent discharges, unmarked minefields around U.S. base camps, the nightly travail experienced by the men on ambush patrol and the chaos that can happen when one actually made contact, all serve to validate Murphy's number one rule of combat: anything that can go wrong, will go wrong.

It's not all negative though, as he describes the precision air-assaults, the bravery of the soldiers, the constructing of an NDP, and the professionalism of the artillery when they set up a fire support base and fired in support of the infantry.[315]

He also gives some insight to the officer's world of the 1st Infantry Division when, after mentioning his service with the 1st Cavalry Division in Korea, the 82d Airborne Division at Fort Bragg, and the Berlin Brigade, he describes the 1st Infantry Division as the "ass-chewingest organization I have ever seen in my twenty seven years in the army."

He singles out BG Bernard Rogers, a future army chief of staff, saying, "If General Roger's definition of help was ass-chewing, then he gave everybody a lot of help." This may account for a common phrase heard among the NCOs of those days, "An ass-chewing is like a drink of water; everyone needs one now and then." It surely accounts for the command climate in the division while I was there.[316]

The whole scheme of officer assignments is described by Shelton when in a conversation with his battalion commander, the commander expresses fear that he is about to be relieved. He tells Shelton that he knows he "had not been wanted" in the 1st Division; he had been "force fed," meaning that someone over General Hay had 'recommended' him for a battalion commander position. Just because you're paranoid doesn't mean they're not after you; the battalion commander was relieved shortly after their conversation.

I really liked Shelton's book. As an officer he did his best to explain life in the 1st Infantry Division and the disaster of October 17th.[317]

## The History Books: II

The second book, published a year after Shelton's, is in a whole other category. "They Marched Into Sunlight," by David Maraniss tells the story of the men of 2-28 Infantry and how they came to be in Vietnam. He tells the story of the battle Ong Thanh in great detail and includes interviews with the VC commander of the 271st Regiment, who by the way, declares that they were the 1st Regiment and never used the designation, 271st.

He blends the battle story with a detailed account of the first violent anti-war demonstrations at the University of Wisconsin, and the Johnson administration in disarray as key members like Johnson and McNamara lose heart for the war that they started and now see as un-winnable. In doing so, Maraniss creates an epic history of the Vietnam War that should be studied for years by those interested in the subject.[318]

## The History Documentary

As to how the men really felt about the battle, this is vividly portrayed in the documentary, "Two Days In October," which was aired on PBS in 2005. It was based on Maraniss' book. Shelton, Captain George, commander of Alpha Company, Lieutenant Clark Welch, commander of Delta Company, and several other soldiers speak candidly about their resentment of the way Westmoreland and Hay 'explained' the battle to both them and the press. In archival footage, Westmoreland is seen telling the press that, "We have a pretty good idea of the enemy troops in this area. We have quite a bit of intelligence on this particular regiment."

The soldiers gave their perspectives of the command and control methods. Tom Hinger, a medic, said, "The company commanders are encouraging the platoon leader to get the platoon moving. And the battalion commander is encouraging the company commander to get his company moving faster." A squad leader, Gerald Thompson said, "Colonel Allen, he's up there flying around in a little bubble-chopper, and he'd say 'pick up the pace, you're going too slow' and you're carrying 50 pound packs, and not knowing when somebody's going to ambush you." Mike Troyer, a sergeant said, "He was mad because we weren't going through the jungle fast enough. Well, get your big ass out of that helicopter and come down here and try it."

When the survivors were brought back to Lai Khe, they were interviewed by the press. Tom Hinger said, "We were ordered to make ourselves available in front of the Alpha Company area. They had set some chairs up." Another one, Mike Arias said, "We were debriefed before we went into the hooch to interview with CBS news, that we were not to mention that it was an ambush. From my perspective, I was pissed because it was an ambush. I felt at that time and I still do now, that there was a cover up."

General Hay, when asked by a reporter what would happen next said, "What happens now? What happens now is we continue to work on them until we destroy them. This is what I had hoped we could do for a long time is get them to stay in one place." Shelton said, "I understand why General Hay didn't want to use the word 'ambush,' because an ambush means you're incompetent. The problem was what was said about it was a spin, which made it sound like this battle was part of something bigger which was very successful."

Back in the States, a nightly TV news anchor reported, "In Vietnam, the 1st Infantry Division in a costly bitter battle with the Viet Cong in the Iron Triangle forty miles northwest of Saigon, has reportedly smashed a guerrilla plan to overrun Saigon itself. The battle took place yesterday between fifteen hundred Americans and twenty-five hundred Viet Cong. Before the fighting ended, fifty-eight Americans were dead including Lieutenant Colonel Terry Allen Jr., son of the World War II general who commanded the First Division in Europe."

Clark Welch described what happened at the hospital, "I remember vaguely waking up enough to know that there's General Westmoreland…then I believe General Westmoreland, fine old man, leaning down and saying, "Well, son, I'm glad, eh, I'm glad you're all right. Tell me what happened that day." And I recall then that I said, sir, I will tell you what happened today. The god-damned Army is 'blanked' up from the President of the United States on down to my boss the Colonel, and I'm glad he's dead."'

Clark's first sergeant, Bud Barrow, described his visit with the General: "General Westmoreland came into the ward, and shook hands and said, "Congratulations." Barrow said, "Are you congratulating me or the enemy? We lost that battle….Sir, we got ambushed." "Oh, no, no, no," he said, "No," he said, "That wasn't no ambush." And I said, "Well, General, then I don't know what happened to the other people out there, but, by God, I was ambushed."[319]

**Lessons Learned**

The Army sent Major John Cash, a military historian, to Lai Khe to conduct a special investigation. When he arrived, no one at Division HQ was eager to see him. The 1st Division was "very uptight" and refused to make the daily staff journals and duty officer's logs available to him. When he finally did see them, he suspected that some entries had been altered.[320]

He interviewed thirty soldiers and officers. One issue kept coming up: the half hour period early in the battle when Allen had his troops hold their positions in the jungle instead of withdrawing, with the artillery check-fired and no air support yet.[321]

Cash was unable to determine if Allen or the higher-ups made the decision not to withdraw, but he was certain that the artillery check-fire order came from someone above the battle. He concluded that the 2-28 Infantry was ambushed, and the body-count was false. From my own armchair quarterback position it looked like Deja Vu all over again. Just like August 25th, 1966: there were men in helicopters making tactical decisions instead of the leaders on the ground.[322]

Major Michael Mahler, a 1st Brigade officer, said, "It quickly became apparent to even a casual observer that our generals had too little to do and too much communications equipment with which to do it...Thanks to the helicopter and the radio, they now had the ability to micromanage the small actions, even down to how the soldiers were holding their mine-sweeper equipment...they found the temptation to get involved in whatever little action was going on to be more than most of them could stand...From their position overhead...the solutions appeared simple...and simple instructions were issued. When the response was not instantaneous ...more irate radio transmissions took place, with more confusion following."[323]

According to Mahler's account, General Hay insisted on airstrikes. Even though artillery was immediately available, Mahler witnessed an earlier instance of troops being denied artillery support because the division commander over-ruled the commander on the ground, and made them wait thirty minutes for air support. General Hay had insisted that battalion commanders be on the ground, but he didn't do anything about the 'great squad leaders in the sky.'[324]

Just like June 17th, 1967, Shelton makes it clear that the troops and their leaders were exhausted from field conditions and lack of sleep. Just like most of the battles in Vietnam up to that point, the command said it was a victory and the body-count was inflated beyond any reasonable calculation.

Of course there were the decorations, some to the non-participants, as usual. MG Hay received a Silver Star, and by all accounts, he wasn't even there until the very end when he arrived by helicopter from Saigon. Hay said that though he would have relieved Allen of command if he had lived, he awarded LTC Allen a DSC for both his bravery, and because he was Terry Allen's son.[325]

Major Donald Holleder, the 1st Brigade Ops officer, received a DSC, posthumously, for attempting to lead some medics back into the battle. He was a West Point football star and took off running toward the battlefield like he was back on the football field. The VC shot and killed him before he reached 100 yards. Lieutenant Harold Durham Jr., the artillery FO of Delta Company was awarded the Medal of Honor. Despite serious wounds, he continued to adjust artillery fire on attacking VC soldiers until he was killed in action.[326]

In his interview for the documentary, BG Shelton said, "It was a total fabrication of what really happened. It kind of, like it showed, like a victory. The Americans held them off, blah, blah, blah, blah, 103 enemy killed and all this stuff, and that haunted me. I'm not a cynic, but I started to become one, you know, of history, you know. What the hell, who the hell knows what really happened if that's the way history is written."[327]

I wish General Shelton could have been there when one of our men educated an officer in our company after the battle of August 25th, 1966. He responded to the officer's question of why he didn't like the army by saying, "Because they're always handing you a bucket of shit and telling you it's a basket of roses."

*For sorrow according to God works repentance unto salvation,*
*which is without regret;*
*but the sorrow of the world works out death*
*2 Corinthians 7:10*

# Chapter 20-Between the Wars: 1967-1989

### Back in the World

The country had changed dramatically since I left in the fall of '65. My high school surfing friends introduced me to the 'brave new world' that they were exploring. Most of them had abandoned the dream of the 'endless summer.' Now they were flying to distant locales in their minds, with the 'League of Spiritual Discovery,' and 'Lucy in the Sky….'

My closest friends were sharing what they called a "crash pad." It was a 'safe house' for the revolution that was in progress across the nation. One day they came to my house and took me there. When I walked through the door, they shoved a joint in my mouth and stood there watching me until I took a long pull and inhaled. There was an expensive stereo with big speakers and there were mattresses on the floor. One of them pulled a long playing record out of a colorful jacket and put it on the record player. The hissing coming out of the speakers was loud, so I should have known, but I was starting to feel the effects of the smoke.

The blast of sound that followed was so strong, and the music was so strange that I was stunned on several levels. I picked up the record jacket. There was a fish-eye lens picture of three freaks wearing faggoty clothes; the one in the middle was black. The title was "The Jimi Hendrix Experience-Are You Experienced?"[328]

The sounds were so different that it was like listening to the music of an alien species that had suddenly appeared. As the singer was describing the effects of something called 'purple haze' doing strange things to his brain, I too was having some trouble with sensory overload that afternoon. My buddies spent the rest of the afternoon playing strange music and talking, initiating me into the secrets of the underground, the secret society of the great rebellion of the sixties.

### The Old Guard

I reported to Fort Myer and the 1st Battalion, 3d Infantry, "The Old Guard," on 21 October, the day of the huge anti-war demonstration at the Pentagon. The hippies were going to levitate it, and that was OK with me. With the Pentagon out of the way, we might have a chance to win the war. 'The Old Guard,' was the Army's ceremonial unit that was spending most its time at Arlington National Cemetery "doing drop jobs in the boneyard," which was the way one of the sergeants described our duties to me. The war had greatly increased the workload, and daily you could hear the bulldozers clearing away trees and brush to open new sections for the cemetery. I was assigned to the Army drill team; but they didn't need a sergeant who had lost perspective. So after a few months they ran me off, and I ended up working out of an office in the Pentagon, giving travel information at the Washington National Airport.

It was an intense time in Washington DC during that fall and winter and the spring of '68. At the end of January, the VC conducted coordinated attacks all over South Vietnam. This was the Tet Offensive that Giap was counting on to instigate a nationwide general insurrection, but that didn't happen. The pageant that the VC presented to the American people however, had the effect Giap was looking for. On his nightly news program, Walter Cronkite told the country that we were "mired in a stalemate...that the only rational way out then will be to negotiate, not as victors, but as an honorable people who lived up to their pledge to defend democracy, and did the best they could." With that, the will to win the war was gone. In March, Lyndon Johnson bailed on the war he had started and refused to run for re-election. In April, Martin Luther King Jr. was assassinated and DC burned. My friends in the 'Old Guard' were sent downtown to guard the government offices with live ammunition in their weapons.[329]

While I was in DC, I made one attempt to find Robert Pointer in the Germantown section of Philadelphia. After searching the phone book and drawing a blank, I asked around in a couple of bars since Bob had always enjoyed a beer or two. The bartenders were black, and since the only thing a white guy wanted with a black man in Germantown was to arrest him, I never found him.

After several arrests for drunk and disorderly conduct, the Army relieved me of my responsibilities as a sergeant and made me a PFC. I appealed the bust, double jeopardy was an issue, and got my rank back. At the same time I got my stripes back, my mother called and told me my father was dying of cancer. The army gave me a compassionate reassignment to Fort MacArthur, California.

## Changes

I drove to California. On the way, I stopped at a town in Georgia and asked for Donnie Gunby. The attendant at the gas station directed me to his house. Donnie answered the door and we caught up. He had been badly wounded when the 'friendly' grenade blew Jose's leg off, and he was walking with a slight limp. After an hour, I had to go. That was the last time I saw him for forty-five years.

My next stop was at Fort Benning, Georgia to see Sergeant Magee. I went to the Post Locator. He was assigned to the G3 Test Committee and I found him at a test site. He had finally been promoted to SFC in spite of the trench fiasco at Bunard SF Camp. He introduced me to his team and told them how I had stopped him from stepping on a butterfly bomb in the VC camp during Cedar Falls.

He invited me to spend the night in his bachelor quarters. He was on emergency leave during the battle of June 17th, so I guessed that he was divorced. We talked a little about this and that until we were tired, and I fell asleep on his couch. The next morning we said goodbye. I never saw him again.

I continued west and stopped in Houston to find Jose Garcia. I went to a phone booth and opened the white pages to 'Garcia.' I called all the Jose 'Garcia's' but no luck, so I went to the A. 'Garcia's' and started dropping dimes. I told whoever answered that I was looking for a Jose Garcia who lost his leg in Vietnam. When the third number answered, he said that Jose was his cousin.

The cousin gave me Jose's phone number, and shortly after that, I was knocking on his door. He greeted me and gave me a hug as is the custom in Texas. I followed him to the dining room table. He limped and was using a cane. I asked him about the night he lost his leg. Jose repeated the details I knew and then gave he gave me the rest of the story.

**Jose Garcia:** *"Donnie and I were hit bad. That grenade blew my leg completely off. The sergeant was freaking out and the rest of the troops were stunned. I told the men to set up security. Then I told the medic to use my belt for a tourniquet. After he stopped the bleeding I told him to take care of Donnie and I told the sergeant to shut-up and call for a medevac.*

*"I could feel myself going numb at my feet and then the numbness started moving up my body. I knew that if it reached my head I would die. By the time it got to my chest I began to direct it to go back down. It got all the way to my neck before I turned it around. I was using all my will to make the numbness retreat, and it did. The numbness tried to come back two more times on the helicopter and I did the same thing."*[330]

A beautiful young woman came into the room and he introduced me to Janie, his fiancée. They were planning their wedding, and I was touched with their care for one another. If anyone deserved some happiness after coming out of that world of hurt that Jose had been in and survived, it was them.

Eventually, I came to know the story of their love. They had fallen for each other before Jose had gone into the service. They wrote each other constantly while Jose was in Vietnam. One day, Janie got a letter from him telling her that the wedding was off and that she should forget about him.

Janie was stunned, but she was also stubborn. And, though it took a while, she managed to track Jose to a hospital in Japan. She contacted him, and after he told her about his injuries and why they would prevent them from being married, she let him know that she didn't fall in love with his beautiful legs. They were married, and the last thing Jose said to me when I left them in Houston was that he was going to dance with Janie at their wedding.

## California

I came home and found my father dealing with his terminal case of lung cancer by staying drunk and chain smoking. "What the hell?" he said, when I asked about the smoking. I lived at home and drove daily for an hour each way to Fort MacArthur in San Pedro, near LA. At Fort MacArthur I was assigned to the duties of training NCO in the garrison admin company. The place was a zoo.

The CO, a young captain recently returned from Vietnam, spent most of his days chasing after his run-around wife, a Hollywood starlet, and trying to get a Bronze Star medal that he claimed was awarded to him; but the paperwork was lost. Many of the troops were stoners from Southern California and had not entered into the spirit of the army. When the first sergeant couldn't make the morning formation, I took it and we tried to hold things together.

I reconnected with my surfing buddies, now deep in the underground and still living in the safe house they were in when I returned from Vietnam. While I was running around with them one day, I was arrested for possession of marijuana. This time I was found not guilty by the civilian court, and court-martialed by the army. They got all my stripes but since there were few experienced soldiers, I was returned to duty as the training NCO. I helped get the admin company through an IG inspection and received rave reviews for my records, which I had totally fabricated in desperation over the mess left by the sergeant before me.

When my father died, I applied for 'Project Transition' and spent my last six months in the army on the beach in San Diego, while supposedly learning to be a book buyer. In June of '69, I received an honorable discharge and quoted the raven, "Nevermore!"

### Surfing

I caught a ride to Trestles with a fellow who asked me to show him how to sneak past the Marine MPs. President Nixon's Western White House was on a bluff overlooking the north end of the beach and the MPs were extra vigilant. We hid the car in some vegetation and were walking down a dirt road when I heard the sound of a vehicle behind us. We ducked into some bushes just before an MP sedan drove past. Remembering the time they caught me, I decided to give them a little pay-back. I had been schooled in the art of booby-trapping by the best.

There was a large tree limb laying next the road and several strands of commo wire draped over some nearby bushes. I enlisted the aid of my companion and we carried the tree branch down the road to a spot where there was a pass through the trees. After propping the branch against a tree, using the Iwo Jima flag raising method, I ran over to the commo wire and grabbed a strand. Tying one end to the branch, about eighteen inches off the ground, I made a loop and tied the other end to a tree across the road. My buddy watched all this with a look of foreboding and asked me what I was doing. "We're giving the Marines some guerrilla warfare training," I said, "now get back in the bushes, they're coming."

Right after we ducked into the bushes, the sedan came back, moving at a good rate of speed, too fast for the driver to see the thin, black strand of commo wire stretched across the road. 'Crash!' The branch landed on the roof of the sedan. I heard the doors open and it was quiet until one MP exclaimed, "What are we going to tell them at the motor pool?" They cleared the branch and wire and drove away. Me and my buddy went to the beach and rode some waves.

### The War

The war dragged on. In July, the Army arrested and court-martialed a group of Green Beret officers, including the 5th Group commander, for murder. In November the newspapers broke the story of the My Lai Massacre; it completely blew my mind that American soldiers could do such a thing. Of course I always felt compelled to explain to anyone who asked, that the soldiers I knew would never do something like that.

I worked for a while, went to college on the GI Bill and bombed out, got married, tried to become a musician, got divorced, and left the country. I spent several years in Mexico and Central and South America before returning to California for a short time and working for a rock band. I was there in the spring of '75 when the final act of the Vietnam tragedy was played out on TV.

### The End of The Road

On the 30th of April, 1975, Saigon fell. As the North Vietnamese Army entered the city, I watched the end on the evening news. The U.S. Embassy was evacuated by helicopter. Once the so-called great 'enabler' of our counterinsurgency strategy, the choppers were now enabling us to get out of Dodge. As soon as they unloaded their passengers, they were pushed off the decks of U.S. Navy ships into the sea. Six years and eleven months before, I was jumping out of one of those Hueys onto the ground of LZ George and participating the next day in one of the most lopsided victories of the Vietnam War. Now, we had lost it.

## Post-Traumatic Stress Disorder

In 1967 when I returned to the states, I occasionally thought about combat—the orders I had given and the things that had happened as a result. At random times, 'film clips' would pop into my mind, and I would relive those moments, clenching my teeth while trying to will an alternate ending to the grim consequences of those orders. I could be with a group of people or by myself, when these images would push aside whatever else my mind was involved in, and I would find myself back in Vietnam.

PTSD is a hot topic these days. Our information age society has become so sensitive to their feelings that there is a lot of hand-wringing by the talking-head psychologists, the substitutes for the religious TV hosts of my youth, the ones who insisted that they understood the un-understandable complexities of the age.

The concern for the Afghanistan and Iraq veterans PTSD, which in some people's eyes makes them walking time bombs, liable to do unspeakable things to those around them when they finally snap, is probably a valid one. Those same psychologists and the psychiatrists have managed to dumb-down many of the troops with anti-depressant medications, the long-term effects or 'unintended consequences' of which are yet to be manifested, except for the record high number of suicides in the armed forces.

After the battle of Xom Bo II which is what the military history people called it, nobody in our platoon was saying much, and I was feeling terrible. June 17th had changed me. Before that battle, I was a youthful sergeant living in a fantasy world I had created, based on a plethora of war movies and the war books that came out in the 1940s and 50s. I had been immortal and proud; all that was finished now.

I had survived the battle, but I was carrying the bodies of Carl, John, Alan, and others on my back. I hadn't fired a shot in the fight, mainly because I hadn't seen any enemy soldiers; given my luck with rifles, if I only had one shot, I wanted it to count. I had directed the defense of the left flank of the company, but no one was saying anything to me, one way or the other, about that.

There was a time when one of the men from the platoon accused me of letting John bleed to death, and I guess I did, even though I thought he was already dead. Eventually, I was forced to conclude that everyone's death in that sector of the battle was either directly or partially my fault. I began a mental activity of continually re-living my role in the battle, the mistakes I made, the thoughts of what I should have done, my moments of cowardice, and guilt, guilt, guilt. This mental preoccupation with the past has been called the 'soldier's heart' in earlier wars, then it was Post Traumatic Stress Syndrome, and more recently, PTSD.

The little things were damning, like: if I had been a better NCO, I would have noticed the signs and alerted my platoon leader; I would have made sure that the ammo bearers kept their ammo with them all the time, no matter what; I would have, I should have, I could have...Long after these events, I was able to sort some things out, but without confirmation by the others, those who were there, there was no comfort in my reasonings.

According to doctrine, for leadership to improve in combat units, after action reviews must be done so that the lessons can be learned, failures can be identified, and corrective actions taken. In this situation, that was impossible. The CO and our platoon leader were wounded, and I never saw either of them again. Our acting platoon sergeant was also wounded and gone. The few of us who remained were in a state of shock. After I got out, I wasn't able to talk about these things with anyone, so I joined the ranks of the silent veterans who 'didn't like to talk about the war.'

**Texas**

Surfing and everything else that California had to offer no longer soothed my restless soul. Texas seemed like it would be a change of pace; Rodney lived in Austin and told me it was a great place. I hitchhiked across the southwest on Interstate Highway 10 and arrived in Austin in 1976. I found a job working on a drilling rig. The 'Outlaw' country music scene had established itself there, and I did my best to enjoy it.

**The Texas Army National Guard**

After working on drilling rigs, I became a mechanic's assistant. He told me I could make better money as a mechanic. When I asked him how he learned, he told me about going to a trade school which was expensive. Then I saw an ad for the Texas National Guard.

Just like malaria, military service gets into your blood, and it never completely goes away. I went by their headquarters and talked to a recruiter. Of course, they would teach me all about diesel mechanics and pay me too; so I signed up. It was springtime. Shortly after that, I joined my new unit, a heavy maintenance battalion, for their annual foray to Fort Hood.

The first week was spent at a motor pool in a garrison setting. As usual, what the unit did was not what the recruiter told me. Yes, there were diesel engines and, yes we were supposed to do something when they needed repair. The mechanics would get to take off the engine mounting bolts and disconnect the wires before the engine was lifted out of the vehicle, dropped into a shipping container and sent to an ordinance depot for repair.

After a week in the garrison motor pool, underneath a truck, lying on my back on a creeper, where I'd been ordered to hide whenever an officer came to the motor pool, we went to the field. I was pissed off about my being fooled by the recruiter. The sergeants that ran the unit were getting tired of my complaining and gave me make-work.

I was finished with one of those tasks and sitting on a log with my head in my hands when a jeep pulled up. It was the chaplain. He asked me my name and how things were going. I guess my need to let off steam overrode my aversion to chaplains; so after a few prodding questions, I unloaded my woes.

When I was finished, the chaplain smiled sympathetically and reached in his pocket for his wallet. I watched him as he opened it and pulled out a business card. "Hmmm," I thought, "he wants me to go to his church, no way."

Then he reached into his front pocket with his other hand and pulled out a single hole punch. He put the edge of the card in the hole punch and squeezed, punching a hole in the card. He handed me the card with a smile, hopped in his jeep and drove away.

I looked at the card. In the center was the chaplain's name and in big letters "Official TS Card." There was a border of numbers, and where the number one had been was a hole. I started laughing and my whole mood changed. Not only was I impressed that he didn't give me a religious message, he too was a student of American military history. Many of the memoirs that I had read by infantrymen in WWII had mentioned sergeants telling someone who was complaining to go to the chaplain and get their 'tough shit' card punched.

As soon as we returned from Fort Hood I looked for another unit. I had no intention of remaining in the maintenance battalion, but since I was in, I decided to look for an infantry unit. There was only one in the Austin area, a recon platoon in Troop D (Air), 124 Cavalry. They were short-handed, and the maintenance unit was happy to see me go; so I transferred.

There were many Vietnam vets in the Air Cav. We probably joined the Guard for a kind of catharsis. On Saturday night during drill weekends, we would get drunk and tell stories about the strange and funny things that happened to us in the war. We never talked about the other thing, except in an off-handed manner.

The only thing that I could see to do was to try and redeem myself by being a better sergeant. I pushed my way into the training planning, hoping to use the lessons I had learned to train the next generation of eager beavers in the Blues Platoon. My recommendations were deemed extreme by the officers, and eventually I found myself standing at attention in front of the troop commander.

He tried to placate my demands for more realistic training, first by telling me that he was going to promote me to staff sergeant, and then, when I reminded him of the need for training, offering to send me to OCS. When I replied, "That's fine sir, but what about the training," his face got red and he said, "I want you out of my unit, Sergeant Murry, you're too good a soldier and you don't belong here!"

Now I had a new mantra, "I want you out of my unit; you're too good a soldier." This was the ultimate military conundrum. Good soldiers were held at a premium and a commander would never get rid of someone for being too good. With those words ringing in my ears, I went to Camp Mabry and filed a complaint with the IG. He listened sympathetically and offered to get me into another unit, but refused to touch the basis for my complaint.

I decided to fight the Major. I let it be known to the first sergeant that if they wanted me out of the unit, they would have to throw me out. I was transferred from Recon to the refuelers in the HQ platoon. The next drill was pretty lonely until the refueler NCOIC, a black sergeant, took me aside and welcomed me to his section. All the refuelers were black. He knew a little about my case and decided that I was being squashed by the system; he was a veteran of that war.

### Books

On the Monday following drill, I was sitting in my tumble-down house out in the country on the north side of Austin. I was looking at a couple of paperback books. One was called "Franny and Zooey," by J.D. Salinger. I can't tell you why I had that book because I only read military history.[331]

In the story about Franny, a college girl, she talks to her boyfriend about reading a book called "The Way of a Pilgrim." She tells him that the book is about a Russian peasant who wandered across Russia until he found the 'Jesus Prayer,' "Lord Jesus Christ, have mercy on me a sinner." Her boyfriend is interested in other things and finds her behavior disturbing. The story ends with her praying, and her boyfriend leaving. How I read the whole story, I can't say, but I did.

The second book I had found in the Service Club at North Fort Hood during our last summer camp (AT). It was "The Way of a Pilgrim." When I saw it, I was amazed. I thought the book mentioned in Salinger's story was some kind of literary device. The Service Club was giving these books away, so I grabbed it and took it home at the end of AT. I read the book and found the Jesus Prayer. [332]

That Monday, I was feeling pretty discouraged. For the past year I had been considering a run at Ranger School. There were no slots for Ranger School in the refuelers, and today was a running day. I had a five mile course that took me through the countryside of north Austin. I ran that course three times a week, and after I found the book, as I ran, I said the Jesus Prayer to the cadence of my feet hitting the ground.

### The Question of Questions

I heard the sound of a car driving into my yard, and when I looked through the screen door, I saw my first sergeant get out of his car and walk toward the house. "What are you doing here, Top?" I asked as I held the door open for him to come in. He didn't say anything as we walked over to some chairs. I sat down and looked up at him.

The atmosphere had changed, and I was like one in a trance. He stood there, gently swaying. "Murry, you ever been saved?" he asked, slurring his words slightly. "No," I said, not really knowing what he was talking about, but knowing. "Do you want to get saved?" Without hesitation, I said, "Yes!" and like a mighty rushing wind, the Lord Jesus came in!

As the Spirit came in, the tears flowed out, and I began to weep. Eventually I was saying, "Thank you, Lord, thank you, Lord," without any conscious realization of who I was thanking or why. The first sergeant didn't seem to consider my behavior unusual, and after a few moments said, "Well, come along with me and I'll get you saved."

He led me out to his car, and we drove towards Austin. I was weeping and thanking the Lord, and he was trying to drive to some place that he hadn't as yet revealed to be our destination. As he was weaving down the road, I was able to discern the fact that he was actually pretty drunk. Normally, I might have offered to drive or at least remonstrated with him as he careened through the city streets, but today was different, and I was above those petty concerns.

We reached our destination and pulled into the parking lot of one of the larger Baptist church meeting places in Austin. There was a lot of activity for a Monday afternoon. The first sergeant told me to follow him, and we joined the people walking toward the main building. He led me to a man in a suit standing by the entrance and introduced me to the pastor, saying, "I brought this man here to get saved." I was still weeping, and the pastor probably knew what was going on with me. The fact that the first sergeant was drunk didn't seem to upset him. He told him to take me up to the front and seat me on the front pew. I had no idea what was going on, but I wasn't alarmed.

Something had happened to me that I couldn't explain, but whatever it was, it was beyond the realm of good and evil. I sat there gently weeping while some men gave me forms to fill out. One was an application to join their congregation, another offered me a number of choices regarding my 'ministry,' whatever that was, and a third was for my address so they could send me some collection envelopes. I filled them out, weeping and thanking the Lord, still clueless as to what had happened.

The pastor started the service. It was the first meeting of a week-long revival. He introduced a speaker who proceeded to entertain the congregation with story after story from the Bible. He gave each story a humorous slant, before turning it around and slapping us upside the head with the facts of our sinful condition. At the end there was a call to come forward, and one of the men sitting nearby escorted me up to join a small group of men and women. I was still weeping and repeated the prayer of the speaker along with the others.

Then the whole congregation was invited to come forward to welcome us into the fellowship. Several pilots from the Air Cavalry Troop were among those who came forward and shook my hand. One of them, Bobby Boyd, was a pilot in the Recon Platoon and he appeared to be delighted to see me, weeping my eyes out in front of this large crowd of people.

The first sergeant took me home after the service. He bought me a chicken dinner and dropped me off. I continued to weep until I fell asleep that night. The next morning when I woke up I decided to return, and for the rest of the week, I listened to speaker after speaker as they attempted to revive the congregation. I don't know about the rest, but on Friday, the honeymoon was over and I was as dead as a door nail. All that week however, I had not been troubled by Vietnam.

## The Church

I came to the realization that I needed to drop my feud with the Air Cavalry. I went back to Camp Mabry and transferred to G Company, (Airborne/Ranger), 143 Infantry (LRRP). By 1980, when I joined G Company, my PTSD had pretty much taken over my mind, and there were few moments that I wasn't back in the Nam trying to undue my mistakes, my decisions, and especially the orders I gave that resulted in the deaths of those men.

After a couple of drills, I met Allen, a Vietnam veteran of the 173d Airborne Brigade. We were talking, and he asked me if I was a Christian. I remembered Jimmy Carter saying that he was a born-again Christian when he was running for president, and by now, I realized that I also was one after my regeneration experience of a few months earlier.

"Yes, I am," I replied. "Would you like to go to a Christian meeting sometime?" he asked. "Yes," I said. "Would you like to go to one tonight?" For the third time I answered yes and later that evening, I was sitting on the back row of a small meeting hall in south Austin.

The man in the front was saying that Christians were people who called on the name of the Lord. I was sitting in the back being hammered by every flashback I had ever entertained. It was like an endless barrage of direct hits, each one worse than the one before, with the main theme being that whatever happened, it was my fault.

I sat there and quietly said, "Oh Lord Jesus!" Immediately, the flashbacks were gone, and I was experiencing peace. I had found the Lord again, like that day when I wept and couldn't stop. I didn't start weeping this time, but I was enjoying Him. From then on, every time I had a flashback, I called out, "Oh Lord Jesus!" and in about three years I was healed from the 'soldier's heart,' PTSD.

This was the fulfillment of Paul's words in Romans 10:9-13 "That if you confess with your mouth Jesus as Lord and believe in your heart that God has raised Him from the dead, you will be saved; for with the heart there is believing unto righteousness, and with the mouth there is confession unto salvation. For the Scripture says, Everyone who believes on Him shall not be put to shame. For there is no distinction between Jew and Greek, for the same Lord is Lord of all and rich to all who call upon Him; For whoever calls upon the name of the Lord shall be saved;" and, 1st Corinthians 1:18 which says, "For the word of the cross is to those who are perishing foolishness, but to us who are being saved it is the power of God."

## The National Guard, Again

I remained in G Company for almost a year until my enlistment was up. I was sure I would never serve in the military again when I got out in 1980, but my military malaria came back in 1988 when I was a police officer in Austin, Texas.

My supervisor was a captain in the National Guard, and had recently been given command of a brand new unit that was being formed, the Long Range Surveillance Detachment. He asked me if I wanted to go back in and hang out with him. I went to the recruiter, signed up for the try-one-year program, took a physical in San Antonio and was cleared for enlistment in the Texas Army National Guard.

I had to take the ASVAB test which is used for job placement. When I asked the recruiter how I did, he said, "You can do anything you want." I asked to see my scores and was surprised to see that they had dramatically improved from when I took the same test twelve years before. I knew I wasn't any smarter, so I had to thank the Lord for his word in Romans 12:1 "Be renewed in the spirit of your mind."

I was first assigned to the communications section of the detachment and then as the operations sergeant. It was kind of fun to go to drill once a month and put my shoulder to the wheel with these eager young paratroopers who all wanted to be 'airborne rangers' and 'live a life of danger.' The cold war was on its last legs, and the chances of our going to war looked pretty slim. I tried to do my duty and insert realism into all the training exercises. I didn't know it yet, but I had two more wars coming my way.

## Epilogue

I lost track of everyone else I knew from Alpha Company that was still alive; the dead stayed on my mind. In 1968 I ran into Dennis Howley in the Washington National Airport. He had been to a meeting at the Pentagon and was returning to Fort Bragg and the Special Forces. He remained in Special Forces and eventually retired to Florida where, among other things, he taught scuba diving.

Two years after I got out of the army, Peter Clark called me out of the clear blue one day. He had heard from Rodney who told him where I lived. We were both surprised, me because he had found my number, and he because he thought I was killed on June 17th, which was true in a sense. Peter went on to law school and serves in government.

Bill Williamson recovered from his wounds, remained in the Army and raised a family. When I spoke with him on the phone after I started writing this, he asked me where I went after I left Vietnam. I told him that I went to this 'show business' infantry unit in Washington DC and hated it. He started laughing. I thought that he was just amused with my well-deserved discomfort, but no, he said, "I commanded the 'Old Guard' in the 1980s." He was an advisor to the director when the great movie "Gardens of Stone," was made at Fort Myer by the same guy who made "Apocalypse Now."[340]

Rodney Floutz retired in Texas and raises cattle. Jack Hyland is a lawyer in the mid-west. Donnie Gunby still lives in Georgia. About six months after my visit in 1968, he started having trouble with his joints, and after several trips to the doctor he was diagnosed with rheumatoid arthritis. The arthritis developed to the point that he was confined to a wheel chair. He went to the VA, but was told that since it happened more than a year after his discharge, it wasn't service connected and they sent him away. He married and raised a family and is now a grandpa.[341]

Don Gilliland left our unit on 11 June, six days before the fight on the 17th. His brother was a Navy Seabee and volunteered to serve in Vietnam so Don could come home. The military had a policy that no two family members need serve in a combat zone at the same time. Don went home but his brother John was killed in a plane crash at the end of his tour. Don said that he sees that crash every day.

I was with Jose Garcia forty-eight years later when he buried Janie, the love of his life. Together they had raised three children and were now grandparents. She had some serious health problems in the last few years of her life, and Jose was her full-time caregiver, still doing the work of a hero, still doing what needed to be done.

All the rest of the men that I was so close to back then have become like a vapor, gone to flowers, every one.

This is the end of book one.

Please look for:
Content With My Wages, A Sergeant's Story: Book II-Drug War
Content With My Wages, A Sergeant's Story: Book III-Afghanistan

See us on our website at: noendtopublishing.com
Email me: greg@noendtopublishing.com

# Appendix 1: Confessions

***Whenever a man has cast a longing eye on [offices] a rottenness begins in his conduct***
***Thomas Jefferson***

### The Politician

Lyndon B. Johnson retired from political life by refusing to run for re-election. By the time he left office in 1968, there were 500,000 U.S. troops in Vietnam and 36,900 U.S. dead. He spent his last years on his ranch in Stonewall, Texas where he drank, grew a ponytail, and poured out his troubles to a psychiatrist. There is no public knowledge of what he 'confessed' to that man, but the main subject of speculation has been his role in the murder of Kennedy; I wonder though, did he ever forget the chanting of the protesters in '68, "Hey, hey, LBJ, how many kids did you kill today." Johnson died in 1973.[333]

***...Render the account of your stewardship, for you can no longer be steward.***
***Luke 16:2***

### The Accountant

Robert McNamara was 'retired' by President Johnson in 1967, after he lost the will to win in Vietnam. In 1995, he published a book, "In Retrospect-The Tragedy and Lessons of Vietnam." This was the first 'confession' made by a senior member of those administrations, and the leading architect of the U.S. strategy in the Vietnam War. Arthur Schlesinger, Jr. wrote, "Can anyone remember a public official with the courage to confess error and explain where he and his country went wrong?" It stunned the veterans and the rest of their generation with its admissions. When he told JFK that he wasn't qualified to be Secretary of Defense, Kennedy should have listened.[334]

***Seek Responsibility and Take Responsibility For Your Actions***

### The U.S. Army Generals

**General Earl Wheeler**. General Wheeler gave an oral history to the LBJ Library in 1970. He held the party line and said nothing that would indicate that he knew or had done anything other than his duty. He died in 1975.[335]

**General Harold K. Johnson.** General Johnson served as Army Chief of Staff until 1968 when he was succeeded by General Westmoreland. In later years he wrote that his act of moral cowardice, not resigning when President Johnson refused to call up the reserves for Vietnam, would haunt him the rest of his life.[336]

**General William Westmoreland.** General Westmoreland died unrepentant for his role in the Vietnam War. Prohibited from conducting a maneuver war for territory, he chose a strategy of attrition and was forced to play the numbers game. In February of 1966, McNamara established the benchmark for success, the 'crossover point,' which was a numerical calculation showing that the U.S. was killing the Viet Cong at a faster rate than the VC could replace them.

In August of 1967, Westmoreland's headquarters staff briefed the press that the 'crossover point' had been reached. Later that month in a conference in Washington, DC, Westmoreland's representatives refused to add the CIA's number of VC political cadre and militia to the number of 'military forces' in their order of battle assessment. Those numbers would have shown McNamara and the President that the ranks of the insurgents were growing in spite of our attrition.[337]

After the war, Westmoreland sued CBS News for alleging that he had 'cooked the books' with regard to the number of Viet Cong he was facing in August of 1967. Testifying, Major General Joseph McChristian, Westmoreland's Intelligence Officer (J2) between 1965 and 1967 stated, "I think for a military man to withhold a report based on political implications would be improper."

Westmoreland withdrew his lawsuit, and General McChristian said that Westmoreland, "in being loyal to the President, was disloyal to his country." When asked, was he [Westmoreland] also being self-serving? "Yes," concluded McChristian. During an interview in 1990, he said, "DePuy and Chaisson asked me to change the reporting to indicate that we had reached the crossover point. We did not reach it. Phil Davidson came in after me and said we had."[338]

**General William DePuy.** General DePuy looked back on his time in Vietnam and confessed in an interview, "I guess I was surprised a little bit, too, after I took over the division, about the difficulty we had in finding the VC. We hit more dry holes than I thought we were going to hit, they were more elusive than I had expected, they controlled the battle better. They were the ones who usually decided whether or not there would be a fight…

"I wish that we had all been smart enough to say in 1965, when we went in, "That's what they are going to do to us." If we had been that smart then maybe we wouldn't have gone in…But, I don't remember anybody saying that, do you? Not even the experts, the scholastics, or the academics said that. Oh, there was one who did, Francois Sully, who is now dead. Now, the reason he did is because he had been through it before with the French. He told me and he told others. He said, 'You're never going to win it. You're not going to be able to find them. You're going to thrash around and you're only going to fight the battles that they win.' Well, he wasn't quite right. He wasn't right in every detail, but he was right in net and sum."

He later continued, "I guess my biggest surprise, and this was a surprise in which I have lots of company, was that the North Vietnamese and the Viet Cong would continue the war despite the punishment they were taking, I guess I should have expected that. I guess I should have studied human nature and the history of Vietnam and of revolutions and should have known it, but I didn't. I really thought that the kind of pressure they were under would cause them to perhaps knock off the war for a while, as a minimum, or even give up and go back north, I understand that from 1965 to '69 they lost over 600,000 men. But, I was completely wrong on that. That was a surprise."[339]

These are interesting words coming from the man that the army appointed to the positions of Director, Counterinsurgency, Special Warfare (DCSOPS) and Special Assistant for Counterinsurgency and Special Activities (SACSA). But, once again, that aura coming from his stint in the 'secret world' dazzled the eyes of the uninitiated.

## Appendix 2: General DePuy's Commanders Notes # 1-2

(Extract from the 1st Infantry Division Operational Report and Lessons Learned, dated:1 January-30 April 1966.)

HEADQUARTERS, 1ST INFANTRY DIVISION
Office of the Commanding General
APO San Francisco 96345

AVID-CG 27 March, 1966

Subject: Commanders Notes - #1

To: See Distribution

1. This is the first of what will be a series of Notes based on the observations of the Division Commander during operations, training, and base camp operations.
2. Training: Rotation, battlefield casualties, sickness and other causes is already high and may increase. The turn-over is greatest at the level of the squad, section and platoon where the greatest number of casualties are taken and where sickness and other disabilities are most prevalent. There is a great store of combat experience in the 1st Division, but that experience can quickly disappear. Therefore the division is faced with the problem of fighting and training at the same time. All commanders will devote their personal attention to training at every available opportunity. Emphasis will be at the squad, section, platoon level. Experience and lessons learned must be pushed down to brigade, battalion, company, troop and battery commander through an imaginative, continuous aggressive training program. Nothing will be taken for granted.
3. Operations:
a. Henceforth no rifle company in the 1st Division will advance either in the open or closed terrain with three platoons on line. Each commander at company and battalion level will always have a reserve element in hand, under control, prepared for immediate commitment.
b. The term or phrase "pinned down" is no longer part of the vocabulary of the 1st Division. Troops must anticipate that meeting engagements with the VC will involve a heavy volume of initial VC fire. At this time, naturally, commanders and troops will not be able to walk freely along the battle front. However, they will not regard themselves as pinned down but rather will accept this condition as the normal and natural initiation of close infantry combat. Forward elements closely engaged will automatically become a base of fire. Commanders at the squad and platoon level will advance their men into the base of fire positions, by crawling if necessary. A heavy volume of fire will be returned by all hands and at any time the VC fire either slackens or stops, the base of fire will improve its position by moving forward-even if forward movement is only a matter of 5 meters at a time and the mode of advance is by crawling. ***Under NO circumstances, repeat, NO circumstances will the forward element in contact withdraw in order to bring artillery fire on the VC. The base of fire will stand fast and reinforce if***

***necessary. Contact will be maintained if necessary throughout the night.*** (Italics mine)

c. Upon initial contact, company commanders will immediately commit their reserve platoons around one flank or the other and will immediately begin artillery and mortar fire to their front. In the jungle, this fire may be started some distance in front of the position and walked back toward the position until safety requires that it be brought no further. This artillery fire even though it may be hind the forward VC elements in contact, will be continued. It will prevent the VC from reinforcing, withdrawing or maneuvering. At no time will company commanders lose control of their forward elements or battalion commanders of their companies, so that the maximum fire power can be brought into the VC position to the immediate front.

d. During the first 5 to 10 minutes of a meeting engagement, the chances are the VC will have the advantage. He will initiate combat at the place and time of his choosing--usually from prepared positions. After the first 5 to 10 minutes, the combat advantage will begin to shift rapidly in favor of 1st Division forces as additional fire power is brought to bear. The maximum casualty producing weapons are light, medium, and heavy artillery and airstrike. Commanders of companies, battalions, and brigades, upon engagement, will immediately analyze the situation on the map and by visual observation and will bring airstrikes and artillery into all areas through which the VC may be withdrawing, reinforcing or maneuvering. An ample quantity of artillery ammunition is available and will be used. I expect that hundreds of rounds of ammunition will be fired into the vicinity and on VC positions. The battalion and brigade commanders will bring in continuous airstrikes and they will use imagination in the selection of targets.

e. Once the VC is engaged, all commanders will use initiative and imagination to commit all available forces and block all possible routes of withdrawal within their capabilities. Until such times as the routes of withdrawal can be physically blocked, they will be blocked by interdiction. Encirclement will be maintained until the VC is eliminated. There will be no pulling back into a perimeter at night during such an action.

f. SATURATION PATROLLING: Increasingly, battalions will be assigned the mission of saturation patrolling in extensive areas as large as 10 kilometers on a side. Progressively, units will learn to operate independently down to platoon level. Initially, platoon operations will be done in the day time, pulling back into company perimeters at night and after a reasonably short period of experience in this mode platoons will operate independently night, and day. The greatest payoff for platoon operations will be at night. The safety of a rifle platoon operating independently depends on two things:

(1) Repeated movement, including movement after dark so that VC forces cannot conduct a planned attack, but rather must conduct an open tactical maneuver, This is not their most effective method of operating, and during such engagements they are extremely vulnerable to artillery and mortar fire. All platoon leaders and platoon sergeants will direct and adjust artillery fire during such operations. (2) While operating independently, then contact is always imminent, platoon leaders will control and maneuver their elements so that at least a squad base of fire covers all advances across open terrain toward positions which may or may not be occupied by the VC.

g. In temporary defensive positions two man emplacements will be constructed so that there is a berm to the front and firing positions on either side with about a 45 degree angle of cross fire. This will permit the regaining of fire superiority without exposing each soldier to direct fire from the front when an attack is initiated by the VC with a heavy volume of small arms and recoilless rifle fire.
h. It will be a normal operating procedure in the 1st Division to position artillery batteries and single rifle companies in forward bases of fire. These positions will be moved with sufficient frequency so that they will normally not be susceptible to coordinated attacks by large forces. However, they will be subject frequently to probes and attacks of up to company size. The troops must be cautioned to expect and to handle this size of engagement. Additionally, combat reconnaissance by platoon and company size elements will be normal. Rifle platoons are expected to be able to handle VC companies; companies to handle battalions and battalions to handle regiments during initial engagements of 4 – 6 - 10 hours until reinforcements can be brought in.

HEADQUARTERS, 1ST INFANTRY DIVISION
Office of the Commanding General
APO San Francisco 96345

AVID-CG 18 April, 1966

Subject: Commanders Notes -#2

To: See Distribution

1. During the Division's operation in Phuoc Tuy, a wide variation in the quality of battalions was noticeable. There were many reasons for this, but the most obvious cause was a difference in the utilization of non-commissioned officers. In those battalions, companies, and platoons in which the non-commissioned officers had been given responsibility and authority, the troops were habitually alert, properly dug in, weapons were clean, security was out and morale was up.
In those battalions, companies and platoons in which the senior non-commissioned officers either were not present or had not been given responsibility and authority, troops tended to be more sluggish, bivouac areas were unkempt, defensive positions were either not dug or not adequate, and security was lax. It is apparent at a moment's notice whether or not the NCO system is working in a unit.
Hereafter, First Sergeants and Sergeants Major will always accompany their units to the field, commanders at all echelons will delegate to the non-commissioned officers the necessary authority to perform their duties and will hold the non-commissioned officers responsible for discharging those duties satisfactorily. Corrections will be made through the NCOs. Those NCOs who are performing well will be recommended immediately for promotion and those who do not measure up will be reported for reassignment or reduction.
2. Generally speaking, company size units are not placing security out at a sufficient, distance to protect themselves against surprise, or even to locate nearby VC forces. Patrolling by company size units for their own defense is still not

adequate. As a consequence, certain units have afforded the VC opportunity to deploy around them in strength, undetected, with grievous consequences to the units involved.

3. The nature of the war in Vietnam is conducive to the relaxation of appropriate security measures. All commanders, from squad up, must require patrolling, local security and digging in even though they know that 99 times out of 100, the VC may not attack or be in the vicinity. The individual soldier will not take these measures voluntarily and this is the great challenge to leadership inherent in the war in Vietnam, On the other hand, each soldier who is hospitalized or killed because of the laxness of his commander who may not have required him to take the necessary protective stops would have chosen in retrospect to have been forced to do so.

4. The vast majority of American fighting men are brave and tenacious in battle. They take care of their buddies and when pressed to the wall, will fight like tigers even after suffering multiple wounds. This fact was again demonstrated during the valiant fight by C Company, 2d Battalion, 16th Infantry north of Binh Gia, It is the responsibility and constant preoccupation of all commanders to see to it that those soldiers are given every conceivable advantage over the Viet Cong and that every military precaution is taken to avoid surprise and resulting casualties. Battalions and brigades must further improve their technique of calling in quickly and accurately the massive supporting fires available. The techniques for continuing these fires during medical evacuation must be developed with imagination and ingenuity. Battalion and brigade staffs, particularly S2, S3, S3 Air, and Air and Artillery Liaison officers, must not become preoccupied with the tactical play-of infantry units so that they fail to perform their own decisively important function of fire support.

5. Air mobile operations have often been nothing more than an air lift exercise rather than a carefully planned, well executed heliborne assault operation. Battalion commanders and company commanders have not been brought sufficiently into air mobile planning, but rather have too often been merely passengers on an administrative air movement. Hereafter, except in extreme emergencies, infantry commanders will be given one hour prior to a heliborne assault to coordinate with the air lift commander for the details of an assault operation. Brigade commanders may coordinate, but will not cut the battalion level out of the planning or execution phase. For each operation there will be an air lift commander who personally will coordinate down to battalion level. Flight leaders are not a substitute for the air lift commander.

W.E. DePuy,
Maj Gen, USA
Commanding

Incl 5 to Operational Report on Lessons Learned, 1 Jan-30 Apr 66

## Appendix 3: General Hay's Fundamentals of Infantry Tactics

DEPARTMENT OF THE ARMY
HEADQUARTERS 1ST INFANTRY DIVISION
APO San Francisco 96345

AVDB –CG                                                                                    25 August 1967

SUBJECT: Fundamentals of Infantry Tactics

TO: Brigade, Battalion, and Company Commanders

1. Swift and enduring lessons in tactics are taught by the Viet Cong, but combat experience is a hard and costly school. I am concerned that as our leaders rotate, our battle-won wisdom shrinks. However, I am convinced that if we help successor leaders to grasp a few tactical principles and basic techniques, victory--and comparatively inexpensive victory--will invariably crown our future undertakings. Therefore, I have asked a group of seasoned officers to draw up the enclosed compendium based on their combat experiences. I direct each of you to study it carefully, and to use it as your guideline for operations and training.
2. I will expect to find in your command, at the minimum, evidence of your attention to and emphasis upon:
a. Exploiting artillery and air firepower for all missions.
b. Maintaining security and dispersion under all circumstances.
c. ***Moving to contact with particular care to find the enemy with scouts.***
d. Controlling advanced elements tightly, so that at any time precise position of units is known, and immediate use of air and artillery is possible.
e. Searching the battlefield with system and thoroughness.
f. Digging defensive positions which are well fortified to the front and overhead, with weapons sited painstakingly for maximum surprise and flanking fire upon an assaulting enemy.
3. The hallmarks of 1st Division leaders, our distinctive professional traits, have been (1) violent, massive firepower; (2) firm control of maneuver at all times; (3) security under all conditions; (4) cloverleaf patrolling and (5) deep foxholes with full frontal berm overhead cover, and 45 degree firing ports

That future leaders of the Big Red One are similarly endowed is my most serious responsibility, and yours.

J.H. HAY
MG, USA
Commanding

1. The Enemy
2. Big Red One Battle Principles
3. Defense
4. Offense

## THE ENEMY

1. INTELLIGENCE IS FOR ALL COMMANDERS: The tactical area of interest (TAOI) of the 1st Division encompasses BINH DUONG Province-the seedbed of armed communism in Vietnam-eastern War Zone C, western War Zone D, and the infiltration routes through BINH LONG and PHUOC LONG Provinces. Table I identifies the principal Viet Cong formations operating within the TAOI, both main force and local force. 1st Division leaders should take advantage of every available opportunity to learn about these units, and their strengths and weaknesses. In this war, intelligence cannot be relegated to staff specialists; it governs our tactics no less than our plans and operations.

2. MAIN FORCE UNITS:

a. Since 1962 the Viet Cong have relied strategically on main force units of regiment and division size, composed of full time soldiers. The 9th Light Infantry Division, among the oldest and most successful of the VC main force organizations, operated during 1965 north of SAIGON down to the metropolitan suburbs. Since 1965 operations of the 1st Division have driven the 9th Division northward, away from the centers of population, into the jungles of War Zones C and D. A series of tactical defeats by the 1st Division have seriously depleted the regiments of the 9th Division, and its original South Vietnamese soldiers have been replaced by North Vietnamese to a significant degree, especially among the cadre and leaders.

b. Main force units normally operate in elements no smaller than battalion, and are well equipped with a full range of modern infantry weapons, including heavy machine guns, mortars, and recoilless rifles. Within the War Zones, 120am mortars have been encountered, and artillery and artillery rockets also must be expected. Unit communication equipment largely wire, with some radios-is adequate. Some weaknesses may lie in the morale, motivation, and state of training of the VC soldiers within main force units stemming from tensions between Northerners and Southerners, continued deprivation of the pleasures of civilization, lack of familiarity with the terrain, disease, and in some instances starvation. These occasionally detract from unit efficiency, but not dependably so.

3. LOCAL FORCE UNITS: The Viet Cong continue to wage intensive war with full time guerrillas (organized usually into district companies or provincial battalions), part-time guerrillas (usually district companies), and village militia (clandestine activists). Local force units are often, but not always, poorly equipped in most respects, but the local force guerrilla can be a better trained, more resolute foe than his main force counterpart. The style of the main force is regimental attack or ambush; that of the local force a two-man claymore attack or a road mining. The strength of the local force is the guerrilla's ability, through long familiarity with his own neighborhood, to merge with the populace or fade quickly into a base camp once he strikes.

4. BASE CAMPS:

a. For both main force and local force units, base camps are essential for survival. Deeply rooted in Communist doctrine is the importance of a "secure base area" for guerrilla operations. The local force units tend to place their reliance on numerous small camps dispersed throughout their areas of operations. In BINH

DUONG Province virtually every patch of woods conceals at least one small circular entrenchment with associated bunkers and tunnels, and each local force unit has at least one elaborately fortified refuge; larger units have a tunnel complex in which their hospital and headquarters are located. Some of these tunnels are more than 20 years old, and many are hundreds of meters in length. Local force base camps are usually extensively booby trapped, and often protected by punji pits. Main force base camps are usually not so well guarded by mines; they are, of course, larger, and frequently include training facilities, such as rifle ranges and classrooms. Having constructed numerous, well-fortified, pre-stocked base camps throughout his area of operations, the enemy may shift his forces as the situation dictates, either for offensive or for defensive reasons.

b. Any defended Viet Cong base camp presents a formidable problem to attackers. One local force squad has been known to withstand assault by two US infantry companies, and even a VC sniper or two, firing from within a mined camp, can inflict numerous casualties on a maneuvering force. Obliteration of local base camps and surrounding jungles using bulldozers has unquestionably been effective. However, our attempts to demolish base camps, using explosives, have been comparatively unsuccessful. Evidence suggests that the enemy soon re-enters and restores partially damaged base camps unless constant patrolling, or other US counter-action prevents him.

5. COMMUNICATION-LIAISON ROUTES: The military organization of the enemy is patterned after the cellular organization of the Communist party. General dissemination of combat intelligence, and even information on Viet Cong dispositions is rare; leaders are discouraged from inquiring into situations beyond their own unit and area of operation. Accordingly, fixed communication liaison routes assume great importance to the Viet Cong units moving from one zone to another, since they must usually follow an established chain of base camps using a series of guides to pass from one area to the other. Supply parties and messengers follow the same routes; frequent "out-outs" and transfer points are prescribed. US interdiction of such routes invariably causes confusion and dismay.

6. VC ATTACKS: Viet Cong offensive operations are usually launched from a base camp, and participating troops are well rehearsed in withdrawal routes, primary and alternate, from the point of attack to the same or another base camp. It is important to appreciate that all enemy military doctrine is couched in offensive terminology. Viet Cong "counter sweep" operations-the posture the Viet Cong assume to defend against large search and destroy operations-are described in their orders and other documents in terms of attacks by small groups upon the advancing enemy. In practice, this means the enemy units dispatch small elements to conduct harassing counter-attacks with mortars, rifle grenades, claymores, and other mines as the situation permits. This tactic is intended to maintain close contact with our forces, thus reducing vulnerability to our fires. Counter-sweeps also visualize the gradual intensification of harassing actions up to and including all out attacks upon our forces once they appear fatigued or depleted, and their strengths and vulnerabilities have been accurately appraised. The terminology "attack" embraces any means of producing casualties among allied forces, including setting pressure mines in the road. Mortar attacks on US bases, both artillery field positions and our permanent bases, is a preferred Viet Cong mode of offensive action. A meeting engagement outside fortifications with Viet Cong

forces larger than platoon is rare, but there have been at least three instances in the past year of a Viet Cong force engaging, by what appeared to be an impromptu ambush, a US rifle company patrolling in the jungle. The Viet Cong prefer better odds and more carefully reconnoitered and planned operations. One favored form is the regimental ambush of a vehicular column on a road-a tactic to which the 9th Light Infantry Division resorted three times in the course of two months in the summer of 1966. Another preference is a regimental assault upon a US defensive position. Post-battle analysis suggests that the enemy plans his maneuver basically on terrain information, that is, knowing we were occupying a position in a given clearing, he maneuvered into position to attack the clearing. However, usually his attack was preceded by ground reconnaissance and probes designed to single out locations of our automatic weapons, and identify weak points in our defense. Invariably, his attacks were preceded by intense mortaring and numerous volleys from direct fire weapons. His assault, when it was launched, was delivered over a wide front, but he concentrated a large mass of his infantry in considerable depth upon one small sector of our position in an effort to penetrate at that point. A number of these large scale attacks were launched in the early morning hours, as though the attackers expected to capitalize upon the first daylight during the latter stages of their assault, when they had penetrated our position. The assault itself was intense and aggressively pressed, with heavy reliance being placed on hand grenades as well as the submachine gun. All these attacks were markedly unsuccessful; enemy initiated ground attacks were the greatest single source of enemy losses over the past year.

**TABLE I: PRINCIPAL VIET CONG FORCES IN THE 1ST INFANTRY DIVISION TAOI**

**MAIN FORCES, [Their] AREA OF OPERATIONS-REMARKS**

**9th VC Division**: A highly mobile light infantry division which normally conducts regimental size operations. Oldest VC division in the III Corps Tactical Zone, this division has been the 1st Infantry Division's primary opponent. Its AO is War Zones C+D.
271st VC Regiment
272d VC Regiment
273d VC Regiment

**7th NVA Division:** Elements of this division entered the Corps Tactical Zone in 1965. It is believed the division was formed during 1966. Ridden with disease, this unit is only just beginning to be a combat effective unit. It's AO is PHUOC LONG and BINH LONG Provinces War Zone C
52d NVA Regiment
141st NVA Regiment
165th NVA Regiment

**101st NVA Regiment:** Independent mobile regiment formerly under the operational control of the 9th VC Division.

## LOCAL FORCES

**PHU LOI Battalion:** AO is BINH DUONG Province. A well trained, high morale provincial battalion. The 1st Infantry Division has had frequent contacts with this battalion. It is the principal local force battalion in the division area.
Viet Cong district companies which vary in strength from 50 to 120 men. These companies are armed with mixed weapons. Their combat effectiveness varies from the highly proficient with high morale to those which are combat ineffective in other than platoon level operations. These companies operate within their districts and reinforce the hamlet and village guerrillas.
C61 Company South BEN CAT District
C62 Company CHANH THANH District
C63 Company LAI THIEU District
C64 Company DAU TIENG District
C70 Company BINH LONG
C81 Company North BEN CAT District

## POLITICAL HEADQUARTERS, AREA OF OPERATIONS-REMARKS

**COSVN**: Located in War Zone C. Political and military headquarters directing all military and political elements of the Viet Cong effort in the majority of South Vietnam.

**Military Region I**: Located in War Zone D. Subordinate to COSVN. Controls and directs VC activity in all of the III Corps area except SAIGON, BINH LONG, BINH TUY, and PHUOC LONG areas.

**Military Region IV**: Located in Southeastern BINH DUONG Controls VC activity, political and military, in SAIGON and its surrounding district.

**Military Region 10**: Probably located in PHUOC LONG New region in two northernmost provinces of III Corps area-BINH LONG and PHUOC LONG. Training and recuperation base for infiltrating units.

## BIG RED ONE BATTLE PRINCIPLES

1. Infantry, armor, and Army aviation find the enemy.
2. Air and artillery kill the enemy.
3. Battalion commanders must know unit locations within 10 meters at all times.
4. Keep plans and schemes of maneuver simple.
5. Put your back to a landing zone.
6. Foxholes are deep, properly sited, camouflaged, have full overhead cover and a frontal protective berm.

## DEFENSE

**1. TEAMWORK**: The 1st Division has earned well a reputation for building sound defenses, and fighting from them magnificently. But reputation will never defeat an attacking Viet Cong force. Perhaps more than any other type of operation, successful defense hinges on sound planning, hard preparatory work, vigorous execution, and aggressive follow-up at every level:

*The rifleman whose shovel, muscle, weapon, and courage are the foundation of the defense.

*The NCO whose know-how shapes and ties together the position, who leads the defenders at the point of decision.

*The company officer who lays out the position, and controls the infantry weapons.

*The battalion commander who selects key weapon positions, arranges artillery concentrations, and pre-planned air, and commands the fight on the ground.

*The brigade commander who supervises preparation, and manages from the air fires and exploiting maneuver.

**2. THE US COUNTER TO ENEMY ATTACK**: The Viet Cong are a tough and wily foe from whom surprises are to be expected. Nonetheless, their doctrine and training seems to compel them to follow a pattern. Usually their attacks are preceded by reconnaissance and light probes designed to delineate our positions, locate our key weapons, and identify weak spots in our line. They then bring their mortars and recoilless rifle well forward, and lay them directly on specific US weapons whose positions they fix during the reconnaissance. Their attack itself is heralded by intense fires from these heavy weapons, followed by a frontal assault of the US line. The assault infantry are normally led by submachine gunners firing continuously from the hip as they run, supplemented by grenadiers. 1st Division defenses are designed to frustrate both enemy heavy weapons, and enemy infantry assault. Table I outlines the means by which we counter specific enemy tactics.

**(Table One-Omitted)**

**3. FIGHTING POSITIONS**: The Big Red One fighting position adheres to the following principles:

a. A frontal protective berm to deflect direct fire.

b. Forty-five degree firing ports.

c. Full overhead cover.

d. Camouflaged to blend into the background.

e. Low silhouette.

f. Permits "Bee Hive" rounds to be fired without endangering occupants.

g. Is continually improved so long as position is occupied.

**4. SITE SELECTION**: Difficulty with an individual position-inability to perform mission or extensive labor--usually starts with poor choice of site. Leaders must look for the ground with best command of long graze in their sector, and emplace their automatic weapons there. They should also look for natural cover and concealment for positions, and use it well. Each machine gun should be protected by at least two rifle positions. Positions should be sited in depth, that is, displaced from front to rear 1O-50 meters from one another, as in the following idealized diagrams (figures 1 and 2). It is not sufficient for a company commander, platoon leader, or squad leader to simply locate his unit upon the general trace of a perimeter and begin to dig. These leaders must develop sensitivity for the defense possibility of any piece of ground their unit occupies. They must visualize how the defense of their assigned sector will develop. They must be alert to the slightest changes in the lie of the terrain; by moving the tentative location of a position as little as five feet, a fine field of fire may develop, or there may be provided a site offering classic cover and concealment. Leaders must develop the facility to visualize the role each position will play in the defense, and how the whole sector will interlock into a coordinated system of mutually supporting positions. They must walk the terrain, identify avenues of approach, and calculate how to defeat enemy assault on those approaches. In selecting his position the commander will, if possible, avoid pushing the defensive perimeter out to the tree line at the edge of a clearing. Well dug-in positions in the open, covered by listening posts in the forest, take advantage of available fields of fire, and are also less vulnerable to attack by mortars since tree bursts cannot impact directly upon the unit. The commander will site his fighting positions to form a perimeter in depth, avoiding a lineal or regular circle configuration, and to interlock positions for maximum mutual support by flanking and covering fires among individual positions. He will take steps to insure that every soldier will know his own field of fire and that of supporting positions, and that each of the subordinate leaders will know the same information for all the positions under his command, plus the planned mortar and artillery fires (to include planned "bee-hive" fires) which can support his area- of responsibility. Normally, he will establish a unit SOP for the defense and follow it, but any SOP must provide for siting or checking key positions by the defense commander, and his designating which shall be two, three, or four man positions.

**5. SEQUENCE OF WORK**:

a. Select site. Primary concern is fields of fire, but look also for natural cover and concealment for each position. Walk key machine gun final protective lines to check the selected position, and to identify dead space.

b. Plan camouflage. Calculate tow position will be blended into background, and establish paths for approaching site, for pitching tents, and for passing forward to clear fire lanes.

c. Dig a foxhole throwing up spoil to form a -berm, which is progressively packed, formed and apertured.

d. Clear (or preferable selectively thin out) fields of fire, to provide fire lane down each FPL, and observation over the whole assigned sector.

e. Complete walking FPL's and prepare range cards.

f. emplace claymores; a minimum of one per men. Emplace wire. A frontal perimeter barrier line of trip flares, plus concertina (if available), and obstacles along the friendly side or each FL.

h. Continue to improve foxhole. Stock hole with ammo, providing storage niches.

i. Put overhead cover on foxholes,

j. Complete camouflage of front,

k. Dig entrance trench, and supplementary hole(s), and camouflage them.

l. Camouflage tents and paths.

m. Dig communications trenches and reserve positions and camouflage. Camouflage will be replaced as needed, berm improved as appropriate, covered

**There was a break in the pages of the document. Pages 17 to 30 were missing. On page 31 he is describing tactical movement by small units.**

fire team will use overwatch within the fire team (half moving and half over-watching). The forward movement is by bounds. This type of movement again allows the minimum number of men to become engaged by the same source of firepower at once, and someone to return fire immediately. When this squad has moved 100 to 200 meters depending on terrain, the squad leader will set up a defense position and send his fire teams, one at a time, to the flanks in a cloverleaf. The fire team (clover-leafing) will advance using the overwatch within the fire team (half moving and half in a position over-watching). The other team will always be over-watching. When this action is completed, he will call the platoon leader who will displace the platoon forward, followed by the company until contact is made with the point. As soon as contact is made with the point, it will move out again repeating the same steps, the company will, upon closing on the point squad, set out security immediately and then send patrols out to the flanks. (Each rifle platoon will send a patrol to both flanks.) The patrols will go out, depending on terrain, no less than 40 meters. The rear platoon will, in addition to clover-leafing, send security to the rear. The platoon directly behind the company Hq group should send security to secure the command group. When all clover-leaf patrols have returned, the company commander must be notified so that he can move the company forward upon the call from the point element. This type of movement is slow and requires practice, good control and lots of patience: however, time and again, units using the cloverleaf have scouted out the enemy, destroyed him by fire, and then maneuvered in upon his positions without serious casualties. The cloverleaf method is slow. The company depicted (Figure I) will cover only about 2000 meters in eight hours of advancing. Some commanders who have elected to advance otherwise have taken heavy casualties in their lead platoon and suffered more attempting to extricate them. It is difficult to outline the application of the clover-leaf principle which would correspond to every situation. The preceding example is merely illustrative. Occasions will arise when greater speed of movement will be dictated by mission, terrain, or enemy situation. The clover-leaf principle holds that the rifle company will advance preceded by patrols in all directions. Successful employment of the clover-leaf principle requires intense practice: sand tables or chalk drills at platoon and company level, and practical exercises on terrain, as often as possible. Success also require patience of commanders at battalion level and above, for they must accept the inherently slower pace of advance which adherence to the clover-leaf principle demands.

**4. ACTIONS UPON CONTACT.** Enemy contact in the jungle usually occurs at point blank range, and more often than not the enemy will enjoy advantages of fortifications, snipers in trees, communication trenches, and minefields to his front and flanks. It is imperative that upon contact, at all echelons, teamwork begins as follows:

a. Company in contact. High volume of fire in direction of enemy, not neglecting trees. Immediately mark most advanced elements and flanks with smoke. Report direction (magnetic azimuth) to enemy, and range from one marking. Initiate artillery fire mission. ***Withdraw to place at least 50 meters between most forward element and enemy.*** Straighten line parallel to enemy line, or to desired airstrike

runs. Report estimated enemy strength, equipment, and direction withdrawal (if any).
b. Battalion commander. Immediately request FAC, airstrikes, and artillery observer. Locate precisely by map grid point of contact and mark for FAC. Initiate artillery blocking fires, if company FO has not done so. Alert reserves, medical evacuation aviation, and emergency resupply. Control airstrikes if company commander not in position to do so.
c. Commanders at all echelons. Aggressive instincts to flank the enemy position must be curbed. Once the enemy position is established, all commanders must strain their resources to bring available fires to bear on the enemy. Each commander from company on up must be capable of employing air and artillery, practiced in utilizing the channels of communications for each, and quick to initiate action to bring each into play. The most crucial information which the unit in contact must supply is the direction in which the enemy is withdrawing. Based on this sensing, commanders at higher echelons deliver fires to block the avenue of enemy withdrawal or reinforcement. Fires are shifted outward from the point of contact progressively, and are discontinued only when, in the judgment of the battalion or brigade commander, the enemy has escaped. The inception of a heavy volume of artillery fire, and sustained fire can be facilitated by:
(1) "walking" fires in advance of and to the flanks of the unit as it moves to contact, and (2) keeping the artillery shooting despite use of air in the target area. Upon contact, time should not be wasted on prolonged attempts to fix precise targets. It is imperative that the supporting fires be initiated immediately. They can be initiated at a greater distance and subsequently is worked toward the unit as the situation clarifies. Battalion and brigade commanders must continually keep informed of the location of friendly fire support bases, and periodically war game the simultaneous employment of air and artillery in the event of contact. As a rule, artillery should never be cut off to facilitate delivery of air; rather, it should be shifted to augment the air in a blocking role. Constantly adjusted air-artillery fire control lines can be employed, Experience confirms that once artillery is cut-off in favor of air, excessive time is lost in resuming fire. Experience also –underscores the importance of the battalion commander choosing correctly among the relative advantages of air and artillery in each given situation. In general, air is the preferred instrument in dense jungle, or against base camps, because it can be delivered dependably very close to troops. Napalm is a fine close support weapon, but should always be delivered parallel to the friendly front. CBU is deadly against enemy fortifications, and should also be delivered parallel. Bombs are the answer to VC emplacements. Light artillery is generally ineffective against fortifications, but is-a fine, high volume antipersonnel weapon capable of achieving local fire superiority if nothing else. Light artillery and mortars can, of course, be fired in close support, but these too perform more reliably fired parallel to friendly front. Medium and heavy artillery must be echeloned in depth from friendly troops, but can effectively destroy VC fortifications. The mastery of fire control and fire coordination is the most important challenge faced by battalion and brigade commanders in Vietnam. Delegation of fire coordination is impossible; only the commander or the S-3 has the feel for the situation required.
**5. FOLLOW-UP TO FIREPOWER:** When in the judgment of the commanders concerned fires on the enemy have been effective, the advance will be resumed.

Security to front and flanks is restored, and the unit enters the enemy position. At this time the mission of the infantry is thorough police of the battlefield. The Viet Cong are adroit at concealing personnel, arms, documents, and other valuables, and care and imagination are necessary for the searchers to ferret out the fruits of victory. Prisoners are especially valuable in this conflict, and pains should be taken to capture, safeguard, and treat medically any VC who survive our bombardment. Any documents, no matter how unimportant appearing they may be, should be evacuated. It should be a matter of pride to any infantry unit that an area it has searched is left devoid of intelligence.

**6. ROAD CLEARING OPERATIONS**: Offensive operations frequently entail securing a road for use as an MSR. In undertaking to clear a road, infantry commanders should commence operations by passing troops in V formation down the road, with the opening of the V in the direction of advance. The ends of the wings echeloned forward and outward from the road should be at least 100 meters away from the ditch-line, and the soldiers therein should be carefully instructed to search for wires and other signs of command detonated mines or claymores. At the point of the V, on the road itself, about 200 meters rearward, should be mine sweep teams. Experience establishes that the best mine detector we possess is an alert infantryman with a keen eye, noticing tracks, disturbances in the surface of the road, or wires. Once the initial clearing patrol moves down the road, the road must be secured against re-mining and snipers. Troops or armor assigned the securing mission must penetrate into the vegetation alongside the road to beyond-the limits of visibility, and must patrol actively. Above all, troops engaged in road clearing must remain alert and dispersed at all times; in any other posture, their court multiple casualties from claymores or other command detonated mines.

## Appendix 4: My Lessons Learned.

General. The duties of a sergeant are many. They can be divided into three categories: The Mission, The Men, and Me.[342]

**Communication** is the weak link in all military operations. Before a sergeant can begin his mission planning he must ensure that both he and his chain of command are on the same page with regard to the commander's intent. If there are questions, after issuing a warning order to his element, he must push for clarification from at least two levels above him. The LT may not be able to grasp the possible problems and he must be persuaded to seek answers from above.

**The mission** requires a sergeant to master many skills and to teach them to his subordinates. Map Reading and more importantly, orienteering are critical skills. If the GPS is down, you're screwed if you didn't bring or can't use a map.

Calling for fire, close air support, and medical evacuation are perishable skills that require constant practice. Use of radios, improvised antennas, and commo procedures should be second nature for a leader. Small unit tactics and movement techniques—immediate action drills have to be rehearsed incessantly.

**Leadership**. The officer/sergeant relationship has continued to evolve. At the heart of the matter is the phrase, "Centralization of Command and Decentralization of Execution." Officers should tell their subordinates what they want done, not how to do it. This concept of leadership is based on a cohesive unit and habitual relationships. It requires a continual interaction between all members of a unit. Commanders must insure that their intent is understood so brief-backs are a useful tool.

**Marksmanship**. Every soldier should first be an expert with his weapon. This can be achieved by intensive marksmanship training with downrange feedback for every round that is fired. The sergeant must identify the strong shooters and develop them as coaches for the weak ones. Once the sergeant's element is able to shoot straight, then he must add conditions of stress to the marksmanship program. Physical stress to include heavy physical fitness events must be added prior to shooting.

**Rules of Engagement.** ROE training needs to be completely revamped. Counterinsurgency warfare is usually much closer to police work than mid-intensity combat. Shoot/No Shoot scenario training is critical. Changing the mindset of the infantry and others who will respond with small arms fire to perceived threats is at the heart of the transition and it must be done by experienced professionals and driven from the top. In doing these things he begins to take care of the men while insuring that the mission will continue to be in the forefront of his element. The men are the sergeant's element and he must endeavor to know them and care for their needs. After he has done all he can for the mission and the men, the sergeant needs to care for himself by seeking self-improvement.

Self-improvement includes many subjects; besides professional development courses and physical fitness, the one critical focus for a sergeant or an officer is the study of military history. Within military history, one must study the human element. Memoirs and thinly disguised 'novels' are best for this kind of study. As SLA Marshall said, "the study of war is the study of human nature.".

## Appendix 5: Stilwell, DePuy, and the Vietnam War

**Now it is not good for the Christian's health to hustle the Aryan brown,**
**For the Christian riles, and the Aryan smiles and he weareth the Christian down;**
**And the end of the fight is a tombstone white with the name of the late deceased,**
**And the epitaph drear: "A Fool lies here who tried to hustle the East."**[343]

It was fifty years ago that our government was contemplating its next move in Vietnam. The presidential elections were in November and President Johnson was doing everything he could to present himself as the peace candidate, "We are not about to send American boys 9 or 10 thousand miles away from home to do what Asian boys ought to be doing for themselves." Now, the 2014 mid-term elections have passed and there are calls for war in the Middle-East. It's like Deja vu all over again.[344]

The debate about who was responsible for the United States losing the war in Vietnam has raged for almost forty years. I have to confess that I, like many other veterans, was not able to put the war behind me and spent an inordinate amount of time reading the many books that have tried to explain how we won or lost the war. Then the thought came to me one day: Who started the war?

When did the war start? When did our involvement in yet another country struggling to define itself in the post-colonial chaos turn into combat operations for our regular forces? It seemed right to point to the events leading up to the Gulf of Tonkin Resolution. President Lyndon Johnson used those incidents to justify deploying U.S. combat troops to Vietnam.

The Gulf of Tonkin episodes have been intensely scrutinized: Were there torpedo boats attacking U.S. destroyers? Were there torpedoes in the water? We're not concerned with those questions here.

This is not about conspiracies either, but about covert operations and something known as 'plausible deniability.' It's also about two actors on a stage in Southeast Asia during America's entry into the first war we lost. Both of these men came from humble beginnings. Both went through the great depression and fought in WWII. They both saw the army as a place where they could make their way to high positions with the attendant benefits.

These actors were soldiers emanating the 'special' aura that is associated with men who have come from the 'secret world' of espionage and covert operations. "They were skilled in combat operations and they also excelled at bureaucratic infighting which is not simply about coming out on top but the ability to so cover one's tracks as to appear utterly blameless."[345]

This is also about why history repeats itself, and learning lessons is beyond the capacity of most professional soldiers. My thesis was developed, when in 2003, I watched the U.S effort in Afghanistan almost mirror the early part of the Vietnam War. Much of our bungling in Afghanistan and Iraq can be traced backed to the machinations of these two men.

For me, it's also personal. One of these 'actors' ran me and my battalion ragged for months at a time as we beat the bushes looking for 'Charlie.' That in itself wasn't problematic, other than his ruthless disregard for our rest and recovery; but knowing that he referred to us, his sergeants and privates, as his 'little people' infuriates me to this day.

## Covert Operations

Covert operations were codified in National Security Council Directive (NSC 10/2) of 18 June, 1948, which established the Office of Special Projects. In it, the NSC, recognizing the need to counter the covert operations of the USSR, directed the Office of Special Projects, later renamed the Office of Policy Coordination (OPC) of the CIA, to plan and execute certain operations.

These operations were to be planned and executed in such a way, "that any US Government responsibility for them is not evident to unauthorized persons and that if uncovered the US Government can plausibly disclaim any responsibility for them."

These operations would include: "propaganda, economic warfare; preventive direct action, including sabotage, anti-sabotage, demolition and evacuation measures; subversion against hostile states, including assistance to underground resistance movements, guerrillas and refugee liberation groups, and support of indigenous anti-communist elements in threatened countries of the free world."[346]

The OPC began recruiting from Wall Street, the 'old boy' network of former OSS operatives, and the armed forces. One of the first recruited from the military was Richard Stilwell, a colonel in the U.S. Army. Stilwell was a West Point graduate and a veteran of WWII. He served as the operations officer (G3) for the 90th Infantry Division which saw combat in Normandy and was part of Patton's Third Army. In 1947 he was a military advisor to the U.S. Ambassador to Italy which was going through a tumultuous struggle against communist efforts to take power. The communists were thwarted in part by one of the first successful OPC operations, and when Richard Stilwell left Italy he was with OPC.[347]

## The Korean War (in China)

Stilwell was appointed chief of the Far East Division, and when the Korean War broke out, he began recruiting 90th Division men he knew and could trust. One of these men was LTC William DePuy. DePuy had held several staff positions and was a battalion commander in the 90th Infantry Division. Highly decorated, DePuy chose to remain in the army after the war and requested intelligence duty. He took a one year Russian language course and was trained to be a military attache in Moscow, but was sent instead to Hungary where he impressed his superiors with the performance of his duties. When the Korean War started, he was recovering from a broken leg so instead of going to Korea, he was detailed to the OPC.[348]

DePuy's biographer covers these activities with a broad brush, no doubt due to DePuy's own reluctance to give any details. DePuy described them saying, "It was a very active life and rather exciting. I have to say in retrospect that it was not all that productive, but everyone was working hard...So, I'll go this far: we were involved in a very covert operation against China."[349]

DePuy was chief of the China Branch of OPC. The covert operation DePuy referred to had at least two components: commando raids on the southern coast of mainland China under the Western Enterprises Incorporated (WEI) cover and Operation Paper.

LTC Ray Peers, former commander of OSS Detachment 101 in Burma during WWII, an experienced unconventional warfare specialist, ran the WEI commando raids from Taiwan, but used various small islands along the China coast from which to strike the mainland. Later, Peers became famous as the investigator of the My Lai massacre during the Vietnam War.

Among his helpers was Robert Barrow, a future commandant of the Marine Corps, and several other 90th Division veterans. These men trained local Chinese to be commandos. Some were dropped by parachute, but most of them took part in over-the-beach, hit-and-run raids.[350]

Samuel Halpern, a senior CIA officer, while serving in the Far-East Division of OPC had this to say about Operation Paper: "Somebody in the Pentagon…had the bright idea that the way to draw Chinese Communist forces away from Korea would be to attack China through the back door, as they called it: from Burma into Yunnan Province…They're talking about creating this army for the attack by using Chinese Nationalist forces from Taiwan plus those who might have escaped out of China into Burma and into northern Thailand.

"We would support and ferry these Chinese Nationalists from Taiwan to Bangkok to the back door of China in Burma. Chinese Nationalist troops were flown from Taiwan…and then we dropped them into northern Burma. From there they invaded China. The Chinese Communists let them walk in and then destroyed them. The OSO (CIA Office of Special Operations)…discovered that the chief radio operator for the Li Mi troops happened to be a Chinese Communist agent."

Halpern goes on to say, "Bill DePuy honestly believed that Jiang Jieshi (Chiang Kai-Shek) had a million guerrilla forces waiting on the Chinese mainland to rise against the Chinese Communists." Then Halpern says that DePuy, when told that the OSO was collecting against the Chinese Nationalists to learn of their intentions said, '"How dare you try to penetrate and spy on our friends and allies."'[351]

The culmination of Stilwell's and DePuy's adventures with the OPC was a closely guarded fiasco known in the CIA as the 'Thailand Flap.' It started when the DCI had ordered an investigation of opium trading under the cover of trying to overthrow the Communist government.

Then came the murder by an OPC officer, of the OSO officer who was investigating drug flows through Thailand. According to R. Harris Smith, a former CIA officer, "Bedell Smith (DCI)…summoned the OPC's Far East director, Richard Stilwell, and in the words of an agency eyewitness, 'gave him such a violent tongue lashing' that 'the colonel went down the hall in tears.'"[352]

Bedell Smith's final word on the whole affair was: "There is no point in bemoaning opportunities lost…nor attempting to alibi past failures," he wrote in a letter to General Matthew B. Ridgway, MacArthur's successor as chief of the Far East Command, "I have found, through painful experience, that secret operations are a job for the professional and not for the amateur."[353]

### Intelligence

The 'secret world' of western intelligence has been bedeviled with increasing frequency by covert action military enthusiasts since WWII. The British, faced with a shrinking empire, used their intelligence services to generate smoke, and wave mirrors, creating the illusion that Britain was still a world power. After all, for several hundred years, they had played the 'Great Game' with Russia for world domination.

Not everyone was impressed with the 'intelligence' from the spy agencies of those times: "You listen too much to the soldiers...You should never trust the experts," said Lord Salisbury to the Viceroy of India in 1877. "If you believe the doctors, nothing is wholesome, if you believe the soldiers, nothing is safe."[354]

## The OSS

At the beginning of WWII, British Intelligence was largely responsible for educating and training the founders of America's first spy agency, the Office of Strategic Services (OSS). This 'special relationship' continues to this day. The OSS conducted intelligence gathering and special operations in Europe, Asia, and Africa during the war. Its founder, Major General William 'Wild Bill' Donovan, tried to keep his organization intact when the war ended. But President Truman disbanded it and then reformed it as the Central Intelligence Agency (CIA).[355]

## The CIA

Some wartime intelligence personnel stayed on with the new agency and some returned to the military. Others went back to the business and academic worlds where they all formed a network which Eisenhower later called the Military-Industrial Complex. It would have been better named the Military-Industrial-Intelligence Complex.

The CIA was intended to be an information analysis agency, but as the Cold War heated up, they were soon conducting covert and clandestine operations. From the beginning, military personnel were 'seconded' or transferred to the CIA. There they entered into the 'secret world' of 'plausible deniability' where accountability was minimal and everything was classified. The CIA inscribed a verse from the Gospel of John on a wall in the lobby of their headquarters, "and ye shall know the Truth and the Truth shall make you free." But in their collective heart was their real motto, "Admit nothing, deny everything, and make counter-accusations"[356]

Duty, Honor, Country doesn't blend well with admit nothing, deny everything, etc. When career considerations and self-esteem are mixed in, it takes the highest character to resist the temptations to avoid accepting responsibility for one's actions by conveniently covering one's mistakes with a security classification and moving on.

The military officers who did tours with the civilian intelligence community were 'made men' when they returned to the armed forces. Many of them played major roles, though often behind the scenes, in the events leading up to and during the Vietnam War. Richard Stilwell and William DePuy were leading players.

Stilwell and DePuy were dilettantes in the 'secret world' of foreign intelligence. Like most military men they considered each problem to be a nail for which they had a hammer. Because of the need for strategic and tactical information necessary for national defense, military men are often brought into the 'secret world,' but most fail to see much further than the nail.

## Made Men

After leaving the CIA, Stilwell commanded the 15th Infantry Regiment for five months at the end of the Korean War. He taught at the War College and served as a strategic planner at the Allied Powers European Headquarters. He did a stint at the Pentagon and then served as commandant of cadets with General Westmoreland at West Point. While at the Pentagon, he wrote a paper dealing with the army's counterinsurgency capabilities and doctrine. This paper identified him as a 'counterinsurgency expert' and his next assignment was Vietnam.[357]

After several schools and troop assignments, DePuy went to the Pentagon in 1956, where his biographer, Henry Gole says, "He joined the clever chaps in Washington who were at the top of the Army hierarchy." He wrote a paper for Major General William Westmoreland, a 'fast burner,' who remembered DePuy later when Westmoreland commanded the war in Vietnam. Gole closed this chapter of DePuy's life by saying, "His stint in the Pentagon, close to the power centers, taught him political infighting, ways to get things done in a bureaucracy…"[358]

After leaving the Pentagon he went to the British Imperial Defense College and then commanded an infantry battle-group in Germany. Back in the Pentagon in 1962, DePuy was Director of Counterinsurgency and Special Operations for the Deputy Chief of Staff for Operations. He must have realized that Vietnam was where he could make his mark. Since the airborne 'mafia' under the Chairman of the Joint Chiefs of Staff General Maxwell Taylor and General Westmoreland were running the war, he became airborne qualified at forty-three years of age and was promoted to Brigadier General.

DePuy never served with an airborne unit and where he went to jump school is not clear. There used to be an airborne training course at Fort Bragg for senior officers, and he and Richard Stilwell may have gotten their wings there. His next assignment was in Vietnam where he would serve as Richard Stilwell's deputy before taking Stilwell's place as Westmoreland's Operations Officer or J3. These two were Westmoreland's most influential assistants.[359]

## Covert Operations

***[A covert operation, like] a conspiracy, is rarely, if ever, proved by positive testimony…A witness swearing positively may misrepresent the facts or swear falsely, but the circumstances cannot lie.***[360]

Richard Stilwell arrived in South Vietnam in April, 1963. He became chief of the Military Assistance Command-Vietnam (MACV) Army Support Group before being made MACV operations officer (J3) and then MACV chief of staff. Operation Switchback was underway, a change of command from the CIA to MACV for covert operations in North Vietnam. Switchback was the result of the CIA fiasco at the Bay of Pigs, and President Kennedy wanted the military to handle large paramilitary and unconventional warfare operations.[361]

The CIA operations were run by William Colby, a former Jedburgh operative with the OSS, who jumped into France and Norway to organize resistance movements and blow up bridges. His operations included parachute drops of South Vietnamese unconventional warfare teams, commando and small boat raids along the coast, and psychological warfare operations. In sum, these operations were total failures.[362]

The internal security system in North Vietnam and its agents in the south insured that every team dropped into the north was met on the drop zone by security service personnel who captured the teams and persuaded many of the radio operators to send deceptive messages to their controllers. Maritime operations were usually met by North Vietnam patrol boats that shot them up and captured the survivors. During a meeting with Secretary of Defense, Robert McNamara, Colby told him of the failure of covert operations in the north, but was ignored.[363]

Colby's only success was the use of Special Forces teams to create the Citizen Irregular Defense Group (CIDG) in a classic counterinsurgency operation. It would soon be terminated by MACV who took the SF teams out of the villages and put them on the border doing 'offensive' operations. That the Special Forces commander, Colonel George Morton, insisted on reporting to Stilwell, rather than to the MACV J3, per MACV regulation, indicates that Stilwell was the MACV 'go to guy' for any 'special warfare' issues.[364]

## MACSOG

McNamara was unconvinced by Colby's assessment that the covert operations in North Vietnam were doomed to failure. No doubt, advised by Maxwell Taylor that the military could do what the CIA couldn't, a new organization was formed in February, 1964 called the MACV Special Operations Group, later changed to the 'Studies and Observations Group' or MACSOG. Taylor and Westmoreland also had the man for the job, Richard Stilwell.

This is a perfect example of the 'mystique' being more powerful than the reality. Stilwell's monumental failure in running covert operations in China ten years earlier had been covered up by security classifications, and all that was known was that he was one of 'those guys' who had been in the CIA and therefore 'knew the deal.'

When you read the MACSOG official histories, the redacting can be disconcerting. For the purpose of this presumption, the redacted material has to contain references to the men who had learned to keep their names out of anything that might come back and bite them later. Annex A of the MACSOG Command History states, "SOG was organized on 24 January, 1964 as the Special Operations Group under the direct supervision of the Chief of Staff, MACV…the overall plan was designated MACV OPLAN 34A." Richard Stilwell became the chief of staff and the MACV covert operations against North Vietnam began. They were almost a mirror image of his operations against China while working for the CIA twelve years earlier.

Richard Stilwell is mentioned by name once when Special Forces commander, Colonel Theodore Leonard said, "I was called to Saigon during one of Secretary McNamara's visits and without any warning I was brought into the conference where he was consulting with General Westmoreland, General Stilwell, Ambassador Lodge, and General Taylor; also present was Ambassador Unger. Out of a clear blue sky I was asked how soon I could launch operations into Laos."[365]

## Good Money after Bad

MACSOG was presented with the failure of the unconventional warfare teams that had been dropped into North Vietnam by the CIA and were now under North Vietnamese control. Under pressure from Stilwell, twelve more teams were sent north by SOG and disappeared into the hands of the North Vietnamese. Colonel Clyde Russell, the first SOG commander said, "[the] people we were going to infiltrate into North Vietnam, unfortunately, were of questionable capability and we found none who wanted to go. As a matter of fact, we forced them into the airplanes on numerous occasions and even then they did not want to go back to North Vietnam."[366]

Meanwhile, there had been a change in thinking about the use of covert operations. Previously the CIA had used them at President Kennedy's behest to 'send a message' to Hanoi, telling them to stop supporting the insurgency in South Vietnam. Johnson and his advisors didn't seem to understand that the North Vietnamese were replying with a message of their own: "If the Americans want to make war for twenty years then we shall make war for twenty years. If they want to make peace, we shall make peace and invite them to afternoon tea."[367]

Ho's message was conveyed in victory after victory when the VC fought the South Vietnamese Army, and with various covert operations of their own, such as bombing the American officer's quarters in Saigon. Now it appeared that the covert operations would be intensified with the purpose of provoking North Vietnam to attack U.S. naval vessels in the Gulf of Tonkin.

## Enter DePuy

DePuy joined Stilwell in the spring of 1964. By then, Stilwell was the MACV chief of staff and DePuy became the J3. He had already been out there in 1962 while serving as Director, Counterinsurgency and Special Warfare (DCSOPS). "In 1962, I went over to Vietnam with Colonel George Morton to establish the Special Forces headquarters at Nha Trang. The Central Intelligence Agency had taken over a number of Special Forces "A" Detachments and had inaugurated a program up at Ban Me Thuot, with the Rhade tribe of Montagnards… We thought Special Forces had a role to use its own troops, but we didn't want them to play it under the Agency. The Army wanted to play its own game. So, that was the beginning of setting up the Special Forces Command in Vietnam."[368]

## The Gulf of Tonkin

As MACV J3 under Stilwell, DePuy was able to take the burden of covert operations off of Stilwell's shoulders. MACSOG built their own staff, but their 'go to' man was DePuy. The optempo of coastal raiding greatly increased after he arrived: everything from capturing North Vietnamese fishing boats and blowing bridges, to small scale commando raids on storage facilities and barracks. Using Norwegian 'Nasty' PT boats, with Norwegian mercenary captains, the crews shot up North Vietnamese PT boats and their bases.[369]

At the same time SOG was directing the covert raiding of the North Vietnamese coast, the U.S. Navy was running communication intelligence gathering missions along the same coast. These operations were known as DESOTO patrols. On 28 July of 1964, SOG conducted shore bombardment missions in the vicinity of a DESOTO patrol being conducted by the destroyer USS Maddox. The Maddox continued its patrol, and on 2 August it was attacked in broad daylight by three North Vietnamese PT boats.

The Maddox fired a warning shot and the PT boats fired torpedoes. After a brief battle which included airstrikes from the carrier USS Ticonderoga, which sank one of the PT boats, the North Vietnamese returned to their base. Several nights later two U.S. Navy destroyers on DESOTO patrols reported that they were under attack by four PT boats. Aircraft were launched, but no PT boats were seen. This was the Gulf of Tonkin incident that President Johnson used to get congressional authority to go to war in Vietnam.[370]

### The War Fighter

DePuy must also take as much responsibility for losing the war as anyone. He and Stilwell have been 'credited' with being General Westmoreland's chief architects of the attrition strategy and the 'search and destroy' tactics used to attain it. DePuy reasoned that American firepower could overcome North Vietnamese willpower before America ran out of political will. In 1965, Richard Stilwell left Vietnam and went to Thailand. There he commanded the U.S. effort in that country. DePuy remained in Vietnam.[371]

After serving as the MACV J3 for two years, he took command of the 1st Infantry Division in March of 1966. There he endeavored to take the fight to the main force VC units that were threatening Saigon. He wasted no time putting his stamp on the division. Ten days after taking command, he rewrote the division's tactical SOP, demanding that his soldiers stand their ground when meeting the enemy in the jungle instead of pulling back and calling for artillery and airstrikes. After the battle of August 25th, during Operation Amarillo, he changed the SOP again, basically, back to what it had been before he arrived. He would later say, "I presided over that very gory and unsuccessful operation, the VC made monkeys out of us." He had relieved a number for battalion commanders for incompetence, claiming that they were killing American soldiers. I wonder why he didn't relieve himself after that fiasco.[372]

When he looked back on his command of the division he said in an interview, "I guess I was surprised a little bit, too, after I took over the division, about the difficulty we had in finding the VC. We hit more dry holes than I thought we were going to hit, they were more elusive than I had expected, they controlled the battle better. They were the ones who usually decided whether or not there would be a fight…

"I wish that we had all been smart enough to say in 1965, when we went in, "That's what they are going to do to us." If we had been that smart then maybe we wouldn't have gone in…But, I don't remember anybody saying that, do you? Not even the experts, the scholastics, or the academics said that. Oh, there was one who did, Francois Sully, who is now dead. Now, the reason he did is because he had been through it before with the French. He told me and he told others. He said, 'You're never going to win it. You're not going to be able to find them. You're going to thrash around and you're only going to fight the battles that they win.' Well, he wasn't quite right. He wasn't right in every detail, but he was right in net and sum.[373]

He continued, "I guess my biggest surprise, and this was a surprise in which I have lots of company, was that the North Vietnamese and the Viet Cong would continue the war despite the punishment they were taking, I guess I should have expected that. I guess I should have studied human nature and the history of Vietnam and of revolutions and should have known it, but I didn't. I really thought that the kind of pressure they were under would cause them to perhaps knock off the war for a while, as a minimum, or even give up and go back north, I understand that from 1965 to '69 they lost over 600,000 men. But, I was completely wrong on that. That was a surprise."[374]

These are interesting words coming from the man that the Army appointed to the positions of Director, Counterinsurgency, Special Warfare (DCSOPS) and Special Assistant for Counterinsurgency and Special Activities (SACSA); but, once again, that aura coming from his stint in the 'secret world' dazzled the eyes of the uninitiated.

## Exit DePuy

DePuy's career was on a dead-end street when he returned from Vietnam in 1967. General Westmoreland took credit for saving DePuy's career when he asked General Wheeler, the Chairman of the Joint Chiefs to keep DePuy out of the reach of the army chief of staff, General Harold K. Johnson, by putting DePuy to work for the Joint Staff. He became the Special Assistant for Counterinsurgency and Special Activities (SACSA).[375]

DePuy was highly regarded for his way with words. He wrote the "Report of the Chairman, JCS, on the situation in Vietnam and MACV Requirements" for General Earle Wheeler while he and Wheeler returned from a post-TET assessment for President Johnson. Westmoreland had characterized the VC TET offensive as the destruction of the Viet Cong organization, but the briefing that DePuy and Wheeler gave to President Johnson's group of 'wise men,' was described by DePuy in 1979 as a too dismal picture of the situation.[376]

DePuy said, "However, I must say that the briefings were not encouraging at that time. And, perhaps those of us who gave the briefings were suffering a little bit from the Washington point of view, as opposed to the field point of view, despite the fact that some of us had just been out there." The next day, these 'wise men' told Johnson that the war was lost. Johnson was furious and accused the briefers of 'poisoning the well' and demanded to hear the same briefing from them. After that briefing, DePuy said later that he thought Johnson had already decided the war was lost.

It appears to me that DePuy saw which way the wind was blowing in Washington and distanced himself from Westmoreland and the conduct of the war that he had a big hand in creating. He wrote Westmoreland's end of tour report entitled "Report on Operations in South Vietnam…" After Westmoreland became Chief of Staff of the Army, he chose DePuy to be his assistant vice chief of staff.[377]

Stilwell returned to Vietnam in 1968 and served as XXIV Corps commander until 1969 when he was appointed Deputy Chief of Staff for Operations in Washington, DC. From there he went to Korea as commanding general and then he retired. He was appointed Deputy Under Secretary of Defense for Policy where he played a heavy hand with issues regarding special operations and military intelligence.[378]

## TRADOC

General Creighton Abrams, who succeeded Westmoreland, made DePuy the first commander of the Training and Doctrine Command (TRADOC) where he took on the task of rebuilding the Army after Vietnam. DePuy was fixated on the Warsaw Pact's massive conventional force in Eastern Europe. The Europeans were not interested in a nuclear exchange, and so he reasoned that the west would have to fight an active defensive campaign to stop a Russian invasion.[379]

In his efforts to rebuild the army, a noble effort, but ironic in that he bore much of the responsibility for destroying it in Vietnam, DePuy determined that the U.S. Army should not fight another counterinsurgency war. In the post-war army of the 70s and 80s, Vietnam was a non-event with no useful information for the next generations of soldiers.[380]

He staffed TRADOC with many of the men who served under him in the 1st Infantry Division. Out of that TRADOC synergy DePuy took the army back to where Vince Lombardi would start with 'This is a football.' They revamped the army schools and training programs, created the Common and MOS specific skill Manuals, the "How to Fight" manuals, the Army Training and Evaluation Program, and the National Training Center. They also described the need for a new tank, an infantry fighting vehicle, two helicopters and an anti-aircraft system, 'the big five.'[381]

He and his disciples wrote the 1976 edition of FM 100-5 (Operations), the basic manual of how the army fights. They built an entire system of training and education to prepare the army for 'winning the first battle,' using what DePuy called the 'active defense.' "Force ratios, superior fire power, attrition, and toe-to-toe slugfests characterized DePuy's Field Manual," said James Burton, one of reformer John Boyd's acolytes.[382]

DePuy went to the rebuilding task with his usual enthusiasm, and the result was what the world saw during Operation Desert Storm. President George H.W. Bush announced, "It's a proud day for America. And, by God, we've kicked the Vietnam syndrome once and for all." Many professional soldiers gave credit to DePuy and his TRADOC team that took the lead in rebuilding the army after Vietnam.[383]

The next version of 100-5, known as the Air/Land Battle was something that Heinz Guderian and George Patton would have recognized. Borrowing from Boyd's OODA loop theory, the army, while defending the front, would attrite the enemy's second echelon and follow-on forces by using fast moving maneuver forces on the ground and deep strikes from the air. Boyd's emphasis on attacking the enemy's mind verses DePuy's attack on men and material was a step away from the traditional American way of war; but both men failed to recognize the need to consider the civilian population and its response to the presence of a foreign army.[384]

In 1987 Andrew F. Krepinevich, Jr. published a scathing exposition of the Vietnam War entitled, "The Army and Vietnam." General DePuy was quick to denounce it in a review published in Army magazine as, "A superbly researched book is flawed by the doubtful premise around which it is organized…the "concept" of the U.S. Army for fighting wars. This concept is described as an ineradicable fixation of the Army on European-type war—a prodigious consumption of resources to avoid the spillage of American blood—and to borrow from the demonology of the military reform movement a strong preference for firepower and attrition."[385]

After being appointed Secretary of Defense, Donald Rumsfeld, pressed for an expeditionary force capable of deploying quickly by air to various places in the world where the U.S. had an interest in projecting its power. Apparently, not realizing that expeditionary warfare would automatically put U.S. troops into insurgency situations, the Army training continued with General DePuy's vision. The Army complied by buying some smaller, wheeled, fighting vehicles, and then sent the troops to do what they always have done: fire, receive and return fire. Supported by the unprecedented precision of bombs and missiles, they swept away any conventional force that tried to fight them.[386]

The enemy however, having learned many of the lessons from the Vietnam War, responded with classic insurgency moves such as hiding within the population and mining the roads with command detonated bombs, now much more lethal, called improvised explosive devices (IEDs.) The bottom line has been presented by numerous captured Taliban fighters, "The Americans have the watches but we have the time." Once again, thanks to short-sighted thinking, we would squander the two most important resources, lives and time, in futile efforts to bring our enemies to battle, so we could destroy them with our technology.[387]

Many of us 'old soldiers' were sorrowfully amused when the U.S. Army announced the impending publication of a new "Counterinsurgency" manual for the troops in Afghanistan and Iraq. FM 3-24 includes many of the hard-learned lessons from Vietnam and other 'brush-fire wars' of the last century. The manual was put together by General David Patraeus and LTG James Amos (USMC) when it appeared we were about to lose the war in Iraq. After the apparent success of the surge of 2007 with Patraeus at the helm, the advocates of counterinsurgency doctrine were satisfied that the army had turned the corner.[388]

The new president pulled the troops out of Iraq and sent Patraeus to Afghanistan to work his magic there. Meanwhile the naysayers were whispering their disdain for this. When Patraeus was retired and sent to CIA, his protégé, General Stanley McChrystal, was forced to endure a long policy review with the opposers demanding a counter-terrorism strategy. After a short time McChrystal was relieved of his command, and the army was able to toss the new manual into the trashcan.[389]

Whenever soldiers have to operate amid a civilian population, they must be more like well-trained local police. This is the information age. Every 'friendly fire' incident will be in the social media before rigor mortis has set in. Every death perceived by the locals to be unjustified turns another extended family or tribe against us. This requires extensive language and cultural training. Already proficient at the use of deadly force, they have to empathize with a population that doesn't look like, act like, or think like they do. These skills should not be limited to Special Forces.

Can this be done? Yes, but it is a slow process. Training the trainers is the critical task, lest you have the blind leading the blind. Unfortunately, for the fast moving, hooah-hooah DePuy army of today, it's impossible. As the U.S. continues to lose its credibility and retreats from its interventions in old world activity, resuming its isolationist ways, the Middle East will continue to implode: Then the end will come.

# Bibliography


The Holy Bible ***(Recovery Version)*** Living Stream Ministry, Anaheim, CA 1997

Allen, George W. ***(None So Blind)*** Ivan R. Dee, Chicago, IL: 2001

Ambrose, Stephen E. ***(Ike's Spies-Eisenhower and the Espionage Establishment)*** Doubleday, New York: 1981

Appleman, Roy E. ***(South to the Naktong, North to the Yalu)*** Center of Military History, Washington DC: 1992

Bacevich, Andrew ***(The Pentomic Era-The U.S. Army Between Korea and Vietnam)*** The National Defense University, Washington, DC: 1986

Bank, Aaron ***(From OSS to Green Berets)*** Presidio Press, Novato, CA: 1986

Berman, Larry ***(Perfect Spy)*** Harper Collins, New York: 2007

Birtle, Andrew J. ***(Years of Stalemate July 1951-July 1953)*** Center of Military History, Washington DC: 2000

Blaber, Pete ***(The Mission, The Men, and Me-Lessons From a Former Delta Force Commander)*** Berkley Publishing, New York: 2008

Boehm, Roy and Sasser, Charles W. ***(First SEAL)*** Pocket Books, New York: 1997

Bowman, John S. ed ***(The Vietnam War Almanac)*** Barnes and Noble, New York: 2005

Brandli, Lt Col Hank USAF Ret. ***(The Use Of Weather Satellite Photos In Vietnam War)*** http://libertyyes.homestead.com/files/TheUseOfWeatherSatellitePhotosInVietnamWar.htm

Brownlee, Romie L. and Mullen, William J. III ***(Changing an Army-An Oral History of General William E. DePuy)*** Center of Military History, Washington DC: 1988

Bui Tin ***(Interview 1981)*** http://openvault.wgbh.org/catalog/vietnam-f729b0-interview-with-bui-tin-2-1981

Caplan, Bryan ***(Vietnam's 300 Days of Open Borders: Operation Passage to Freedom)*** 2012 http://econlog.econlib.org/archives/2012/07/vietnams_300_da.html

Carland, John M. ***(Stemming the Tide-May 1965 to October 1966)*** Center of Military History, Washington, DC: 2000

Camp X ***(The History of Camp X)*** http://www.camp-x.com/historyofcampx.html

Carroll, James ***(The House of War-The Pentagon and the Disastrous Rise of American Power)*** Houghton Mifflin, New York: 2006

Chapman, F. Spencer ***(The Jungle Is Neutral)*** The Lyons Press, Guilford, CT: 1948

Clay, Steven E. ***(Blood and Sacrifice-The History of the 16th Infantry Regiment From The Civil War To The Gulf War)*** Cantigny First Division Foundation, Wheaton, IL: 2001

Colvin, John *(Volcano Under Snow)* Quartet Books, London: 1996

Cosmas, Graham A. *(MACV The Years of Escalation, 1962-1967)* Center of Military History, Washington, DC: 2006

Creighton, George E. Jr. *(The Battle of Xom Bo II (LZ X-Ray))* 17th Military History Detachment, 1st Infantry Division, 1 August, 1967

Davidson, LtGen Phillip B. *(Vietnam at War-The History 1946-1975)* Presidio Press, Novato, CA: 1988

DeForest, Orrin and Chanoff, David *(Slow Burn: The Rise and Bitter Fall of American Intelligence in Vietnam)* Simon & Schuster, New York: 1990

Derks, Tracy and Holland, James G. *(The Battle of Bong Trang)* Vietnam-Weider History Group, Leesburg, VA: October 2007

Dick, Ron and Patterson, Dan *(Aviation Century: War and Peace in the Air)* Boston Mills Press Buffalo, NY: 2006

Egersdorfer, Rudolf H. *(Video Tape Interview)* First Division Museum at Cantigny, February 1996 Blue Spaders-The 26th Infantry Regiment, 1917-1967 Cantigney First Division Foundation

Fall, Bernard *(Street Without Joy-The French Debacle in Indochina)* Stackpole Books, Mechanicsburg, PA: 1994

Fitzgerald, Frances *(Fire in the Lake)* Little, Brown, and Company, New York: 1972

Flynn, George Q. *(The Draft 1940-1973)* University Press of Kansas, Lawrence, KS: 1993

FM 21-13 *(The Soldier's Guide)* Department of the Army, Washington, DC: 1961

FM 22-100 *(Military Leadership)* Department of the Army, Washington, DC: 1961

Fremantle, Arthur *(Three Months in the Southern States: April, June, 1863)* 1864, http://docsouth.unc.edu/imls/fremantle/fremantle.html

French, R.M. *(The Way Of A Pilgrim)* Ballantine Books, New York: 1977

Gephardt, Major James F. USA Ret *(Eyes Behind the Lines: US Army Long Range Reconnaissance and Surveillance Units)* CSI Press Fort Leavenworth, Kansas: 2005

Gleason, Robert L. *(Air Commando Chronicles)* Sunflower University Press, Manhattan, KS: 2000

Gole, Henry G. *(General William E. DePuy-Preparing The Army For Modern War)* University Press of Kentucky: 2008

Gorman, Paul F. General *(Interview)* Cardinal Point: An Oral History-Training Soldiers and Becoming a Strategist in Peace and War. CSI Press: 2011

Grahame, Kenneth *(The Wind in the Willows)* Walt Disney Productions 1949

Hackworth, David and Sherman, Julie ***(About Face)*** Touchstone, New York: 1989

Hackworth, David and England, Eilhys ***(Steel My Soldiers' Hearts)*** Touchstone, New York: 2002

Haig, Alexander M. Jr. ***(Inner Circles-How America Changed The World)*** Warner Books, New York: 1992

Hairston, Jester ***(Song: Amen)*** Curtis Mayfield and the Impressions-ABC-Paramount Records: 1964

Hall, Simon ***(Rethinking the American Anti-War Movement)*** Routledge, New York: 2012

Hay, John H Jr. ***(Vietnam Studies-Tactical and Material Innovations)*** Center of Military History, Washington DC: 1972

Hendrix, Jimi ***(Song: Are You Experienced)*** 1967

Herbert, Anthony B. and Wooten, James T. ***(Soldier)*** Holt, Rinehart, and Winston-New York: 1973

Herrington, Stuart A. ***(Silence Was A Weapon-The Vietnam War In The Villages)*** Ballantine Books, New York: 1982

Holland, James G. ***(The Battle Of Bong Trang-Written account)*** http://www.quarterhorsecav.org/pg4g1b.htm

Holober, Frank ***(Raiders of the China Coast)*** Naval Institute Press, Annapolis, MD: 1999

Horne, Alistair ***(A Savage War Of Peace)*** Viking Press, New York: 1977

House Armed Services Committee ***(Report on the special subcommittee on the M-16 rifle program)*** October 19, 1967

Hubbs, M.E. ***(With the Black Scarves at Bong Trang-Part II)*** http://erasgone.blogspot.com/2012/11/with-black-scarves-at-bong-trang-part-2.html

Hunter, Charles ***(Galahad)*** Naylor Publishing, San Antonio, TX: 1962

James, Robert Rhodes (ed.), ***(Winston S. Churchill: His Complete Speeches 1897-1963 Volume II: 1943-1949)*** Chelsea House Publishers, New York: 1974

Johnston, John Harold ***(Battle-of-Bong-Trang)*** 8/6/2011-http://secinfreg.websitetoolbox.com/post/ronald-lee-watson-battle-of-bong-trang

Joint Publication 1-02, ***(Department of Defense Dictionary of Military and Associated Terms)***

Just, Ward S. ***(Military Men)*** Knopf, New York: 1970

Kelly, Col. Francis J. ***(U.S. Army Special Forces 1961-1971)*** U.S. Army 1973

Kenner, Robert ***(Two Days In October-PBS Documentary)*** Robert Kenner Films: 2005

Krepinevich, Andrew F. ***(The Army and Vietnam)*** The John Hopkins University Press, Baltimore, MD: 1986

Languth, A.J. ***(Our Vietnam-The War 1954-1975)*** Touchstone, New York: 2000
LeGro, William ***(Interview)*** The Texas Tech University-Vietnam Archive Oral History Project: Conducted by Laura Calkins, Ph.D. October 31, 2005

Loehr, Charles T. ***(War History of the Old First Virginia Infantry Regiment)*** Richmond, VA: 1884 https://archive.org/stream/cu31924032779047#page/n5/mode/2up

Long, Lonnie M. and Blackburn, Gary B. ***(Unlikely Warriors: The Army Security Agency's Secret War in Vietnam 1961-1973)*** iUniverse, Bloomington, IN: 2013

MacGregor, Morris J. Jr. ***(Integration of the Armed Forces 1940-1965)*** Center of Military History, Washington DC: 1985

Mahler, Michael D. ***(Ringed In Steel)*** Presidio Press, Novato, CA:1986

Maraniss, David ***(They Marched Into Sunlight)*** Simon and Schuster, New York: 2003

Marshall, S.L.A. ***(Ambush-The Battle of Dau Tieng)*** Nelson Doubleday, New York: 1969

Marshall, S.L.A. ***(Men Against Fire-The Problem of Battle Command)*** William Morrow, New York: 1947

Marshall, S.L.A. and Hackworth, David ***(Vietnam Primer)*** DA Lessons Learned: 1967

McAleese, Peter ***(No Mean Soldier: The Story of the Ultimate Professional Soldier in the SAS and Other Forces)*** Cassell, London: 2001

McClellan, Barr ***(Blood, Money, and Power)*** Hannover House, New York: 2003

McChristian, Joseph A. ***(Vietnam Studies-The Role of Military Intelligence 1965-1967)*** Center of Military History, Washington DC: 1974

McCoy, Alfred W. ***(The Politics of Heroin-CIA Complicity in the Global Drug Trade-revised from The Politics of Heroin in Southeast Asia)*** Lawrence Hill Books, Brooklyn, NY: 1972-1991

McMaster, H.R. ***(Dereliction of Duty-Lyndon Johnson, Robert McNamara, The Joint Chiefs Of Staff, And The Lies That Led To Vietnam)*** Harper Collins, NY: 1997

McNamara, Robert S. ***(In Retrospect-The Tragedy and Lessons of Vietnam)*** Times Books, New York: 1995

Morrison, Wilbur H. ***(The Elephant and the Tiger-The Full Story of the Vietnam War)*** Hippocrene Books New York: 1990

Myer, Charles L. ***(Vietnam Studies-Division Level Communications 1962-1973)*** Department of the Army, Washington DC: 1982
Myrer, Anton (***Once an Eagle)*** Holt, Rinehart, Winston, New York: 1968

National Archives ***(Defense Casualty Analysis System)*** http://www.archives.gov/research/military/vietnam-war/casualty-statistics.html

National Security Council ***(NSAM 131-Training Objectives for Counter-Insurgency)*** 13 March 1962 https://history.state.gov/historicaldocuments/frus1961-63v08/d128

Oakes, Guy ***(The Imaginary War-Civil Defense and American Cold War Culture)*** Oxford University Press, New York: 1994

1st Infantry Division Long Range Reconnaissance Patrol ***(History)***- http://www.75thrra.com/history/i75_hx.html

Patton, Charles D. ***(Colt Terry, Green Beret)*** Texas A+M University Press, College Station, TX: 2005

Pipes, Richard ***(Communism-A History)*** The Modern Library, New York: 2001

Philby, Kim ***(My Silent War)*** MacGibbon & Kee, London: 1968

Prochnau, William ***(Once Upon A Distant War-Young War Correspondents And The Early Vietnam Battles)*** Times Books, New York: 1995

Prunier, Henry A. ***(Obituary)*** New York Times-17 April, 2013 http://www.nytimes.com/2013/04/18/world/asia/henry-a-prunier-army-operative-who-helped-trained-vietnamese-troops-dies-at-91.html

Rottman, Gordon L. ***(Mobile Strike Forces in Vietnam 1966-70)*** Osprey Publishing: 2007

Rogers, LTG Bernard ***(Cedar Falls-Junction City: A Turning Point)*** Department of the Army, Washington, DC: 1974

Salinger, J.D. ***(Franny and Zooey)*** Bantam, New York: 1964

Secretary Of Defense ***(The Pentagon Paper***s) https://archive.org/details/thepentagonpapers

Seeger, Peter and Hickerson, Joe ***(Song: Where Have All The Flowers Gone)*** Columbia Records 1964

Shamir, Eitan ***(A Very Sharp Eye: Moshe Dayan's Counterinsurgency Legacy in Israel)*** http://portal.idc.ac.il/he/schools/government/research/documents/shamir.pdf

Shapley, Deborah ***(Promise and Power-The Life and Times of Robert McNamara)*** Little, Brown & Company, New York: 1993

Shelton, BG James E. ***(The Beast Was Out There)*** Cantigny First Division Foundation, Wheaton, IL: 2002

Schlight, John ***(The War in Vietnam-The Years of the Offensive)*** Air Force History and Museum Program: 1999

Simpson, Howard R. ***(Dien Bien Phu-The Epic Battle America Forgot)*** Potomac Books, Washington, DC: 1994

Sorley, Lewis ***(General Harold K. Johnson and the Ethics of Command)*** University Press of Kansas, Lawrence, KS: 1998

Sorley, Lewis ***(Westmoreland-The General Who Lost Vietnam)*** Houghton Mifflin Harcourt, New York: 2011

Stewart, Richard W. ***(The Korean War-The Chinese Intervention)*** Center of Military History, Washington, DC: 2000

Stone, Oliver ***(Platoon)*** A semi-biographical movie by a combat infantry veteran of Vietnam MGM: 1987

Summers, Harry G. Jr. ***(On Strategy-A Critical Analysis of the Vietnam War)*** Presidio Press, Novato, CA: 1982

Taubman, William ***(Khrushchev: The Man and His Era)*** W.W. Norton, New York: 2003

Taylor, Maxwell D. ***(The Uncertain Trumpet)*** Harper & Brothers, New York: 1960

The Desk Encyclopedia of World History, Oxford University Press, New York: 2006

Time Magazine ***(The Pentagon's Whiz Kids)*** The Nation-3 August, 1962

Tourison, Sedgwick D. Jr. ***(Talking With Victor Charlie-An Interrogators Story)*** Ballantine Books, New York: 1991

Valentine, Donald E. ***(Strap Hanger)*** 1997 http://www.don-valentine.com/1st Group and White Star.htm

Verrier, Anthony ***(Through The Looking Glass)*** W.W. Norton-London: 1983

von Clausewitz, Carl , eds./trans. Michael Howard and Peter Paret, (***On War)*** (Princeton: Princeton University Press, 1976/1984)

Weiner, Tim ***(Legacy of Ashes)*** Doubleday, New York: 2007

Wellborn, Charles ***(History of the 86th Mountain Infantry in Italy)*** http://10thmtndivassoc.org/86thhistory.pdf

Wilkins, Warren ***(Grab Their Belts to Fight Them: The Viet Cong's Big Unit-War Against the U.S., 1965-1966)*** Naval Institute Press, Annapolis, MD: 2011

Williams, Juan ***(Eyes on the Prize-America's Civil Rights Years 1954-1965)*** Penguin Books, New York: 1988

**After Action Reports-Lessons Learned**

Bamford, Major Charles M. II ***(CAAR-Operation Junction City)*** 2d BDE, 1ID:6 May 1967

Berry, Colonel Sidney B. Jr. ***(CAAR-Operation Amarillo)*** 1st BDE, 1ID 18 Dec 1966

Fife, LTC Thomas ***(CAAR-Operation Williston)*** 1-4 Cav, 1ID 19 February 1967

Marks, Colonel Sidney M. ***(CAAR-Operation Danbury)*** 3d BDE, 1ID 12 October 1966

Marks, Colonel Sidney M. ***(CAAR-Operation Healdsburg)*** 3d BDE, 1ID 1 January 1967

Marks, Colonel Sidney M. ***(CAAR-Operation Santa Cruz)*** 3d BDE, 1ID 18 January 67

Marks, Colonel Sidney M. ***(CAAR-Operation Cedar Falls)*** 3d BDE, 1st ID 10 Feb 1967

Marks, Colonel Sidney M. ***(CAAR-Operation Tucson D)*** 3d BDE, 1st ID 16 March 1967

Marks, Colonel Sidney M. ***(CAAR-Operation Junction City)*** 3d BDE, 1st ID 25 Apr 1967

Marks, Colonel Sidney M. ***(CAAR-Operation Bluefield)*** 3d BDE, 1st ID 27 June 1967

Marks, Colonel Sidney M. ***(CAAR-Operation Billings)*** 3d BDE, 1st ID 16 July, 1967

DePuy, BG William ***(Or-LL)*** 1st Infantry Division 1 January-30 April 1966

DePuy, MG William ***(OR-LL)*** 1st Infantry Division 1 November 1966-31 January 1967

Hay, MG John ***(OR-LL-Operation Junction City)*** 1st Infantry Division 8 May 1967

Hay, MG John ***(OR-LL)*** 1st Infantry Division, 1 May-31 July 1967

**Reports and Studies**

Combat Studies Institute ***(Sixty Years of Reorganizing for Combat: A Historical Trend Analysis)*** USACGSC Fort Leavenworth, KS: 1999

MACV Office of Information ***(Summary of MACV News Events 1966)***

U.S. Air Force ***(Contemporary Historical Evaluation of Combat Operations-Short Rounds)*** HQ PACAF 28 September 1967

U.S. Army War College ***(Study on Military Professionalism)*** 1970 http://www.carlisle.army.mil/usawc/dclm/pdf/study1970.pdf

USARV Seminar Report ***(Attack of Fortified Positions in the Jungle)*** 2 January 1968

# End Notes

1--1 John 1:6 Recovery Version of the Holy Bible, footnote 6: The word truth is used in the New Testament more than one hundred times. Its denotation in each occurrence is determined by its context. The Greek word means reality (the opposite of vanity), verity, veracity, genuineness, sincerity. It is John's highly individual terminology, and it is one of the profound words in the New Testament, denoting all the realities of the divine economy as the content of the divine revelation, conveyed and disclosed by the holy Word as follows: In John 5:33 and 18:37, according to the entire revelation of the Gospel of John, truth denotes the divine reality embodied, revealed, and expressed in Christ as the Son of God. John 18:38

2--S.L.A. Marshall ***(Bringing Up The Rear)*** Page 72 Presidio Press 1979
S.L.A. Marshall ***(Men Against Fire)*** William Morrow 1947
John E. Morrison and Larry L. Meliza ***(Foundations of the After Action Review Process)*** Special Report 42, U.S. Army Research Institute for the Behavioral and Social Sciences July 1999

3--FM 22-100 ***(Military Leadership)*** Page 22, Department of the Army, Washington, DC: June 1961 This is the leadership doctrine of the Army going into Vietnam.
FM 21-13 ***(The Soldier's Guide)*** Page 127, Department of the Army, Washington, DC: August 1961

4--***Black's Law Dictionary Free Online Legal Dictionary 2nd Ed.*** http://thelawdictionary.org/conscience/

5--Definition of Criminal Intent http://thelawdictionary.org/criminal-intent/
Spiritual explanation of the function of the conscience-from a note in Acts 23:1 The Recovery Version New Testament. After man's fall and his being sent out of the garden of Eden (Gen. 3:23), God in His dispensation wanted man to be responsible to his own conscience. But man failed to live and walk according to his conscience and fell further into wickedness (Gen. 6:5). After the judgment of the flood, God ordained that man should be under human government (Gen. 9:6). Man failed in this also. Then, before fulfilling His promise to Abraham concerning the blessing of the nations in his seed, Christ (Gen. 12:3; Gal. 3:8), God put man under the test of the law (Rom. 3:20; 5:20). Man failed this test utterly. All these failures indicate that man has fallen from God to his conscience, from his conscience to human government, and from human government to lawlessness; that is, man has fallen to the uttermost.
Definition of Conscience http://thelawdictionary.org/conscience/
Definition of a Confession http://thelawdictionary.org/confession/

6--Bui Tin (***Interview 1981***) http://openvault.wgbh.org/catalog/vietnam-f729b0-interview-with-bui-tin-2-1981

7--The OSS or Office of Strategic Services. The forerunner of the CIA.
PFC Henry A. Prunier ***(Obituary)*** New York Times-17 April, 2013
http://www.nytimes.com/2013/04/18/world/asia/henry-a-prunier-army-operative-who-helped-trained-vietnamese-troops-dies-at-91.html
***The Pentagon Paper***s-Part II A-2 Page A-35 In the first post-war decade, France was relatively weak and depended upon the United States through NATO and the Marshall Plan for its military security and economic revival. But neither NATO nor the Marshall Plan offered usable fulcrums for influencing French policy on Indochina.
Both were judged by the U.S. Government and public to be strongly in the American national interest at a time when the Soviet threat to western Europe, either through overt aggression or internal subversion, was clearly recognizable. A communist take-over in France as a real possibility. (The French Communist Party was the largest political party in the nation, and, at the time, quite militant in character.) Thus, an American threat to to metropolitan France if it did not alter its policies in Indochina was not plausible.
To threaten France with sanctions in NATO or through the Marshall Plan would have

jeopardized a U.S. interest in Europe more important than any in Indochina.
8--*The Pentagon Papers*-Part 4 A-2 Page 15, By February 3, 1953, the United States had shipped 137,200 long tons of material (224 ships' cargoes); by July 1954, approximately 150,000 long tons had been sent, including 1,800 combat vehicles, 30,887 motor transport vehicles, 361,522 small arms and machine guns, 438 naval craft, 2 World War II aircraft carriers, and about 500 aircraft. By the conclusion of the Geneva agreements in July, 1954, the U.S. had delivered aid to Indochina at an original cost of $2,600 million.
Howard R. Simpson ***(Dien Bien Phu-The Epic Battle America Forgot)*** Pages 86-87, Potomac Books 1994
***The Pentagon Papers*** Part IV A-5 Page 34: The U.S. aid program-economic and military-for South Vietnam was among the largest in the world. From FY 1946 through FY 1961, Vietnam was the third ranking non-NATO recipient of aid, and the seventh worldwide. In FY 1961, the last program of President Eisenhower's Administration, South Vietnam was the fifth ranking recipient overall. MAAG, Vietnam, was the only military aid mission anywhere in the world commanded by a lieutenant general, and the economic aid mission there was by 1958 the largest anywhere.
A.J. Langguth ***(Our Vietnam-The War 1954-1975)*** Page 320 Touchstone, NY 2000
***LBJ Campaign speech*** at Akron, Ohio 21 October, 1964
9--Richard Pipes ***(Communism-A History)*** The Modern Library New York 2001
10--Robert Rhodes James (ed.), ***(Winston S. Churchill: His Complete Speeches 1897-1963 Volume VII: 1943-1949)*** Pages 7285-7293, Chelsea House Publishers, New York: 1974
11--***(American Military History)*** Page 529, CMH, Washington, DC: 1989
George Q. Flynn ***(The Draft 1940-1973)*** University Press of Kansas 1993
Morris J. MacGregor Jr. ***(Integration of the Armed Forces 1940-1965)*** CMH Washington DC 1985
12--Juan Williams ***(Eyes on the Prize-America's Civil Rights Years 1954-1965)*** Penguin Books, New York: 1988
Jose Garcia ***(Conversation with author)*** 2013
13--Guy Oakes ***(The Imaginary War-Civil Defense and American Cold War Culture)*** Page 53 Oxford University Press New York 1994
14--S.L.A. Marshall ***(Men Against Fire-The Problem of Battle Command)*** Page 21, William Morrow, New York 1947
Roy E. Appleman ***(South to the Naktong, North to the Yalu)*** CMH Wash DC 1992
15--Henry Soloman ***(Victory at Sea)*** NBC, New York: 1952
***(The Big Picture)*** ABC, New York: 1951
16--Simpson ***(Dien Bien Phu-)*** Pages xix-xxv
17--Bernard Fall ***(Street Without Joy-The French Debacle in Indochina)*** Page 185, Stackpole Books, Mechanicsburg, PA: 1994
18--John S. Bowman ed ***(The Vietnam War Almanac)*** Pages 44-45, Barnes and Noble, New York: 2005
19--Bryan Caplan ***(Vietnam's 300 Days of Open Borders: Operation Passage to Freedom)*** 2012 http://econlog.econlib.org/archives/2012/07/vietnams_300_da.html
20--Wilbur H. Morrison ***(The Elephant and the Tiger-The Full Story of the Vietnam War)*** Page 39, Hippocrene Books New York: 1990
Bowman ***(The Vietnam War Almanac)*** Pages 37-48
21--Kenneth Grahame ***(The Wind in the Willows)*** Walt Disney Productions 1949
22--Juan Williams ***(Eyes on the Prize-America's Civil Rights Years 1954-1965)*** Penguin Books 1988
23--Ibid
24--Audie Murphy ***(To Hell and Back)*** Universal Pictures 1955
25--Andrew Bacevich ***(The Pentomic Era-The U.S. Army Between Korea and Vietnam)*** Page 106 The National Defense University, Washington, DC 1986
Lewis Sorley ***(Westmoreland-The General Who Lost Vietnam)*** Page 48, Houghton Mifflin Harcourt, New York 2011

[26]--Maxwell D. Taylor ***(The Uncertain Trumpet)*** Harper & Brothers, New York: 1960
James Carroll ***(The House of War-The Pentagon and the Disastrous Rise of American Power)*** Pages 220-228, Houghton Mifflin, New York: 2006
H.R. McMaster ***(Dereliction Of Duty-Lyndon Johnson, Robert McNamara, The Joint Chiefs Of Staff, And The Lies That Led To Vietnam)*** Pages 9-17, Harper Collins, NY: 1997
[27]--Bowman ed ***(The Vietnam War Almanac)*** Pages 37-48
[28]--William Taubman ***(Khrushchev: The Man and His Era)*** Page 487-488, W.W. Norton, New York: 2003
Warren Wilkins ***(Grab Their Belts to Fight Them-The Viet Cong's Big Unit War Against The U.S.)*** Page 7-10, Naval Institute Press, Annapolis, MD: 2011
[29]--John F. Kennedy ***(Remarks at West Point to the Graduating Class of the U.S. Military Academy)*** 6 June, 1962
Harry G. Summers Jr. ***(On Strategy-A Critical Analysis of the Vietnam War)*** Page 73, Presidio Press, Novato, CA: 1982
***(NSAM 131-Training Objectives for Counter-Insurgency)*** 13 March 1962 https://history.state.gov/historicaldocuments/frus1961-63v08/d128
Roy Boehm and Charles W. Sasser ***(First SEAL)*** Page 150, Pocket Books, New York: 1997
Robert L. Gleason ***(Air Commando Chronicles)*** Page 8, Sunflower University Press, Manhattan, KS: 2000
[30]--Languth ***(Our Vietnam-The War 1954-1975)*** Page 108,
Bowman ***(The Vietnam War Almanac)*** Pages 51, 54
[31]--Ibid Pages 54-58
William Prochnau ***(Once Upon A Distant War-Young War Correspondents And The Early Vietnam Battles)*** Page 240, Times Books, New York: 1995
[32]--George Q. Flynn ***(The Draft 1940-1973)*** University Press of Kansas 1993
[33]--Ward S. Just ***(Military Men)*** Knopf, New York: 1970
[34]--Sorley ***(Westmoreland-The General Who Lost Vietnam)*** Page 70
[35]--Bowman ***(The Vietnam War Almanac)*** Page 86
[36]--LBJ ***(Speech)*** Akron University, Akron, Ohio (October 21, 1964);
[37]--Bowman ***(The Vietnam War Almanac)*** Pages 64-100
[38]--Ibid Pages 104, 108, 114
[39]--S.L.A. Marshall ***(Pork Chop Hill)*** MGM, Hollywood, CA: 1959
[40]--John Colvin ***(Volcano Under Snow)*** Pages 211-215, Quartet Books, London: 1996
Sorley ***(Westmoreland-The General Who Lost Vietnam)*** Page 91
[41]--Written by Elmer Bernstein and Ernie Sheldon and performed by Glenn Yarbrough. RCA Victor 1965
[42]--Chris Kenner ***(Land of a Thousand Dances)*** Cannibal and the Headhunters, Rampart Records: 1965
[43]--Barry Sadler and Robin Moore ***(The Ballad of the Green Berets)*** RCA Victor 1966
[44]--Carl von Clausewitz, eds./trans. Michael Howard and Peter Paret, ***(On War-Book One, Chapter 1, section 25.)*** (Princeton: Princeton University Press, 1976/1984)
[45]--Frances Fitzgerald ***(Fire in the Lake)*** Chapters 1-2, Little, Brown, and Company, New York: 1972
[46]--Bowman ed ***(The Vietnam War Almanac)*** Page 493,Barnes and Noble, New York: 2005
[47]--Ibid Page 482
[48]--Wilkins ***(Grab Their Belts To Fight Them-)*** Pages 7-9
[49]--Bowman ed ***(The Vietnam War Almanac)*** Pages 33, 50, 131
[50]--Robert S. McNamara ***(In Retrospect-The Tragedy and Lessons of Vietnam)*** Page 24, Times Books, New York 1995
Time Magazine ***(The Pentagon's Whiz Kids)*** The Nation-3 August, 1962
Lewis Sorley ***(Westmoreland-The General Who Lost Vietnam)*** Page 44, 123,
[51]--FM 22-10 ***(Leadership)*** Page 3, U.S. Army: 1951

[52]--Seek Responsibility and Take Responsibility For Your Actions-A leadership principle found in: FM 22-10 (Leadership) Page 10, 1951 and every leadership manual since.
FM 22-100 ***(Military Leadership)*** Page 28, Principals of Leadership 1961. This is the manual we took to Vietnam
[53]--H.R. McMaster ***(Dereliction Of Duty-Lyndon Johnson, Robert McNamara, The Joint Chiefs Of Staff, And The Lies That Led To Vietnam)*** Page 110
[54]--Lewis Sorley ***(General Harold K. Johnson and the Ethics of Command)*** Page 304, University Press of Kansas, Lawrence, KS: 1998
[55]--Sorley ***(Westmoreland-The General Who Lost Vietnam)*** Pages 4-24
[56]--Ibid Pages 25-31
[57]--Ibid Pages 41-47
[58]--Ibid Pages 48-72
[59]--Ibid Pages 62-148
[60]--Bowman ed ***(The Vietnam War Almanac)*** Pages 76, 116, 158, 205
Kathleen Lockwood ***(Vietnam Magazine)*** June 1999
[61]--James Scott Wheeler ***(The Big Red One-America's Legendary 1st Infantry Division From World War I to Desert Storm)*** Page 415, University Press of Kansas, Lawrence KS: 2007
[62]--Ibid Pages 416-419
[63]--Ibid Pages 419-420
[64]--Warren Wilkins ***(Grab Their Belts To Fight Them-)*** Page 9,
[65]--Ibid Pages 16-17
[66]--Larry Berman ***(Perfect Spy)*** Pages 15-16, Harper Collins, New York: 2007
McChristian ***(Vietnam Studies-The Role of Military Intelligence 1965-1967)*** Pages 138-146
[67]--Sedgwick D. Tourison, Jr. ***(Talking With Victor Charlie-An Interrogators Story)*** Pages 269-280, Ballantine Books, New York: 1991
John Colvin ***(Volcano Under Snow)*** Page 7 Quartet Books, London: 1996
[68]--John M. Carland (Stemming The Tide) Page 166
[69]--Charles L. Myer ***(Vietnam Studies-Division Level Communications 1962-1973)*** Pages 65-67 Department of the Army, Washington DC 1982
[70]--Lt. Col. Anthony B. Herbert with James T. Wooten ***(Soldier)*** Holt, Rinehart and Winston, NY 1973
Col David H. Hackworth and Julie Sherman ***(About Face-The Odyssey Of An American Warrior)*** Pages 348, 449-450, 831, Touchstone Books, NY: 1989
[71]--U.S. Army War College ***(Study on Military Professionalism)*** Pages vii, 17, 22, 28, Carlisle Barracks, PA: 1970
[72]--Hank Brandli USAF Ret. ***(The Use Of Weather Satellite Photos In Vietnam War)*** http://libertyyes.homestead.com/files/TheUseOfWeatherSatellitePhotosInVietnamWar.htm
John Kovacs, USAF (Ret.) et al ***(SAC Reconnaissance in the Vietnam Conflict)*** Page 2, http://www.55wa.org/Heritage/SAC%20Recon%20in%20Vietnam%20final.pdf
John Schlight ***(The War in Vietnam-The Years of the Offensive)*** Page 7, Air Force History and Museum Program 1999
Lonnie M. Long and Gary B. Blackburn ***(Unlikely Warriors: The Army Security Agency's Secret War in Vietnam 1961-1973)*** iUniverse, Bloomington, IN 2013
Hay ***(Vietnam Studies-Tactical and Material Innovations)*** Pages 78, 80
[73]--DeForest, and Chanoff, ***(Slow Burn: The Rise and Bitter Fall of American Intelligence in Vietnam)*** Simon and Schuster, New York: 1990
Hay ***(Vietnam Studies-Tactical and Material Innovations)*** Page 123-124
[74]--McChristian ***(Vietnam Studies-The Role of Military Intelligence 1965-1967)*** Page 111
[75]--Long and Blackburn ***(Unlikely Warriors:)***, Chapter 7-Enter the Direct Support Units
Sorley ***(Westmoreland-The General Who Lost Vietnam)*** Page 98-99
[76]--Wheeler ***(The Big Red One-)*** Page 423

77--Ibid Page 423
78--Ibid Page 424
79--Ibid Page 428
80--Ibid Page 429
81--Gole ***(General William E. DePuy-Preparing The Army For Modern War)*** Pages 75, 97, 138, University Press of Kentucky, Lexington, KY: 2008
82--Ibid Pages138-142
William E. DePuy ***(Changing an Army-An Oral History)*** Page 130, CMH, DC 1988
83--Ibid Page162
84--Wilkins ***(Grab Their Belts To Fight Them-)*** Pages 22, 39
85--Brig. Gen. William DePuy ***(Commanders Notes #1)*** HQ, 1st ID, 27 Mar March 1966 See Appendix 1 for the complete Notes #1-2
86--Gole ***(General William E. DePuy-)*** Page 169
87--DePuy ***(Changing an Army-An Oral History)*** Page 138
88--Gole ***(General William E. DePuy-)*** Pages 170-171
89--Ibid Pages 170- 171,173,180-181
90--Ibid Page 170
91--Wheeler ***(The Big Red One-)*** Page 435-436
92--Ibid Pages 437-442
93--William LeGro ***(Interview)*** Pages 335-337 The Texas Tech University Vietnam Archive Oral History Project Conducted by Laura Calkins, Ph.D. October 31, 2005
Wheeler ***(The Big Red One-)*** Page 440-442
94--Hay ***(Vietnam Studies-Tactical and Material Innovations)*** Page 32
Gole ***(General William E. DePuy-Preparing the Army for Modern War)*** Page 181
95--DePuy ***(Changing an Army-An Oral History)*** Page 160
96--John M. Carland ***(Stemming the Tide-May 1965 to October 1966)*** Page 325- Center of Military History, Washington, DC 2000
97--Fn 48-ORLL, l Aug- 31 Oct 66, 1st Inf Div, n.d. pp. 4- 7, Historians files, CMH.
98--Fn 49-AAR, Opn AMARILLO, 1st Bde, 1st lnf Div, 18 Dec 66, pp. 1-2, Historians files, CMH; AAR, Opn AMARILLO, 1st Bn, 2d Inf, 11 Sep 66, pp. [1-2]
Harry G. Summers Papers, Bowie, Md.
99--Fn 50-AAR, Opn Amarillo, 1st Bde, 1st Inf Div, p. 5
100--Fn 51-Annual Hist Sum, 1966, 1st Bde, 1st Inf Div, 25 Mar 67, p . 2, box 5, 81/469, RG 338, NARA.
101--Fn 52-Memo, Lt Col Richard L. Prillaman, CO, 1st Bn, 2d Inf, for 1st Inf Div Dist, 3 Sep 66, sub: Journal Summary, 24- 26 August 1966 (Operation AMARILLO), Summers Papers; Annual Hist Sum, 1966, 1st Sqdn, 4th Cav, p. 2l
102--Fn 53-Memo, Prillaman for 1s t Inf Div Distribution, 3 Sep 66, sub: Journal Summary, 24-26 August 1966 (Operation AMARILLO); Ltr, Col Sidney B. Berry, Jr. to Anne F. Berry, 28 Aug 66, Sidney B. Berry Papers, Arlington, Va. Interv, Brownlee and Mullen with DePuy, 26 Mar 79, sec. 6, p. 16.
103--Fn 54-Ltr, Berry to A. Berry, 28 Aug 66.
104--Fn 55-AAR, Opn AMARILLO, 1st Bde, 1st Inf Div, p . 6.
105--Peter Clark ***(Correspondence with author)*** 2013
106--Fn 56-Interv, author with Brig Gen William J. Mullen III 24 Feb 94, Historians files, CMH. See also Interv, Brownlee and Mullen with DePuy, 26 Mar 79, sec. 6, pp. 16- 17.
107--Fn 57-Interv, Brownlee and Mullen with DePuy, 26 Mar 79, sec. 6, pp. 15, 17; Interv, author with Lt Gen Sidney B. Berry, Jr., 15 Mar 95, Historians files, CMH.
108--Fn 58-Annual Hist Sum, 1966, 1st Sqdn, 4th Cav, pp. 21- 22.
109--Fn 59-Intervs , author with Mullen, 24 Feb 94, and with Berry, 15 Mar 95, plus Brownlee and Mullen with DePuy, 26 Mar 79, sec. 6, p. 17.
110--Fn 60-Memo, Prillaman for 1st Inf Div Distribution, 3 Sep 66, sub: Journal Summary, 24-26 August 1966 (Operation AMARILLO); Daily jnl, 1st Bde, 1st Inf Div, 25 Aug 66, Historians files, CMH.

[111]--Fn 61-Annual Hist Sum, 1966, 1st Sqdn, 4th Cav, p. 18; Memo, Prillaman for 1st lnf Div Dist, 3 Sep 66, sub: Journal Summary, 24- 26 August 1966 (Operation Amarillo).

[112]--Peter Clark ***(Correspondence with author)*** 2013

[113]--Fn 62-Ltr (quoted words), Berry to A. Berry, 28 Aug 66; Harry G. Summers, Jr., "Would You Believe ...? p. 46, sidebar to Quentin L. Seitz, Jr., "Phu Loi Cornered," Vietnam 5 (April 1993): 42- 49; Memo, Prillaman for 1st Inf Div Distribution, 3 Sep 66, sub: Journal Summary, 24-26 August 1966 (Operation AMARILLO) AARs, Opn AMARILLO, 1st Bn, 2dInf, p. 13], and 1st Bde, 1st Inf Div, p. 7.

[114]--Fn 63-AAR, Opn AMARILLO, 1st Bde, 1st Inf Div, p. 6; Memo, Prillaman for 1st lnf Div Distribution, 3 Sep 66, sub: Journal Summary, 24- 26 August 1966 (Operation AMARILLO); Annual Hist Sum, 1966, 1st Sqdn, 4th Cav, p. 18.

[115]--Fn 64-Annual Hist Sum, 1966, 1st Sqdn, 4th Cav, pp. 19- 20.

[116]--Fn 65-Ltr, Berry to A. Berry, 28 Aug 66; Memo, Prillaman for 1st Inf Div Dist, 3 Sep 66 sub: Journal Summary, 24-26 August 1966 (Operation AMARILLO).

[117]--Fn 66-lnterv, author with Berry, 15 Mar 95; Daily Jnl, 1st Bde, 1st In f Div, 25 Aug 66; Ltr, Berry to A. Berry, 28 Aug 66.

[118]--Fn 67-Ltr (quotation), Berry to A. Berry, 28 Aug 66; AAR, Opn AMARILLO, 1st Bde, 1st Inf Div, p. 18.

[119]--Fn 68-AAR, Opn AMARILLO, 1st Bde, 1st Inf Div, pp. 7, 16.

[120]--Dennis Howley ***(Correspondence with author)*** 2013

[121]--Peter Clark ***(Correspondence with author)*** 2013

[122]--Fn 69-Summers, "Would You Believe...?," p. 46.Fn 70-AAR, Opn AMARILLO, 1st Bde, 1st Inf Div, pp. 7, 16; Paul F. Gorman, "Daring DOBOL, 1966-1967: Part III of the Story of 1st Battalion, 26th Infantry Regiment," p.33, copy in Historians files,CMH.

[123]--Peter Clark ***(Correspondence with author)*** 2013

[124]--Fn 71-ORLL, 1 Aug-31 Oct 66, 1st Inf Div, p. 7; Seitz, "Phu Loi Cornered," pp. 47-48.

[125]--Dennis Howley ***(Correspondence with author)*** 2013

[126]--Peter Clark ***(Correspondence with author)*** 2013

[127]--Fn 72-Seitz, "Phu Loi Cornered," p. 48.

[128]--Fn 73-Ltr (quotations), Berry to A. Berry, 28 Aug 66; Daily Jnl, 1st Bde, 1st Inf Di v, 25 Aug 66.

[129]--Peter Clark ***(Correspondence with author)*** 2013

[130]--Fn 74-AAR, Opn AMARILLO, 1st Bde, 1st Inf Div, p. 8.

[131]--Peter Clark ***(Correspondence with author)*** 2013

[132]--Ibid

[133]--Fn 75-Ltr, Berry to A. Berry, 28 Aug 66; Interv, Brownlee and Mullen with DePuy, 26 Mar 79, sec. 6, p. 18; AAR, Opn AMARILLO, 1st Bde, 1st Inf Div, p. 8; Seitz, "Phu Loi Cornered," p. 49.

[134]--Fn 76-ORLL, l Aug- 31 Oct 66, 1st Inf Div, p. 1; AAR, Opn AMARILLO, 1s t Bde, 1st Inf Div, pp. 8- 9; Ltr, Berry to A. Berry, 28 Aug 66.

[135]--Peter Clark ***(Correspondence with author)*** 2013

[136]--Fn 77-AAR, Opn AMARILLO, 1st Bde, 1st Inf Div, pp. 2, 12.

[137]--Fn 78-Ibid., p. 15.

[138]--Dennis Howley ***(Correspondence with author)*** 2013

[139]--Fn 79-AAR, Opn AMARILLO, 1st BI1, 2d Inf, p. [4]. Fn 80-Ltr, Lt Gen Sidney B. Berry, Jr., to BG William J. Mullen III, 26 Dec 94, copy in Historians files, CMH.

[140]--Warren Wilkins ***(Grab Their Belts to Fight Them:)*** Pages 103-104, COL Sidney B. Berry Jr. ***(Operation Amarillo-Combat After Action Report)*** Page 2 18 DEC 1966

[141]--William E. DePuy ***(Changing an Army-An Oral History)*** Page 150

[142]--British Army slang for a 'technical attack' or 'bugging' a weapon or piece of equipment for the purpose of tracking it.

William LeGro ***(Interview)*** Page 349, 350

[143]--Paul Gorman ***(Interview)*** Page 41, Cardinal Point: An Oral History. Combat Studies Institute, Fort Leavenworth, KS: 2011
Berry ***(CAAR)*** Page 5
(The "Wildcat" Lerps) that was attached to D (Air) Troop, 1-4 Cavalry http://www.75thrra.com/history/i75_hx.html
[144]--***(Conversation with author)*** 1989
[145]--Major James F. Gephardt, USA Ret ***(Eyes Behind the Lines: US Army Long-Range Reconnaissance and Surveillance Units)*** Page 66, Combat Studies Institute Press, Fort Leavenworth, Kansas 2005
[146]--Berry ***(CAAR)*** Page 2
James G. Holland ***(Written account)*** http://www.quarterhorsecav.org/pg4g1b.htm
Tracy Derks and James G. Holland ***(The Battle of Bong Trang)*** Pages 36-39, Vietnam-Weider History Group, Leesburg, VA: October 2007
[147]--Oliver Stone ***(Platoon)*** A movie by a combat infantry veteran of Vietnam. MGM:1987
[148]--Berry ***(CAAR)*** Pages 3, 5
Holland ***(Written account)***
Derks and Holland ***(The Battle of Bong Trang)*** Pages 36-39
Berry ***(CAAR)*** Pages 3, 5
[149]--**(Conversation with author)** August, 2014
[150]--Berry ***(CAAR)*** Pages 3, 5
[151]--Holland ***(Written account)***
[152]--Derks and Holland ***(The Battle of Bong Trang)*** Pages 36-39
[153]--DePuy ***(Changing an Army-An Oral History)*** Page 158
[154]--Pete Seeger and Joe Hickerson ***(Where Have All The Flowers Gone)*** Columbia Records: 1964
DePuy ***(Changing an Army-An Oral History)*** Page 158
Carland ***(Stemming the Tide-May 1965 to October 1966)*** Page 228
[155]--Herbert and Wooten ***(Soldier)*** Page 263
Hackworth and Sherman ***(About Face)*** Page 563
[156]--Alexander M. Haig, Jr. ***(Inner Circles-How America Changed The World)*** Pages 159-160 Warner Books, New York: 1992
[157]--Joint Special Operations Command-Command and Control for SFOD-D (Delta Force)
Pete Blaber ***(The Mission, The Men, and Me-Lessons From a Former Delta Force Commander)*** Chapters 17-19, Berkley Publishing, New York: 2008
[158]--Carland ***(Stemming the Tide-May 1965 to October 1966)*** Page 330
DePuy ***(Changing an Army-An Oral History)*** Page 158
USARV Seminar Report ***(Attack of Fortified Positions in the Jungle)*** Page 33-35 2 January 1968
[159]--Gorman ***(Interview)*** Page 44
[160]--M.E. Hubbs ***(With the Black Scarves at Bong Trang-Part II)*** http://erasgone.blogspot.com/2012/11/with-black-scarves-at-bong-trang-part-2.html
[161]--Gorman ***(Interview)*** Pages 45, 102
[162]--***John Harold Johnston*** 8/6/2011 http://secinfreg.websitetoolbox.com/post/ronald-lee-watson- battle-of-bong-trang
http://www.virtualwall.org/ds/SmithFx01a.htm
http://www.virtualwall.org/dg/GlasscockCL01a.htm
[163]--Rudolf H. Egersdorfer ***(Video Tape Interview)*** First Division Museum at Cantigny, February 1996 Page 173 Blue Spaders-The 26th Infantry Regiment, 1917-1967 Cantigney First Division Foundation
[164]--LeGro ***(Interview)*** Page 350
[165]--Ibid Page 349
[166]--LeGro ***(Interview)*** Page 350
DePuy ***(Changing an Army)*** Page 150

[167]--Berry ***(CAAR)*** Page 11
LeGro ***(Interview)*** Page 293
[168]--DePuy ***(Changing an Army)*** Page 164
[169]--Alistair Horne ***(A Savage War Of Peace)*** Page 142, Viking Press, New York: 1977
DePuy ***(Changing an Army)*** Page 138, 140
[170]--Berry ***(CAAR)*** Page 11
[171]--Hackworth and Sherman ***(About Face)*** Page 560
U.S. Army War College ***(Study on Military Professionalism)*** Page B-1-10 1970
http://www.carlisle.army.mil/usawc/dclm/pdf/study1970.pdf
[172]--Berry ***(CAAR)*** Page 15
[173]--Berry ***(CAAR)*** Page 18
Haig , Jr. ***(Inner Circles-How America Changed The World)*** Page 161
[174]--USARV Seminar Report ***(Attack of Fortified Positions in the Jungle)*** Page 33-35
[175]--DePuy ***(Changing an Army-An Oral History)*** Page 157
LeGro ***(Interview)*** Pages 351-352
[176]--Charles T. Loehr ***(War History of the Old First Virginia Infantry Regiment)*** Page 38 Richmond, VA: 1884
https://archive.org/stream/cu31924032779047#page/n5/mode/2up
[177]--Arthur Fremantle ***(Three Months in the Southern States: April, June, 1863)*** Pages 135-136: 1864 http://docsouth.unc.edu/imls/fremantle/fremantle.html
[178]--DePuy ***(Changing an Army-An Oral History)*** Page 157
[179]--Anton Myrer ***(Once An Eagle)*** Page 810-817, Holt, Rinehart, Winston, New York: 1968-The book's author, Mr. Myrer said his combat service in World War II had the greatest impact on his life. ''I enlisted imbued with a rather flamboyant concept of this country's destiny as the leader of a free world and the necessity of the use of armed force,'' he once wrote. ''I emerged a corporal three years later in a state of great turmoil, at the core of which was an angry awareness of war as the most vicious and fraudulent self-deception man had ever devised.'' New York Times-
MEL GUSSOW Published: January 23, 1996
[180]--Gole ***(General William E. DePuy-Preparing the Army for Modern War)*** Pages 170
[181]--Ibid Page 191
[182]--DePuy ***(Changing an Army-An Oral History)*** Pages 152-153
[183]--Gole ***(General William E. DePuy-Preparing the Army for Modern War)*** Page 190
Hackworth ***(About Face)*** Page 562
[184]--S.L.A. Marshall ***(Ambush-The Battle of Dau Tieng)*** Pages 109-126
Nelson Doubleday, New York: 1969
[185]--Hackworth ***(About Face)*** Pages 556, 561-563
S.L.A. Marshall and David Hackworth ***(Vietnam Primer)*** DA Lessons Learned 1967
[186]--Attributed to John Paul Vann, a military advisor in the early years and a major figure in the Civil Operations and Revolutionary Development Support or CORDS program
[187]--Dennis Howley ***(Correspondence with the author)*** 2013
[188]--Harry G. Summers Jr. ***(On Strategy-A Critical Analysis of the Vietnam War)*** Page 73
Presidio Press, Novato, CA: 1982
[189]--Audie Murphy **(To Hell and Back)** Universal Pictures 1955
[190]--Stuart A. Herrington ***(Silence Was A Weapon-The Vietnam War In The Villages)*** Page 215 Ballantine Books, New York: 1982
[191]--Jose Garcia ***(Correspondence with the author)*** 2013
[192]--Jose Garcia ***(Correspondence with the author)*** 2013
[193]--Colonel Sidney M. Marks ***(CAAR-Operation Danbury)*** 3d BDE, 1st ID12 Oct 1966
[194]--DePuy ***(Changing an Army-An Oral History)*** Page 95, 118
[195]--Robert F. Dorr ***(Chopper: A History of America Military Helicopter Operators from WWII to the War on Terror)*** Pages 1-17, 18-71, 86-106, Berkley Books, NY: 2005
Charles R. Shrader ***(The First Helicopter War: Logistics and Mobility in Algeria, 1954-1962)*** Page 2, Praeger, CT: 1999

[196]--Old Army term for a home for non-performers
[197]--Dennis Howley ***(Correspondence with the author)*** 2013
[198]--Ibid
[199]--Peter Clark ***(Correspondence with the author)*** 2013
[200]--Dennis Howley ***(Correspondence with author)*** 2013
[201]--Jimi Hendrix ***(Are You Experienced)*** Polydor Records, London, UK: 1967
[202]--Jose Garcia ***(Correspondence with author)*** 2013
[203]-- Stone ***(Platoon)***
[204]--F. Spencer Chapman ***(The Jungle Is Neutral)*** Chatto and Windus, London: 1949
[205]--Jose Garcia ***(Correspondence with author)*** 2013
[206]--Ibid
[207]--Ibid
[208]--Gole ***(General William E. DePuy-)*** Page 179-180
[209]--James Jones ***(From Here To Eternity)*** Random House, NY: 1951
[210]--Dennis Howley ***(Correspondence with author)*** 2013
[211]--Jose Garcia ***(Correspondence with author)***
[212]--The Army fired twelve 155mm rounds 180 degrees off at Fort Hood, TX in 2000
http://greenspun.com/bboard/q-and-a-fetch-msg.tcl?msg_id=002TS9
[213]--Gole ***(General William E. DePuy-)*** Page 95
[214]--Ibid Pages 177-179
[215]--Dennis Howley (Correspondence with the author) 2013
[216]--Dennis Howley ***(Correspondence with author)*** 2013
[217]--Steven E. Clay ***(Blood and Sacrifice-The History of the 16th Infantry Regiment)***
Page 202, Cantigny First Division Foundation, Wheaton, IL: 2001
[218]--Sidney M. Marks ***(CAAR-Operation Healdsburg)*** 3rd BDE, 1st ID 1 JAN 67
[219]--Ibid
[220]--***(Report on the special subcommittee on the M-16 rifle program)***
House Armed Services Committee, October 19, 1967 Pages 5369-5370
[221]--Sidney M. Marks ***(CAAR-Operation Santa Cruz)*** 3rd BDE, 1st ID 18 JAN 66-[67]
[222]--Col. Charlie Beckwith ***(Conversation with author)*** 1989
[223]--S.L.A. Marshall ***(Ambush)*** Pages 109-126
[224]--Peter McAleese ***(No Mean Soldier: The Story of the Ultimate Professional Soldier in the SAS and Other Forces)*** Cassell, London: 2001
[225]--Jose Garcia ***(Correspondence with author)*** 2013
[226]--Flynn ***(The Draft-1940-1973)*** Pages 134-258
[227]--Simon Hall ***(Rethinking the American Anti-War Movement)***
Pages 51-52, 81, 117, 131, 148 Routledge, New York: 2012
[228]--Jester Hairston ***(Amen)*** Curtis Mayfield/the Impressions ABC-Paramount Records:1964
[229]--LTG Bernard Rogers ***(Cedar Falls-Junction City: A Turning Point)*** Page 74-78
Department of the Army, Washington, DC: 1974
[230]--Sidney M. Marks ***(CAAR-Operation Cedar Falls)*** 10 February 1967
William DePuy ***(OR-LL: 1 November 1966-31 January 1967)*** 1st ID: 1967
[231]--Ibid
[232]--Ibid
[233]--LTC Thomas Fife ***(CAAR-Operation Williston)*** 1-4 Cavalry 19 February 1967
http://www.quarterhorsecav.org/pg44c.htm
[234]--Carl White, Al Frazier, Sonny Harris, Turner Wilson Jr. **(Papa Oom Mow Mow)**
Liberty Records, Hollywood, CA: 1962
[235]--Bill Williamson ***(Correspondence with author)*** 2014
[236]--Jose Garcia ***(Correspondence with author)*** 2013
[237]--Bill Williamson ***(Correspondence with author)*** 2014
[238]--Neil Skiles ***(Conversation with author)*** 2014
[239]--Bill Williamson ***(Correspondence with author)*** 2014
[240]--Jose Garcia ***(Correspondence with author)*** 2013

[241]--Sidney M. Marks ***(CAAR-Operation Tucson D)*** 3d Brigade 16 March 1967
[242]--Jose Garcia ***(Correspondence with author)*** 2013
[243]--Sidney M. Marks ***(CAAR-Operation Tucson D)*** 3d Brigade 16 March 1967
[244]--Rogers ***(Cedar Falls/Junction City-A Turning Point)***
[245]--Sorley ***(Westmoreland-The General Who Lost Vietnam)*** Pages 110-111
Rodney George ***(Vietnam Magazine-October 2004)*** page 56 Letter to the Editor
[246]--MG John Hay ***(OR-LL-Operation Junction City)*** 1st Infantry Division 8 May 1967
[247]--Lou Murray ***(Conversation with author)*** 2010
[248]--Jose Garcia ***(Correspondence with author)*** 2013
[249]--Hay ***(OR-LL-Operation Junction City)*** 1st Infantry Division 8 May 1967
[250]--Sidney M. Marks ***(CAAR-Operation Junction City)*** 3d Brigade 25 April 1967
[251]--Ibid
[252]--Ibid
[253]--Major Charles M. Bamford II (***CAAR Junction City)*** 2d BDE, 1st ID: 6 May 1967
[254]--Ibid
[255]--Gordon L. Rottman ***(Mobile Strike Forces in Vietnam 1966-70)*** Page 88, Osprey Publishing: 2007
[256]--Aaron Bank ***(From OSS to Green Berets)*** Pages 139-204 Presidio Press, Novato, CA: 1986
[257]--Charles D. Patton ***(Colt Terry, Green Beret)*** Pages 63-64, Texas A+M University Press, College Station, TX: 2005
[258]--Bank ***(From OSS to Green Berets)*** Page 175
[259]--Kim Philby ***(My Silent War)*** Page viii MacGibbon & Kee, London: 1968
[260]--Bank ***(From OSS to Green Berets)*** Page 187
[261]--Charles D. Patton ***(Colt Terry, Green Beret)*** Page 64
[262]--Col. Francis J. Kelly ***(U.S. Army Special Forces 1961-1971)*** Page 10 U.S. Army: 1973
[263]--Ibid Pages 6-7, 10
[264]--Donald E. Valentine ***(Strap Hanger)*** Chapter 6: 1997 http://www.don-valentine.com/ 1st Group and White Star.htm
[265]--Andrew F. Krepinevich ***(The Army and Vietnam)*** Pages 69-71 The John Hopkins University Press, Baltimore, MD: 1986
[266]--Kelly ***(U.S. Army Special Forces 1961-1971)*** Pages 4, 56
[267]--Ibid Page 45
[268]--Valentine ***(Strap Hanger)*** Chapter 5:
[269]--Donald Duncan ***(The New Legions)*** Random House, NY: 1967
[270]--Ron Dick and Dan Patterson (***Aviation Century: War and Peace in the Air)*** Page 161 Boston Mills Press Buffalo, NY: 2006
[271]--Sidney M. Marks ***(CAAR-Operation Bluefield)*** 3d Brigade, 1st ID 27 June 1967
[272]--Ibid Page 7
[273]--John Hay ***(OR-LL-1 May-31 July 1967)*** Pages 8-9, 1st ID: 25 August, 1967
[274]--Sidney M. Marks ***(CAAR-Operation Billings)*** Page 4, 3d Brigade, 1st ID 16 July, 1967
[275]--Peter Clark ***(Correspondence with author)*** 2014
[276]--Marks ***(CAAR-Operation Billings)*** Page 4
[277]--Peter Clark ***(Correspondence with author)*** 2014
[278]--Ibid
[279]--Jose Garcia ***(Correspondence with author)*** 2013
[280]--Peter Clark ***(Correspondence with author)*** 2014
[281]--Ibid
[282]--Ibid
[283]--Jose Garcia ***(Correspondence with author)*** 2013
[284]--Peter Clark ***(Correspondence with author)*** 2014
[285]--Jose Garcia ***(Correspondence with author)*** 2013
[286]--Peter Clark ***(Correspondence with author)*** 2014
[287]--Ibid

[288]--Ibid
[289]--Jose Garcia ***(Correspondence with author)*** 2013
[290]--Peter Clark ***(Correspondence with author)*** 2014
[291]--Ibid
[292]--Donnie Gunby (Conversation with author) 2013
[293]--Jose Garcia ***(Correspondence with author)*** 2013
[294]--Ibid
[295]--Ibid
[296]--Peter Clark ***(Correspondence with author)*** 2014
[297]--Jose Garcia ***(Correspondence with author)*** 2013
[298]--Ibid
[299]--Ibid
[300]--Peter Clark ***(Correspondence with author)*** 2014
[301]--John Hay ***(OR-LL-1 May-31 July 1967)*** Pages 95
[302]--Wilkins ***(Grab Their Belts to Fight Them-)*** Page 58
[303]--Bill Williamson ***(Correspondence with author)*** 2014
[304]--Francis Ford Coppola ***(Apocalypse Now)*** Zoetrope Studios, United Artists: 1979
[305]--Hunter ***(Galahad)*** Preface
[306]--Eitan Shamir ***(A Very Sharp Eye: Moshe Dayan's Counterinsurgency Legacy in Israel)*** Page 18
http://portal.idc.ac.il/he/schools/government/research/documents/shamir.pdf
[307]--See Appendix A
[308]--Charles Wellborn ***(History of the 86th Mountain Infantry in Italy)*** Page 3
http://10thmtndivassoc.org/86thhistory.pdf
[309]--Pete Seeger and Joe Hickerson ***(Where Have All the Flowers Gone?)*** Columbia Records, New York: 1964
David Hackworth and Eilhys England ***(Steel My Soldiers' Hearts)*** Page 53 Touchstone, New York: 2002
[310]--MG John Hay ***(OR-LL: 1 May-31 July 1967)*** 1st Infantry Division
[311]--Oliver Stone (Platoon)
[312]--BG James E. Shelton ***(The Beast Was Out There)*** Page 142, Cantigny First Division Foundation, Wheaton, IL: 2002
[313]--Ibid Page 142
[314]--Ibid Pages 93, 19-20, 44, 95, 61
[315]--Ibid Pages 35, 40, 63-64, 83-84, 39, 46, 48-51, 58, 98-101, 80
[316]--Ibid Page 27, 73
[317]--Ibid Page 41
[318]--David Maraniss ***(They Marched Into Sunlight)*** Simon and Schuster, New York: 2003
[319]--Robert Kenner ***(Two Days In October)*** Robert Kenner Films: 2005
[320]--Maraniss ***(They Marched Into Sunlight)*** Pages 413-415
[321]--Ibid Page 414
[322]--Ibid Page 414
[323]--Michael D. Mahler ***(Ringed In Steel)*** Page 21 Presidio Press, Novato, CA:1986
[324]--Ibid Pages 22-23
MG John Hay ***(Fundamentals of Infantry Tactics)*** 1st ID: 25 August 1967
[325]--Maraniss ***(They Marched Into Sunlight)*** Pages 483-484
[326]--Maraniss ***(They Marched Into Sunlight)*** Page 484
Shelton ***(The Beast Was Out There)*** Page 174, 248
[327]--Kenner ***(Two Days In October)*** Robert Kenner Films: 2005
[328]--Jimi Hendrix ***(Are You Experienced?)*** Polydor Records, London: 1967
[329]--Walter Cronkite **(CBS Evening News)** February 27, 1968
[330]--Jose Garcia ***(Conversations with author)*** 1968-2013
[331]--J.D. Salinger ***(Franny and Zooey)*** Bantam, New York: 1964
[332]--R.M. French ***(The Way Of A Pilgrim)*** Ballantine Books, New York: 1977

[333]--Letter to Tench Coxe 21 May 1799
National Archives ***(Defense Casualty Analysis System)***
Barr McClellan ***(Blood, Money, and Power)*** Pages 3-5 Hannover, NY: 2003
[334]--Robert S. McNamara ***(In Retrospect-The Tragedy and Lessons of Vietnam)*** Times Books, New York 1995
[335]--Earle Wheeler ***(Oral History Project)*** LBJ Library http://web2.millercenter.org/lbj/oralhistory/wheeler_earle_1969_0821.pdf
[336]--Sorley ***(General Harold K. Johnson and the Ethics of Command)*** Page 304
[337]--LTG Phillip B. Davidson ***(Vietnam at War-The History 1946-1975)*** Pages 400, 123, 246, Presidio Press, Novato, CA: 1988
George W. Allen ***(None So Blind)*** Page 249, Ivan R. Dee Chicago, IL: 2001
[338]--Sorley ***(Westmoreland-The General Who Lost Vietnam)*** Page 294, 292, 164
[339]--DePuy ***(Changing an Army-An Oral History)*** Page 160-161
[340]--Francis Ford Coppola ***(Gardens of Stone)*** Zoetrope Studios, Tri-Star Pictures: 1987 and ***(Apocalypse Now)*** Zoetrope Studios, United Artists: 1979
[341]--Donnie Gunby ***(Conversations with author)*** 1968-2013
[342]--Blaber ***(The Mission, the Men, and Me)***
[343]--Rudyard Kipling-The Naulahka
[344]--LBJ ***(Speech)*** Akron University, Akron, Ohio (October 21, 1964)
[345]--Quote of Scott Anderson ***(Lawrence in Arabia: War, Deceit, Imperial Folly and the Making of the Modern Middle East)*** Page 233, Doubleday, NY: 2013
[346]--National Security Council Directive on Office of Special Projects ***(NSC 10/2)*** 18 June, 1948 https://history.state.gov/historicaldocuments/frus1945-50Intel/d292
[347]--Department of the Army ***(Stilwell Obituary)*** 3 February, 1992
[348]--Gole ***(General William E. DePuy-)*** Pages 25-85
[349]--Brownlee and Mullen III ***(Changing an Army-)*** Pages 105-106
[350]--Frank Holober ***(Raiders of the China Coast)*** Pages 7, 10, 60-87, 123, Naval Institute Press, Annapolis, MD: 1999
[351]--Ibid Pages 3, 108
Ralph Weber-Editor ***(Spymasters: Ten CIA Officers in Their Own Words)*** Pages 119-120, Scholarly Resources Inc. Wilmington, DE: 1999
[352]--Peter Dale Scott ***(American War Machine: Deep Politics, the CIA Global Drug Connection, and the Road to Afghanistan)*** Page 85 Rowman and Littlefield, Lanham, MD: 2014
[353]--Tim Weiner ***(Legacy of Ashes)*** Page 61 Doubleday, New York 2007
[354]--Anthony Verrier ***(Through The Looking Glass)*** Pages 1-6, 16, W.W. Norton-London 1983
[355]--Thomas Moon and Carl F. Eifler ***(The Deadliest Colonel)*** Page 49 Vantage Press, New York: 1975
Camp X ***(The History of Camp X)*** http://www.camp-x.com/historyofcampx.html
Weiner ***(Legacy of Ashes)*** Page 5-31
[356]--Weiner ***(Legacy of Ashes)*** Page 25
Porter Goss, former DCI ***(Speech at Tiffin University)*** Toledo Blade 2006
[357]--Krepinevich, Jr. ***(The Army and Vietnam)*** Page 43-44
[358]--Gole ***(General William E. DePuy-)*** Pages 101, 110, 113
[359]--Ibid Pages 75, 95-97 115-142
Sorley ***(Westmoreland-The General Who Lost Vietnam)*** Page 77 ***(Photo)***
Stilwell, General Richard Giles https://deeppoliticsforum.com/forums/showthread.php?1534-Gen-Richard-Giles-Stilwell#.UtQfSPRDuSo
Graham A. Cosmas ***(MACV The Years of Escalation, 1962-1967)*** Page 138, CMH Washington, DC 2006
[360]--John A. Bingham ***(The Trial of the Conspirators-1865)*** Page 52 http://babel.hathitrust.org/cgi/pt?id=yale.39002028089267;view=1up;seq=22

[361]--Kenneth Conboy and Dale Andrade ***(Spies and Commandos-How America Lost The Secret War In North Vietnam)*** Page 84 University Press of Kansas, Lawrence, KS: 2000

[362]--William Colby ***(Honorable Men)*** Pages 33-50 Simon and Schuster, NY: 1978

[363]--Sedgwick Tourison **(Secret Army-Secret War)** Page 100-101, Naval Institute Press, Annapolis, MD: 1995

[364]--Thomas L. Ahern, Jr. ***(The Way We Do Things: Black Entry Operations Into North Vietnam, 1961-1964)*** Page 1-5, 11, 13-14, 26, 41, 49-50 Center for the Study of Intelligence Washington, DC: May 2005

Thomas L. Ahern, Jr ***(CIA and Rural Pacification in South Vietnam)*** Page 45-60, 112, Center for the Study of Intelligence Washington, DC May 2001

[365]--Joint Chiefs of Staff ***(MACSOG Documentation Study Appendix D Cross-Border Operations in Laos)*** Page D-8

[366]--Tourison **(Secret Army-Secret War)** Page 127

Joint Chiefs of Staff ***(MACSOG Documentation Study)*** Pages B-Q-7, 8, ANX Q to APX B 16 July 1970

[367]--Marilin Young ***(The Vietnam Wars 1945-1990)*** Page 172 Harper Collins, NY: 1991

[368]--Brownlee and Mullen III ***(An Oral History of General William E. DePuy)*** Page 118

[369]--Edwin E. Moise ***(Tonkin Gulf and the Escalation of the Vietnam War)*** Pages 13-14, 17, The University of North Carolina Press, Chapel Hill, NC: 1996

[370]--Conboy and Andrade ***(Spies and Commandos-)*** Pages 113-123

[371]--Department of the Army ***(Stilwell Obituary)*** 3 February, 1992

Gole ***(General William E. DePuy-)*** Pages 170-173

[372]--DePuy ***(Commanders Notes #1)***

Gole ***(General William E. DePuy-)*** Page 176

[373]--Ibid Pages 160-161

[374]--Brownlee and Mullen III ***(An Oral History of General William E. DePuy)*** Page 118

[375]--Gole ***(DePuy-Preparing the Army for Modern War)*** Page 197

[376]--Ibid Page 207

[377]--Brownlee and Mullen III ***(An Oral History of General William E. DePuy)*** Page 169

[378]--Susan Lynn Marquis ***(Unconventional Warfare: Rebuilding U.S. Special Operations Forces)*** Pages 156-158, Brookings Institution Press, Washington, DC: 1997

[379]--Gole ***(General William E. DePuy)*** Page 197, 212

[380]--Colonel Richard M. Swain ***(Selected Papers of General William E. DePuy)*** Page 372-373 Combat Studies Institute, U S. Army Command and General Staff College, Fort Leavenworth, Kansas: 1994

[381]--Frank N. Schubert and Theresa L. Kraus, General Editors ***(The Whirlwind War-The United States Army in Operations DESERT SHIELD and DESERT STORM)*** Pages 25-33, Center Of Military History, Washington, D.C.: 1995

[382]--Major Paul H. Herbert ***(Deciding What Has To Be Done: General William DePuy and the 1976 Edition of FM 100-5, Operations)*** Pages 7, 9, Combat Studies Institute, Fort Leavenworth, KS: 1988

James Burton ***(The Pentagon Wars)*** Page 52 Naval Institute Press, Annapolis, MD: 1993

[383]--President George H.W. Bush ***(Remarks to the American Legislative Exchange Council March 1, 1991)***

[384]--Burton ***(The Pentagon Wars)*** Page 52

[385]--Krepinevich, Jr. ***(The Army and Vietnam)***

Swain ***(Selected Papers of General William E. DePuy)*** Page 372

[386]--Bradley Graham ***(By His Own Rules-The Ambitions, Successes, and Ultimate Failures of Donald Rumsfeld)*** Page 208, Public Affairs-Perseus Books, NY: 2009

[387]--Seth G. Jones ***(Take the War to Pakistan)*** New York Times: December 3, 2009

[388]--FM 3-24/MCWP 3-33.5 ***(Counterinsurgency)*** 2014

[389]--Bob Woodward ***(Obama's War)*** Pages 85, 188, 373-374, Simon & Schuster, NY: 2010

# Index

Made in the USA
Lexington, KY
26 March 2016